D1002901

GREEN UNPLEASANT LAND

GREEN UNPLEASANT LAND:
CREATIVE RESPONSES TO RURAL BRITAIN'S
COLONIAL CONNECTIONS

CORINNE FOWLER

PEEPAL TREE

First published in 2020 by
Peepal Tree Press Ltd
17 King's Avenue
Leeds LS6 1QS
England

ISBN13: 97818452324829

Supported using public funding by
ARTS COUNCIL
ENGLAND

To Rafael
and all the children on the Colonial Countryside project

CONTENTS

ACKNOWLEDGEMENTS

Books are always a collective effort. First of all I want to thank Jeremy Poynting, the founder and managing editor of Peepal Tree Press. Thanks to Jeremy's efforts, I have been able to incorporate considerably more historical and literary material than I would otherwise have done. He also urged me to think more deeply about the importance of class to the analysis. In particular, his editorial interventions allowed me to connect, and evidence, rural poverty at home with colonial activity abroad. The existence of Peepal Tree clearly demonstrates the importance of quality independent presses. I also want to thank Jacob Ross, the associate editor, for his judicious and forensic editorial input to the creative material and to Hannah Bannister for keeping everything on track no matter what.

This book represents one of many efforts to provide a sound basis of evidence as a resource to inform public discussions about British colonial history. Once again, this is a collective effort. I wish to thank a list of exceptional people for the insights that they have contributed through their work and for the Colonial Countryside project: Robert Beckford, Caroline Bressey, James Dawkins, Misha Ewen, Radikha Holstrom, Rozina Misrah, Sumita Mukherjee, Shawn Sobers, Florian Stadtler, Anthony Tibbles and Kristy Warren. My close colleagues have given sound advice and offered timely support: Rabah Aissaoui, Gowan Dawson, Lucy Evans, Zalfa Feghali, Clive Fraser, Martin Halliwell, Sarah Knight, Mary Ann Lund, Suzanne MacLeod, Richard Thomas, Richard Sandell, Philip J. Shaw and Victoria Stewart. In the heritage sector itself are many talented and brave colleagues whom I admire: Dominique Bouchard, Rhian Cahill, Laura Carderera, Matthew Constantine, Alison Dalby, Emile de Brujin, Liz Green, Andrew Hann, Emma Hawthorne, Charlotte Holmes, Tom Freshwater, Indy Hunjan, Nadia Hussain, Sally-Anne Huxtable, John Orna-Ornstein, Polly Schomberg and Nino Strachey.

There is another group of people to thank who have provided moral support and applied their fine minds to this book's topics, making me see things anew. They are Clare Anderson, Kavita Bhanot, Joanna de Groot, Katie Donington, Madge Dresser, Elisabeth Grass, Marian Gwyn, Sarah Longair, David Olusoga, Raj Pal and Laurence Westgaph. I particularly want to thank the amazing Miranda Kaufmann, the generous and clear-sighted lead historian of Colonial Countryside. For giving me moral support and courage, I want to thank Hamida Ara, Desiree Baptiste, Jane Baron, Steve Baron, Yannick Guerry, Halgurt Habeel, Peter Kalu, Carol Leeming, Hari Matharu, Edy Motta, Henderson Mullin, Kevin Ncube, Yewande Okulele, Raj Pal, Lynne Pearce, Harry Whitehead and Binnie Sabharwal. Finally, to my long-suffering parents, Malcolm and Yvonne Fowler and my twin sister Naomi Fowler.

PREFACE

A hand shot up. My questioner looked quizzical. I pointed at him and he said, 'Doesn't this sort of approach undermine your position as a literary critic? Writing a book with poems and short stories in it?'

I expected the question, but it's taken me a while to formulate an answer. For this academic, I had crossed a line. To him, creative writing is expressive, not analytical. He felt that this book would be fatally compromised because I saw my stories and poems as integral to its commentary. I was supposed to write *about* writers, not *with* them. His tone was confident, his question a statement. I was reminded of the writer, Graham Mort, who once remarked that university literature specialists view creative writing as 'an interesting cultural secretion'. Having betrayed my own propensity to secrete poems and stories, my impartiality was now in question.

I *should* have replied that writing both critically and creatively has respectable antecedents. The Welsh novelist and critic Raymond Williams observed that research topics are invariably linked to personal stories. See the topic and you see the person. Williams did not consider this a bad thing. Most academics accept that impartiality is an illusion. When personal motivations animate scholarship, it is a bad idea for these to remain unconscious, unexamined and undeclared because they cause intellectual distortion. I take comfort in the fact that Williams wrote *Border Country* (1962), an account of his childhood and youth as well as *The Country and the City* (1973).[1] We at least share the same theme, and – more than this – Williams's work shaped that of Edward Said, author of *Orientalism*[2] and a parent of postcolonial studies, my own area of study.

Here is my story. I became obsessed with country houses' colonial connections whilst writing an article about them. I pre-ordered every forthcoming book. I kept *Slavery and the British Country House* (2013)[3] and *Country Houses and the British Empire, 1700-1930*[4] beside my bed. One night I dreamt about Charlecote Park. In another dream I walked a grassy track leading from Penrhyn Castle to Erdigg, where I later saw a portrait of a Black coach-boy. I started staying up long after midnight writing poems and stories. Realising that reading and writing about country houses had become strangely compulsive, I decided to contact my cousin Yannick, who dabbles in family history, to ask if he knew of any blood connections to empire or to country houses. Yes, he replied, the French side of our family

– the De Caradeucs – profited from Caribbean sugar wealth. One branch of the family lived at the Château de Caradeuc at Bécherel in Brittany, which they built with sugar money. This branch did business with another family member who owned plantations in St. Domingue (Haiti). Jean-Baptiste De Caradeuc was Governor General of San Domingo. At the onset of the Haitian Revolution, he fled the island with 62 enslaved people – including a wet nurse known by the family as 'mama monkey'.[5] He was known to be cruel. He is almost certainly the character Citoyen C in Victor Hugo's short novel *Bug Jargal* (1826),[6] about the revolution. De Caradeuc impaled babies on sticks outside his plantation at Croix-des-Bouquets.[7] He received compensation from the French government for the loss of the people that he had enslaved, and he used the money to develop plantations in South Carolina. His mixed-race descendent, Carole Ione, wrote a book about her experiences called *Pride of Family: Four Generations of American Women of Color.*[8]

The colonial connection did not stop there, my cousin told me. Another branch of my family were the Poidloüe, naval people who captained East India Company ships. My relatives sailed from Lorient, leaving docks from which 150 slave-trading ships also departed. My family had both East and West Indies links. Only then did I understand in the fullest, most personal sense, why I was compelled to write this book, which unites historical work on the Caribbean and the East India Company as though joining two halves of my family history. And only then did it occur to me – since I arrived at this understanding through a creative process rather than an academic one – that creative instincts possess an intelligence of their own.

I make no claim to neutrality. Even if Jean Baptiste de Caradeuc is *not* the Citoyen C of Hugo's novel, my own family history reveals an aspect of imperial Britain's repressed story. Britain's colonial legacy is not simply expressed by chinoiserie, statues, monuments, galleries, warehouses and stately homes. For Britons with roots in all continents, people's ancestral stories stray far beyond British shores. Our relatives either profited from empire, or were impoverished by it. This history lives on. An eerie parallel to my own story is that of Ripton Lindsay, a British resident. Ripton Lindsay is the three times great grandson of an enslaved woman named Susanna, and Alexander Lindsay (1794-1801), the Scottish Lieutenant Governor of Jamaica and an owner of plantations worked by enslaved Africans. Having investigated his family history for years, Ripton Lindsay arranged a meeting with Alexander Lindsay's descendants, who live in Britain today. In his account of this encounter he writes: 'I would like to... create a greater understanding of how Alexander became the man he was and why I believe that the recognition of this is important in the reconciliation of the past and, along with creating a wider understanding of the harsh impact of slavery's legacy, I believe that in sharing these stories we can help forge a better future for us all.'[9]

My parents gave me a love of country walking. We went on long walks every Sunday in all four seasons. I had no idea, then, that rural England had any relationship to the British Empire, of which I had learned little at school. As a child I experienced those woods, villages and valleys as quintessentially English. I was then wholly ignorant of my family connection to transatlantic slavery and the East India Company. I did not see that the countryside could express colonial wealth. I did not associate the landscape with people of African or Asian descent. I had no idea that my untroubled relationship with nature was not universal. Nor did I see the historical connection between slave-ownership and enclosure's hedgerows, or colonial wealth and rural philanthropy. *Green Unpleasant Land*, therefore, begins at home and extends outwards to empire but circles back to the English countryside. The book is purposely reparative. It respects the ghosts of people encountered on my journey towards understanding that "England's green and pleasant land",[10] to quote William Blake, is not just about agriculture and estates, but about colonialism and a long-standing Black presence. The book includes creative work because I have indeed crossed a line. I embrace the academic principles of originality, significance and rigour, but it is time to declare an interest. This book lays aside any pretence that I am not involved. I am involved, and this story belongs to all of us.

I have organised this book to tell several parallel stories. The first two chapters provide overviews of the relevant work done by others so far, and the following four offer more detailed discussions of the specifics of landscape and the countryside, country houses, moorlands, plants and gardens, in which I include allotments and public parks.

Chapter One focuses on the responses to two attempts to tell different kinds of national stories: Danny Boyle's opening ceremony for the 2012 Olympic Games and the National Trust's publication of a report on the colonial connections of properties they manage. The chapter presents a rationale for bringing together histories of empire, the place of rural Britain in that history and the presence of Black and Asian Britons as both experiencers of, and writers about, the countryside. I acknowledge the existing research this book attempts to build on and argue that the determined opposition to an anti-colonial history suggests a nation at the crossroads: either prone to comforting nationalist myths, or a country ready to embrace its fuller histories and the global connections of its people.

Chapter Two explores the changing features of rural Britain in historical and contemporary reality, the shifts in attitudes towards the countryside in social commentary and literary portrayal, and it introduces the book's focus on writing by Black and Asian Britons about that aspect of Englishness which seems most exclusionary.

Chapter Three situates English rural writing in a global setting, a re-contextualisation that reveals the limitations of concepts such as pastoral, georgic, anti-pastoral and even postcolonial pastoral. In the context of rural writing's colonial dimensions, I then acknowledge the scope and significance of contemporary rural writing by Black and Asian Britons whose work draws on both rural literary tradition and personal experience to join, reanimate and deepen England's longstanding literary conversation about the colonial countryside. This book investigates changes in literary writing about the rural landscape and rural activities. The chapter examines how established poetic traditions of the pastoral and the georgic defined most writing about the countryside until at least the 18th century and suggests that as generalising and abstracted forms, these still enter our views at a mythic level. The chapter examines how this body of work, from the 17th to the 20th century, has engaged with, or can be read against, the impact of colonial activities on the economy, society and culture. I track a shift from the pastoral and the georgic and consider the challenge to these generally elite views of the landscape from plebeian and women's perspectives. Here, in particular, I look at the writing that responded to enclosure and the loss of commoners' rights. The chapter examines other challenges to views of the countryside that derives from classic Greek and Latin literature from that revolution in sensibility – equally part of our contemporary consciousness – that we identify by the label of romanticism. Another focus concerns views of the rural that deal with the individual, cultural and psychological roots of perception and the particularity of place. I look at these traditions within the context of empire and show how Black and British Asian writers have engaged with English traditions of rural writing, sometimes in dialogue with it, sometimes quarrelling with it, sometimes ignoring it altogether.

In Chapter Four I consider the country house, its associated literature and the way the genre of the country house poem provided a screen for the reality of how many such houses were involved with both the West and East Indies. I look for traces in fiction and poetry of how writers responded to imperial histories, in particular through the genre of the gothic. I also look at the rare attempts to see the country house world from below. I see Jane Austen's *Mansfield Park* and the debate about her work stimulated by Edward Said as central to the kind of national 'culture wars' discussed in Chapter One. From here I explore how Black writers are re-imagining the country house's connections to the hidden world of the Caribbean plantation and those actual Black presences in Britain, including domestic servants, mostly young enslaved children, who can be seen in hundreds of country house portraits of the 17th, 18th and early 19th centuries.

Chapter Five looks at moorlands, so very opposite from the artfully tended grounds of country house estates. In the context of examining changing ideas about the cultivated and the wild, the picturesque and the sublime, the civilised and the savage, I focus on Emily Brontë's *Wuthering Heights* (1847). I consider the novel's location in the economy of empire and the aftermath of emancipation in the West Indies. The chapter investigates the debate about Heathcliff's ethnic identity and discusses contemporary filmic and literary responses to Emily Brontë's novel, including Andrea Arnold's eponymous film and the intertextual novels of V.S. Naipaul, Caryl Phillips and Maryse Condé. I also record efforts by groups of Black walkers to take their own possession of the moors both through walking and through making a play about the experience.

Chapter Six focuses on and explores the cultural history of gardens as shaped by empire and migration. I review how researching gardens reveals the colonial-era transportation of new edible and ornamental plants to Britain and the notable examples of slave-gotten wealth that funded the late 18th and early 19th-century passion for botany and plant collecting. The chapter looks at the role of institutions such as Kew Gardens in imperial commerce and its activities that made possible the expansion of empire into Africa. But I also look at how a love of plants spread beyond the elites, as reflected in the poetry of John Clare, in particular. The chapter also tells a counter story: how enslaved Africans changed the foodways of the Americas by bringing grains and vegetables with them on the slave ships, foods that enabled them to survive, maintain their culture and establish the distinctive creole cuisine of the Caribbean that is now also part of British culinary culture. The chapter also looks at those aspects of the vernacular garden – allotments, public parks and the suburban garden – that engaged the majority of the population. The chapter sees poetry about gardens as one of the most floriferous zones of writing by Black and Asian Britons.

The second half of the book contains my own response to this topic in fiction and poetry that explores the colonial aspects of other rural phenomena: country estates, fields, flowers, graveyards, hills, parks, village pubs and woodlands. If rural England's relationship to empire was once self-evident, later generations have largely forgotten it. These creative pieces are written in the recognition that no academic study can do justice to the human stories which are routinely lost in historical writing.

The terms Black British and British Asian are used throughout the book in preference to BAME or other formulations. As socially constructed categories, the terms Black British and British Asian do, of course, risk conflating peoples of diverse origin, class and identifications into ludicrous single categories. Nonetheless, use of the term Black, particularly, gestures towards earlier positive constructions of Black identity. Wherever possible, the book is precise about the cultural heritage of the people it discusses.

Endnotes

1. Raymond Williams, *Border Country* (London: Chatto & Windus, 1960) and *The Country and the City*, (London: Chatto & Windus, 1973).
2. Edward W. Said, *Orientalism*, (New York: Pantheon, 1978).
3. Madge Dresser and Andrew Hann (eds.), *Slavery and the British Country House* (London: English Heritage, 2008).
4. Stephanie Barczewski, *Country Houses and the British Empire, 1700-1930*, (Manchester: Manchester University Press, 2016,).
5. Musée de Lorient, 'Traite et Esclavage', https://musee.lorient.bzh/collections/traite-et-esclavage/,accessed 9th November, 2020. Thanks to Yannick Guerry, independent researcher, for providing this information.
6. Victor Hugo, *Bug Jargal* (Paris: J. Hetzel, 1826).
7. David P. Geggus (ed.), *The Impact of the Haitian Revolution in the Atlantic World* (Columbia: University of South Carolina Press, 2001), p. 232.
8. Carole Ione, *Pride of Family: Four Generations of American Women of Color*, (South Carolina: iUniverse, 2001).
9. Ripton Lindsay, 'Alexander Lindsay and Jamaica', file:///C:/Users/csf11/AppData/Local/Microsoft/Windows/INetCache/Content. Outlook/6EWB7WB2/Alexander%20Lindsay%20and%20Jamaica%20(2019%20Edition).pdf, p .27. Accessed 28th September, 2020.
10. William Blake, Preface to *Milton, a Poem*, Edited by Robert N. Essick and Joseph Viscomi ([1810] Princeton: Princeton University Press, 1993).

PART ONE

EMPIRE, LITERATURE AND RURAL ENGLAND

CHAPTER ONE
NATION AT THE CROSSROADS

'Thank God the athletes have arrived! Now we can move on from leftie multi-cultural crap. Bring back Red Arrows, Shakespeare and the Stones!' (Tweet by MP Aiden Burley, Olympics Opening ceremony, July 2012).

It was Friday night on 27 July, 2012. The London sky was overcast and a BBC commentator worried aloud about the prospect of rain. There was tension in the air: Britain was about to be showcased to a worldwide television audience of over 900 million people. As the countdown began to the official opening of the Olympics Ceremony, viewers were reminded that 'Isles of Wonder' was choreographed by Danny Boyle, the celebrated director of *Trainspotting* (1996) and *Slumdog Millionaire* (2008).[1] The choice of Boyle as creative director had been announced two years previously. Back then, news media coverage of the impending spectacle was cautiously optimistic. The *Guardian* went so far as to express 'delighted astonishment' at the choice of Boyle.[2] But none of this could quite dispel the air of trepidation: would London's opening ceremony rival Beijing's 2008 offering? 'Isles of Wonder' came with a high price-tag. At £27M it had consumed twice its original budget, yet at £65M the Chinese had spent considerably more.

As nine o'clock loomed, the BBC's aerial cameras zoomed in on the Olympic Stadium's blazing lights. As Big Ben's amplified chime faded, 'Isles of Wonder' began with *Journey Along the Thames*, a two-minute BBC film directed by Boyle. As the film's title and length imply, the River Thames is followed at high speed from its source in a Gloucestershire field to the heart of London. This journey is full of references to rural representation, from the English idyll to more radical depictions of the countryside by film-makers that Boyle admired, such as Michael Powell and Emeric Pressburger whose film, *A Canterbury Tale* (1944), depicted rural Britain as a place of labour and a place of change (landgirls in the fields), but also a place resistant to change. In its opening frames, *Journey Along the Thames* follows an improbably blue dragonfly as it flits along the water's surface. Insofar as the dragonfly evokes hot, bygone summers, it belongs to the symbolic terrain of England's pastoral idyll. Yet its ultramodern electric-blue colouring gives an early indication that the film is concerned with updating established ideas about rural England. The film itself is speeded-up, a device which indicates the passing of time as though to indicate progress from traditional mind-sets. Below, I examine two scenes from the opening ceremony to understand why some spectators were so provoked by it. Their anger is symptomatic of widespread lack of awareness that England's coastlines, country houses, moorlands, villages and woodlands have multiple global and colonial connections, which this book explores.

Successive images in *Journey along the Thames* unfold to the accompaniment of 'Surf Solar', by a two-piece, mixed-race pop band called Fuck Buttons. Their soundtrack underlines the film's concern with diversifying images of rural Britain. Boyle's letter in the ceremony's official guide hints at this agenda:

> 'This is for everyone' is the theme of the opening ceremony... We can build Jerusalem. And it will be for everyone.[3]

The concept 'for everyone' was soon afterwards adopted by the National Trust in its efforts to make the organisation more inclusive. The reference to 'Jerusalem' – the song which is commonly considered England's 'true national anthem', based on a poem by William Blake – calls for the creation of a better world, built on 'England's green and pleasant land', a land which – in the context of the opening ceremony – belongs to all, regardless of ethnicity. Yet, as studies of rural racism have consistently shown, rural England is a fiercely guarded site of belonging.[4]

Early on, *Journey to the Thames* presents its viewers with two white boys playing in the river with nets and jam-jars. The boys are immersed in a soundscape of birdsong, sloshing water and echoing laughter. It probably refers to a scene in *A Canterbury Tale* where boys are playing by a river. Two elements of this scene suggest its historical provenance: the receding echoes of laughter and the once-popular pastime of collecting specimens. Its fleeting image is calculated to evoke nostalgia for a lost era of unsupervised play in English meadows. The notion of the rural idyll is evoked by Kenneth Grahame's riverside classic *The Wind in the Willows* (1908) when Ratty, Mole and Toad flash on to the screen. The camera passes under a Cotswold bridge before returning to the theme of childhood exploration with a medium close-up of a child brushing his palm against ears of corn. This last image is also given a historical flavour, viewed through a keyhole as though through a doorway to the rural past. These prepare the ground for the film's concern with dislodging tenacious images of England's countryside as a white preserve.

The film's first black face appears as the outskirts of London are reached. A mixed-race woman opens a garden umbrella outside a riverside pub. This is followed by a brief close-up of a smiling Black schoolboy before the camera pans across a field and hovers above an Intercity 125 train. Inside the carriage, an Indian family is seated at a table. The teenage daughter reads the official gold-coloured guide to the opening ceremony.[5] A split-second shot of a Black cricketer, a bowler – dressed in traditional cricket whites with a cloth cap and spotted necktie – appears at a culturally sensitive moment, coming straight after shots of the Oxford-Cambridge boat race and the Eton boating song, both of which epitomise elite expressions of Englishness. In this context, the image of an early 20th-century Black bowler is disruptive, not merely reminding supporters that Britain's colonial masters have frequently been beaten at their own game,[6] but because the way he is dressed suggests a historical, rather than recent, Black presence in the countryside. Whether Boyle intended it or not, the image is more complex than it might seem. There was a class tradition where the Marylebone Cricket Club employed professional bowlers as servants to bowl at the gentlemen batsmen,[7] and the Caribbean trope of the Black fast bowler and the white batsman persisted at least into the 1930s.[8] The only Black cricketers on a 1900 West Indies tour to England were bowlers; all the batsmen were white. But the presence of a Black cricket player is historically appropriate. There was the famous Indian prince, Kumar Shri Ranjitsinhji (1872-1933) who played for both Sussex and England between 1895-1904;[9] there was Charles Ollivierre (1876-1949) who came with the 1900 West Indian team to England, and thereafter was recruited by the Derbyshire County Cricket club for whom he played between 1901 and 1907;[10] and there was Kumar Shri Duleepsinhji (1905-1959), another Indian prince who also played for Sussex and England between 1929 and 1931.[11] But almost certainly the film's reference is to Learie Constantine (1901-1971), a Trinidadian all-rounder who toured England with the West Indies in 1923 and later played in the Lancashire League (perhaps explaining the cloth cap). In Lancashire, Learie Constantine was an immensely popular figure who immersed himself in local radical Labour politics. He later became a formidable influence on racial equality campaigns and legislation. Eventually he became Britain's first Black peer.[12] Yet the Black cricketer might have been *seen* by the Olympic audience that night as unlikely because this figure challenges collective historical amnesia about Black people's longstanding and influential association with England's countryside as well as the nation more generally. In fact, as this book explores, the history of Black and Asian people in Britain before the 1940s was almost as much rural and coastal as it was urban.

That night in July, 'Green and Pleasant Land' was the first live spectacle in the stadium. 7,346 square metres of real grass and crops simulated a pastoral, pre-industrial setting. Farmers and milkmaids tended sheep, horses, ducks, goats and geese. The scene featured a cricket match – again including a Black bowler in cricket whites – and four Maypole dances, with a handful of Black children. Actors moved around the white cottages and hedgerows to the accompaniment of choristers singing Parry's 'Jerusalem'.

On the surface, the *Official Guide* commentary on 'Green and Pleasant Land' seems relatively innocuous:

> This is the countryside we all believe existed once. It's where children danced around the Maypole and summer was always sunny. This is the Britain of *The Wind in the Willows* and *Winnie the Pooh*.[13]

The statement is actually a gentle reproof which rejects outmoded visions of the past. England's rural idyll is presented as a nostalgic falsehood ('the countryside we all *believe* existed'), a falsehood fed to us by the classic stories we heard as children. This fiction, the commentary implies, has left a rose-tinted imaginative legacy ('summer was always sunny'). Depictions of idyllic rural childhoods are – the booklet suggests – freighted with nostalgia, a beautiful lie. This lie is undermined by the commentary's appeal to our contrasting experiences of overcast skies or recurrent summer rain. The use of the singular ('*the* Britain') immediately implies that there are multiple 'Britains' with which its citizens variously identify.

From a historical perspective, Boyle did well to place Black Britons in the pre-industrial countryside, since he offered an alternative lens through which to view the nation's rural past. Yet, in Boyle's presentation (although the Black cricketer probably recalls Constantine), the presence of Black maypole dancers, farmers and milkmaids in the stadium cannot be seen as wanting to reflect any historically genuine Black rural presence in the 18th and 19th centuries. Rather it is presented as a utopian dream for the future ('we will build Jerusalem'). Boyle might easily have drawn on established historical knowledge to justify his vision of a multiracial rural past. Instead, Boyle's 'Green and Pleasant Land' is a well-meaning reaction against elitist and exclusive forms of English self-fashioning more than any genuine acknowledgement that – to quote Caroline Bressey – 'black histories of England are intimately connected to the rural'.[14] Wills, parish records and court records testify to this presence. So do paintings. Few exhibition halls would be big enough to exhibit all the paintings that include African and Asian servants which currently hang in historic houses.[15] As the words of the Parry's anthem 'Jerusalem' imply, the scene advocates national unity by means of an inclusive collective return to nature. The countryside is 'for everyone'. Boyle's multicultural vision of rural England was a healing gesture, given the use of the 'green and pleasant land' metaphor to the anti-immigration speeches of Conservative MP Enoch Powell in the late 1960s and 1970s and – by the time of the London Olympics – the UK Independence Party, which was then at its height of popularity.[16] In Boyle's contemporary response, however, 'Green and Pleasant Land' missed the opportunity to justify its representation of a historical Black presence when it failed to provide genuine references to this presence in England well before the days of empire.

Had 'Green and Pleasant Land' had greater historical precision, it might have been less of an easy target for the resultant hostile reviews in blogs and newspapers. 'Pandemonium', the Industrial Revolution scene in the pageant – named after John Milton's 'hell' and Humphrey Jennings's book with that title[17] – contains black industrialists in top hats – a phenomenon without any historical justification – which provoked Scott Gronmark to write: 'I knew we were in for some social re-engineering when a black Victorian industrialist popped up complete with top hat in the Kenneth Branagh... section.'[18] 'Pandemonium' underlined the fact that England's historical Black presence was presented as fanciful rather than real.

Boyle may have intended to include everyone, but the reality of the event was very different. Despite the ceremony's celebration of diversity, Britain's largest black newspaper, *The Voice*, was denied access by the Media Accreditation Committee on the grounds that there was only space for 400 journalists to cover the ceremony. A further irony was that *The Voice* offices are situated close to the Olympic stadium.[19]

One of the 900 million-strong audience members was the Conservative MP, Aiden Burley, who kept up a running commentary of his responses to 'Isles of Wonder' on Twitter. After viewing 'Green and Pleasant Land' he tweeted: 'The most leftie opening ceremony I have ever seen – more than Beijing, the capital of the communist state!' His later, now notorious, tweet expressed affront at the presence of so many Black people in the artistic reconstruction of Britain's past:

> Thank God the athletes have arrived! Now we can move on from leftie multi-cultural crap. Bring back Red Arrows, Shakespeare and Stones![20]

The tweet caused a political row, prompting Burley to offer an explanatory tweet: 'Seems my tweet has been misunderstood. I was talking about the way it was handled in the show, not multiculturalism itself.' On Saturday 28 July, The *Guardian*'s Nicolas Watt commented:

> Burley's outburst will fuel suspicions that some members of the Conservative party have unreconstructed views which fail to recognise the pivotal contribution to society made by black and minority ethnic Britons. Boyle illustrated this with a section devoted to *MV Empire Windrush*, the ship which brought many passengers from Jamaica to start a new life in Britain.[21]

While these words are offered in defence of multiculturalism, they promote an inaccurate but widely-held belief that the postwar era was *the* moment when black people arrived in Britain. Watt fails to address the deeper cause of Burley's offence, hinted at in his defensive tweet: 'I was talking about *the way it* [multiculturalism] *was handled* in the show' [my italics]. What evidently offended Burley was the vision of Black people in the countryside, a phenomenon that he saw as incongruous. Burley's tweets imply that the countryside has always been, and ought to remain, a white sanctuary. In the same vein, and on the same weekend, an anonymous tweeter wrote the following response to the ceremony: 'Apparently, in the pre-industrial revolution bit, some of the white sheep were pretending to be black sheep'.[22] Whiteness, the logic goes, is native to the English countryside: anyone else is an outsider and an impostor. Other commentators, too, characterised 'Isles of Wonder' as a farcical minstrel show. Gronmark wrote in his blog: 'I'm surprised Boyle didn't ask Paul McCartney to black up to sing "Hey, Jude"'.[23] Gronmark's irritation is similarly triggered by the ceremony's portrayal of devolved Black Britishness. A stadium-based choir composed of black and white children sing 'Jerusalem' but hand over to their Northern Irish counterparts standing on the Giant's Causeway. Next, the camera visits a third children's choir positioned near Stirling castle. As they offer a regionally-accented rendition of 'Flower of Scotland', the camera pans across the front row, where a Black boy is prominently placed. As another implicit celebration of blackness in a semi-rural location, this again provoked Gronmark, who complained that, in Boyle's vision of multiculturalism, Black people were 'punching well above their demographic weight'. He similarly objects to the presence of a Black Scottish singer: 'A Scottish female singer with an extremely unsuitable voice later sang "Abide With Me", obviously she was black too.'[24] Like Burley, Gronmark objects to the *way* multiculturalism was depicted. The implicit suggestion is that the countryside does not belong to all.

As this book explores, the countryside is widely viewed as having everything to do with whiteness and little to do with empire, and suggestions to the contrary typically encounter strong opposition. A recent *Daily Mail* article about the National Trust's attempts to address its colonial connections provoked nearly 500 comments, all hostile.[25] One reader wrote, 'There is a coordinated attack on British values, culture [and] heritage', conveying a belief that the heritage sector ought to promote monocultural versions of the rural past. Another reader called Rosie accused the National Trust of starting a 'campaign to make Britons ashamed of their glorious heritage.' For another reader, the idea of a rural white preserve is enduringly potent: 'It is high time all the descendants of slaves returned to the birthplace of their ancestors and stayed there, as they are not doing themselves any favours trying to besmirch our ancestors and heritage.' Made in the context of country houses, this comment indicates that what is being disturbed is an unsubstantiated illusion of historic rural England as having been self-contained, isolated from the world.

Other *Mail* readers of the article accused the Trust of trying to 'change the past'. One comment reads: 'The National Trust is supposed to preserve our history, not change it.' In the mind of this reader, and many others who left similar comments, to revisit this aspect of the past is to falsify and corrupt history itself.

But to preserve without asking new questions is to fossilise. If the heritage sector is a custodian of history, it is incumbent upon professional interpreters of that history to explore stories which emerge from new research. Historic houses predominantly tell the story of family, but such properties have many more stories to tell.[26] One *Mail* reader asserted: 'The fact is that there were never any slaves in Britain.' To counter this denial is to be met with suspicion: the attempt is seen as ideologically motivated rather than evidence-based. There is widespread reluctance to hear local historical evidence of colonial links, such as the 1771 slave 'auction' in Lichfield in which the *Aris's Gazette* advertised the sale of 'a NEGROE BOY, supposed to be about ten or eleven years of Age'.[27] There are hundreds more escaped slave notices recorded by the Runaway Slaves project at the University of Glasgow.[28] In one sense, however, *Mail* readers' remarks on the subject of the Black rural presence missed the point. As the article made clear, the heritage sector is primarily interested in the *legacies* of colonialism (not just slavery) – financial, cultural and curatorial. For many, simply researching colonial connections is an affront. When Cambridge University announced its intention to investigate its slavery links, the news was widely condemned. 'Seldom', David Olusoga wrote, 'have so many people taken to print and the airwaves to make the case for academic incuriosity.'[29] Moreover, when the National Trust published its report on colonialism and historic slavery connections in September 2020, the Leader of the House of Commons, Jacob Rees-Mogg, objected in a parliamentary speech, the Culture Secretary condemned the report in the press, the Common Sense Group of Conservative MPs called a debate on 'The Future of the National Trust' in Westminster Hall and the Charity Commission wrote to the National Trust to ask 'how the trustees consider its report helps further the charity's specific purpose to preserve places of beauty or historic interest.'[30] Widespread attempts to repress historical research – and to incorporate colonial history into heritage sites – are often made in the name of free speech and celebrating the nation's past.

In response to one of many *Daily Mail* articles on the subject, one objector states, 'it is *history* and should be left there' [my italics].[31] Another writes: 'nothing can be done to change history, so what in earth [sic] is to be gained?' Yet these comments suggest that, in this context, the term *history* can actually be taken to mean 'unpalatable elements of the national story'. What require preserving, the logic goes, are familiar, established accounts of the past. Specialists in British imperial history are viewed as ideologues, trespassers on hallowed ground. Research findings on this topic are presented as political and emotional rather than rational in motivation. Another comment under a *Mail* article declared: 'this self-punishment must stop'. Another calls it 'self-flagellation'. Such statements communicate unexamined emotional responses, an unnamed fear that new facts threaten old ones. Given the paucity of information in the school curriculum on Britain's four colonial centuries that most British adults have received, it is unsurprising that it should come as a shock that the country-side has so many colonial connections.

Such comments reveal inconsistent attitudes to the past. As the historian Rajwinder Singh Pal remarks, few Britons would wish to destroy the sites of German Nazism or Italian Fascism. Neither are there objections to com-memorating Waterloo, or even Peterloo.[32] Olusoga observes that 'the parts of the past that it seems unhealthy to dwell on tend to be those in which non-white people were exploited or exterminated. It's always too long ago or not appropriate.'[33] The idea that new information amounts to 'politically correct revisionism' (as one *Mail* reader asserted) – actual falsification of the past – reminds us that England's 'green and pleasant land' is sensitive terrain. This book attempts to explain the sources of rural mythologies themselves.

It is worth pointing out that the views noted above do not exist only on the pages of *The Mail*. *The Telegraph* has run many negative articles about the 2020 National Trust report since its release, and ran an opinion piece entitled 'National Trust must listen to members' in which it argued that questions 'about the wisdom of the Trust's "woke agenda" need to be heeded, not ignored.'[34] Academic historians such as Andrew Roberts have offered more sophisticated versions of the same proposition, selling many books promoting his view of the benefits (with a few regrettable lapses) of colonialism.[35] Roberts, and many of the commentators in *The Mail*, hold the view that we cannot judge the imperial past by the values of the enlightened present. One descendant of a family who built a country mansion from the proceeds of active involvement in transatlantic slavery said, 'raking through the past is not particularly helpful', and implied that the existence of slavery was a blot on everyone.[36] Perhaps, but it is worth remembering that slave-ownership involved 6% of the British population (those whose claims show up in the emancipation compensation records). This is only a slightly greater percentage of the population than those who formed the electorate before 1832 and who could have chosen the MPs who decided the fate of slavery.[37] It is an argument that is profoundly ahistorical, as is shown in Jack P. Greene's *Evaluating Empire and Confronting Colonialism in Eighteenth Century Britain* (2013) and Priyamvada Gopal's *Insurgent Empire: Anticolonial Resistance and British Dissent* (2019). Through-out the colonial period, there were always well-informed and ethically unambiguous critics, not merely of empire's more indefensible outrages (though there were always defenders to be found), but also of the sources of its profits from slavery and the activities of the East India Company.

The historian Catherine Hall has pointed out that, even after abolition and emancipation, British literary figures with (little-discussed) links to slave ownership applied their writing talent to present versions of the past that justified chattel slavery and promoted racial hierarchies. Thomas

Carlyle's infamous racist tract, *Occasional Discourse on the Nigger Question* (1853) asserted that emancipation had been a huge mistake. Carlyle was not alone. Following the killing of African Jamaican peasants after the Morant Bay rebellion of 1865 on the order of Governor Eyre, the 'cream' of literary England took Carlyle's side when he set up a committee to defend Eyre from liberals such as Charles Darwin and John Stuart Mill who wanted to see him prosecuted for murder. Charles Dickens, Lord Alfred Tennyson, Charles Kingsley and John Ruskin were amongst those who supported Carlyle in defending Eyre.[38]

Priyamvada Gopal records similar divisions in Britain over the bloody aftermath of the Indian rebellion of 1857, between those who approved of the retribution visited on suspects who were blown to pieces from the mouths of English cannons, and those like the Chartist Ernest Jones who believed that the rebellion was a justified struggle for nationhood.[39]

I have discussed at length the phenomenon of Boyle's film and grand Olympic pageant and the response to it because it illustrates that, for a long while, Britain has been at a crossroads. There have been recent attempts both to open up *and* to resist a discussion about the way Britain has been shaped by its history as an imperial power. The corollaries of once being an imperial power do not simply concern the presence of people from the former empire in the 'motherland', but the imprint of empire on contemporary attitudes to nationhood, sovereignty and the idea of (English) exceptionalism. Danny Dorling and Sally Tomlinson's book, *Rule Britannia: Brexit and the End of Empire* (2019) makes some of those connections. The choice between nostalgia and egalitarianism is also identified by Paul Gilroy in the subtitle of his book *After Empire: Melancholia or Convivial Culture* (2004). My book weighs in on the side of a rich, convivial culture.

This book attempts to bring three points of departure into connection and dialogue. The first is the phenomenon of empire and colonisation as a set of activities at home and abroad – administrative, economic, military, political, and rhetorical. The second point of departure is the relationship between empire and rural Britain. Here this book unites discussions by researchers of the East India Company and Black Atlantic studies. It makes sense to join these often distinct scholarly domains because the worlds they study are often interwoven. Stately homes illustrate this point. Through successive generations and owners, many properties have links with both the East and the West Indies, which is the case with many of the 93 houses named in the 2020 National Trust report into its places' colonial links. The histories of persons are also often intertwined. In *Children of Uncertain Fortune*, Daniel Livesay tells the story of the Jamaican plantation owner, John Morse. Three of his mixed-race children – the descendants of an enslaved mother – moved from Jamaica to London and, from there to India, where the son worked for the East India Company in Calcutta. The daughters also travelled from London to India, each marrying East India Company servants (officials) in Calcutta, coming back to England and featuring in a painting by Johann Zoffany called *The Morse and Cator Family* (1784).[40] The third point of departure is the long historical presence of Black and Asian people in Britain, including their particular relationship to the countryside. From these three starting points, the book sets out to explore the connections between historical studies and imaginative literary attempts to rethink English rurality. It demonstrates how Black British and British Asian writers (who are inevitably also readers) have addressed and challenged a sense of rural exclusion within the context of shifting sensibilities about the countryside in writing from the sixteenth-century to the present.

Writing in the Footsteps of Pioneers

As in any book of synthesis, I have intellectual debts. These include C.L.R. James's book *The Black Jacobins* (1938) which provided an influential account of the Haitian revolution, the first significant countermovement for colonial freedom in the modern Atlantic and global world.[41] The book's original preface summarised the achievements of the enslaved, led by Toussaint L'Ouverture: 'The slaves defeated in turn the local whites and the soldiers of the French monarchy, a Spanish invasion, a British expedition of some 60,000 men, and a French expedition of similar size under Bonaparte's brother-in-law.'[42] Inspired by this account, Eric Williams's *Capitalism and Slavery* (1944) argued that slave-produced wealth allowed Britain to accumulate the necessary capital for the industrial revolution. Slave-trading stimulated manufacturing through the goods used as barter for enslaved people and the manufacture (in Birmingham in particular) of the chains and items of torture used to discipline enslaved people.[43] Though some subsequent historians dismissed this as an exaggerated claim, Williams's thesis has received well-documented defences in a book such as Joseph E. Inikori's *Africans and the Industrial Revolution in England* (2002).[44] More recently, the work of Nicholas Draper, *The Price of Emancipation: Slave Ownership, Compensation and British Society at the End of Slavery* (2010) demonstrates that the profits of slavery did not end after its abolition and that the direct benefits of slave-ownership produced further capital, some of which was invested in infrastructural projects such as railway construction. Draper's book and a major research project led by Catherine Hall, called *Legacies of British Slave-Ownership* (2014), suggests that Williams's thesis was substantially correct.[45] The project and its accompanying database identify the recipients of £20M worth of compensation money paid to former slave-owners from around 1837 into the 1840s. Administered by the misleadingly-named Slave Compensation Commission, this enormous sum, estimated at £17 billion in today's money, was finally paid off by the British taxpayer in 2015.[46] *Legacies of British Slave-Ownership* allows researchers to trace the money received and spent by the recipients of this compensation money. Catherine Hall observes: 'all the way through to the 1830s and indeed beyond we can see wealth derived from slave-ownership being redeployed into country-house building, connoisseurship and philanthropy in Britain'.[47] Recent research has extended work on empire into family histories such as Katie Donington's work on the slave-owning Hibbert family, which reveals how power and wealth was passed down the generations.

The history of the careers of five members of the Beckford family neatly brings together the complex of wealth, power, literary idealisation, sporting recreation and the aestheticised proceeds of fortunes gained from slavery. Peter Beckford (1643-1710) was the founder of the dynasty as acting governor and owner of around twenty estates in Jamaica. His grandnephew, William Beckford (1709-1770), inherited Jamaican estates, but himself lived most of his life in London, when he was not at his country estate, Fonthill, in Wiltshire. He was reputed to be London's wealthiest citizen, became lord mayor twice and ardently supported the bourgeois liberties of the subject against the crown, and the colonist's right to enslave colonised people.[48] His son, also William (1760-1844), was the author of what is now seen as the founding novel of the queer gothic, *Vathek* (1786). He was the aesthete who squandered the wealth accumulated by his father, collecting art and building the gothic folly of Fonthill Abbey, most of which collapsed in 1825 only eighteen years after it had been built.[49] There was Peter Beckford (1740-1811), grandson of the Jamaican acting governor, who also inherited Jamaican estates but never visited them. He spent his time and money engaged in rural sports and wrote one of the first books about hunting. He was reputedly much embarrassed by the reputation of his cousin, the gothic writer, who had at one time to flee from England because of a homosexual scandal.[50] There was a third William Beckford (1744-1799), the illegitimate nephew of the lord mayor, who inherited five smaller sugar estates and lived in Jamaica for 13 years, failed as a planter and was imprisoned for debt in London in 1786. To earn some money he wrote two volumes of *A descriptive account of the island of Jamaica* (1790), which combined an ardent defence of slavery with a pastoralisation of the plantation landscape, that is 'chiefly considered in a picturesque point of view', meaning he represented it as if it had been an English landscape.[51] There was a further Beckford, Henry, an ex-slave and abolitionist, who appears in the painting of an anti-slavery convention in London, by Benjamin Robert Haydon (1840).[52] Henry Beckford was a deacon in St Ann's Bay, Jamaica, the location of many of the Beckford estates. The Forebears website tells us that one in every 330 Jamaicans (8689) is a Beckford.[53]

I am by no means the first to explore the relationship between empire, slavery, the countryside and British literature. Raymond Williams's study, *The Country and the City* (1973), was pioneering in the way it connected the ideas of C.L.R. James and Eric Williams to fundamental ideas about land and its relationship to capitalist development.[54] Focusing on English stately homes as the subject of a long tradition of literature, Williams writes: 'important parts of the country house system, from the sixteenth to the eighteenth centuries, were built upon the profits of [imperial] trade.'[55] At the time of writing *The Country and the City*, Williams was not able to elaborate very precisely upon these connections, but since then, as noted above, country house historians have identified specific and multiple links with both Caribbean and East India Company wealth.

Following the work of Raymond Williams, there has been an increasing trend in British imperial history to see colonial profits as being as much a rural as an urban phenomenon. In *Slavery and the British Country House* (2013), Andrew Hann and Madge Dresser argue that country houses are a potent 'symbol of ...connoisseurship and civility... and an iconic signifier of national identity'.[56] This is an argument explored across a wider range of cultural practices in Simon Gikandi's important book, *Slavery and the Culture of Taste* (2011). Gikandi's book argues that far from being anomalies, the brutality of slavery and the promotion of polite culture (of manners and concern with aesthetics) were both deeply intermeshed in ideas about race and social and economic development. These were the ideas that justified the colonisation of the lands of other peoples who were believed not to have any sense of property or civility, and the right of those people who had those qualities to own Africans as chattel slaves.[57] Further critical contributions have been made to discussions of the countryside in James Walvin's *Fruits of Empire: Exotic Produce and British Taste, 1660-1800* (1997); Stephanie Barczewski's *Country Houses and the British Empire, 1700-1930* (2014) and David Olusoga's *Black and British: A Forgotten History* (2016). These authors reveal rural Britain's colonial connections to be many and various.

This book also refers to work on writers' social station and gender, in publications such as Donna Landry's *The Muses of Resistance: Laboring-Class Women's Poetry in Britain, 1739-1796* (1990) and William J. Christmas's *The Lab'ring Muses* (2001). It includes work that investigates the literary traditions of pastoral and georgic such as John Gilmore's *The Poetics of Empire* (2000) and Rachel Crawford's *Poetry, Enclosure, and the Vernacular Landscape 1700-1830* (2002). Other critics have connected writers' perceptions of landscape to actual agricultural change and to the relationship between land and empire. Helpful contributions here come from Beth Fowkes Tobin's *Colonizing Nature* (2005), Jill H. Casid's *Sowing Empire: Landscape and Colonization* (2005), and in particular Saree Makdisi's *Romantic Imperialism: Universal Empire and the Culture of Modernity* (1998). Increasingly, rural writing has been read in the context of visual culture, especially the aesthetics of the picturesque and the sublime, aesthetic ideas that still influence the way we see the countryside today. John Barrell, for instance, in *The Idea of Landscape and the Sense of Place: An Approach to the Poetry of John Clare* (1972) identifies a shift from general and idealised perceptions of landscape, to portrayals of the rural world that are individual and specific, a shift that he locates in the writing of John Clare.

For me as for many other authors, Peter Fryer's respected work *Staying Power: The History of Black People in Britain* (1984) remains a key foundational text.[58] Fryer's book was by no means the first. Before it came Paul Edwards's first modern edition of Equiano Olaudah's autobiography in 1967.[59] There was also James Walvin's *The Black Presence: A Documentary History of the Negro in England* (1970) and Edward Scobie's *Black Britannia: A History of Blacks in Britain* (1972), the first panoptic history, which goes back to the Elizabethan period, marking the beginnings of British colonial activity.[60] There was also F.O. Shyllon's *Black Slaves in Britain* (1974). But though not the first, Fryer's book reached and influenced more readers and is widely acknowledged as having demonstrated how long Black people have resided in Britain. *Staying Power* begins with Roman centurions on Hadrian's Wall, and only a relatively slim section of the book postdates the 1948 arrival of the *SS Empire Windrush* in Tilbury Dock, an event which is persistently and incorrectly held to have inaugurated Black Britishness. Important subsequent texts include Gretchen Gerzina's *Black England. Life Before Emancipation* (1995), which also explores the rural black presence. Another foundational work is Rozina Visram's *Ayahs, Lascars and Princes: Indians in Britain, 1700-1947* (1986),[61] the first book to deal with the historical experience of South Asians in the British Isles.

As Fryer suggested, it was not always the case that black people came to Britain as a consequence of empire. As Miranda Kaufmann argues, the lives of those she writes about in *Black Tudors: The Untold Story* (2017) fall outside the colonial framework. They include a royal trumpet player, a diver, a porter, a silk-weaver and a mariner.[62] Research about 18th century England and Wales makes a related point about ordinary lives. Kathleen Chater's book *Untold Histories: Black People in England and Wales during the period of the British Slave Trade c. 1660-1807* (2009) draws extensively from official records to argue that Black people led active working lives in a range of professions. They were tradespeople, shopkeepers, government officials and entertainers. They did not always live 'in the shadows of... aristocratic famil[ies]'.[63]

Going even further back, developments in isotope technology and radio carbon dating have led archaeologists to take ancient British skeletons out of cupboards, only to discover that 'white' bones are sometimes African bones, including those of some of the seamen who perished with the *Mary Rose* in 1545.[64] This 'archaeology of Black Britain' is providing a growing body of evidence to suggest that parts of the countryside – in this case the area around York – once had larger black populations than they do today.[65] The archaeologist Rebecca Redfern writes that Roman Britain was 'a highly multicultural society which included newcomers and locals with black African ancestry and dual heritage, as well as people from the Middle East'.[66] Scientists have studied well over a hundred skeletons from the Roman period and found that, contrary to the idea that pre-modern populations were immobile, some British towns had migrant populations – from other cities and sometimes other countries – of up to thirty percent.[67]

A rurally-based Black British writer, the poet Louisa Adjoa Parker has documented the Black presence in *Dorset's Hidden Histories* (2007). Kevin Le Gendre's *Don't Stop the Carnival: Black Music in Britain* (2018) profiles the career of the virtuoso violinist and orchestral composer, Joseph Antonio Emidy (1775-1835) who was part of a significant population of Black people on the southwest coast. They settled in that area as part of its military presence, at a time when Black people were commonly recruited into the army and navy as musicians (Emidy was press-ganged for this purpose). Emidy rose to be leader of the Falmouth Harmonic Society and the Truro Philharmonic. As a sad note on the limits of possibility for even a virtuoso, Emidy's introduction to London society seems to have foundered on his blackness, he having been described by one member of this elite as 'the ugliest Negro I have ever seen.'[68]

Repressed histories only *appear* contentious because they feel unfamiliar. Until recently, the histories and legacies of Britain's colonial era seem to have all but faded from wider public memory. This is especially true of the nation's involvement with transatlantic slavery. In *Devon and the Slave Trade*, for example, Todd Gray points out that the most authoritative text on the county's history, written by W.G. Hoskins (*Devon and Its People* (1959)), fails to mention slavery even though England's first slave-trading vessels set sail from Plymouth harbour in 1562.[69]

For decades, knowledge of African, Caribbean and Indian connections have been restricted to the academic field of British imperial history. Now, the wider public is awakening to these legacies. It is learning, for example, that not only did Sir Francis Drake participate in John Hawkins's third slave-trading voyage on a royal ship, but – as Miranda Kaufmann discovered – he depended upon an African circumnavigator, Diego, to guide and advise him. Diego was not the only African aboard Drake's ship. *The Golden Hind* carried an enslaved African named Maria, whom Drake eventually abandoned on an Indonesian island. She was pregnant and there was no water source. As Kaufmann points out, this cruelty is likely explained by the need to keep up appearances. Had the protestant crew returned to Plymouth with a heavily pregnant woman, the captain and his sailors would have had some explaining to do.[70]

Later periods tell their own varied stories. A key rural protagonist is George Nathaniel Curzon, whose name adorns many Derbyshire buildings, including Curzon Primary School.[71] His childhood home, Kedleston Hall, has an architectural counterpart in India, where it was once Government House in Calcutta.[72] The Curzon example connects empire with domestic history, since British rule over colonial India was used as a pretext for Curzon's opposition to women's suffrage in his home country. In a pamphlet, Curzon argued that giving women the vote would demean Englishmen in the eyes of Indians. New information disturbs established versions of the past. Two princesses at West Midland's Wightwick Manor connect with forgotten stories about Indian women's contribution to Britain's suffragette movement, while also reminding us that it was a global, not merely a local, movement.[73]

Places tell their stories, but so does cultural production. Classical music is often used to evoke the English countryside, particularly in heritage films and costume drama. Yet this music, too, is implicated in empire. George Frideric Handel (1685-1759) invested in the slave-trading Royal African Company and there are links between 18th-century music and slave-ownership. Musicologist David Hunter discovered that the profits of slavery paid for the purchase of musical instruments, and performers' fees for London operas. He also found that the Beckford family, which made its money from sugar plantations, invested in an expensive new organ for the palladian mansion at Fonthill and bought other valuable musical instruments.[74] But there were also 18th century Black musicians and composers, such as Ignatius Sancho (1729?-1780) and Joseph Emidy, as noted above.

This book is unapologetically materialist, not least because material culture is key to understanding the relationship between the countryside and empire. This is especially true of upper-class settings, since record-keeping and inventories provide detailed information about houses' contents over time. A common item in country houses was 18th-century mahogany – including much Chippendale furniture – which was invariably felled by enslaved Africans in Jamaica, and Central and South America. As James Walvin observed, Africans dragged the trunks through rainforests and floated them down rivers to ports. It was the demand for luxury goods which first propelled colonial fortune-seekers to source and transport goods such as bone-china, Persian carpets, fine silks, exotic wood and Chinese wallpaper. Colonialism's environmental cost is little discussed, but the demand for woods such as mahogany and coromandel brought about deforestation. By the 1740s, the prized Jamaican mahogany forests were depleted and the English had to import their timber from elsewhere in the Americas.[75] Tiger-hunting – always popular with Indian rulers – escalated under the British Raj and there is a direct link between colonialism and the decimation of tiger populations. By the 1930s, the Van Ingen taxidermy firm were processing 400 big cat skins a year.[76] Elephant populations also diminished as European markets increasingly opened up for ivory products at the height of empire. A standard feature of English upper-class domestic settings was the billiard table: it took eight elephant tusks to make a single set of ivory balls.[77]

Such objects belong to a heritage industry that welcomes millions of visitors a year. It collects money from them and aims for repeat visits. In this context, history easily becomes confused with public relations. Accordingly, heritage sites have conventionally withheld information which might risk alienating their members. As an example, until very recently, Harewood House made no mention in its brochures of its financing by the Lascelles family's involvement in all aspects of slave trading, financing the slave trade, the ownership of Caribbean sugar plantations and enslaved people. Information given by guides explained that the extensive rebuilding of the property in the 1840s was the result of a profitable marriage, but the rebuilding costs almost exactly equated to the compensation money the family received for giving up their human property.[78]

Now questions are increasingly being raised about whose stories are being told and to whom such heritage belongs. Strikingly, archival research on the colonial countryside is often carried out by local historians and black history projects outside universities.[79] This raises real and practical questions about where the expertise lies, and which forums are best suited to discussions of recent historical findings. Academics accrue authority by association with Higher Education institutions, but local historians are in danger of being overlooked by museums and heritage organisations which require assistance to interpret their collections in more expansive ways: in a Covid-19 world of budget cuts, it is cheaper to ask salaried academics for help. Increasingly, too, museum and heritage professionals realise that it is unethical not to pay unsalaried experts, but the necessary budget is not always provided and the status quo persists. Yet the custodians of history have a responsibility not to withhold facts. No one should knowingly tell half a history.

Knowledge of the countryside's colonial links is not restricted to historians alone. Writers are increasingly alert to the countryside's imperial dimension. Since the 1980s there has been a distinct rural turn in literary expression by British Asian and Black writers whose forays into rural landscapes parallel recent discoveries by historians of the legacies of imperial Britain. Beginning in the 1980s, with V.S. Naipaul's *The Enigma of Arrival* (1987) and David Dabydeen's *Disappearance* (1993), *Green Unpleasant Land* explores how, and to what end, English rurality is being reimagined by poets, fiction-writers, playwrights and novelists. Whilst 18th and 19th century writing registers the imperial reach into rural England, contemporary Black writers are interested in the colonial past precisely because it disturbs the countryside's persistent association with English soulhood. In this, they join their voices with a long line of earlier anti-pastoral poets who rejected this association for their own reasons.

Like anyone English writing about Britain, I am conscious that *Green Unpleasant Land* focuses mainly on *English* links to empire. I am very conscious of the casual English habit of speaking of Britain but meaning England. I am conscious, too, of the fact that England's relationship to Scotland, Wales and Northern Ireland is one that still bears the imprint of what Michael Hechter calls 'internal colonialism.'[80] This is not to dismiss the role of Scotland and Wales (and Ireland) as themselves actors in empire and colonialism. Scotland was enriched by tobacco and sugar wealth and many estate managers were Scottish.[81] The Caribbean connection is so strong that fewer Scots bear the surname Campbell than their Jamaican counterparts, whose families were forced to take on slave-owners' names.[82] Similarly, the name Ross has many branches in Grenada. Researchers are also discovering that there was a larger 18th century Black presence in Scotland than previously thought. Records examined by the 'Runaway Slaves' project show that at least 67 enslaved people tried to escape their Scottish owners during this period.[83] James Robertson's novel, *Joseph Knight* (2003) is an important work of fiction about slavery in Scotland. Gordon Napier's film, written by Morayo Akandé, entitled *1745: An Untold Story of Slavery*, is based on documentary evidence of two African sisters who escaped to the Highlands after being transported from the Caribbean. Released in 2017, the film has been described as 'Scotland's *12 Years A Slave*'.[84] Meanwhile, Scottish nabobs often left behind 'second families' in India but sometimes brought back their illegitimate children. Little is known about these children, but Deborah Cohen's book *Family Secrets: The Things We Tried to Hide* (2014) tells the story of the half-Indian daughter of Robert Bruce, named Margaret Stuart, who was brought to Falkland and eventually built a house with 'Oriental hints'.[85]

Wales also has strong Caribbean connections. In North Wales, the vast Penrhyn estate is described by historian Marian Gwyn as a 'slavery landscape': its roads, railway lines, port and slate-workers' cottages were financed by the profits of the Pennant family plantations in Clarendon, Jamaica.[86] Today, Penrhyn Castle displays little trace of the sugar wealth which funded its opulence except for a painting of the family's Jamaican plantations. In a letter to his Jamaica agent, Lord Penrhyn chillingly equates enslaved people with livestock while also fashioning himself as a benevolent slave-owner. He writes: 'I do not wish the cattle nor the negroes to be overworked'.[87] Yet the agent's records tell a different story: people who worked on Penrhyn's plantation suffered from 'yaws', 'ulcers' and 'bad feet'. On one record, Marian Gwyn discovered that 47 enslaved people were described as too 'weak' to work.[88] Wales has other economic links to slavery. Chris Evans's book *Slave Wales: Welsh and Atlantic Slavery 1660-1850* shows that woollen fabric and copper were traded for Africans. These profits bolstered Welsh industrial development.[89] A new Heritage Lottery project (in collaboration with Evans) reveals further links between working-class labour and empire. 'Sheep to Sugar: Welsh Wool and Slavery' is run by community research volunteers who are investigating 18th century woollens called Welsh Plains, produced by impoverished Montgomeryshire and Merionethshire families to make 'negro cloth' for enslaved people to wear on Caribbean sugar plantations.[90] The legacy is also experienced personally, as explored in Charlotte Williams's book *Sugar and Slate*, about growing up in North Wales in the 1950s as the daughter of a father from Guyana and a Welsh mother.[91] Her own father, the artist, archaeologist and novelist, Denis Williams, wrote an experimental novel called *The Third Temptation* (1968),[92] set in the Welsh seaside resort he calls Caedmon, a fictional version of Colwyn Bay. In his novel, Denis Williams refers to the nearby African Training Institute, in Colwyn Bay, otherwise known as Congo House, one of the few missionary establishments that respected African cultures.

In naming this book after the phrase 'green and pleasant land' from the poetic preface to William Blake's prophetic *Milton, a poem*, I wanted to reflect on some of the ironies of the poem's subsequent use: the gap between the poem's context in *Milton* and later political and cultural contexts of interpretation. *Milton, a poem* is a complex epic in which Blake works out his mixed admiration for the poet John Milton, because Milton was a brave republican and supporter of regicide, and his quarrel with Milton's Calvinist belief that there was a spiritual elect, a variety of Christianity that Blake believed showed an empty, self-regarding moralism.[93] Blake's poem was popularised by Sir Hubert Parry, who, as the result of a commission that he grew increasingly reluctant to deliver, set it to the familiar hymn-like music we know. Parry had been asked by the British poet laureate Robert Bridges to compose it for a group called Fight for Right, but he was alarmed to discover the group's jingoistic and ultra-nationalist leanings. Parry was relieved when the National Union of Women's Suffrage Societies asked to use his song at a suffrage rally, and he assigned the copyright to the NUWSS, happy that it be sung as a 'women voters' hymn'.[94]

'Jerusalem's' modern-day resonances might well have upset Blake, the prophet against empire, the wearer of the red cap of liberty for the French revolution, and the man who was tried for sedition in 1803.[95] How did his poem come to serve so many disparate and incompatible ends? For Blake, 'England's green and pleasant land' refers to something that once existed in the deep past and could exist again, but only through immense mental and physical struggle. This was a fight against the evils that he believed lay within the thought processes of individuals, but were also embedded in a society corrupted by kings, priests and the law. Blake wrote from a millennialist tradition that welcomed the French revolution as a sign of a world turned upside down. He wanted to see the end of monarchy, the hierarchical clericalism of 'thou shalt not', and of the institutions of law designed to protect private property from the propertyless – and he believed that achieving this would herald the imminent return of Christ. Nowhere does the poem indicate that the green and pleasant land still exists. The poem's 'dark Satanic Mills' are less about the beginnings of industrialisation, but rather the mills of that strand of rationalist, enlightenment thought (Locke and Newton were his particular enemies) that Blake saw as creating the global oppressions of universal empire.

Despite Blake's call to 'love the human form/ in heathen, turks and jew', 'Jerusalem' has been enlisted to support racially exclusive visions of rural England as a space of whiteness which has supposedly always been that way and should remain as such. It is hard not to wonder what Blake himself would have made of Danny Boyle's Olympic opening ceremony and its political fallout.

Parry's 'Jerusalem' shows what can happen when words are removed from their original context. This book makes the same point about the way that the English countryside, country houses, moorland and gardens are misconceived when, both deliberately and by more unwitting amnesia and ignorance, those sites of Englishness are removed from their complex global histories.

Endnotes

1. Danny Boyle, dir., *Trainspotting,* (Polygram) and Danny Boyle and Loveleen Tandan, directors., 2008, *Slumdog Millionnaire* (20th Century Fox).
2. Lyn Gardner, 'Stephen Baldry and Danny Boyle to run the Olympics spectacle? Huzzah!', *The Guardian* June 17th, 2010.
3. Danny Boyle, 'Isles of Wonder', *The Olympics Opening Ceremony. Official Guide* (London: 2012), p. 11.
4. Neil Chakraborti and Neil Garland, eds., *Rural Racism*, (London: Routledge, 2012). And see Kye Askins, 'Crossing Divides: Ethnicity and Rurality', *Journal of Rural Studies* 25, 2009, 365-375.
5. 'Green and Pleasant Land', *The Olympics Opening Ceremony. Official Guide* (London: 2012), p. 20. The guide also refers to 'Green and Pleasant Land' as 'British meadow'.
6. Those days are rarer, but there were the two famous 'Blackwash' series when the West Indies beat England 5-0 in 1984 and 1986.
7. This was continued in the tradition of Gentlemen v Players matches that lasted until 1962. Professionals (players) were listed on scorecards just by their initials, whilst Gentlemen (amateurs usually of independent means), had the prefix 'Mr' See Neil Wigglesworth, *The Story of Sport in England* (London: Routledge, 2007).
8. For an account of race and colour in West Indian cricket, see C.L.R. James, *Beyond a Boundary* (London: Hutchinson, 1962).
9. See Alan Ross, *Ranji: Prince of Cricketers* (London: Collins, 1983).
10. See Barry Ricks, *Duleepsinhji, A Prince of Cricketers* (Parrs Wood Press, 2005).
11. See Jeffrey Green, *Black Edwardians: Black People in Britain 1901-1914* (London: Routledge, 1998), pp. 167-169.
12. For Learie Constantine in Nelson, see Harry Pearson, *Connie: The Marvellous Life of Learie Constantine* (London: Little Brown, 2017), and for Constantine himself on race, see Learie Constantine, *Colour Bar* (London: Stanley Paul, 1954).
13. 'Green and Pleasant Land', *The Olympics Opening Ceremony. Official Guide.*
14. Caroline Bressey, 'Cultural Archaeology and Historical Geographies of the Black Presence in Rural England', *Journal of Rural Studies* 25, 2009, 386-395.
15. See Chapter 4, pp. 135, 156-157. And see Beth Fowkes Tobin, *Picturing Imperial Power: Colonial Subjects in the Eighteenth-Century* (Durham: Duke UP, 1999), pp. 27-55.
16. Enoch Powell's words in his infamous speech of 16 November 1968 were: 'recreating in Britain's green and pleasant land, the

haunting tragedy of the United States'. www.enochpowell.net/fr-83.html.

17. A reference to Humphrey Jennings, *Pandaemonium, 1660-1886: The Coming of the Machine As Seen by Contemporary Observers* (London, Icon, 1985). As the opening date suggests, Jennings took his title from its invention in Milton's *Paradise Lost*, as the capital of Hell. Humphrey Jennings was a documentary film-maker, a contemporary of Powell and Pressburger, the British film-making duo whose films of the 1940s and 1950s are admired by Danny Boyle. Jennings, too, was concerned with shaping a non-elitist sense of national identity.

18. Scott Gronmark, 'The Olympics Opening Ceremony - "none more than black"!', Saturday 28 July, 2012, http://scottgronmark. blogspot.co.uk/2012/07/the-olympics-opening-ceremony-none-more.html#more, accessed 5 July, 2013.

19. Kunbi Tinuoye, 'Britain's Largest Black Newspaper Barred from the Olympic Stadium' July 17, 2012. http://thegrio.com/2012/07/ 17/ the-voice-silenced-britains-largest-black-newspaper-barred-from-olympic-stadium/, accessed 12 April 2018.

20. Tweet referenced in Nicolas Watt, 'Olympics Opening Ceremony was "Multicultural Crap" MP Burley Tweets', *The Guardian*, Saturday 28 July, 2012.

21. Nicholas Watt, 'Olympics Opening Ceremony was "multicultural crap", Tory MP tweets', 28 July 2012, accessed 3 November 2013.

22. Anonymous tweet, 28 July 2012.

23. Gronmark, 2012, *op. cit.*, accessed 5 July 2013.

24. Gronmark, 2012, *op. cit.*, accessed 4 July 2013.

25. Julie Henry and Eleanor Harding, 'Now National Trust probes slave trade links of its stately homes and wants children as young as TEN to advise staff on explaining Britain's imperial history to visitors', *The Daily Mail,* 6 May 2019.

26. See Chapter Four, pp. 127-135.

27. Cited in Barbara Willis-Brown, *Scawdi. In the Beginning,* (Birmingham: Birmingham City Council, 2008), p. 11.

28. The 'Runaway Slaves in Britain: bondage, freedom and race in the eighteenth-century' project is based at Glasgow University and the website can be found at www.runaways.gla.ac.uk/, accessed 13 May 2019. Evidence of the Lichfield slave sale was discovered by the Whose Story project, based at the University of Birmingham in 2008.

29. David Olusoga, 'Why are so many afraid to confront Britain's historical links with the slave trade?', *The Guardian,* 5 May 2019.

30. Amit Roy, 'National Trust Faces Heat for Revealing Buildings' Colonial Past', *Asian Times*, 11 November 2020, p. 19.

31. *Daily Mail*, online, 6 May 2019.
32. I am grateful to Rajwinder Singh Pal for pointing this out in response to the *Daily Mail* article responses.
33. David Olusoga, *Black and British: A Forgotten History* (London: Pan, 2017), p. 8.
34. Telegraph View, 'National Trust must listen to members', *The Telegraph*, 10th November, 2020.
35. Andrew Roberts's *A History of the English-Speaking Peoples since 1900* (2019) finds ways to excuse the Amritsar massacre and the appalling treatment, including mass hangings and torture, of Kenyan detainees during the British war of suppression against the Kenyan uprising to end colonialism in the 1950s.
36. *Yorkshire Post*, 7 May 2019.
37. Nicholas Draper, *The Price of Emancipation: Slave Ownership, Compensation and British Society at the End of Slavery* (Cambridge: Cambridge UP, 2009). And see Michael Taylor, *The Interest: How the British Establishment Resisted the Abolition of Slavery* (London: Bodley Head, 2020), pp. 232-249, for the relationship between the 1832 Reform Act and the campaign to abolish slavery.
38. See Bernard Semmel, *The Governor Eyre Controversy* (London: MacGibbon and Kee, 1962).
39. See Gopal, *Insurgent Empire*, Chapter Four.
40. Daniel Livesay, *Children of Uncertain Fortune. Mixed-Race Jamaicans in Britain and the Atlantic Family, 1733-1833* (Williamsburg: University of North Carolina Press, 2018)
41. C.L.R. James, *The Black Jacobins: Toussaint L'Ouverture and the San Domingo Revolution* (London: Secker and Warburg, 1938).
42. *The Black Jacobins*, p. ix.
43. Eric Williams, *Capitalism and Slavery* (North Carolina: University of North Carolina Press, 1944).
44. Joseph E. Inikori's book, *Africans and the Industrial Revolution in England: A Study in International Trade and Economic Development* (Cambridge: Cambridge UP, 2002)
45. Catherine Hall, Nicholas Draper, Keith McClelland, Katie Donington and Rachel Lang, *Legacies of British Slave-Ownership: Colonial Slavery and the Formation of Victorian Britain* (Cambridge: Cambridge UP, 2014).
46. See David Olusoga, 'The Treasury's tweet shows slavery is still misunderstood', *The Guardian* 12 February 2018. https://www.theguardian.com/commentisfree/2018/feb/12/treasury-tweet-slavery-compensate-slave-owners, accessed 2 February 2019. As Olusoga argues in his article, an ill-judged tweet from the Treasury announced this news as a #FridayFact, which read: 'Did you know?

In 1833, Britain used £20 million, 40% of its national budget, to buy freedom for all slaves in the Empire? The amount borrowed for the Slavery Abolition Act was so large that it wasn't paid off until 2015. Which means that living British citizens helped pay to end the slave trade'. As David Olusoga points out in his article, the money was paid to slave-owners rather than slaves, it was paid long after Abolition, and enslaved people worked without wages for a further 6 years.

47. See Catherine Hall et al, *Legacies of British Slave-Ownership*, pp. 11-12.

48. See Perry Gauci, *William Beckford: First Prime Minister of the London Empire* (New Haven: Yale UP, 2013).

49. See Timothy Mowl, *William Beckford: Composing for Mozart* (London: John Murray, 1998), and James Lees-Milne, *William Beckford* (London: Century, 1976).

50. See A. Henry Higginson, *Peter Beckford Esquire: A Biography* (London: Collins, 1937), and see Donna Landry, *The Invention of the Countryside: Hunting, Walking and Ecology in English Literature, 1671-1831* (London: Palgrave, 2001), pp. 63 ff.

51. For William Beckford the jailbird, see below in this book p. 230.

52. On Henry Beckford see Paul O'Keefe, *A Genius for Failure: The Life of Benjamin Robert Haydon* (London: Bodley Head, 2009), pp. 486-487.

53. See http://forbears.io/surnames/beckford and see Robert Beckford, Bloodlines: Branding with Another Iron (25 July 2005). http://www/open.edu/openlearn/history-the-arts/history/heritage/bloodlines-branding-another-iron.

54. Raymond Williams, *The Country and the City* (London: Chatto & Windus, 1973).

55. *The Country and the City*, p. 279.

56. Dresser and Hann, *Slavery and the British Country House*, p. xiii.

57. Simon Gikandi, *Slavery and the Culture of Taste* (Princeton: Princeton UP, 2014).

58. Peter Fryer, *Staying Power: The History of Black People in Britain* (London: 1984)

59. Paul Edwards, ed. *Equiano's Travels: His Autobiography* (London: Heinemann, 1967)

60. Edward Scobie, *Black Britannia: A History of Blacks in Britain* (London: Johnson Pub. Co., 1973).

61. Rozina Visram, *Ayahs, Lascars and Princes: Indians in Britain, 1700-1947* (London: Pluto Press, 1986).

62. Miranda Kaufman, *Black Tudors: The Untold Story* (London: Oneworld Publications, 2017).

63. Kathleen Chater, *Untold Histories: Black People in England and Wales during the period of the British Slave Trade c. 1660-1807* (Manchester: Manchester UP, 2009), p. 222.

64. Recent examples include the 'Ivory Bangle lady', who grew up in Britain and was buried with expensive jewellery, suggesting that she was of high status. Meanwhile, the 'Beachy Head Lady' was found in a box labelled 'Beachy Head, something to do with 1956 or 1959', but showed that the skeleton belonged to a Roman African. See Jo Seaman, 2018, 'The Mystery of Beachy Head Lady: A Roman African from Eastbourne', https://museumcrush.org/the-mystery-of-beachy-head-lady-a-roman-african-from-eastbourne/, accessed 8th May 2019. The 'Cheddar Man' was found in Somerset. A Mesolithic hunter-gatherer, his skin pigmentation was darker than conventionally expected, revealing a shade normally associated with Sub-Saharan Africa (Kerry Lotzof, 'Cheddar Man: Mesolithic Britain's Blue-Eyed Boy www.nhm.ac.uk/discover/cheddar-man-mesolithic-britain-blue-eyed-boy.html?gclid=EAIaIQobChMI34nx_sqa4AIVCIbVCh1OMgxDEAAYASAAEgIAX_D_BwE), accessed 1 February 2019. And see Richard Paul Benjamin, 'Black British Heritage Internet Resources', Article 6, African Diaspora Archaeology Newsletter Vol.8, issue 1, May 2005, Available at: https://scholarworks.umass.edu/adan/vol8/iss1/6, accessed 14 February 2019.

65. Steve Bird, 'Analysis of Roman grave reveals that York was a multicultural society', *The Times,* 27 February 2010.

66. Rebecca Redfern, 'The Roman Dead: new techniques are revealing just how diverse Roman Britain was', *The Conversation*, May 24, 2018. http://theconversation.com/the-roman-dead-new-techniques-are-revealing-just-how-diverse-roman-britain-was-95243, accessed 14 February 2019.

67. Runnymede Trust, 2017, 'Early and Medieval Migrations, AD43-500: The Ivory Bangle Lady', https://www.ourmigrationstory.org.uk/oms/roman-britain-the-ivory-bangle-lady, accessed 2 February 2019

68. Todd Grey, *Devon and the Slave Trade: Documents on Enslavement, Abolition and Emancipation from 1562 to 1867* (Devon: Mint Press, 2007).

69. Miranda Kaufmann, *Black Tudors: The Untold Story* (London: Oneworld Publications, 2017), p. 86.

70. Curzon Primary School participated in the Arts Council and Heritage Lottery-funded project 'Colonial Countryside: National Trust Houses Reinterpreted' (2018-2020), in which 100 primary pupils raised public awareness of country houses' Caribbean and East India Company connections.

71. David Olusoga, *Civilizations: First Contact. The Cult of Progress.* (London:

Profile Books, 2018). See also James Best, 1804., 'Plan of the principal storey of the New Government House, Calcutta', British Library catalogue.

72. Women and Power exhibition at Kedleston Hall, Derbyshire. Viewed 11th May 2018. Women and Power was the National Trust's Cultural Programme theme for 2018 and Kedleston Hall was one of the properties which participated in the programme. The princesses, from Cooch Behar in India, married two Mander brothers of Wightwick Manor. See Sumita Mukherjee, *Indian Suffragettes. Female Identities and Transnational Networks* (Oxford: OUP, 2018).

73. David Hunter, 'The Use of the Profits of Slavery to Support Musical Activity in Eighteenth-Century Britain and its Colonies', paper given at 'What's Happening in Black British History VIII' conference, 10 May 2018; and David Hunter, 'The Beckfords in England and Italy: A Case Study in the Musical Uses of the Profits of Slavery', *Early Music* Volume XLVI, no. 2, 2018, pp. 285-299, p. 286.

74. James Walvin, *Slavery in Small Things: Slavery and Modern Cultural Habits* (Chichester: John Wiley and Sons, 2017), pp. 82-103.

75. J. Sramek, "Face Him like a Briton": Tiger Hunting, Imperialism, and British Masculinity in Colonial India, 1800-1875, *Victorian Studies*, 48(4), 2006, pp. 659-680.

76. Walvin, *Slavery in Small Things*, p. 90.

77. Research is often carried out by community organisations and small history local projects, such as the SCAWDI (Sparkbrook Caribbean and African Women's Development Initiative). http://www.localtrust. org.uk/big-local/environment/environment-case-studies/sparkbrook-caribbean-african-womens-development-initiative-scawdi-birmingham/, accessed 4 April 2018. SCAWDI trained a number of members to search the work with archivists to find evidence of a black presence in the Midlands in 2011-12.

78. See Michael Hechter, *Internal Colonialism: The Celtic Fringe in British National Development, 1536-1966* (London: Routledge, 1975).

79. Glasgow port is central to the story of Scottish slavery. Stephen Mullen's seminal book, *It Wisnae Us: The Truth About Glasgow and Slavery* (Edinburgh: EUP, 2009), documents the impact of the city's Virginian tobacco and Jamaican sugar wealth. Stephen Mullen, published by The Royal Incorporation of Architects in Scotland, 2009. See also *Recovering Scotland's Slavery Past* by T.M. Devine (Edinburgh University Press, 2015).

80. David Pott, 'Jamaica: the country with more Campbells per head of population than Scotland', *For the People of Glasgow. Evening Times*, 11 October 2015. www.flagupscotjam.uk, accessed 14 February 2019.

81. 'Runaway Slaves in Britain: bondage, freedom and race in the

eighteenth century' is funded by the Leverhulme Trust and based at the College of Arts at University of Glasgow, UK. See www.runaways.gla.ac.uk.

82. See www.1745film.com.

83. Ellen Filor, 'William Rattray of Downie Park', an East India Company at Home case study. See blogs.ucl.ac.uk/eicah/case-studies-2/william-rattray-of-downie-park/, accessed 2 July, 2018.

84. Marian Gwyn, 'Interpreting the Slave Trade: The Penrhyn Castle Exhibition', (2007, PDF available via https://www.academia.edu/9632929/Interpreting_the_Slave_Trade_The_Penrhyn_Castle_Exhibition, accessed 14 February 2019).

85. The Pennants of Penrhyn Castle owned sugar plantations for over 300 years. Colonial Countryside project has collaborated with historian Marian Gwyn to make the castle's slavery connections better known. One of the children on this project, Anne, made a video about the plantation painting, which received over 7,300 views on Twitter. Gwyn has researched the Jamaican connection for a quarter of a century by reading the papers of Richard Pennant, Lord Penrhyn. Pennant's agent in Jamaica kept detailed records of enslaved people on the estate and sent regular reports back to Wales, which have proved an invaluable historical source.

86. In 2018, these words were fashioned into a piece of embroidery by Manon Steffan Ross at the National Trust exhibition called '12 Stories', Penrhyn Castle 2017. For details of the exhibition see https://www.nationaltrust.org.uk/penrhyn-castle/features/manon-steffan-ros—12-stories, accessed 14 February 2019.

87. Gwyn, *op cit.*

88. Chris Evans, *Slave Wales: Welsh and Atlantic Slavery 1660-1850* (Cardiff: University of Wales Press, 2010).

89. See article by Evans on 'Sheep to Sugar: Welsh Wool and Slavery', www.welshplains.cymru/index.asp, accessed 24 April 2019.

90. Charlotte Williams, *Sugar and Slate* (Planet Books, 2002)

91. Denis Williams, *The Third Temptation* ([1968] Leeds: Peepal Tree Press, 2010).

92. *Milton a poem* (London: Tate Publishing, 1995).

93. On the themes of Milton, see David Bindman's introduction to the Tate edition.

94. On Parry's 'Jerusalem', see wikipedia: wiki/And-did-those-feet-in-ancient-time.

95. See David V. Erdman, *Blake: Prophet Against Empire* (Princeton: Princeton UP, 1977).

96. See Saree Makdisi, *Romantic Imperialism: Universal Empire and the Culture of Modernity* (Cambridge: CUP, 1998), pp. 154-172.

CHAPTER TWO:
GREEN UNPLEASANT LAND

I will not cease from mental fight
Nor shall my sword sleep in my hand
Till we have built Jerusalem
On England's Green and Pleasant Land
William Blake, from the Preface to *Milton a Poem,* 1804-1809

In the 11th century, William the Conqueror ordered a survey of landownership and audit of livestock. The resultant document was the *Domesday Book.* Now over 900 years old and housed in the National Archives, it is the first central record of English rural life, and includes some Welsh regions. The survey, completed in 1086, provides a detailed picture of eleventh-century social order. It shows that, following the Norman invasion of 1066, William the Conqueror established a system in which the Norman aristocracy controlled half the land. It evidences a strict social hierarchy, with the king, lords and bishops at the top and serfs at the bottom. Eleventh-century serfs were people who owned no land. However, they did have some access to land to enable their subsistence, but their lives and some of their labour essentially belonged to the landowners.

By the 15th century, the agricultural open field system began to change. Land use was divided among landowners, the bigger tenant farmers and 'cottagers', a hybrid group who were half landless peasants and half wage labourers. The latter maintained a semblance of independent life through access to common land. Between the sixteenth and nineteenth centuries, increasing areas of 'common' land gave way to enclosure. Parliament, dominated by landowners, passed a series of Enclosure Acts (1773, 1801, 1845-1859) whereby wealthy landowners and the bigger farmers bought ground rights and fenced off land that had once been open. For the landowners, who only rarely farmed themselves, enclosing and improving agricultural land allowed them to extract higher rents from tenant farmers and improve the quality of their lives of leisure. Here, the various aesthetics of the natural and the picturesque often involved hiding the evidence of commercialised agriculture behind carefully planted stands of trees to screen these scenes from the stately vista. For the bigger farmers enclosure meant taking more land into agricultural production. For the cottagers, enclosure meant that they lost their rights of access to common land for grazing livestock, growing crops, gleaning or collecting fuel. As the balance between self-subsistence cultivation and waged labour shifted sharply, the supply of rural workers seeking waged work rose and exceeded demand.[1] This had the effect of driving wages down to starvation levels. (It also had the unwelcome consequence for local ratepayers of increasing the costs of poor law support.) It forced many landless people into temporary migrancy, crossing rural England in search of work. Ultimately it drove many off the land into the industrial cities and towns; others left the country as settlers within the British empire. The commons had, at least, enabled a dignified bare subsistence, as opposed to the humiliations of the poorhouse.

What Karl Marx wrote about this process and the attempts to disguise it remains classic. In *Capital*, Marx wrote that the vision of the rural idyll was not just a sentimental and ahistoric evasion of privilege ('Such insipid childishness is every day preached to us in defence of property'), but an attempt to conceal 'the conquest, enslavement, robbery, murder, in short force,' that lay behind landownership. He also saw idealised views of the landscape as disguising the brutal 'primitive accumulation' that enabled the rise of capitalist agriculture through the enclosure of the commons.[2] As Marx wrote ironically, 'In the tender annals of political economy, the idyllic reigns from time immemorial.'[3]

There has been as yet little extensive examination of the connection between enclosure, the abolition of common rights and the creation of the often spacious grounds of country houses. One exception is Timur Tatlioglu's doctoral thesis on Harewood House (*Biographies of People and Place: The Harewood Estate, 1698-1813* [2010]), which records that people who had formerly farmed on land owned by the Lascelles had their tenancies ended, and villagers lost grazing and access rights to Harewood Common when it was enclosed using wealth from plantations in Barbados.[4] Feudal land was rarely bought or sold. The period of enclosure and agricultural improvement was also the period of empire and slavery. Commodifying land and commodifying people went hand in hand.

The history of the connections between rural inequality and colonial empire is of course widely known to those who read works of academic history, but it evidently finds little purchase in the more widely shared myths about the idylls of rural England. This is why Nick Hayes's *The Book of Trespass* (2020) is important. In its engagingly personal tone, it smuggles an anti-colonial historical vision into a multi-genre book that combines personal memoir, literary descriptive writing, potted history, art and polemic to record his incursions on to the vast quantities of private land and rivers that are closed to ramblers and canoeists. Hayes ranges widely to draw connections between the causes of social justice, anti-racism, the necessity to green the economy and a return to the idea of commons (which would entail, of course, a revolutionary policy of deprivatisation and land reform).

Looking from England to the Caribbean, Hayes observes that remnants of feudalism can be seen in the early days of Barbadian plantation activity by families like the Draxes (whose inheritors still benefit from the proceeds of slavery through their huge land-holdings). He notes that James Drax first staffed his tobacco plantations with men and women from English workhouses. In the 1640s, English ships carried 8,000 British vagrants and Irish prisoners of war to work on the tobacco plantations.[5] When Drax's tobacco venture failed, sugar was grown instead, and because the cultivation of sugar was more labour-intensive than tobacco, the sugar plantations turned to the purchase of enslaved Africans. Hayes connects English destitution with transatlantic slavery, which he sees as 'an extreme version of a time-honoured hierarchy in England.'[6] *The Book of Trespass* also charts the actions of returnee planters. When the colonial profits rolled in, the money came home. Following on from Guy Shrubsole's *Who Owns England,* Hayes shows that this West - and East - Indian wealth part-funded an 18th-century land-grab which was legitimised by the 1773 Enclosure Act. This money funded walls and blocked footpaths.[7] Hayes's description of Fonthill, the former estate of the slave-owning Beckford family expresses very vividly this connection:

> The Fonthill estate... is a 9,000 acre beauty, that comprises residential and commercial letting, industrial farming, forestry and an 80-acre stud farm. It offers pheasant and partridge shooting, angling, deer-stalking holiday retreats and a stunning location for filming. It is what the profits of slavery look like today, laundered in time and land.[8]

The term 'laundered' is misleading in legal terms, since slavery did not then break the law. To further illustrate this point, though, Hayes stays with his example of the Drax family, observing that their sugar plantations 'propelled the Draxes into the premier league of landowners', also funding England's longest wall, which runs through Dorset.[9] The wall is one of many examples of slavery's impact on England's built heritage. It also provides a fitting metaphor for the link between empire overseas and enclosure at home: many of England's lengthier walls, hedges and keep-out signs are unrecognised legacies of colonial profiteering.

Hayes further links enclosure to colonial wealth when he observes that Basildon Park's '400 acres of parkland were enclosed by Francis Sykes... whose fortune was amassed through his work for the East India Company.' Sitting in the Berkshire valley, Hayes reflects on how the Basildon estate was once 'unrestricted common land, where you grazed your cattle and kept your bees.'[10] His work echoes the concerns of Oliver Goldsmith, and even William Cobbett, when he observes that the profits of empire 'flooded the countryside' and this 'new money... brought in on the back of African

and Indian labour, was the same money that partitioned English commoners from their livelihood and land.'[11] He notes, for example, that the
Enclosure Act of 1773 coincided with the sway that returnee East India
Company officials and plantation-owners held over Parliament: 'It is
estimated that in 1765 there were forty MPs... with West Indian connections and, by 1784, twenty-nine MPs with direct East Indian connections.'[12] Today, Richard Grosvenor Plunkett-Ernle-Erle-Drax, the owner
of 13,780 acres of Dorsetshire Land, and a substantial sugar estate in
Barbados, is the MP for South Dorset.

Rural Idyll

John Major once predicted that, 'fifty years from now, Britain will still
be the country of long shadows on county grounds, warm beer, invincible
green suburbs, dog lovers and – as George Orwell said – old maids
bicycling to Holy Communion through the morning mist...'.[13] However,
rural Britain (though Major meant England) is far from unchanging,
locally bounded, or, in the past, rarely peaceful. Apart from the likely
truth about the persistence of dog-lovers, the elderliness of the maids
is incongruous with the many itinerant female East Europeans who,
before Brexit, picked the fruit and vegetables that grace our tables.

Major's statement ignored what had actually been happening in the
countryside. In the post Second World War period, mass food production
turned animals – chickens, pigs, cows and dairy cattle – into units of
production. Intensified factory farming methods changed the relationship of
agricultural workers to animal husbandry and required far fewer of them. So
too had the mechanisation of arable farming in the postwar period. Gone
were horses and gone were many hedges (once a visible sign of enclosure).
Many agricultural workers had less sense of a physical relationship to the
land, and though small, family-run farms continued to survive, they did so
precariously. A representative image of this change might be the solitary
driver high in his computerised combine-harvester and wearing earmuffs.

Industrialised farming and escalating environmental destruction ought
to have made naive visions of the countryside hard to sustain. Yet they have
been sustained, and a succession of social histories, personal memoirs and
political manifestos have criticised the continuing pastoral view.

Forty years ago, Howard Newby's Penguin special, *Green and Pleasant
Land? Social Change in Rural England* (1979) challenged a general nostalgia
for the countryside with the reality of mechanised postwar farming. He
wrote about 'agribusinesses' and vast factory farms, producing meat, milk
and eggs. He talked about animals that never saw the light of day. He raised
concerns about monoculture and reliance on artificial fertilizers, observing
that these were endangering insects, birds and wild mammals. Since then,
pressures to protect nature have battled with imperatives to keep food

prices artificially low and maximise profits. The year after Newby's book, Marion Shoard's campaigning *The Theft of the Countryside* (1980) was published with its vision of vast deserts of arable lands from which every hedge has been grubbed up and in which no bird sings. Shoard's book ends, 'And if we fail to save our countryside, we shall have no one to blame but ourselves'.[14] Fraser Harrison in *Strange Land. The Countryside: Myth and Reality* (1982), sees an 'emptiness at [...the] core' of village 'cosiness.'[15] Fraser may *seem* to rue 'a general alienation from rural experience and agricultural practice,' but his book nonetheless insists on the need to de-romanticise rural life by examining the power which has been wielded by landowners ever since the Enclosure Acts. Alun Howkins makes no bones about the nature of rural change by calling his book, *The Death of Rural England: A Social History of the Countryside Since 1900* (2003). His book ends with the catastrophes of BSE (c. 1989-1997) caused by feeding cattle to cattle, and the foot and mouth crisis (2001), accentuated by the practice of moving livestock all over the country. Six million animals were slaughtered and burned. Swathes of countryside were closed to visitors. Howkins notes that this kind of closure is unlikely to happen again, since even during the foot and mouth infection, the economic value of rural leisure and tourism already exceeded that of food production by a ratio of 3:1.[16] Yet forty years later, James Rebanks's *English Pastoral: An Inheritance* (2020) feels forced to repeat almost exactly the same arguments about the threat of industrialised farming methods to the environment.[17]

These 20th and 21st century studies suggest a repeated need to counter persistent and falsely comforting images of the 'country' from the past, and to anatomise a present which makes those images impossible to hold on to. But have those images of a rural idyll ever been true? Martin Empson's *'Kill All the Gentlemen': Class Struggle and Change in the English Countryside* (2018) reminds us that there a peasants' rebellion of 1381 shook much of rural England. He also writes about further upsurges of rural revolt in the 16th and 17th centuries when rural people rose up against religious and economic impositions from the London-based monarchy. There were numerous riots and disturbances against enclosure in the 18th and early 19th centuries. Empson also documents the trade union activities of Joseph Arch in the late 19th century.[18] Other classic historical works – E.J. Hobsbawm and George Rudé's *Captain Swing* (1969), E.P. Thompson's *Whigs and Hunters: the Origins of the Black Act* (1975) and Thompson's *Customs in Common* (1991) – all document the extent to which the working people of rural Britain had a strong sense that their interests were very different from those of landowners, the farmers who employed them, and those in parliament who had ended their customary entitlement to access common land.[19] John E. Archer's *By a Flash and a Scare: Arson, Animal Maiming, and Poaching in East Anglia 1815-1870* (2010) records the bitter guerrilla war that was in progress throughout this period. This war was, he writes, fought with terror on both sides, between the landed and the landless.[20] Rural people were prepared to face the heavy odds of execution or penal transportation under a legal system that protected landed interests. The Captain Swing riots of 1831 were in part focused on destroying the threshing machines that were taking away one of the few sources of paid employment in winter (filthy work where workers flailed corn seeds to remove chaff in dusty barns). After the Swing campaign was ended by the intervention of the army, 252 labourers were sentenced to death, 19 were actually executed (almost all for offences against property), 505 were transported to penal servitude in Australia (only one ever returned) and 644 were imprisoned.[21] In exactly the same year, Black Jamaicans, also mainly agricultural labourers, were fighting to end their enslavement in another part of British rural territory. After the eventual defeat of their rebellion through superior fire power (few enslaved people had guns of any kind), there was a pogrom led by British-Jamaican landowners who also controlled the legal system, in which 312 enslaved men were executed, many in cynical mockeries of the rule of law; numerous others were killed in cold blood without a trial.[22]

We are accustomed to looking at maps showing the location of historic houses, country parks and famous gardens. A very different kind of map is shown in Andrew Charlesworth's *An Atlas of Rural Protest in Britain 1548-1900* (1983).[23] It might be instructive to compare such maps, since common land was frequently enclosed to make way for grand parks.

Even today, of all aspects of social and economic inequality, the ownership of land has the most extreme profile, the deepest national roots and the most lasting consequences. According to the Country Land and Business Association, just 36,000 landowners, only 0.6% of the population, now own half of rural England and Wales.[24] Less discussed is the relationship of these struggles to empire, but Guy Shrubsole estimates that around a third of this rural land is still in the hands of the landed gentry. This includes those who came into title and landownership through the profits of slavery or through colonial activity in India.[25]

The continuing privatisation of rural land is given a more theoretical economic basis in another recent book, Brett Christopher's *The New Enclosures: The Appropriation of Public Land in Neoliberal Britain* (2018). The book argues that the steady erosion of public land ownership (land which was formerly owned by local authorities, formerly nationalised industries and state institutions) has been promoted by successive Conservative and Labour governments since the 1980s. He also points to the increasing financialisation of land (rural, urban and suburban), which is held as an appreciating asset in 'land banks' by financial institutions and owned for its exchange rather than its use value.[26] This has not only discouraged the building of affordable housing but made land so expensive that, as noted later, the size of gardens over the past sixty years has continued to shrink. This practice of land-hoarding is a continuation of a tendency of slave-owners and East Indian nabobs to repatriate their capital in the safest form of savings: ownership of land.

The belated focus on the consequences of unequal land ownership has seen writers revisiting the histories of 'the commons', commoning and enclosure in a number of recent books. Peter Linebaugh's *Stop Thief! The Commons, Enclosures, and Resistance* (2014) links the idea of commons to a wider anti-capitalist struggle, to the literal idea of common wealth in all aspects of life from the domestic to the ecological. As the chapter on gardens examines, Black British writers are beginning to make ecological links between empire, enclosure and gardening or food-growing.

Transatlantic Slavery, The East India Company and Rural England
English coastlines, villages, moors and country estates were integral to the empire's expansion, operation and to its creative imaginary. Coastal ports such as Bristol and Liverpool received cargoes of cotton, coffee, muslin, rum, sugar, tea, tobacco and exotic wood. However, it is only now becoming clear to what extent these ports were portals to imperial wealth and to investing this money in the ports' rural hinterlands. The clues of historic hothouses, naturalised exotic plants and ornamental stone pineapples all provide evidence of the expanding world of colonial trade.[27]

From 1700 onwards, colonial merchants, West India Planters and East India Company men collectively acquired around 789 country estates.[28] From his station in Bengal, the Welshman, George Herbert, wrote that he intended to settle in England's 'pleasant counties'. He wanted to establish himself among the landed gentry.[29] George Hibbert, whose wealth came from Jamaica, similarly wished to secure his family's place among the rural elite but – as with East India Company men John Walsh and John Balfour – rural acquisition also helped him to secure electoral and parliamentary influence. It funded his religious philanthropy and his passion for botany, activities that were designed to gild his record.[30] Today, England's home-counties represent archetypal green and pleasant lands. They were once differently understood. Berkshire was once known as 'England's Hindoostan' because so many East India Company men settled there with newfound fortunes.[31]

In the 17th century William Blathwayt turned Britain's American colonies (including the Caribbean islands) into moneymaking enterprises while living at Dyrham Park, near Bristol. Seeds from the colonies were planted in his gardens and exotic flowers were displayed in his Delft vases.[32] In the same century, Sir Hans Sloane brought hundreds of plant specimens, skins of animals and birds and drawings back from Jamaica. We think of Sloane as a founding father of knowledge about the natural world and the cultural utility of the museum. We think less about his role in Jamaica as a doctor who picked the healthiest Africans coming off the slave-ships and ensured that the enslaved people he treated were returned to work as rapidly as possible, sick or well. It was Sloane who recorded, without any evident dismay, the obscene punishments inflicted on black bodies and justified these as necessary to control 'a very perverse generation of people'.[33]

For the landed gentry, it was convenient that the East India Company was becoming immensely profitable precisely at the point when the Haitian revolution and the growing abolitionist campaign made it less secure to invest in chattel slavery and sugar plantations.[34] A further Indian and Atlantic connection began with the East India Company's rack-renting of land-taxes in areas such as the Central Provinces. This so immiserated the population that two and a half million Indians were driven to emigrate as indentured labour to the plantations of the British empire (including around a million to the Caribbean, with most to Guyana and Trinidad). The favoured commercial space the East India Company gave to businesses such as Gillanders and Arbuthnot in Calcutta enabled this new export of labour to take place. This company organised the first shipment of indentured Indians to British Guiana in 1838, a trade that until 1917 supported the survival of the British West Indian sugar plantations in Trinidad and British Guiana in particular, after emancipated Africans very naturally abandoned the estates after 1838.[35]

For the English theatre-going public there was evidently little distinction between the Caribbean and India. If Richard Cumberland confidently expected his audience to grasp the figure of the 'West Indian' as a symbol of 18th century wealth in his play of that name (1771),[36] Samuel Foote had the same expectation of a rather newer figure in his play, *The Nabob*, written one year later.[37] This entwined history is the territory of *Green Unpleasant Land*, and I have set out to show how both branches of historical expertise are major animating forces behind the rural turn in creative writing by Black Britons since the late 1980s, for instance in Catherine Johnson's novel *The Curious Tale of the Lady Cariboo* (2015) and Caryl Phillips's *The Lost Child* (2015), both books that are discussed in later chapters. Where history leads, writers have followed. The same is true in reverse. Chapter Four of this book, 'Moorlands', observes that the pervasiveness of empire in the Brontë sisters' novels prompted contemporary historians to explore Yorkshire's plantation economy.

Rural Racism

Historically, then, the countryside is a terrain of inequalities, so it should not surprise us that it should be seen as a place of particular hostility to those who are seen as not to belong, principally Black and Asian Britons.

Neil Chakraborti and Jon Garland argue that, even today, rural and urban spaces are routinely perceived as separate, contrasting realities. They observe that the countryside is frequently viewed as 'a sanctuary from the harsh realities of the urban world, [offering] a way of life that embraces a... wholly preferable set of values to the urban such as honesty, kinship, solidarity and paternalism'. Chakraborti and Garland show that modern cities, by contrast, are associated with anonymity and social change.[38] The countryside is contrastingly seen as a 'storehouse' of tradition, virtue and permanence, whereas 20th and 21st century cities symbolise immigration and demographic change. From the Augustans to the Lakeland poets, the countryside is perceived as a refuge from the perceived threat of city life.[39] As documented by Terry Gifford's book *Pastoral*,[40] this idea of sanctuary has never been true for those living in rural poverty.

Nor is it the case that the English countryside is unconnected to the rest of the globe. Rural studies research contests the fallacy that village life is bounded and timeless. Paul Cloke writes that, in modern England, 'rural areas are essentially dynamic... they are reconstructed economically and recomposed socially by the globalised food industry, by the increasing mobility of production and people, by the niched fragmentation of consumption and the commodification of place.'[41] Recent rural studies have focused on issues such as low-income itinerant farm labour or care work in the countryside, often carried out by migrant women.[42] This is also true of the past: the influx of colonial wealth and consumption of colonial goods has long linked the countryside with the rest of the world.[43]

The idea of close-knit rural communities is key to the concept of the rural idyll. David Francis and Paul Henderson write: 'there is no doubt that community, especially when prefixed by "rural" is a[n]... emotive concept... it includes notions of reciprocal human relationships, voluntary effort, interest in local affairs, neighbourliness'. The neighbour is a cultural insider who belongs on the grounds of both physical proximity and who shares, and even shapes, local sensibility.[44] The neighbour is therefore a potent figure of belonging. This concept of a rural community connects with a collective nostalgia for rural spaces which are, to quote James Procter, perceived as existing 'at a cultural remove from multiracial Britain.'[45] Kye Askins argues that rural England tends to exclude 'British multiethnic... values and sensibilities.'[46] These values, the logic goes, will only endure if the village neighbour is white.

The phenomenon of rural racism has so far been studied largely from a criminological or equalities perspective. In a 1992 report called *Keep Them In Birmingham*, Eric Jay found evidence of widespread racial discrimination in South Western England, while a 2007 Attitudes Survey in Cumbria revealed that 50% of respondents strongly agreed that people 'settling in this country should not maintain the culture and lifestyle they previously had.'[47] A 2009 report established that people of colour are 19% less likely to feel they belong in rural England. Other race equality projects have investigated the situation in Cornwall, Devonshire, Lincolnshire, Norfolk, Northern Ireland, Perthshire, Shropshire, Somerset and Wiltshire.[48] These projects provided the foundation for Mohammed Dhalech's report, 'Challenging Racism in the Rural Idyll.' By creating an informal system for reporting racism and discrimination, Dhalech and his colleagues were able to demonstrate high levels of racist crime in the English countryside, such as attacks on mosques and corner shops. The report also evidenced discrimination, such as refusing participation in educational courses on the grounds that applicants 'might not fit in'.[49] Dhalech discovered multiple barriers to accessing other services such as rural health and funding provision. Kye Askins also found that 'visible minorities' frequently feel that the countryside is not for them. Askins provides two explanations for this. For first generation migrants, this sense of not belonging is fuelled by the memories of poverty associated with agricultural work in the global south. It is also driven by the fear of racism.[50] Such studies are borne out by the expressions of alienation from the countryside that are examined in Chapter Three: 'The Pastoral'. Graham Huggan and Helen Tiffin suggest that rural belonging is often predicated on people's sense of historical relationship to the land. It is precisely this sort of historical sensibility which enables white Britons to more easily 'inhabit' the countryside when they visit it, or dwell in it. Huggan and Tiffin argue that a sense of white, rural belonging is expressed as a form of 'patrician privilege' which exceeds mere residential rights and amounts to 'emotional posses-sion'. This feeling of ownership is, they suggest, often 'vouchsafed by romantic appeals to English cultural heritage.'[51]

Since the 1980s, the Black photographer Ingrid Pollard has relentlessly explored the disjunction between the Black presence and white rural entitlement. That is made very clear in the title of her pictorial sequence 'Pastoral Interludes'. This depicts uneasy Black figures in rural settings and one image is captioned: 'the owners of these fields... want me off their GREEN AND PLEASANT LAND'.[52] In referencing a line from 'Jerusalem' and placing it in capitals, as if to mimic the warning notices of landowners against the perceived trespass of people whose faces do not fit, Pollard mocks the apparent innocence of the pastoral vision of a white rural idyll.

This makes it all the more a pity that imaginative work by Black British and Asian British writers is only fleetingly referenced in academic studies about rural racism. Cloke alludes very briefly to literary figures, mention-ing Andrea Levy (who reported feeling self-conscious walking into a country pub), Benjamin Zephaniah (whose countryside jog launched a police helicopter searching for a 'suspicious jogger') and Lemn Sissay (who speaks of the 'incendiary racism that is in the country [of England and] is never challenged').[53] Yet literary works can provide rich details of the experience of rural racism and, as explored in later chapters, Black British writers' expressions of determination to repel feelings of being unwelcome in the countryside. As an example of racist experience, Lemn Sissay's poem, 'A Black Man in the Isle of Wight' (2000), simply reads:

> Faces cold as the stone
> stuck to the sea's belly
> with seaweed for hair
> sculpted into expressions of fear[54]

The white onlookers' sense of shock at seeing a black man is expressed by their arrested movement and their almost literal petrification ('cold as the stone'; 'sculpted into expressions of fear'). The stone simile allows Sissay to depict rural racism as tangible ('stone'), deep ('the sea's belly') embedded ('stuck') and enduring ('sculpted'). Sissay also cleverly reverses the situation. It is the white viewers, shocked at the Black presence, who make themselves monstrous – like some creature from the deep.

Whilst I have no evidence that Sissay was aware of this historical background, research by the economic historian Nick Draper reveals that the Isle of Wight has a connection to slave-ownership. Jamaican slave registers even list a man who was given the name 'Isle of Wight'. Records also reveal a black presence on the island – a servant named Thomas Cyrus in a marriage register of 1822. Draper believes that Cyrus was an African who was shipped to the Isle of Wight from Jamaica. The island has other connections with slavery, including Osborne House (purchased from a slave-trader for Queen Victoria), the Shedden family and the Holford family.[55] Whether or not Sissay knew any of this is not the point, rather that the kind of information provided by Draper and the Legacies of Slave Ownership project will keep on providing fresh contexts for reading, and writing, literary work. Sissay made just this point about the complexity of contextual meaning when he wrote:

> [W]hen I hear of Oasis or Weller, and the great Beatles influence, when I hear of young up-and-coming artists harking back to The Beatles in some kind of retro-chic way, I remember not what they produced in this enlightened summer [of 1967, the year of Sissay's birth] but the misinformation of the time and how black people... were either demonised or hero-worshipped but god forbid they would be accepted as *neighbours*.[56]

The importance of including imaginative literature in any attempt to understand and change perceptions of Black people and rural Britain is reinforced in a sociological report written by Kye Askins, who notes that staff responsible for the management of the countryside tend to view the absence of Black people from the country as evidence of a culturally founded lack of appreciation for nature and wildlife.[57] This is precisely the kind of misapprehension that Camille T. Dungy addresses in her introduction as the editor of a recent anthology, *Black Nature: Four Centuries of African American Nature Poetry* (2009). It is not merely that African American poets have been conspicuously absent from supposedly national anthologies of American nature writing, but they have also been perceived as an urban people, uninvolved with the natural world – a quite ludicrous censorship of history, given the pre-migratory origins of most Black Americans in the rural South. As Dungy notes, whereas much white nature poetry is written from the perspective of the observer, in some of the African American poetry of the past, 'we see poems written from the perspective of the workers of the field.'[58] In Britain, studies of Black and Asian writers have focused almost entirely on the urban street, which is historically defined as the prime locus of Black criminality, political protest and interracial struggle.[59] Despite the wealth of new writing explored in this book, even the best-known photographic images of Black Britons are stubbornly urban. Reviewing Paul Gilroy's *Black Britain: A Photographic History*, Derica Shields notes that 'very few canonical images of Black people in the UK feature us among flora... or in the countryside at all'. Nonetheless, she argues that Black Britons are increasingly depicting themselves in rural settings on social media.[60] For instance, as his career has developed, Lemn Sissay has increasingly depicted himself in and amongst nature. His regularly updated website pictures him in green parks, walking in snow and swimming in the sea. Such images both reveal and breach the territorial limits of multiracial England.

In considering the relationship between empire, migration from former British colonies and the countryside, there is a temptation to overlook the contemporary presence and long historical experience of Britain's oldest and often most persecuted and rural ethnic minority, the Romani people, who arrived in Britain at the turn of the sixteenth century.[61] The 'Gypsies' or Egyptians, as they were once known, were soon outlawed: it was actually illegal – under pain of death – to be a Gypsy until the late 18th century.[62] Before this, Elizabethan law ruled: 'All and every person which... shall be seen or found within the Realm of England and Wales or found in any company or fellowship of vagabonds commonly called or calling themselves Egyptians... shall by Virtue of this Act... suffer pains of death loss of lands and goods as in cases of felony'.[63] Sarah Houghton-Walker observes that this Elizabethan law illustrated both how unacceptable it was to be without fixed employment or abode, but also notes the emphasis in this legislation on foreignness.[64] The Act was repealed in 1783 and, Houghton-Walker argues, Gypsies were increasingly seen as belonging to the British Isles, as part of the English landscape, even while they were being marginalised and persecuted by the law.[65] As representatives of a substantial minority, considered as both rural outsiders and insiders, Gypsies have appeared in rural writing across the centuries: in the poems of William Cowper and John Clare, in Jane Austen's novel *Emma* and in contemporary writing by poets such as David Morley, who acknowledges his own Romani heritage, and draws on the Gypsies of Clare's poetry in his collection, *The Gypsy and the Poet* (2015), which takes the form of a poetic dialogue between Clare and an actual Gypsy whom he encountered called Wisdom Smith.[66]

Max Porter's novel *Lanny* (2019) explores the countryside's history of racism and empire in its unsentimental vision of rural England. Amidst the realities of rural life ('I kill pigs for a living' and 'vomit behind the hall') there are echoes of empire, such as a dog called Walter Raleigh. Embedded in the snatches of conversation overheard in the village is uneasy talk about foreigners: there is mention of a 'Trinidadian', a 'gyppo alert' and an objection to 'Polish adverts in the village mag', a broadening out of older outsiders to new Eastern European arrivals in the area.[67] As the novel progresses, it explores the idea that being native to the English countryside is a fallacy. Reflecting on the ancient spirit of the village, known as Dead Pappa Toothwort, an old villager says: 'Nobody was truly born here, apart from him.'[68]

Many British Black and Asian writers make direct links between rural England and the British empire but *Lanny* is one of the first novels by a white British writer to make any connection between the two. For instance, the old villager, Pete, reflects on received views of pastoral life:

> On the fridge was a postcard... the wonky Westbury horse with the train popping behind. I've treasured it for years. I looked at this image, this lovely English thing, and I felt sick... I hated that quaint image... since I first read those pamphlets about what the brave Englishman did in Bengal, did in Kenya, did in Northern Ireland...[69]

Here, in referencing the partition of Bengal by Lord Curzon, the crushing of the Mau Mau in Kenya and the violent legacy of empire in Northern Ireland, Pete acknowledges both the seductive beauty of the rural idyll and the colonial violence that lies behind it.

Yet so much past British writing betrays a collective amnesia about the role of empire. The celebrated landscape historian W.G. Hoskins makes no mention of empire in his classic work, *The Making of the English Landscape* (1955), although his landmark book was the first to explore 'the historical evolution of the landscape.'[70] And more recently some social geographers have argued that promoting an inclusive view of the countryside cannot be achieved by appealing to history. A recent cultural studies conference paper claimed, 'often these [memories] just aren't there'.[71] Forgotten though it may be, the historical evidence is clear.

Black British and Asian British Writers' Responses to History
This book focuses on Black British and British Asian writers' expressions of affection for local landscapes and the natural world. The focus on local settings simultaneously recognises the wider devolution of Black

English literary culture and endorses Procter's maxim: 'it is not the same to be black in London as it is in Llandudno'.[72] This is too easily forgotten. As Kay, Robinson and Procter argue: 'If alienation, unbelonging and dislocation remain key aspects of black and Asian experiences in Britain, what such terms simultaneously conceal are the rich and manifest attachments to place, region, city and landscape'.[73] Focusing on specific country houses, moors and villages allows colonial connections to emerge in precise ways. In this book, I document the ways in which V.S. Naipaul, David Dabydeen, Shanta Acharya, Grace Nichols, John Agard, Maya Chowdhry, Louisa Adjoa Parker and many others have contributed to debates about rurality. Even routine country pleasures provoke unease. In 'Blackberrying Black Woman', Nichols begins: 'Everyone has a blackberry poem. Why not this?'[74] The question refers to the tension between the 'compulsion' to pick, the 'passing glances' and the sinister undertones of 'blood from the prickling vine'.[75] The barbs amongst the bushes suggest that, for a Black woman, picking English fruit is never straightforward.

This chapter set out to dismiss some common misapprehensions about rural England: firstly, that it has nothing to do with colonialism and, secondly, that Black British and Asian British authors are disconnected from English rurality. As the succeeding chapters show, recent historical research and literary work do not simply interrogate the countryside's Englishness. They call into question the nature of Englishness itself.

Endnotes

1. The best historical account is J.M. Neeson, *Commoners: Common Right, Enclosure and Social Change in England, 1700-1820* (Cambridge: Cambridge UP, 1993). For the contemporary politics of 'commons' and the fight against continuing enclosure see Peter Linebaugh, *Stop, Thief! The Commons, Enclosures, and Resistance* (Oakland: PM Press, 2014). For further discussion in this book see pp. 63, 67-68, 69, 71, 80-82, 142, 184-185.
2. Karl Marx, *Capital* Vol. 1 (London: Penguin Books, 1990), pp. 873-874.
3. Marx, *Capital*, p. 874.
4. See Timur Tatlioglu, *Biographies of People and Place: The Harewood Estate, 1698-1813*, Ph D, University of York, 2010.
5. Nick Hayes, *The Book of Trespass* (London: Bloomsbury, 2020), p. 23. And see Hilary McD. Beckles, *White Servitude and Black Slavery in Barbados* (Knoxville: University of Tennessee Press, 1989) and Gwenda Morgan & Peter Rushton, *Banishment in the Early Atlantic World: Convicts, Rebels and Slaves* (London: Bloomsbury, 2103).
6. Nick Hayes, *op. cit.*, p. 148.
7. Nick Hayes, *op. cit.*, p. 149.
8. Hayes, *op. cit.*, p. 125.
9. Hayes, *op. cit.*, p. 149. For the creation of these tropical Babylons and English society see Susan Dwyer Amussen, *Caribbean Exchanges: Slavery and the Transformation of English Society 1640-1700* (Chapel Hill: University of North Carolina Press, 2007).
10. Hayes, *op. cit.*, p. 149.
11. Hayes, *op. cit.*, p. 134.
12. John Major, speech to the Conservative Group for Europe, 22 April 1993. See www.johnmajorarchive.org.uk/1990-1997/mr-majors-speech-to-conservative-group-for-europe-22-april-1993.
13. Marion Shoard, *The Theft of the Countryside* (London: Maurice Temple Smith, 1980), p. 260.
14. Fraser Harrison, *Strange Land. The Countryside: Myth and Reality* (Witham: Sidgwick and Jackson, 1982), p. 22.
15. Alan Howkins, *The Death of Rural England: A Social History of the Countryside Since 1900* (London: Routledge, 2003), pp. 205-234.
16. James Rebank, English Pastoral: An Inheritance (London: Allen Lane, 2020).
17. Martin Empson, *'Kill All the Gentlemen': Class Struggle and Change in the English Countryside* (London: Bookmarks, 2018). See below in this book pp. 63 ff.
18. E.J. Hobsbawm and George Rudé's *Captain Swing* (London: Readers

Union & Lawrence & Wishart, 1970), E.P. Thompson's *Whigs and Hunters: the origins of the Black Act* (London: Allen Lane, 1975) and Thompson's *Customs in Common* ([1999] London: Merlin Press, 2010).

19. John E. Archer, *By a Flash and a Scare: Arson, Animal Maiming, and Poaching in East Anglia 1815-1870* (London: Breviary Stuff, 2010). Breviary Stuff Publications have an important list of books concerned with working class struggle in rural Britain. See also Harry Hopkins, *The Long Affray: The Poaching Wars in Britain 1760-1914* (London Secker & Warburg, 1985).

20. Hobsbawm and Rudé, *Captain Swing*, pp. 253-280.

21. See Michael Taylor, *The Interest: How the British Establishment Resisted the Abolition of Slavery* (London: The Bodley Head, 2020) and see Mary Reckord, 'Jamaica Slave Rebellion of 1831', *Past & Present*, 40 (1968), pp. 108-125. For a contemporary account of the planter onslaught see Henry Bleby, *Death Struggles of Slavery: Being a Narrative of Facts and Incidents, which Occurred in a British Colony, during the Two Years Immediately Preceding Negro Emancipation* (London: Hamilton, Adams & Co., 1853).

22. Andrew Charlesworth, *An Atlas of Rural Protest in Britain 1548-1900* (Philadelphia: University of Pennsylvania Press, 1983).

23. Guy Shrubsole, *Who Owns England: How We Lost Our Green and Pleasant Land & How to Take it Back* (London: William Collins, 2019), pp. 86-87.

24. Shrubsole, *op. cit.*, pp. 19, 78-84.

25. Brett Christopher, *The New Enclosures: The Appropriation of Public Land in Neoliberal Britain* (London: Verso, 2018). See pp. 63, 67-69, 71, 79-82, 137, 142, 184-185, 240-241, 262 below for further discussion.

26. See in particular James Walvin, *Fruits of Empire: Exotic Produce and British Taste, 1660-1800 (London: Macmillan, 1997)*.

27. See Stephanie Barczewski, *Country Houses and the British Empire 1700-1930* (Manchester: Manchester UP, 2014).

28. Jill Casid, *Sowing Empire: Landscape and Colonization* (Minneapolis: University of Minnesota Press, 2004)., p. 49.

29. On the Hibberts see Katie Donington, *The Bonds of Family. Slavery, Culture and Commerce in the British Atlantic World* (Manchester: MUP, 2020).

30. See Margot Finn and Kate Smith, *The East India Company at Home* (London: UCL Press, 2018).

31. See Rupert Goulding, *William Blathwayt and Dyrham Park* (Gloucestershire: National Trust Guidebooks, 2018).

32. James Delbourgo, *Collecting the World: The Life and Curiosity of Hans Sloane* (London: Allen Lane, 2017), p. 78.

33. See William Dalrymple, *The Anarchy: The Relentless Rise of the East*

India Company (London: Bloomsbury Publishing, 2019).

34. See Hugh Tinker, *A New System of Slavery: The Export of Indian Labour Overseas 1830-1920* (Oxford: Institute of Race Relations, 1974).

35. Richard Cumberland, *The West Indian* in John Hampton ed. *Eighteenth Century Plays* (London: Dent Everyman, c. 1930).

36. Samuel Foote, *The Nabob* in *The Dramatic Works of Samuel Foote* Vol II ([1808] New York: Benjamin Blom, nd.).

37. See Neil Chakraborti and Neil Garland, eds., *Rural Racism*, (London: Willan Publishing, 2012).

38. See Chapter Three and Chapter Four, pp. 77-78, 137.

39. Terry Gifford, *Pastoral* (London: Routledge New Critical Idioms, 2019).

40. Paul Cloke, 'Rurality and racialised others: out of place in the countryside?' in Chakraborti and Garland, *op. cit.,* (2004), p. 20.

41. See Lizzie Collingham, *The Hungry Empire: How Britain's Quest for Food Shaped the Modern World* (London: Vintage, 2018) and James Walvin, *Slavery in Small Things: Slavery and Modern Cultural Habits* (New York: John Wiley and Sons, 2017).

42. David Francis and Paul Henderson, *Working with Rural Communities* (London: Palgrave, 1992).

43. Paul Milbourne in Askins 2009, *op cit.*, p. 373. An excellent example of approach is Sondra Cuban's *Deskilling Migrant Women in the Global Care Industry* (Basingstoke: Palgrave Macmillan, 2013) which examines the work carried out by women migrants in caring for elderly, rural residents in the Lake District.

44. James Procter, *Dwelling Places. Postwar Black British Writing* (Manchester: MUP, 2003), p. 181.

45. Askins, *op cit.*

46. Cumbria County Council, 'Equality for All' report, 2009, https://www.cumbria.gov.uk/equalities/, accessed 14 February 2019.

47. Cumbria County Council, 2009, *op cit.,* p. 6.

48. Mohammed Dhalech, 1999, 'Challenging Racism in the Rural Idyll. Final Report of the Rural Race Equality Project Cornwall, Devon and Somerset 1996 to 1998', National Association of Citizens Advice: Exeter 1999. Thanks are due to Mohammed Dhalech for providing this information. Dhalech was a Race Equalities Officer in multiple regions during this period.

49. Kye Askins, 'Crossing divides: ethnicity and rurality,' *Journal of Rural Studies*, 25(4), 2009, pp. 365-375.

50. Graham Huggan and Helen Tiffin, *Postcolonial Criticism: Literature, Animals, Environment* (London: Routledge, 2010).

51. Ingrid Pollard, *Postcards Home*, (London: Autograph, 2004 [1989], p. 29.

52. Cloke in Chakraborti and Garland, *op cit.* (2004), p. 18.

53. Lemn Sissay, 'A Black Man on the Isle of Wight' in *Rebel Without Applause* (Tarset: Bloodaxe, 1992).
54. Nick Draper, 'A Black Presence in the Isle of Wight' 2017., https://lbsatucl.wordpress.com/2017/11/28/a-black-presence-in-the-isle-of-wight/, accessed 14 February 2019.
55. Lemn Sissay, *Listener* (Edinburgh: Canongate Books, 2008), p. 102. Emphasis added.
56. Askins (2009), *op cit.*, p. 372.
57. Camille Dungy, *Black Nature: Four Centuries of African American Nature Poetry* (Athens, Georgia: University of Georgia Press, 2009), pp. xxii-xxiii.
58. See for instance Sukdev Sandhu, *London Calling: How Black and Asian Writers Imagined a City* (London: Harper Collins, 2003) and Marc Matera, *Black London: The Imperial Metropolis and Decolonization in the Twentieth Century* (University of California Press, 2019).
59. Derica Shields, 'Black Flora', presentation given at ICA London as part of Technology Now: Blackness on the Internet, winter 2016.
60. Houghton-Walker, 2014 *op cit.*, p. 16.
61. Houghton-Walker, 2014, *op. cit.,* p. 15.
62. Houghton-Walker, 2014, *op. cit.,* p. 15.
63. David Morley, *The Gypsy and the Poet* (Manchester: Carcanet, 2015)
64. See David Cressy, *Gypsies: An English History* (Oxford: Oxford UP, 2018).
65. Max Porter, *Lanny* (London: Faber, 2019), p. 22 and p. 33.
66. *Lanny*, p. 85.
67. *Lanny*, p. 97.
68. *Lanny*, p. 85.
69. W.G. Hoskins, *op. cit.*, p. 14.
70. Ben Pitcher, 'Non-Representational theory, landscape, and the ecological politics of race'. Paper given at Re-Imagining Ruralities conference, London. University of Westminster conference, 2015.
71. Procter, *Dwelling Places: Postwar Black British Writing* (Manchester: Manchester UP, 2003), p. 13
72. Kay, Robinson and Procter, *Out of Bounds* (Bloodaxe: Tarset, 2013), p. 13
73. Grace Nichols, *Passport to Here and There* (Bloodaxe: Tarset, 2020), p. 40.
74. *Passport to Here and There.* p. 40

CHAPTER THREE: PASTORAL

'I think landscape is paramount, as it is where our bodies reside. Each is made from the other.' John Siddique (2013)[1]

In his book *Landscape and Englishness*, David Matless asserts that 'a sense of Englishness' is 'essentially rural'.[2] Rurality is certainly a much-loved theme in the English literary tradition. So many rural poems, plays and novels were published during England's four colonial centuries that it would be surprising if some of them did not allude to the impact of empire on rural England and Englishness. Indeed, some works were written by authors who were directly involved in colonial activity, some by those who celebrated colonial enterprise from the sidelines and expanded their rural vision accordingly, and some were written by authors who accused colonially-enriched landowners of confiscating common land and corrupting rural society. Sometimes, though, empire's influence on English rural writing, though present, is harder to see.

Classical Beginnings
Until at least the later 18th century, most rural poetry derived from two distinctive but related genres of ancient Greek and Roman verse, the pastoral and the georgic. The pastoral as a form features shepherds conversing about work, love and the countryside.[3] Key works include Theocritus's *Idylls* (c.316-260 BCE), and Virgil's *Eclogues* (37 BCE). These were immensely influential on the English poetic tradition, though contemporary scholars of classical writing distinguish between such post-Renaissance uses and the more complex motivations and political purposes embedded in the historical Roman meaning of Virgil's *Eclogues*. The *Eclogues* were always seen as a form of poetic artifice whose shepherds were never meant to be thought of as actual shepherds. Their dialogues were a literary device that played on the difference between the sophisticated poet and naive rural singers, in order to criticise present day corruption in comparison to an imaginary golden past. Eclogues were a way of smuggling in political criticisms. They depict a vanished Arcadia, a rural idyll that no longer exists in the degenerate times in which the poet writes.[4] It is worth noting that for Virgil the golden, ancient past contained five major Plebeian uprisings from 494 BCE

down to 287BCE. In his own father's remembered times there had been the Spartacist slave revolt of 73-71 BCE.[5]

The other tradition of rural poetry draws from Hesiod's celebration of husbandry, *Work and Days* (c.700 BCE) and Virgil's *Georgics* (29 BCE). On the surface these are practical, instructional poems about farming, but they also moralise about the 'good life' that is only to be found in agricultural pursuits. The georgic, though, like the eclogue, was the work of poets who were at best onlookers or 'gentleman' farmers.

One further classic Roman literary influence runs through English poetry on rural themes. This draws from the *Epistles* of Horace (Quintus Horatius Flaccus, 65 BCE-8 BCE), of which several (including 10, 14, 16), take the form of letters from the poet as committed countryman to urban friends, extolling the virtues of the retired, natural life in contrast to the false excitements of the city. This idea runs through the several epistles of Alexander Pope and connects to the poetry about elite country houses which is discussed in the next chapter.

A Native Tradition Ignored

There was always an alternative to the pastoral. There was a distinctive, realist tradition in English rural writing that is not best described as anti-pastoral since it was a native tradition with no conscious continuities to the classic literary pastoral or georgic. Its classic expression was the alliterative poetry of William Langland's *Piers Plowman*, and its associations with the Peasants Revolt of 1381. These were in the connections drawn between the folk figure of Piers and the itinerant 'hedgerow' priest, John Ball, who was a figurehead of the revolt.[6] In several of William Chaucer's *Canterbury Tales*, the portrayal of rural figures such as the miller and the reeve are realist in an earthily comic tradition. However, this tradition, particularly from Langland, was not available to later poets because Langland's long poem was rarely in print until 1813 (and there was no scholarly edition until 1886) so it was little studied until the mid to late nineteenth century. As a result, the influence of Langland's alliterative verse and realist perceptions of the rural world did not surface until the poetry of Gerard Manley Hopkins ('Harry Ploughman' and 'Felix Randal'), though Hopkins wrote somewhat dismissively of Langland.[7] As noted later in the chapter, *Piers Plowman* takes on a subsequent postcolonial presence in allusions to it in a poem by the St Lucian poet, Derek Walcott.

Sixteenth and seventeenth-century pastoral

But as noted above, it was Virgil's eclogues that inspired many subsequent works, notably Jacopo's utopian 16th-century *Arcadia*, which laments a lost Golden Age – characterised by pious, honest labour in which the labourer knows his (or her) place and there is no class antagonism between rich and poor. Nostalgia for a lost rural past is a prominent idea in much pastoral writing and can be seen in Philip Sidney's *Arcadia* (c.1580),[8] in Edmund Spenser's *The Shepheardes Calender* (1579) and *The Faerie Queene* (1596). Sidney is writing only thirty years after the tumultuous rural uprisings of 1549 that included the Western Rising (centred on Cornwall) against the imposition of the Book of Common Prayer (written in English, which many rural Cornish men and women did not speak) and Kett's rebellion (centred on Norfolk), which began as a protest against the loss of common land through enclosure and oppression of the rural poor by the rising gentry.[9] As Raymond Williams wryly notes: Sidney's *Arcadia* was 'written in a park... made by enclosing a whole village and evicting the tenants.'[10] Spenser was writing his epic, *The Fairie Queen*, which is told through mostly non-realist tales exploring such virtues as holiness, temperance and chastity, precisely at the time when he was part of an anti-insurgent force repressing the rebellious Irish as a colonial administrator. In the same year that *The Fairie Queen* was published, Spenser was writing *A Vewe of the Present State of Irelande* (1596) in which he argued for the murderous suppression of a barbarous, savage race by the sword. Though he explored the theme of justice in *The Fairie Queen*, he was busily committed to destroying Ireland's agricultural means of survival together with the Irish language and culture – the strategy of all subsequent settler colonialisms and anti-insurgency wars.

This is not to forget significant contributions from other genres of the period, particularly Shakespeare's *As You Like It* (1599), which (alluding to the legend of Robin Hood's egalitarian woodland society – which contrasts pleasingly with life in the royal court), gently satirises the pastoral tradition of courtiers pretending to be peasants.[11] In the 17th century, Robert Herrick (1591-1674), John Milton (1608-1674), Andrew Marvell (1621-1678) and many others wrote on rural themes,[12] and Sir John Denham's (1615-1669) 'Cooper's Hill' introduced a sub-genre of loco-descriptive verse, including, most famously, John Dyer's 'Grongar Hill'.[13] In the earlier 18th century, the Augustan period, rural poetry made further reference to Greek and Roman pastoral, including works by Alexander Pope (1688-1744), Ambrose Philips (1674-1749) and John Gay (1685-1732).[14]

The Real, Empire and the Pastoral
Though written in relation to classical models, it would be wrong to think that this dependence did not allow glimpses of the actual, including the world of empire, even if idealised. Neither does the outwardly pastoral preclude more complex readings. Robert Herrick's 'The Country Life, to the Honoured Master Endymion Porter, Groom of the Bedchamber

to his Majesty' (c. 1635-1640) is framed within the convention of the pleasures of 'sweet country life' in comparison to life in the court where 'lives are others', not their own!'[15] The descriptions of the wise master encouraging the ploughman 'by singing how / The kingdom's portion is the plough' is classical georgic, exploring the rhythms of farming life. The 'enamelled meads' where the master can see 'a present Godlike power / Imprinted in each leaf and flower / And smellst the breath of great-eyed kine, / Sweet as the blossoms of the vine' have the charm of a celebratory pastoral vision. But as a country clergyman, Herrick also has a closer vision of the round of rural festivities that interrupted the grind of agricultural labour:

> Thy wakes, thy quintels, here thou hast,
> Thy maypoles too with garlands graces:
> Thy morris dance; thy Whitsun ale;
> Thy shearing feast, which never fail;
> Thy harvest home; thy wassail bowl,
> That's tossed up after fox i'th'hole;
> Thy mummeries; thy Twelthtide kings
> And queens: thy Christmas revellings...

The poem's reference to the sheep that '...find'st their bellies there as full / Of short sweet grasse, as backs with wool', points to England's greatest source of export wealth at the time. Meanwhile, the close of the poem celebrates the chief delight of the rural gentry, the art of hunting, 'the witty whiles to draw, and get/ The lark into the trammell net;/ Thou hast thy cockrood [a clearing with nets to catch game birds], and thy glade/ To take the precious pheasant made...' These lines are a reminder that the idea and actuality of rural England as a place for leisure and play for the privileged was there centuries ago. The poem also contains lines that only later historical knowledge can really unpack. Herrick congratulates Porter on the fact that:

> Thou never ploughst the ocean's foam
> To seek, and bring rough pepper home;
> Nor to the Eastern Ind dost rove
> To bring from thence the scorchèd clove.[16]

Porter may never have been physically engaged in the new Indian trade, but he was a major investor in Sir William Courteen's Association, a trading company set up to try to break the East India Company's monopoly on trade with India. It is not known whether Porter invested in Courteen's other colonial exploits: his Guinea trading (in enslaved Africans) and his also unsuccessful attempt to seize control of Barbados as a private colony (he fell foul of the Earl of Carlisle who was already there), but the connection between pastoral poetry and empire as early as 1635 is clear enough.

The Eighteenth Century Georgic
In this age of expanding commerce and empire, poets like James Thomson both widened the bounds of writing about nature to more direct observation of the countryside in *The Seasons* (1726-1746) and evoked commercial colonial expansion and the tropical world.[17] Others wrote in the georgic tradition, such as Christopher Smart (*The Hop Garden*), John Dyer (*The Fleece*) and James Grainger (*The Sugar-Cane*), all of whom produced lengthy poems about the rural or imperial trades on which the new prosperity was based.[18]

In the work of James Thomson, writing around eighty years later than Herrick, the connections between the countryside and empire form the core subject matter of his *The Seasons*, once the most read book of rural poetry.

Thomson's origins as a Scottish poet who grew up in the immediate aftermath of the Act of Union (1706-1707) is crucial to his story. He came to London in 1725 to seek his poetic fortune through patrons and book sales whilst London was expanding commercially. He wrote the lyrics for Thomas Arne's nationalist song 'Rule Britannia' (currently a battleground between those who seek to decolonise British culture and their opponents). Thomson's major work *The Seasons* is a compendium of many of the generic possibilities of poetry about the rural world, the gateway through which later poets such as Wordsworth and John Clare were to pass. It is also the very clearest articulation of the connections between empire and the English countryside. It contains examples of the pastoral, the georgic, the poem of Horatian withdrawal, the loco-descriptive, the dominant 18th century mode of the picturesque that obeys the laws of generality found in the paintings of Claude, and poetry that looks forward to the subjective and more locally specific rural poetry of romanticism. *The Seasons* sets out to celebrate the ideals of harmony between man and nature, agriculture and imperial commerce. Thomson saw Britain as being uniquely blessed by a benign deity with the good fortunes of climate, enterprise, liberty and respect for property. As a long poem that went through extensive revisions, it is often at its most interesting when there is least harmony between Thomson's conflicting ideals. Whilst there is much that idealises English rural life, Thomson nevertheless brings fresh perceptions to some of these scenes. On the one hand his depiction of harvest reapers in 'Autumn' belongs to the tradition of the pastoral in its evasive gilding, and is sharply contradicted in the work of Stephen Duck, discussed below:

> At once they stoop, and swell the lusty sheaves;
> While through their cheerful band the rural talk,
> The rural scandal, and the rural jest
> Fly harmless, to deceive the tedious time
> And steal unfelt the sultry hours away.[19]

Thomson's depiction shows that if he had ever witnessed reapers at work it was from a distance. But lines from his 'Spring', makes it possible to believe that the ploughman, released from the workless poverty of winter and from confinement in a damp and smoky cottage, might well have felt a rising of his spirits:

> Joyous the impatient husbandman perceives
> Relenting Nature, and his lusty steers
> Drives from their stalls to where the well-used plough
> Lies in the furrow loosened from the frost...
> Cheered by the simple song and soaring lark.[20]

There is in 'Spring', too, a remarkable eco-poetic sequence where the burgeoning sexuality of birds, beasts, plants and humans is connected in a vision of Spring's recreative growth. But the figure of the ploughman is not simply a respectful nod to the classical pastoral tradition. The ploughman actively contributes to the new national commercial prosperity (though not sharing in it). Thomson urges the reader to 'venerate the plough', while at the same time empire 'Wafts all the pomp of life into your ports'. This is poetry concerned with the balance of payments. It values agricultural exports and the new colonial imports which brought luxury to the rising middle class,

> So with superior boon may your rich soil,
> Exuberant, Nature's better blessings pour
> O'er every land, the naked nations clothe,
> And be the exhaustless granary of a world![21]

But Thomson also knew that empires rise and fall and he is familiar with the commonplace that the Roman empire fell because it was corrupted by luxury and had lost touch with its agrarian base. He urges harmony between the honest stability of the agricultural past, 'the sacred plough', and the new prosperity of empire. Colonial trade is summed up in the phrase 'social commerce', and posits the fallacy that such trade was equally beneficial to all parties. Thomson also peddles the idea that trading nations are 'naked nations', populated by barbarous people blessed by edenic climates where nature provides all and sets 'brown labour free.' The inhabitants of such places, the poem implies, have no skills in husbandry: '...what avails this wondrous waste of wealth, / ... This pomp of Nature', a plenty wasted on Africans as an 'ill-fated race' who lack

> kind equal rule, the governement of laws,
> And all-protecting freedom which alone
> Sustains the name and dignity of man –
> These are not theirs....[22]

Britain's civilised duty is to take charge: '...hence she commands / The exalted stores of every brighter clime, / The treasures of the sun without his rage...' So far, so jingoistic. It is a powerfully expressed version of one of the dominant ideological bases of empire that lasted right through the 19th century. It was the kind of belief that prevented a supposedly scientific observer such as the botanist Joseph Banks, discussed in Chapter Six, from seeing what was right in front of his eyes when he landed in Tahiti with Captain Cook in 1769. Yet Thomson also expresses anxieties about the consequences of imperialism. He writes powerfully of the sharks that follow slave ships,

> And from the partners of that cruel trade
> Which spoils unhappy Guinea of her sons
> Demands his share of prey...[23]

At other times he displaces this colonial anxiety on to the behaviour of others, notably the Catholic Spanish. The 'thou' of the following lines might seem to give credit to the British trader, but the lines are actually addressed to his Muse, and so imply a veiled critique:

> Thou art no ruffian, who beneath the mask
> of social commerce com'st to rob their wealth;
> No holy fury thou, blaspheming Heaven,
> With consecrated steel to stab their peace,
> And through the land, yet red from civil wounds,
> To spread the purple tyranny of Rome.[24]

It is what Thomson does not say that most points to the ideological contradictions he is grappling with. There is no acknowledgement that the 'cruel trade' contributes so substantially to the profits of 'social commerce'. During the years that passed between the first publication of *The Seasons* and Thomson's final alterations (1726-1746), 357,100 enslaved Africans were imported into the British Caribbean and 185,100 into the British colonies in North America. Just three years before Thomson was writing about 'kind equal rule' and 'all-protecting freedom' in the 1726 edition, the British parliament was passing the Black Act of 1723. As one of the most repressive pieces of criminal legislation in British history, this made fifty offences, almost all against property, punishable by death. The Black Act was a brutal response by the ruling class to bitter class protests in the countryside against the consequences of enclosure, particularly when country people were denied access to game. The poem reminds us that colonial expansion and violence coincided with brutal repression at home, often enacted by the same men. Ultimately, Thomson chooses rural pleasures over colonialism's moral risks. In 'Autumn' he decides at one point:

> Let others brave the flood in quest of gain,
> And beat for joyless months the gloomy wave.
> Let such as deem it glory to destroy
> Rush into blood, the sack of cities seek –
> Unpierced, exulting in the widow's wail,

The virgin's shriek, and infant's trembling cry.
Let some, far distant from their native soil,
Urged or by want or hardened avarice,
Find other lands beneath another sun.[25]

He will retire to the 'rural, sheltered solitary scene' and there 'studious...
hold high converse with the mighty dead' who as 'gods beneficent... blessed
mankind/With arts and arms, and humanised a world'.[26] Despite this retreat,
and though Thomson writes against aspects of slavery and naked plunder,
The Seasons expresses confidence that local agricultural traditions can nonetheless coexist in harmony with new global commercial expansion.

By contrast, Oliver Goldsmith in 'The Deserted Village' (1770) sees
nothing but harm in the new commercial spirit. For him there is another
side to the new wealth brought by empire:

Proud swells the tide with loads of freighted ore,
And shouting Folly hails them from her shore;
Hoards even beyond the miser's wish abound...[27]

Goldsmith's poem has been taken as a naively sentimental complaint
against modernity's inexorable drive. It is seen as a conservative and fanciful
pastoral vision of a world that never existed. Such a view forgets that he
arrived penniless in England because he was fleeing the continuing effects of
British (English) colonial rule in Ireland. In England, Goldsmith witnessed
the destruction of a pre-capitalist way of life in the process of enclosure,
which resulted in the privatization of a fifth of English common land after
1750.[28] One can see his 'Auburn' as a precursor, in intention and radical
critique, to William Blake's *Songs of Innocence and Experience*, which appeared
only nineteen years after Goldsmith's poem, in 1789. Indeed, the first lines
of *The Deserted Village* acknowledge the poem's own idealising processes. This
is clear in its knowing use of superlatives: the village is blessed by the *earliest*
spring, the *longest* delayed summer; the place where *every* sport could please,
where humble happiness endeared *each* scene; where the brook *never* fails –
a place of impossible perfection that looks forward to Blake's 'The Ecchoing
Green', 'Laughing Song', 'Nurse's Song' and others. Experience comes as 'all
these charms are fled' when 'One only master grasps the whole domain':

...The man of wealth and pride
Takes up a space that many poor supplied;
Space for his lake, his park's extended bounds,
Space for his horses, equipage, and hounds:
The robe that wraps his limbs in silken sloth,
Has robbed the neighbouring fields of half their growth;[29]

There is some evidence both in the poem and in the historical record
that Goldsmith was thinking of a specific act of enclosure and dispossession
wrought by a returning East India Company nabob. This was not an
enclosure which could be justified by bringing agricultural improvement,

but made in order to display wealth. The figure of the man displaying new riches brought back from the West Indies or India would have been familiar enough to Goldsmith's contemporary readers, or to the audiences of plays such as Richard Cumberland's *The West Indian* or Samuel Foote's *The Nabob*. As in Blake's sick rose, commodity plunder despoils the natural:

> No more thy glassy brook reflects the day,
> But, choked with sedges, works its weedy way;
> [...]
> Sunk are thy bowers, in shapeless ruin all,
> And the long grass o'ertops the mouldering wall...[30]

The poem traces a sequence of negative social developments. The former inhabitants of this imagined village are displaced, just as Goldsmith had been in Ireland. They are transformed from rural villagers with commoners' rights into industrial workers with only their labour to sell, or else colonial emigrants who possess only their bodies and, in the case of tens of thousands of convicts sentenced to transportation to the American and Caribbean colonies, not even that. Goldsmith contrasts the lives of settled rural communities to those of their children, who would be sent into the mines and factories. Meanwhile, former villagers are driven to vagrancy and denied even parish relief:

> For him no wretches, born to work and weep,
> Explore the mine, or tempt the dangerous deep;
> No surly porter stands in guilty state
> To spurn imploring famine from the gate
> [...]
> If to the city sped – what waits him there?
> To see profusion that he must not share [...]
> Here while the proud their long-drawn pomps display,
> There the black gibbet glooms beside the way.[31]

It has been customary to regard Goldsmith's attack on modernity as naive and built on simple binaries. But historical works such as the multiply-authored *Albion's Fatal Tree: Crime and Society in Eighteenth Century England* (1976), and Peter Linebaugh's *The London Hanged: Crime and Civil Society in the Eighteenth Century* (2006) tell a story of rural (and urban) strife that resonates with details in Goldsmith's poem. The rising commercial wealth of the old landed gentry and the newly affluent saw a fierce legal defence of private property via the hangman's 'black gibbet'. Goldsmith might be utopian, but he draws lines that lead unmistakably from colonial wealth to rural poverty. He links empire with enclosure, expulsion from the commons and the death of village traditions:

> Teach erring man to spurn the rage of gain;
> Teach him, that states of native strength possest,
> Tho' very poor, may still be very blest;
> That trade's proud empire hastes to swift decay...[32]

These connections provide the underlying inspiration for two lesser-known long poems, Susanna Blamires's 'Stocklewath; or the Cumbrian Village' (c. 1771)[33] and Ebenezer Elliott's 'The Splendid Village" of 1833.[34] Blamires and Elliott remind us that village England does not reside wholly in the south; Blamires's Stockdalewath (as it is written), where she was born, lies south of Carlisle, whilst Elliott's village lay north of Rotherham in South Yorkshire. Stockdalewath remains a small, remote village, but Elliott's village, once agricultural, was already becoming a suburb of Rotherham, bringing a population change that he deeply lamented. Both Blamires and Elliott connect their villages to the colonial world.

Blamires shares with Goldsmith the idea of villages as places of virtue, 'Foe to the toils which wealth and pomp create'. She says nothing about enclosure (in the main, Cumberland's enclosure was to happen far later) and describes a village where much has stayed the same '…the hot cattle startling cease to graze; / While to the pool, or darkest shade they hie,/ And with the scourging tail whip off th' offending flie'.[35] The changes are superficial and recurrent as the old women complain: 'Look at the girls! – they all dress now-a-days / Like them fine folk who act them nonsense plays!'.[36] But this is still a village where:

Along the path that winds around the hill
You lose the milkmaid – though you hear her still.
At the last fair she caught yon thrilling lay,
And now the woods repeat 'Auld Robin Gray'.[37]

and where there is sturdy dancing on the village green:

Nor form that every Grace was known to bend,
Nor foot that every feathered hour would lend,
Has any merit here; – but feet of sound,
Which tabour-like re-echo on the ground.[38]

'Stocklewath' (as it was probably pronounced) has many neat images like these, but – at the expense of coherence – the poem takes a detour to the village alehouse. Here, a wanderer returned connects distant empire to this Cumberland village. 'Six-pence Harry' (the six-pence a sign of what he has left after he had taken the king's shilling and been pressed into the army) connects the tropes of distant empire to this remote village. Harry demurs from his listeners' assumption that all Britain's enemies are as bad as each other:

You're much mistaken: Goodness I have found
Spring like the grass that clothes the common ground [...]
Nay, 'mongst the Indians [native Americans] I've found kindly cheer,
and as much pity as I could do here![39]

Harry embarks on a tale about being lost and encountering some men 'their faces painted o'er/The wampum belt and tomahawk they bore', who treat him with unexpected kindness – a sign of shared humanity in contrast to the stereotype of savagery, though sometimes of a noble kind. Ludicrously, he tells how in return he taught Native Americans the arts of husbandry and agriculture, including the domestication of animals and Indian corn (maize). It is unclear whether Blamires plants this story to expose Harry or whether she believed in the civilising mission, but the fact that the wife of one of the listeners, 'scolding Nancy to the ale-house flies' and berates her husband 'What are you doing – hearing Harry's lies', suggests the former.

Elliott's 'The Splendid Village' shares this theme of the wanderer returned from seeking his fortune in the empire (Canada), to find his native village not deserted but corrupted by the sharp divisions between rich and poor in the post-enclosure world. He finds his own family reduced to hopeless penury. The honest schoolmaster has been replaced by 'Mister John Suckemwell's Academy', a boarding school for the sons of would-be gentlemen. There's the butcher's son, now the estate steward, 'Red as a lobster, vicious as his horse, /That like its master, worships fraud and force'[40] and the enriched squire, 'Yon mass of meanness, baseness, grease and bone / – Yon jolly soul, that weighs just eighteen stone?' The village has been gentrified: 'Now, where three cotters and their children dwelt / The lawyer's pomp alone is seen and felt', whose three acres of garden, 'uncrops the ground that fed a family'.[41] Gone is the hospitable equality of the ancient inn, now dominated by the constable and bailiff, protectors of the property of the wealthy. Here, too, the rural poor are connected to the ill-effects of empire when their wages are driven down by 'Erin's hordes', the migrant Irish labourers who are fleeing famine, and where the rural poor are themselves driven to emigrate. Elliott, a small factory owner, was no revolutionary, but he was disturbed by rural class antagonisms: 'I look on pomp, that apes a bloated crew/ While beggar'd millions hate the biggen'd few'.[42] Like Goldsmith, the fault lies in enclosure and commercialised agriculture. He asks: 'Where is the Common, once with blessings rich –/ The poor man's Common – like the poor man's flitch/ And well fed ham, which erst his means allow'd,/ Tis gone to bloat the idle and the proud'. It is a world where 'One farmer prospers now, where prosper'd five'. Elliott's sentimental and rough-hewn jeremiad for 1830s' England ends with the narrator's return to 'Niagara's roar', while the line, 'England flames – a "garden" and a hell',[43] makes an explicit reference to Goldsmith's line, 'The country blooms – a garden, and a grave.'

Anti-pastoral

The poems of Goldsmith and Elliott show that the tradition of rural writing does not always mask power and privilege in a wholly self-deceiving way. In *The Country and the City*, Williams identified a number of anti-pastoral poets from the 18th and 19th centuries whose work scorns aristocratic visions of feasts which appear on banquet tables as if by magic.[44] He described the poetry of Stephen Duck, George Crabbe, Oliver Goldsmith, and, to an extent John Clare, as anti-pastoral, though perhaps it would be truer to say that, whilst Clare was influenced by rural literary traditions, including Thomson's *The Seasons*, he established a distinctive tradition that still speaks to contemporary poets and readers.

Literary historical work has reawakened interest in the work of peasant and plebeian poets of the 18th and 19th century, but it is worth drawing attention to Stephen Duck's *The Thresher's Labour* and the response to it by Mary Collier, *The Woman's Labour*. For many agricultural labourers, the only paid work available in winter was threshing – separating wheat from chaff with flails. This was so essential to rural survival that, as noted in Chapter Two, the introduction of mechanised threshing machines pro- voked the Captain Swing campaign of machine-breaking in the 1831. Duck describes how:

> When sooty Pease we thresh, you scarce can know
> Our native colour, as from Work we go;
> The sweat, and dust, and suffocating smoke
> Make us so much like Ethiopians look,
> We scare our wives, when Evening brings us home,
> And frighted infants think the Bug-bear come.
> Week after week we this dull Task pursue... [45]

In the classic pastoral, harvest is invariably portrayed as a time of merriment, but Duck reminds us of the sheer backbreaking physicality of such labour:

> But when the scorching Sun is mounted high,
> And no kind Barns with friendly Shades are nigh,
> Our weary Scythes entangle in the grass,
> And streams of sweat run trickling down apace;
> Our sportive Labour we too late lament,
> And wish that Strength again we vainly spent.[46]

Perhaps Duck's most telling anti-pastoral thrust is against the false bonhomie of the 'harvest home' where the class antagonism between the propertied farmer and landless labourers is drowned in an alcoholic haze, and the sentimental embrace of the cycle of the seasons, which Duck sees as no more than the labours of Sisyphus. At the feast:

> A Table plentifully spread we find,
> And jugs of humming Beer to cheer the Mind,
> Which he, too generous, pushes on so fast,
> We think no toils to come, nor mind the past.
> But the next Morning soon reveals the Cheat,
> When the same toils we again repeat,
> To the same Barns again must back return,
> To labour there for room for next year's corn.[47]

Duck mentions women's labour only once in his poem and that in a dismissive way. Mary Collier wrote *The Woman's Labour: An Epistle to Mr. Stephen Duck* in response to this omission. Her poem was published in 1739, long after Duck had left the fields and was in receipt of royal patronage. Duck had written how during the harvest:

> Our Master comes, and at his Heels a Throng
> Of prattling Females, arm'd with Rake and Prong,
> Prepar'd whil'st he is here, to make his Hay,
> Or, if he turns his back, prepar'd to play. [...]
> And were their Hands as active as their Tongues,
> How nimbly then would move their Rakes and Prongs?[48]

Collier reminds Duck that women labourers worked in the fields before performing the thankless round of domestic labour: cooking, minding the children, washing the clothes, and attending their male lords and masters:

> When Evening does approach we homeward hie,
> And our domestic Toils incessant ply,
> Against your coming home prepare to get
> Our work all done, our House in order set.
> Bacon and Dumpling in the pot we boil,
> Our Beds we make, our Swine we feed the while,
> Then wait at door to see you coming home...[49]

Collier concludes the poem with a witty play on Duck's allusion to the labours of Sisyphus by comparing rural women labourers to the daughters of Danaus who are eternally condemned to fill a perforated container with water as punishment for killing their husbands:

> While you to *Sysiphus* yourselves compare,
> With *Danaus*' daughters we may claim a share;
> For while *he* labours hard against the Hill,
> Bottomless Tubs of Water *they* must fill.[50]

Raymond Williams identifies George Crabbe's *The Village* (1783) as a literary turning point in purposely shifting readers' attention from landowners to labourers, and also consciously assailing the pastoral poetic tradition. Crabbe lived in impoverished coastal Suffolk and was the son of an minor public official who was neither landless labourer nor minor gentry. Crabbe wrote in an explicitly anti-pastoral vein. Writing nearly fifty years after Duck's *The Thresher's Labour*, Crabbe begins *The Village* by announcing:

> Fled are those times, when, in harmonious strains
> The rustic poet praised his native plains:
> No shepherds now, in smooth alternate verse,
> Their country's beauty or their nymphs rehearse;
> [...]
> Yes thus the Muses sing of happy swains

Because the Muses never knew their pains:
They boast their peasants' pipes; but peasants now
Resign their pipes and plod behind the plough;

The Village knowingly rejects the high pastoral mode. It is less concerned with reflecting, as Goldsmith does, on the enclosure-wrought disruption to rural life, but in recording the actuality of a particular place where nature itself is unremittingly hostile to human effort, where the harsh cycle of a life of labour almost invariably ends in the humiliations of the poorhouse. Crabbe's aged labourer complains:

'These fruitful fields, these numerous flocks I see,
Are others' gain, but killing cares to me';[51]

And far from seeing the village as a place of community and social solidarity, Crabbe sees that the poverty of his particular village fosters selfishness: children abandon their parents to the poorhouse when they can no longer work. But *The Village* is a poem of two parts. Book II unwrites the devastating portrait of Book I. Book II blames villagers' miseries on their profligacy, violence and drunken ways. It undercuts the poem's earlier awareness of poverty's oppressions by singing the praises of the local squire – from whom Crabbe sought preferment as a clergyman, his means of escape from Aldeburgh.

Also writing explicitly in the anti-pastoral mode was the Liverpool poet, Edward Rushton, whose experience as the second mate of a slave-ship travelling between Guinea and Dominica made him a passionate abolitionist.[52] Rushton very consciously used the pastoral form, satirically, to stage a series of dialogues in his 'West-Indian Eclogues' between two enslaved men, one quiescent out of fear, the other prepared to sacrifice his life for liberty. Rushton's approach follows in the footsteps of the 'African Eclogues' written by the Bristolian poet, Thomas Chatterton, written in 1770 (themselves influenced by William Collins's *Persian Eclogues* of 1742) and first published in 1784. Like Collins's sequence of poems, Chatterton's eclogues are markedly exotic in language; however the first eclogue is undoubtedly intended as an anti-slavery tract in a heightened heroic mode. Set on the slave coast of West Africa, Heccar seeks to persuade Gaira not to pursue marauding slave traders, whilst Gaira exclaims, 'Heccar, my vengeance still exclaims for blood,/'Twould drink a wider stream than Caigra's flood.'[53] Rushton uses the conventional eclogue form rather more effectively to contrast the beautiful Jamaican landscape at each stage of the day ('Now the huge mountains charm the roving eye/ Their verdant summits tow'ring to the sky') with the horrors they overlook and the dreadful choice that Loango must make after his wife is seized by the white master and he plots his resistance:

'Three, three must fall! for Oh! I'll not survive;
I dread the white man's gibbeting alive,
Their wiry tortures and their ling'ring fires: –

These he escapes, who by the knife expires. [...]
Come pointed blade; – the Tyrant's house is nigh:–
And now for vengeance, death, and liberty!'[54]

Sensibility, Connoisseurship, the Picturesque and the Sublime
One of the poetic directions that later poets found in James Thomson's *The Seasons* was his image of the man of feeling who delights in nature in its least cultivated forms, an image in sharp contradiction to his georgic praise of the plough. In the writing of the later 18th century, there is a discovery of the delights of the natural over the artificial, or at least of the natural that could be arranged in harmony with art. It was a period of enquiry into the aesthetic ideals of the sublime and the picturesque. As Edmund Burke argued in his *Philosophical Enquiry into the Origin of Our Ideas of the Sublime and Beautiful* (1756), the sublime and the beautiful were opposite concepts, though both could give pleasure. Key to Burke's theory was the idea of terror, or at least the capacity of an object to induce intense feeling. The Lakes or the Swiss Alps were important sites for the sublime, as landscapes that were vast and awe-inspiring. It led to a poetry that found beauty in wild places, and also heralded the growth of tourism to the Lake District (discussed further in Chapter Five) and the Wye Valley. The poet Thomas Gray was one of the first to write a travel memoir about the Lake District (see Chapter Five), and he shows that even this wild place could only be appreciated by those trained in the arts of cultivated spectatorship. This was the age of the Claude glass, a plano-convex mirror that converted the actual landscape into a replica of a landscape painting by the French artist Claude Lorrain (1604-1682). Gray records in his journal of a 1769 tour to Westmoreland that he 'fell down on my back across a dirty lane with my [Claude] glass open in one hand, but only broke my knuckles...'.[55]

The picturesque offered gentler pleasures, but again scenes had to be worthy of a painting and viewers trained in the art of looking. Notions of the picturesque were first applied to British landscapes by William Gilpin in his *Observations on the River Wye, and Several Parts of South Wales, etc. Relative Chiefly to Picturesque Beauty; made in the Summer of the Year 1770*. The Wye Valley was within reach of the city of Bath, then the pleasure 'capital' of the Atlantic West,[56] a city where merchants and West Indian planters invested their sugar wealth in a move from Bristol.[57] One of these men was the absentee planter, Valentine Morris, who developed tourism to the area by funding access routes into the Wye Valley. He employed 100 men to build roads to his Piecefield estate and these roads provided the infrastructure for tourists from Bristol to visit his cliff-top walkways and admire the views, a popular pastime because – seen through Gilpin's instruction in viewership – they resembled painted Italianate landscapes.[58] Here is an instance when literature's colonial connections have only recently come to light through historicist and materialist approaches that have revealed empire's less explicit role in creating the context for pre-romantic and some later romantic poetry.

One of these tourists, though he would have hated to be considered as such, was William Wordsworth.[59] The Wye Valley provides the setting for his poem 'Lines Composed a few miles above Tintern Abbey'. At the time of Wordsworth's visit, British landscapes were already being altered by new farming methods and industrial development. The poem reacts to these developments, not by mentioning them, but by envisioning an idealised return to nature. It draws on sublime and picturesque conventions to show the poet communing with nature and restoring him to his purest self. In this, he takes up a long, transcultural idea of nature as a trope of virtue, restoration and escape, although it is important to say that whilst the kind of historicist reading that Marjorie Levinson offers complicates our understanding of the poem, it does so without denying that this is a great poem that explores both a moment of disillusionment over events in France and the joy of being reunited with his sister, Dorothy.[60] As a traveller who reached the area along the river by boat, Wordsworth may or may not have been aware that slave-produced wealth paid for the roads on which many tourists travelled to the Wye Valley. He was certainly surrounded by reminders of the South West's connection to slavery: between 1795 and 1797 he and Dorothy rented Racedown Lodge from the sons of the Bristolian slave-owner John Pinney.[61] With his friend Samuel Taylor Coleridge he was in the process of writing and publishing *Lyrical Ballads* with Joseph Cottle in Bristol in 1798, and Coleridge had given a lecture against slavery in Bristol 'against the falling off of zeal in the friends of the Abolition'.[62] However, as Raymond Williams has observed, Romantic vistas often obscure the logistical structures that grant access to those places: roads, horses, carriages and working-class labour.[63] Slavery can be added to Williams's list. There is no account of a journey to the Wye Valley in 'Tintern Abbey', except in the poem's title, which refers to 'a Tour, July 13, 1798'. To quote from the poem, it is as if the speaker (and the subsequent tourists who seek this Wordsworthian landscape) is magicked into a 'green pastoral landscape'.

The retreat to the countryside sometimes had very practical reasons. This was the case for Wordsworth's and Coleridge's truly radical friend, John Thelwall who retreated from London to a farm in Wales. Thelwall was the chief theoretician of the London Corresponding Society and had been put on trial for high treason (which still carried the sentence of hanging, drawing and quartering). Though he was acquitted, he was still being hounded by government-supporting loyalist thugs who broke up his meetings armed with cudgels and cutlasses. He was abandoned by Wordsworth and Coleridge when a spy (James Walsh, whom Coleridge nicknamed "Spy Nozy") from the repressive Pitt government came snooping around the Wordsworth's rented house in Alfoxden in Somerset where Thelwall was visiting in 1797.[64] In contrast, the retreat of Wordsworth, Coleridge and Southey to the Lake District can be seen as an historical variant on the generalised notion of a rural idyll found in the works of Robert Herrick, Andrew Marvell, Alexander Pope, James Thomson and others discussed above.[65]

The story of colonialism's relationship to Romantic aesthetics is convoluted but instructive. Sugar profits financed the road to Piecefield, which connects to Gilpin, who connects to Wordsworth, who leads to Jane Austen. Austen was an avid reader of Gilpin: her heroine Fanny Price is, Kathryn Sutherland argues, 'formed as a contemporary of Wordsworth and Coleridge' and her schoolroom is modelled as 'a Romantic location, as laden with meaning and restorative power as... Tintern Abbey is for Wordsworth.'[66] Fanny Price's appreciation of Mansfield Park's grounds conforms to picturesque conventions of serene landscapes. She sees 'all that was solemn and soothing and lovely'. Fanny continues, 'When I look out on such a night as this, I feel as if there could be neither wickedness nor sorrow in the world'.[67] This idealised vision overlooks the Antiguan slavery connection that funds Mansfield Park, discussed in the following chapter. In *Mansfield Park* as in 'Tintern Abbey', such raptures are ultimately enabled by sugar barons. As Williams argued, Romantic vistas sometimes conceal the unpleasant preconditions of their existence.

Empire, the Rural and the Romantic Revolt against Modernity
By the turn of the nineteenth century, England's evolution from the commodification of land and imperial trade towards capitalist industrialisation was becoming clearer. As Saree Makdisi explores in *Romantic Imperialism* (1998), turning towards the rural represented an escape from urbanisation but the turn also testified in Wordsworth's case to his sharp awareness of the destructive impact of global capitalist commodification on social relations. Makdisi observes a contrast between Book VII of Wordsworth's *The Prelude*, which reports a painful recoil from the explicitly imperial city of London (including its growing multiracial character), and the memories of a boyhood spent in the uncultivated wilds of the Lake District. Makdisi argues that Wordsworth rejects an alienating modernity that is both capitalist and imperial. In the 'blank confusion' of the city, Wordsworth sees the visible signs of capitalist empire amongst the milling crowds:

> ...from remote
> America, the Hunter-Indian; Moors,
> Malays, Lascars, the Tartar and Chinese,
> And Negro Ladies in white muslin gowns...[68]

Far from welcoming this new diversity, Wordsworth's vision of Britain's capital becomes almost hysterical in its portrayal of Bartholomew Fair's 'anarchy and din/ Barbarian and infernal', including 'The silver-collared Negro with his timbrel' in this 'Parliament of Monsters'.[69]

At the same time, Makdisi reminds us that the delight Wordsworth took in uncultivated nature was an absolute reversal of the disgust that 18th-century land-improvers felt about such wastes. To improvers, such land-scapes could mean nothing to enlightened men. Makdisi quotes Daniel Defoe's denigration of the Lake District as 'the wildest, most barren and frightful of any that I have passed over in England.'[70] As Makdisi argues, the way we see landscape is always historically situated, frequently in reaction to the present. He points to the irony that, though Wordsworth and the other Lakelanders saw these places as a refuge from modernity, they contributed unwittingly to commodifying them for the modernity of tourism. Words-worth no doubt wrote *A Guide through the District of the Lakes* (1810) because he needed the commission, but he later regretted it.[71] In 1844, he campaigned against extending the railway from Kendal to Windermere not only as a desecration of nature in the Lake District, but as 'highly injurious to its morals'. He asserted that the uneducated poor would not benefit 'morally or mentally' from such excursions. Even some of Wordsworth's friends disagreed with this class snobbery. But there was probably a more political objection behind his opposition. When he wrote 'We shall have the whole of Lancashire, and no small part of Yorkshire, pouring in upon us to meet the men of Durham and the borderers from Cumberland and Northum-berland', he signalled that industrial Lancashire and Yorkshire were loca-tions of intense Chartist organisation and activism that had not yet reached the more rural areas to their north.[72] This late conservatism does not tell the whole story. Wordsworth's earlier and more radical work – the *Salisbury Plain* and *Deserted Cottage* poems (1793) – was concerned with unhoused poverty and abandoned wayfarers such as the maimed victims of the Napoleonic wars and a wife abandoned by her soldiering husband.[73] More generally, we can read Wordsworth's rejection of the city as part of his quest to find a more humane world, but one which involved a withdrawal from wider social commitments.

John Clare: Beyond Romantic Subjectivity

One can read in works by 18th and 19th century writers who were identified as 'peasant' (in their own time), and as 'plebeian' in later academic studies, some of the same frameworks within which Black British writing has been produced and read. It was not by accident that the Barbadian novelist George Lamming in his *The Pleasures of Exile* (1960) praised what he called a 'peasant sensibility' in the work of Caribbean writers of the 1950s. He referred in particular to the work of Samuel Selvon, including both his novels of Trinidadian life and his urban masterpiece, *The Lonely Londoners* (1956).[74] Then as now, there were conflicting perceptions of unwelcome literary challenges on the one hand – an invasion of territory marked out for the gentrified, the educated and refined – and the corresponding opportunity to patronise writing that was seen as refreshingly different. In the case of Stephen Duck, Mary Collier, Ann Yearsley (known as Lactilla because she was a milkwoman), and later John Clare, the history of their publication and reception has much to say about the angle of view but also about vexed relationships with publishers and patrons. Inevitably, for the writer in this situation there are intense pressures. Duck's poetry shows a tension between using truthful language that conveys the harshness of farm labour and the pressure to imitate the language of elite poetry. Writing *The Thresher's Labour* (1730) brought Duck to the attention of Queen Caroline, gave him an income and the time and space to write. A new edition of *The Thresher's Labour* appeared in 1736. Duck apologised for the delay and for what he now thought were the imperfections of what he claimed was a pirated (1730) edition. He had spent the time, he wrote, 'in endeavouring to Learn a Language, of which I was then intirely ignorant' – Latin. The 1736 edition loses the burning sun for 'Phoebus rays' and instead of 'Barns well filled' (very explicitly by human labour), it is 'Ceres' Gifts' that reward the farmer. Though he became materially comfortable in later life, and the author of a substantial body of undistinguished, pious and increasingly polished work, Duck committed suicide by drowning in 1756.[75]

In the work of John Clare, writing almost a century later, there is almost an opposite linguistic process. The earlier published collections are those in which one sees Clare's desire to write in approved forms about rural England, collections such as *Poems Descriptive of Rural Life and Scenery* (1820) and *The Village Minstrel and Other Poems* (1821) in which Clare's publisher, John Taylor, 'amended' both Clare's punctuation and his use of specifically local words. The Clare we know today and regard as a major poet is the Clare of the then largely unpublished work that speaks in his own voice without any evident attempt on his part to write for a sophisticated and largely urban audience, though Clare's letters and prose writings display the intensity of his desire to communicate his vision. Like Stephen Duck, Clare suffered mental collapse, but it would be too easy to ascribe this solely to his social situation, to his undoubted distress when the map of his intimate landscape was abruptly altered by the enclosure and privatisation of the common land of his village of Helpston. Nonetheless, his letter about how his rare gift as a poet separated him from his fellow villagers points to what those pressures were:

> I live here among the ignorant like a lost man in fact like one whom the rest seemes careless of having anything to do with – they hardly dare talk in my company for fear I should mention them in my writings

and I find more pleasure in wandering the fields than in musing among my silent neighbours who are insensible to everything but toiling and talking of it and that to no purpose.[76]

At the same time as he was isolated in his own village, he was regarded as a curiosity who could be patronised as 'the Northamptonshire Peasant Poet' by the literary world in London. Perhaps it is possible to see Clare and his struggle to speak in his own voice as a precursor of the Black British poets of our time and of an ongoing struggle by so-called 'regional' writers to throw off the sense that their writing is of strictly local appeal.

The standard edition of John Clare's poetry runs to nine impossibly expensive volumes[77]; the critical work on him fills a good many library shelves[78] and his life and poetry have continued to inspire contemporary works of fiction, poetry and art.[79] He is indeed critical to any discussion of English rural writing. Seen in his own time as a 'peasant' poet in the tradition of Stephen Duck, Robert Bloomfield and others, his work, published between 1820 and 1835 was well-regarded for a time, but went out of fashion following Clare's breakdown and long years of seclusion in mental asylums. An important but unreliable biography of Clare was written by Frederick Martin in 1865. This traces Clare's decline and dwells more on the life than the poetry, though it reveals that he continued to write unpublished poetry during his years of incarceration. The real and lasting revival of interest in Clare began in the 1920s and continues into the present. Clare's poems and prose in manuscript uncover a vastly more complex and important writer than was evident in the published work, which was itself a record of an often uncomfortable relationship between poet and publisher.[80] The range of Clare's work as a whole reveals a writer in dialogue with the rural poetry of the past – James Thomson's *The Seasons* was his first inspiration – but working towards a distinctive perception of the rural world. In this century, his work has come to seem ever more pertinent to our current environmental crisis and to the renewed interest in the idea of material and immaterial commons as part of the radical fight against all kinds of inequalities and exclusions. His poems and writing about Gypsies, for instance, are important in this respect. His poetry also offers a vision of the human place in the 'natural' world that goes beyond the kind of romantic subjectivity that sees that world as somehow intended for human purposes, whether economic or spiritual.

In his poem, 'The Lament of Swordy Well', spoken as if in the voice of the field after its enclosure and transformation into 'productive' land, the field laments:

The bees flye round in feeble rings
And find no blossom bye
They thrum their almost weary wings
Upon the moss and die [...]

There was a time my bit of ground
Made freemen of the slave
The ass no pinard dare to pound
When I his supper gave
The gipseys camp was not afraid
I made his dwelling free
Till vile enclousure came and made
A parish slave of me.[81]

In 'The Village Minstrel', Clare writes of the enclosure and clearing of the scrubby woodland surrounding the village in a way that uncannily foretells Rachel Carson's *Silent Spring* (1962):

The thorns are gone, the woodlark's song is hush,
Spring more resembles winter now than spring.[82]

In his long verse satire, *The Parish* (1820, 1827), Clare, like Ebenezer Elliott, observes how the commodification of land – the purpose behind the Parliamentary enclosures – is changing the relationship between capitalist farmers and landless labourers. Clare satirises 'Young farmer Bigg' who now 'Struts like the squire and dresses dignified'.[83]

This was the kind of observation that was also being made by William Cobbett on his rural rides when he complains that newly enriched outsiders now dominate rural affairs,[84] and of the fact that 'the small gentry... are all gone, nearly to a man, and the small farmers with them.'[85] Raymond Williams quotes Cobbett's remark that the 'Barings [family] alone have swallowed up thirty or forty of these small gentry.'[86] But he misses the full significance of Cobbett's complaint, which he reads as class-based – 'the reduction of intermediate classes in the rural economy' – but Cobbett does not just criticise landowners' changing social profile. Northington Grange estate was purchased partly with sugar plantation wealth from Alexander Barings's father-in-law. Cobbett writes: 'But Mr Baring, not reflecting that woods are not like funds, to be made at a heat, has planted his trees *too large*... this enclosure and plantation have totally destroyed the beauty of this part of the estate.'[87] Cobbett refers to English enclosures and plantations in the same sentence as a description of wealth which has been ('made at a heat'). This is a tropically-inflected accusation if ever there was one. To Cobbett, Baring mismanages his land because he has no prior relationship with it and no true taste in English landscape. It is wholly relevant to Cobbett's observations that, fourteen years before Baring bought the Grange, the Baring Brothers enriched themselves by arranging the purchase of Louisiana from Napoleon Bonaparte, an action which expanded the plantation system in mainland America.[88] Later in *Rural Rides* Cobbett names and shames the planters who have disturbed the social order: 'Mr Laing, a West India dealer of some sort, has stepped into the place of the lineal descendants of Sir William Temple... Alexander Baring has succeeded the successors and heirs of Lord Northington…[and] Sir Thomas Baring…has succeeded the Russells.'[89]

But perhaps Clare speaks even more powerfully to our time in his preoccupation with environmental change. Although Clare's woodlark has recently seen a recovery in numbers as a result of set-aside for scrubland and the felling of non-native evergreen forests, other native birds are in sharp decline: the tree sparrow (by 95%), the starling (by 71%) and the skylark (by 52%). The concerted contemporary efforts to restore wetlands, scrubland, heath and moorland to their state before such 'unproductive' areas were 'improved' by being drained, limed, cleared and cultivated point to Clare's farsightedness.

In addition to his personal dismay when his village, Helpston, was enclosed, Clare was acutely aware that the people most affected by the loss of the commons were the Gypsies who were a regular but elusive part of the rural and village world. As Sarah Houghton-Walker reminds us in *Representations of the Gypsy in the Romantic Period* (2014), right up to 1783, merely to be identified as gypsy ('vagabonds calling themselves Egyptians') could carry the death penalty. By the 18th century, Gypsies tended to be persecuted in less capital ways under the 1744 vagrancy acts.[90] In 2020, the Home Secretary Priti Patel threatened to change the law on trespass, with the power to confiscate Gypsy and Traveller caravans and mobile homes in a way that would make the travelling life impossible – which might have gladdened the heart of the man Clare excoriates in a prose piece:

> An ignorant iron hearted Justice of the Peace at ―――― Sessions whose name may perish with his cruelty […] mixd up this malicious sentence in his condemnation of 2 Gipseys for horse-stealing "This atrosious tribe of wandering vagabonds ought to be made outlaws in every civilizd kingdom and exterminated from the face of the earth".[91]

Clare wrote of his attraction to the Gypsy way of life, learning to play their tunes on the fiddle and 'joining in their pastimes of jumping dancing and other amusements'. He records how 'I became so initiated in their ways and habits that I was often tempted to join them'. He never did because he recognised how impossibly difficult the passage of the enclosure acts had made such lives. They are his canaries in the mine, the symbols of the loss of freedom, the closing down of possibilities. In the *Shepherd Calendar* of 1827, Clare could write of:

> The wild wood music from the lonely dell,
> Where merry Gipseys o'er their raptures dwell,
> Haunting each common's wild and lonely nook[92]

and of the Gypsies' place in the rural community, cutting and selling bullrushes as floor coverings, 'offering to hus wives cheap repairs / Mending their broken bottomd chairs' and being present with a jaunty confidence, 'Wi step half walk half dance & eye / Ready to smile on passers bye', earning their beer by playing the fiddle. They also gained pennies through their reputation as fortune-tellers, a mystery Clare half wants to believe in.

Just fourteen years later, in 1841, Clare wrote his powerful sonnet, 'The Gipsy Camp'. Whilst Clare never romanticises Gypsy attitudes to property, his use of the word 'pilfering' is not judgemental. It is analogous to 'gleaning', another of the commons that the new enclosed farming methods and the courts dominated by landed interests had declared illegal. (The judge, Lord Loughborough, said that granting a right to glean would 'raise the insolence of the poor'.)[93]

> The snow falls deep; the Forest lies alone:
> The boy goes hasty for his load of brakes,
> Then thinks upon the fire and hurries back;
> The Gipsy knocks his hands and tucks them up,
> And seeks his squalid camp, half hid in snow,
> Beneath the oak, which breaks away the wind,
> And bushes close, with snow like hovel warm:
> There stinking mutton roasts upon the coals,
> And the half roasted dog squats close and rubs,
> Then feels the heat too strong and goes aloof;
> He watches well, but none a bit can spare,
> And vainly waits the morsel thrown away:
> 'Tis thus they live – a picture to the place;
> A quiet, pilfering, unprotected race.[94]

In his important work, *The Idea of Landscape and the Sense of Place 1730-1840: An Approach to the Poetry of John Clare* (1972), Barrell seeks to establish Clare as a revolutionary poet who overturns the 18th century concern with the general into a particularity of observation. More recent critical work has examined more closely Clare's extensive reading and the extent to which many of his poems, as well as having the experiential purity that Barrell notes, are often in dialogue with the work of other poets and elite and popular literary sources.[95] Other recent critical work has focused on the position of Clare as a poet of deep ecological insight, who had moved beyond the poetry of nature, the kind at least that John Keats identified in Wordsworth as 'the egotistical sublime', where the natural world stands subservient to the human intellect. In a reading, probably influenced by the open, dialectical ecology of thinkers such as Timothy Morton (in which survival depends on the abandonment of the hierarchies of anthropocentrism),[96] Patrick Bresnihan argues that in a poem such as 'The Lament of Swordy Well', the field is 'never just a field, but always a field-and… a field-and-bees; field-and-rabbits; field-and-freeman; field-and-ass; field-and gypsies', and that none of these relationships is fixed or in any kind of hierarchical position with respect to others.[97]

Just how radical and open-minded was John Clare's portrayal of Gypsies is evident in some of the other literary representations of the time – Wordsworth's 'Wild outcasts of society' and their 'torpid', stationary life – is a failure of perception and empathy if there ever was one.[98] In Jane Austen's *Emma*, Emma finds her protégé Harriet in a state of alarm, leaning on Frank Churchill's arm. Harriet and her friend have come face to face with 'a party of gipsies.' A child asks for money and the friend takes flight, leaving Harriet to be 'assailed by half a dozen children, headed by a stout woman and a great boy, all clamorous, and impertinent in look, though not absolutely in word.'[99] Austen's ironic voice casts doubt on whether or not the young woman's 'exceeding' terror is justified, since – by her own admission – no verbal threats were made, and their judgement is questioned: 'How the trampers might have behaved, had the young ladies been more courageous, must be doubtful'. It is therefore unclear if she truly needed to 'be[g] them not to use her ill.'[100] Although Austen's depiction of Gypsies as raucous and even thieving (they are the prime suspects for a later raid on Mr Woodhouse's hen house), her portrayal is relatively sympathetic for a conservative writer. Houghton-Walker explains this by observing that Austen was writing in a period of heightened anthropological interest in wandering people, when Gypsies came to represent dying country traditions and were correspondingly prone to receive nostalgic literary treatment by romantic writers, conservative and radical alike.[101]

The Victorian Pastoral
John Barrell's and John Bull's *The Penguin Book of English Pastoral Verse* (1974)[102] contains little from the mid- to late 19th century except from the substantial body of William Barnes's (1801-1886) poems in the Dorset dialect. In Barnes's work – the son of a tenant farmer, self-educated and later a country parson – it is possible to see a rare connection between the writer and the rural people he wrote about, where they read him and admired him.[103] Otherwise, apart from Lord Tennyson's poems in the Leicester dialect, Victorian poetry is predominantly urban with the rural as a refuge for leisure and mental recuperation, and the pastoral as an even more artificial form used as a distancing device in poems such as Matthew Arnold's (1822-1888) 'Thyrsis' and 'The Scholar Gypsy' (1855), whose protagonist seeks escape from '...this strange disease of modern life, / With its sick hurry, its divided aims'.[104]

Barrell and Bull find no room for the work of Elizabeth Barrett Browning, though her poem *Aurora Leigh* (1856) emerged as a national favourite in a recent National Trust survey of poetry of the countryside.[105] This was evidently an anthologised extract from what is a long, complex, nine-book narrative poem from the section, 'England'. This relates to the heroine's very gradual appreciation of the English countryside.[106] Aurora comes from Italy after her mother's death, and at nine, aboard ship, approaching land, she wonders 'Could I find a home / among those mean red houses through the fog?' To her '[t]he ground seemed cut up from the fellowship of verdure' and everything seems 'dull and vague'. Eventually, her reading of the classics of pastoral poetry and her discovery of Keats, overcome her Mediterranean resistance. 'I learnt to love that England' Aurora admits, and 'plunged myself / Among the deep hills' of Herefordshire. She celebrates a land of 'the up and down of verdure', 'such nooks of valleys', is 'confused by the smell of orchards' and finally comes to feel 'my father's land was worthy too / Of being Shakespeare's'. Catherine Hall notes that the land featured in *Aurora Leigh* is materially connected to wealth derived from transatlantic slavery. Barrett Browning was descended from a long line of slave-owners and owners of plantations in Jamaica – absentees for quite some time by Barrett Browning's day. Her father's plantations in northern Jamaica brought in an income of £4,000 in 1807 and this enabled him to buy the 500 acre Herefordshire estate on which she grew up.[107] Her mother had Jamaican property too. Barrett Browning was unhappy about her family's association with slavery, though she wrote to a friend expressing real anxiety about the impact of threatened emancipation on her income. That she was in favour of abolition is shown in her powerful anti-slavery poem 'The Runaway Slave at Pilgrim Point', which expresses the grievances of an enslaved woman who escapes to Plymouth Rock, the landing point for the pilgrims. It is hard not to conclude that the generous compensation the Browning family received was part of the story. Though the Herefordshire estate which features in 'Aurora Leigh' was sold in anticipation of lost enslaved labour and declining sugar profits,[108] her father and his business associate received £7,734 for the 'loss' of 397 enslaved Jamaican men and women from the Slave Compensation Commission. Barrett Browning herself inherited £4,000 from her grandmother's Jamaican properties in 1830 together with shares in a West India ship.[109] This resource allowed her to be financially independent from her father. She eloped with Robert Browning (who was himself descended from St Kitts planters) and the couple received further money from the poet John Kenyon, another slave-owner who also received compensation for lost labour.[110] As Catherine Hall argues, while Barrett Browning 'hated slavery... she... lived much of her life on the proceeds of the plantations'.[111] The biography of Aurora Leigh as a Mediterranean child gradually attuning herself to England quite clearly parallels a family history that was both tropical and temperate and is perhaps to be seen as a way of exploring those tensions, though in an evasive way. Sometimes the connections between nineteenth century writing about rural Britain and empire only emerge with later knowledge. These contradictions are richly and sympathetically explored by the Black British writer Laura Fish in her novel, *Strange Music* (2008).[112]

The World We Have Lost: Nostalgia and the Rural World
By the time Thomas Hardy was writing his Wessex novels published
between 1872 and 1895, the rural world he describes in them was long
gone and the novels, such as *The Return of the Native* (1878), written in
the city, express sorrow about disappearing country ways which the
author witnessed as a child and to which no one could return.[113] This
said, Hardy does not sentimentalise rural life and its inequalities of
power. *Tess of the D'Urbervilles* depicts the downfall of the heroine following
her rape by the son of a wealthy family during the 1870s agricultural
depression.[114] The unpopularity of *Jude the Obscure* (1895), evidenced
by the critical and reader response at the time, can be attributed as
much to its absence of nostalgia and the stark portrayal of rural entrapment
as to its sexual frankness.[115] However, that nostalgia for a disappearing
world extends through the writing of the later nineteenth century to
our own time, to Ronald Blythe's *Akenfield: Portrait of an English Village*
(1969) and the works discussed below.

Twentieth-century pastoral
In the early twentieth century, Richard Jeffries (in prose), A.E. Housman
(*A Shropshire Lad*) and Edward Thomas were influential in establishing
enduring links between Englishness and country settings.[116] It is significant
that the one attempt to establish a rural poetic community – in Dymock
on the Gloucestershire/Herefordshire border – occurred immediately
before the First World War. This community broke up even before
one of its leading figures, Edward Thomas, was killed just before the
end of the war. At its height, this 'Muse Community', as its biographer
calls it, was a group of mainly middle-class Georgian poets that included
Rupert Brooke, the American Robert Frost, W.H. Davies (the erstwhile
super tramp), Lascelles Abercrombie, Eleanor Farjeon, Wilfred Gibson
and John Drinkwater.[117] Much later, Edward Thomas's wife, Helen
Thomas, called it a 'poet's holiday in the shadow of the war'.[118] But
the experience of that war also produced some of the best poetry about
rural England. Fine examples include two poems by a Kentish countryman,
Edmund Blunden, 'The Poor Man's Pig' and 'The Pike'.[119] These poems
anticipate the work of Ted Hughes (an admirer of Blunden) in collections
such as *The Hawk in the Rain* (1957), *Wodwo* (1967) and *Moortown* (1979),
the latter a poetry collection about a working Devonshire farm. Until
the emergence of Hughes, the fortunes of rural poetry ebbed and flowed,
but mostly ebbed. After the First World War, it became associated with
a backward-looking Georgianism and was overshadowed by urban
modernism. One of the few notable poetry collections written in the
georgic tradition was Vita Sackville-West's *The Land* (1927), which begins
in Virgilian fashion, 'I sing the cycle of my country's year'. *The Land*

is work of a scion of the aristocratic Sackville family, who had owned
the 1000 acre Knole estate in Kent since Elizabethan times (which Vita,
though the eldest, could not inherit because she was a woman).[120]
Otherwise, few notable 20th century British poets were associated with
the land (in contrast to Ireland with Patrick Kavanagh (1904-1967) and
Seamus Heaney (1939-2013) or the USA with Lorine Neidecker, Robert
Frost and Wendell Berry). The two poets who perhaps are most associated
with rural landscapes (before Ted Hughes) were Vernon Watkins and
R.S. Thomas (Welsh) and Jack Clemo (Cornish) who were not writing
in English contexts. In our own time, Terry Gifford notes how difficult
it has become to see 'nature writing' as anything other than a worn-
out genre. He argues that much contemporary writing has to be 'post-
pastoral', because the writing admires nature without forgetting that
people are busy destroying it.[121] Gifford points in the direction of eco-
poetry and its critical analogue of eco-poetics as its replacement.

   Where the interest in the rural went in the early twentieth century was
into genre fiction. Glen Cavaliero's *The Rural Tradition in the English Novel
1900-1939* (1977) lists well over two hundred novels published in the first
three decades of the twentieth century. The bibliographies of some of the
writers he discusses suggest five or six times as many publications on top of
this. Cavaliero does not provide information about book sales, but it is clear
from his discussion that much rural writing from this period was produced
for a readership that longed for a part of England which was uncontaminated
by industry, trade unions and mass politics. There were the popular novels
of Florence Barclay (1862-1921) who found rural remnants of an otherwise
lost 'spirit of courtesy and gracious manners; the consideration of the rich for
the poor; the respectful deference of the poor towards the rich.'[122] Other
writers presented rural England as a place of primitive passions in contrast to
suburban respectability. Such stereotyped depiction encouraged the kind of
purple prose that Stella Gibbons parodied in *Cold Comfort Farm* (1932), her
targets being Mary Webb, Sheila Kaye-Smith and Eden Phillpotts (1862-
1959). Philpotts authored around 150 novels and collections of short stories,
many set in rural Dartmoor. Their portrayal of moorland displays the
influence of Emily Brontë and Thomas Hardy. Arnold Bennett's preface to
a collected edition of this work says: 'What a district for a novelist – compact,
complete, withdrawn, exceptional, traditional, impressive, and racy! Eden
Phillpotts found it and annexed it.'[123] Others, such as the Herries novels of
Hugh Walpole (1884-1941) set in Cumberland, and Sheila Kaye-Smith's
Sussex novels, found a readership keen for a fiction of regions that car
ownership was opening up to tourism. Publishers such as Blackie with their
32 brief guides to 'Beautiful England' (published between 1910-1925 but
remaining in print until the 1950s), were quick to capture this market. In this
series, beautiful England was almost exclusively rural, with the exception of

cathedral cities like York, Bath and Wells. Elsewhere, it is evident that rural England provided a post-romantic flight from modernity – including the democracy that had returned Labour governments in 1924 and 1929. In the case of Henry Williamson, author of *Tarka the Otter*, which is still widely read, there was the complication of a genuine literary talent entangled with an enthusiasm for Hitler and a longtime political association with the fascist Oswald Mosley.[124]

Fiction about rural England in this period was not all motivated by reactionary responses to the contemporary world. The novels of Winifred Holtby came out of the political Left, and the work of the farmer-novelist Adrian Bell has drawn recent critical attention and reprints. The popular novels and short stories of H.E. Bates, particularly his Larkin family stories (serialised for television between 2000 and 2003), have remained almost continuously in print.

Whilst this period produced powerful works of memory that locate the pastoral spirit in childhood experience, such as Dylan Thomas's poem 'Fern Hill', or Laurie Lee's prose memoir, *Cider with Rosie* (1959), the times when the connections between rurality and Englishness have been at their most intense were in times of approaching or actual war, when there were existential fears for national survival. Three examples are Virginia Woolf's novel *Between the Acts* (1941), set in 1939, on the day of the annual village pageant at Pointz Hall. Woolf's novel reflects on the challenges of telling the English, predominantly rural story in the stage pageant devised by Miss La Trobe. The novel's characters, performers in the pageant, sense that nothing will ever be the same. In T.S. Eliot's *The Four Quartets* (1936-1943) the world shifts from the city landscapes of *Prufrock* (1917), *Poems 1920* and *The Waste Land* (1922) to a rural manor house in the Cotswolds and the rural villages of East Coker (Somerset) and Little Gidding (Cambridge-shire). In *East Coker*, Eliot portrays a bucolic village festival, almost as if it were the rural English equivalent of a rain dance, a desperate plea for the continuation of a world under the direst threat:

> Round and round the fire
> Leaping through the flames, or joined in circles,
> Rustically solemn or in rustic laughter
> Lifting heavy feet in clumsy shoes,
> Earth feet, loam feet, lifted in country mirth
> Mirth of those long since under earth
> Nourishing the corn. Keeping time,
> Keeping the rhythm in their dancing
> As in their living in the living seasons...[125]

There was also the Britain in Pictures series, published by William Collins between 1941 and 1949, lavishly illustrated 48-page books selling originally at 3/6d, and produced as a conscious attempt to boost national morale. Edmund Blunden in his *English Villages* (1941), after making the admission 'that the pilgrim will often find it horribly difficult to get a reasonable meal there...' also more seriously asserts '...of one thing I am profoundly persuaded, and that is that to the man or the woman who is desirous of finding the best in this country I commend the English village.'[126] For quite some time past, and still, this series of 126 titles has been very collectable, another instance of the kind of sentiment that explains the popular success of Flora Thompson's republished *Lark Rise to Candleford* (1945, 1979) which was dramatized as two plays and a later television series (2008-2011).

The Traumatised Pastoral
As noted in Chapter Two, in the post millennial world, we look back on at least forty years of industrialised farming practice that has changed landscapes and shifted the perception of agriculture from being the custodian of the countryside to being its potential destroyer. This environmental threat lies behind Robert Macfarlane's interrogation of the rural idyll from a contemporary creative perspective. He detects an 'eerie' quality in much contemporary writing, music and film about the English countryside. These brooding and uncanny depictions express an anti-pastoral 'hauntology', of which Macfarlane provides many examples. Among these is *A View from a Hill* (2005), a film based on M.R. James's (1862-1936) short story of that name (first published in book form in 1925), in which rolling hills and summer meadows are replaced by gibbets and corpses whenever the protagonist peers through his binoculars.[127] This 'traumatised pastoral', Macfarlane argues, runs through music – he lists P. J. Harvey, Julian Cope, These New Puritans – and also films – *Robinson in Ruins*, *A Field in England* and *Catch Me Daddy* (which I discuss in Chapter Five), all of which find something uncanny and disturbing beneath the surface of rural England.[128] To this list should be added Sam Peckinpah's 1971 film, *Straw Dogs*, in which a reluctant hero overcomes bloody violence directed against his wife and Cornish farmhouse. The film was controversial, principally because of an explicit rape scene, rendered all the more incongruous for taking place in scenic Cornwall; while rural America is a recognisable site of the violence of genocide and slavery, violence is supposedly anathema to rural England. Fundamentally, Macfarlane sees such productions as reacting against the conservatism of much pastoral writing, and what he describes as 'hauntology' as an expression of fears over the excesses of late capitalism, over-surveillance and environmental destruction rather than being cynical about the natural world.[129]

Strangely, as an admirer of Ted Hughes, Macfarlane does not mention Hughes's short story 'The Rain Horse' (*Wodwo*, 1967) in his article. It was as perhaps too well-known and written too long ago for an article reviewing recent work, but Hughes's story of nature's hostility and malevolence has probably lain fertile in the minds of its many readers, particularly because it was once part of a much-taught anthology of short stories in schools.[130] In 'The Rain Horse', a suited man bypasses the 'pleasantly remembered... lanes' of an English idyll to find himself mired in mud and 'holding himself tensely against the cold.' The man expects his experience to fall in line with pastoral: 'some pleasure, some meaningful sensation' but instead he sees 'bare fields, black and sodden as the bed of an ancient lake after the weeks of rain.'[131] The vast lapse of time ('ancient') denies him a relationship with the land, born of personal memory. The nostalgic experience of the landscape he once played in as a boy is denied him: he experiences 'nothing but the dullness of feeling nothing. Boredom.' Instead of belonging to the countryside, he is alienated from it. He sees himself as a 'trespasser' and an 'outcast'.[132] When he spots a black horse running in his direction, he is instantly unsettled by it. Menacingly, it stands stock still and watches him and then charges at him: 'its head stretching forwards, ears flattened and lips lifted back from the long yellow teeth. He got one snapshot glimpse of the red-veined eyeball as he flung himself backwards around the tree.'[133] The discoloured teeth and bloodshot eyes – together with the animal's malice – defy the conventional depiction of horses as elegant and noble creatures. Convinced that the animal is intent on doing him harm, he arms himself with stones and sees the encounter as 'open battle'. The countryside has revealed itself to him as a hostile, uncomfortable place. Taking refuge in some outbuildings, his boyhood memories return, but they are far from romantic: 'paraffin, creosote, fertilizer, dust – all was exactly as he had left it... He remembered three dead foxes hanging in a row from one of the beams, their teeth bloody.'[134] Smells are artificial and wildlife is associated with death. In this brooding and muddy morass, the man realises he has been changed too much by his absence to be able to deal with nature in all its otherness, its separateness from human will. Nature requires intimacy and work. Now he feels lobotomised, and the story leaves him sitting 'staring at the ground, as if some important part had been cut out of his brain.'[135]

Robert Macfarlane's 2015 essay both takes on the idea of the English pastoral and discusses the important work of the Black photographer, Ingrid Pollard and her exhibition of photographs, *Pastoral Interlude* (1988). Yet English pastoral writing continues to be both much anthologized and monocultural. Recent popular anthologies include Owen Sheers' *A Poet's Guide to Britain* (2009) and Samuel Carr and Jo Bell's book, *Ode to the Countryside. Poems to Celebrate the British Landscape* (2010).[136] Both anthologies foreground Romantic writing and celebrate the pastoral's 'distinguished ancestry' but recognise, as Jo Bell states in her introduction, that such writing frequently expresses 'nostalgia for a world that never was'.[137] Black writers are absent from both these anthologies, collections designed for the fringes of the poetry market. But as Terry Gifford has argued, nature poetry as pastoral can no longer have any credibility in our environmental crisis, and has had to give way to the concerns of eco-poetry.[138] Peter Abbs in his edited *Earth Songs* (2002), a transatlantic *Resurgence anthology of contemporary eco-poetry*, finds room for only one poet of colour, Sujata Bhatt, in his selection. African American poets do not appear. Neil Astley does much better in his *Earth Shattering: Ecopoems* (2007), an anthology generous in its dimensions through time and geography, where poems by Jean Binta Breeze, Patience Agbabi and Benjamin Zephaniah appear alongside poems by Derek Walcott, Ken Saro-Wiwa, Jayne Cortez and native American poets such as Paula Gunn Allen and Joy Harjo.[139] Even so, the work of such Black British writers is generally overlooked by academic researchers on the pastoral, the one exception being Dominic Head's *Modernity and the English Rural Novel* (2017), which finds the space to discuss V.S. Naipaul and David Dabydeen alongside the usual suspects. I address such omissions in my poem 'A New Chronology', in Part Two of this book, and in the sections that follow.

One recent novel that follows very much in the vein of Macfarlane's traumatised pastoral is, as noted in Chapter Two, Max Porter's *Lanny* (2019). In it an older villager, Peggy, discusses local history with the boy Lanny and the artist Pete:

> Do you know, she says, what the Domesday book has to say about this place?... It says the bishop holds this place. It says it answers for ten hides, land for sixteen ploughs, twenty-nine villagers and five slaves.
> Slaves? I ask, because that doesn't sound right.
> Peggy tuts, Slaves just meant folk with no land, Peter.[140]

Peggy uses a vocabulary which relates to feudal England but which also strangely evokes the later history of English contact with the Atlantic world. Her reference to feudal ownership of people puzzles Peggy's listeners, since the word 'slave' evokes the more modern history of Europeans enslaving West Africans. In such subtle and passing ways the novel invites the perception of connections between the colonised Atlantic world and working-class resistance to the landed gentry.

Rural writing by Black and Asian Britons

The remainder of this chapter considers how Black and Asian British writers have begun to reshape the pastoral. Accordingly, the chapter discusses the utility, or otherwise, of labels such as pastoral, anti-pastoral or even the postcolonial pastoral. It looks at what has drawn such authors to write about the countryside and considers the reshaping of some classic tropes of the English pastoral terrain: flora, fauna, rivers and Morris dancing.

When Black writers intervene in the tradition of rural poetry, they are effectively challenging the idea that multiculturalism and rurality are mutually exclusive. I prefer to characterise much of this writing as post-pastoral rather than anti-pastoral (though some writers engage with the pre-romantic pastoral and anti-pastoral tradition), because much of the writing expresses an affiliation with the countryside, rather than alienation from it. As Jackie Kay and her fellow editors argued in *Out of Bounds. British Black and Asian Poets*, many black writers 'open up the counties and countries of Britain to their post-colonial heritage'. There may be anti-pastoral elements to poems such as Lorna Goodison's 'At The Keswick Museum' (2005), which foregrounds the 'recorded' deaths of local people and 'all categories of malevolent spirits',[141] but more generally, as Kay, Robinson and Procter point out: 'if alienation, unbelonging and dislocation remain key aspects of black and Asian experiences in Britain, what such terms simultaneously conceal are [...] rich and manifold attachments to...landscape'.[142] The strength and extent of these attachments has gone largely unnoticed. Rural pleasures run through writing by Black and Asian poets. As stated in chapter Two, Grace Nichols declares that '[e]veryone has a blackberry poem'.[143] Louisa Adjoa Parker's poem 'An Afternoon in August' confirms this assertion, praising the 'bright juice' of blackberries which she describes as 'jewels'. For her, blackberry picking is a family bonding experience: 'there is peace to be found in foraging'.[144]

Postcolonial Pastoral
Rob Nixon coined the term 'postcolonial pastoral' in his argument that V.S. Naipaul's Wiltshire-based novel, *The Enigma of Arrival* (1987), 'invents postcolonial pastoral' because he flirts with romantic perspectives on the English landscape, asserts his 'postcolonial presence', and puts the geographies of an English country estate and Trinidadian sugar plantations side by side.[145] As Graham Huggan and Helen Tiffin observe, the utopianism of pastoral writing holds an attraction for postcolonial authors worldwide, because – frequently in the context of dispossession – it allows them to 'creatively refashion their relationship with the earth'.[146] For the most part, academic work on the concept of the postcolonial pastoral has focused on Africa or Australia. In the light of the rural turn in writing by Black Britons in the last three decades, now is a good moment to address the English context. By embracing romantic ideals of nature as a healing force, I argue, black Britons have reformed the English pastoral.

The earliest reflection by a postcolonial writer on the English landscape perhaps comes from the St Lucian poet, Derek Walcott. His poem 'XXXV', from *Midsummer* (1984), recounts a journey by car from Wales to England, giving a traveller's eye-view of ridges and fields, where that journey culminates in a visit to a roadside café with some companions. Walcott's poem belongs to a category of writing which, in the words of Kay, Procter and Robinson, 'compose[s]... landscape not from the perspective of the native or settled speaker, but *en route*, on the move, between places.'[147] Even so, Walcott's experience of the landscape is heavily mediated by the poetry he studied at school, a detailed knowledge derived from the colonial education system. Walcott was well aware that such an experience could be described as cultural imperialism,[148] but he also makes it clear that he transforms the pastoral for his own purposes. His literal journey becomes a literary one. The passing fields conjure up Arthurian England (Avalon), William Langland's narrative poem *Piers Plowman* (c. 1370-90), and no doubt Virgil's *Georgics*, with the ploughmen as symbol of humble communion with nature.[149] At first, even this lowly form of communion is unavailable to Walcott, who feels estranged from the English countryside. There are the 'gusts of rain', 'puddles' and 'drizzle', symbols of England's often forbidding, chilly landscapes. Walcott experiences the countryside at some remove, watching it through the 'rain-seeded glass' of a car window and later finding his view obscured by 'mist on the [café] window'. But the poetry of the English landscape lives inside him. Literary tradition interposes itself between Walcott and his view of the hills. Walcott is not so much Langland's ploughman as the planter of seeds who comes after him. In the first line of the poem, he offers the image of 'the sucking heel of the rain-flinger', the person who casts seeds to the earth with a flick of the wrist. His own 'flinging wrist' hurts and his 'veins ache in a knot', though he also satirises himself in fancifully connecting to Arthurian legend in seeing 'helmets of wet cars in the parking lot'.[150]

Walcott's choice of the fourteenth-century narrative poem *Piers Plowman* shows that he knows England's literary geography. *Piers Plowman* criticises the gentry who barred public access to common grazing land.[151] Whilst Langland condemns proprietorial attitudes towards land, Walcott condemns territorial attitudes to poetry and claims pastoral verse as his poetic birthright, regardless of birthplace. By doing so, he lays the foundations of an English postcolonial pastoral.

The earlier days of Black British rural writing tended to produce transrural visions of the landscape, in which the landscape of one country is overlaid by the landscape of another.[152] In V.S. Naipaul's novel *The Enigma of Arrival,* an account of Naipaul's eleven-year stay on the grounds of a Wiltshire country estate, a snowdrift is compared to a Caribbean sand dune.[153] An Englishman with a hoe evokes memories of 'green things growing' in Trinidad.[154] Debjani Chatterjee's more recent book, *Daughters of A Riverine Land* (2003), compares English and Indian rivers.

But if *The Enigma of Arrival* begins with that kind of double vision, it goes beyond it. Presented as a work of fiction, it is a narrative about the Wiltshire countryside perceived in ways that Naipaul continually wonders about. Does he still see in ways that are influenced by his Trinidadian origins, or were those origins already infused with Englishness? In a preface written for the 2002 reissue of the book, he wrote: 'My concern as someone from the colonies was… how, through a longing for metropolitan material, the writer or narrator misses his big subject.'[155] This 'big subject' combines Naipaul's place in the English literary tradition with ideas of Englishness. Into these reflections, memories of rural Trinidad surface with an intensity and affection that is striking given Naipaul's repeated assertions of his disconnection from his country of birth.

The Enigma of Arrival has its critics. Nixon asserts that, although Naipaul reshapes the pastoral, his novel 'screens out the violent decrepitude of… inner cities', allowing the author to 'mus[e] with delicate melancholy on the England of… Camelot'.[156] Ian Baucom similarly charges Naipaul with retreating from multiracial cities, and expressing 'post-imperial nostalgia' for country houses and the colonial might which such houses symbolise.[157] Both critics seem to imply, albeit unconsciously, that rural England is no fit subject for Black writers. As Lucienne Loh argues, *The Enigma of Arrival* inserts Naipaul 'within a pastoral tradition that would readily have denied him a place.'[158] Nixon and Baucom are no doubt right that Naipaul is shunning urban Britain, but both critics nonetheless underestimate the significance and impact of Naipaul's achievement.

Nevertheless, Nixon considers *The Enigma of Arrival* important because it acknowledges the role of colonial education in making its author admire pastoral verse and – at times – prefer rural England to rural Trinidad.[159] Not only is Naipaul familiar with writing, but also with artistic depictions of the English countryside: he knows Salisbury Cathedral because he first saw it in a Constable painting, which was 'reproduce[ed]… in my third-standard reader'.[160] Inevitably, then, Naipaul – as with later writing by Black and Asian Britons – accesses the countryside via the romantic tradition and sees the landscape with a 'literary eye' (p. 18). To others he is a victim of cultural imperialism (something Naipaul himself would have denied), but, wandering in 'solitude' from 'valley to crest' gives him solace (p. 18). Though his education has made him deeply English, to the English he is a brown foreigner. *The Enigma of Arrival* teases out this contradiction, away from England's old imperial capital, in the deepest countryside.

Naipaul links stately homes with sugar plantations. As I discuss in the Country House chapter, to make this connection is entirely justified but the links that he draws are imprecise. Naipaul links the Wiltshire manor house that he writes about to the memory of his exploited indentured Indian ancestors. He makes this connection solely because he is reflecting on his own physical presence on the country estate. Vague though it is, this association is important. As Huggan and Tiffin observe, the postcolonial

pastoral implicitly criticises earlier English pastoral poets for ignoring the
people who work the land, since it is highly conscious of the exploitation of
migrant transnational labour.[161] Naipaul subtly connects the Wiltshire manor
to Trinidad by overlaying one scene with another when he writes how some
plants 'jumped the path... and seeded themselves in the lawn...[like] a
sugar-cane fire jumping a firebreak and sending arrows of flame into the
adjoining green field' (p. 221). Earlier in the novel, this connection is
articulated in personal, human terms when he dwells on the manor's
Edwardian builders, who 'could not have imagined, with their world view,
that at a later time someone like me would have been in the grounds' (p. 55).
Their 'world view' would, he assumes, be an imperialist one. Such statements make the link between sugar and stately homes, but they do so in
general and symbolic terms. Naipaul does not substantiate the link by
referring to country estates with direct connections to the Caribbean plantation economy, such as Bowden House near Laycock in Wiltshire, nor does
he write about the East India Company, which shaped upper-class domestic
interiors and funded properties like Daylesford House or Sezincote Manor,
a two-hundred year-old Moghul palace in the English Cotswolds. In truth,
little of this information was readily accessible at the time Naipaul was
writing; for instance at the time of emancipation, 69 separate claims for
compensation for the loss of enslaved people as property came from Wiltshire. Wilsford Manor, where Naipaul rented a cottage, was not built until
1906; probably its only imperial connection was Edward Tennant's director-
ship of the Mysore Gold Company, which Naipaul does not mention.[162]

   Despite seeing the English countryside through the lens of a colonial
education, Naipaul is repeatedly afflicted by a sense of his own foreignness.
He describes this experience as 'tearing at an old scab' (p. 8), the experience
of racism he later acknowledges in *Reading and Writing* (2002), but which he
had written openly about in the letters to his family, later published as
Letters Between a Father and a Son (2003). The feeling arises when he converts
two former agricultural cottages into a single house, upsetting an old
woman who used to live there. Naipaul feels 'embarrassed to be... an
intruder, not from another village or country, but from another hemisphere; embarrassed to have destroyed the past for the old lady' (p. 347).
This sense of being 'an intruder' arises from his awareness that some of the
villagers have an entrenched belief that only white people legitimately
belong to such settings. Such moments undermine his sense of satisfaction
that his presence in Wiltshire is a consequence of British colonialism, an
irony which permeates his prose. This feeling leads him to re-interrogate
his first impressions of the place, including his neighbour, Jack, whom he
initially sees as 'genuine, rooted, fitting: a man fitting the landscape' (p. 14).
This idea of Jack unravels as Naipaul realises that pastoral myths have
misled him: 'it did not occur to me that... the past around his cottage might

not have been his past; that he might at some stage have been a newcomer to the valley' (p. 14). Naipaul comes to realise that he has been mistaken: 'Jack's style... suggested to me (falsely, as I got to know soon enough) the remnant of an old peasantry... surviving somehow the Industrial Revolution, deserted villages, railways, and the establishing of the great agricultural estates in the valley' (p. 17). This list and the allusion to Oliver Goldsmith's 'The Deserted Village' indicates precisely how the illusion has been created in Naipaul's mind. Naipaul may be misreading Goldsmith as uncomplicatedly epitomising naive nostalgia for a lost rural past. Nonetheless, by referencing Goldsmith in this way, Naipaul implicitly blames the pastoral tradition for his own misunderstanding of Jack.

Naipaul's close observation of his neighbours' relationship to this piece of the countryside pays off. He becomes critical of the locals' belief that Wiltshire is their 'historical inheritance' or birthright. He writes that '[t]hese people' – though they had come, many of them, from other places – still had the idea of being successors' (p. 53). He displaces such views by appealing to the distant past, remembering ancient patterns of settlement in the village of Waldenshaw: 'the very name spoke of invaders from across the sea and of ancient wars and dispossessions here, along the picturesque river and the wet meadows.' (p. 98). He disturbs any straightforward sense of 'historical inheritance' by harking back to far earlier periods of immigration.

Though the connections Naipaul makes between rural England, empire and immigration are loose ones, the larger achievement of *The Enigma of Arrival* is to dissociate rural England from 'racial, and historical, and cultural virtue' (p. 221). He accomplishes this by interrogating activities which perpetuate a false sense of virtue. One of his targets is historical preservation, which Naipaul identifies as contributing to a false 'assurance of continuity, the sense of something owed to oneself' (p. 53). This was farsighted: when the National Trust announced its intention, in 2020, to incorporate colonial history into its interpretation of heritage sites, it was accused of betraying its primary purpose, to conserve. As *The Telegraph* opinion column put it: 'its job is to conserve, not comment – to pass things on to future generations in a spirit of intelligent affection for what the nation holds dear.'[163] Back in the 1980s, then, Naipaul recognised the pastoral's role in constructing consoling mythologies of Englishness.

Ultimately, though, Naipaul's claim on the Wiltshire countryside is personal and cultural rather than historical or political. He becomes increasingly familiar with its appearance and character, finding himself 'in tune with the landscape in a way I had never been in Trinidad or India' (p. 221). The irony that this affinity originates in his colonial education is not lost on him. Steeped in rural poetry, he takes pleasure in 'Wordsworthian' walks (p. 18). However, Naipaul inherits more than romantic solitude from Wordsworth. He adopts Wordsworth's anti-tourist stance, which

distinguishes sophisticated observers from ignorant tourists.[164] A similar
rhetoric surfaces in Naipaul's description of Stonehenge. Though he lives
a short distance from that site, Naipaul depicts himself as viewing it from
afar. He writes that 'the tourist crowd, from a distance, was noticeable only
because of the red dress or coat that some of the women wore' (p. 19). This
may have been an innocent observation, but it conforms to a tradition of
denigrating women travellers. As James Buzard observes, (more strident)
misogynist rhetoric evolved in the context of mass tourism, when women
were often represented as interlopers on the masculine European tour.
Naipaul contrasts the women tourists' conspicuous clothing with his own
muted presence. They stand out. He is immersed in the landscape.

Another example of Naipaul's anti-tourism can be found in his depiction
of Constable's beech-lined water meadows beside the railway station as 'the
scenic drive the taxi drivers of the town took visitors along' (p. 204). By
emphasising that 'visitors', not locals, are driven along the tourist route, he
contrasts himself with tourists. However, we later learn that he frequently
rides taxis along the same route (p. 264). Naipaul's novel may be postcolonial
and post-pastoral, but it inherits and perpetuates a gendered, Wordsworthian
view of the landscape. It is a view that can be compared with Kamau
Brathwaite's despairing protest that 'hotels are squatting on my metaphors',[165] a protest against commercialisation and ecological displacement,
whereas Naipaul's complaint has more to do with class and snobbery.

On the one hand, Naipaul unconsciously inherits romanticism's privileged rural gaze; on the other, he deconstructs the pastoral. Yet he also
embraces aspects of romantic rural writing as a deliberate strategy when
writes how his encounter with the English countryside alleviates his sense of
being an outcast. His country walks allow him 'to shed the nerves of being
a stranger in England' (p. 18). Echoing the place-based precision of John
Clare, Naipaul acquires a growing vocabulary to describe Wiltshire in
specific terms: 'I was able to think of the flat wet fields with the ditches as "water
meadows"…and the low, smooth hills…as "downs"' (p. 3). This growing
familiarity amounts to a form of 'emotional possession', another characteristic
of the postcolonial pastoral. Naipaul's encounter with local country scenes is
intimate. He repeatedly describes the experience in terms of 'heal[ing]' and
'awakening': 'I was beginning to heal. For me, a miracle had occurred in this
valley' (p. 111). Wiltshire offers him a 'second life', an 'awakening to the natural
world' (p. 105). In this respect, his work is akin to the romantic tradition but
also to the regional sensibilities of less privileged poets like Clare.

Though more implicit than explicit, the transrural dimension of *The
Enigma of Arrival* is healing because it looks in two directions. On the one
hand, Naipaul repeatedly connects Wiltshire with his place of birth,
describing 'the gladiolus which, to my delight, flourished in both the
climate of England and the tropical climate of Trinidad' (p. 31). This flower

analogises his experience as an immigrant: he can take root in both places. The idea of taking root is critical. Communing with nature brings healing and awakening. Since these are recurrent metaphors, it is hard to agree with Huggan and Tiffin that the postcolonial pastoral is 'a medium for painful cultural memory rather than comforting cultural myth'.[166] It is of course true that Naipaul presents rural England as a mythologised, overprotected site of white belonging. It is also true that he situates this rurality in the context of empire, immigration and, initially, belonging. But Huggan and Tiffin's characterisation of the postcolonial pastoral fails to capture Naipaul's rural writing, since most of the book explores the experience, albeit non-naive, of being soothed, stimulated and accommodated by rural Wiltshire. But the experience of Wiltshire also leads Naipaul back to Trinidad, and the expression of a greater sense of at-homeness in its landscape than anywhere else in his writing. There is the death of a much loved sister that draws him back, but there is also the way that Naipaul writes about the cows he sees in Wiltshire and compares them to those he remembers from his childhood in Trinidad:

> Our few cows (perhaps like Gray's or Goldsmith's herds) were poor things compared to the healthy, big animals on the downs. But these animals on the downs, even with their beauty, were without sanctity, the constant attention of men, which as a child I thought cows craved. These cows in railed pastures or meadows had numbers scored into their rumps. No sanctity at birth, and none at death..." (p. 81).

Perhaps, David Dabydeen's novel *A Harlot's Progress*[167] comes closest to Nixon's definition of postcolonial pastoral in its act of brutal destruction of the English pastoral. This is most striking in the depiction of the real-life sadist slaver, Thomas Thistlewood (1721-1786) whose cabin is hung with pastoral paintings. These idyllic images evidently soothe Thistlewood's troubled conscience but they do not stop the sexual and sadistic abuse of the slaves under his control. Indeed, *A Harlot's Progress* compares pastoral verse to the construction of a slave-ship: 'every inch of deck needed to be plotted to maximize the cargo... consider the perfection of Mr. Dryden's couplets, which give new order to the English page.'[168] Dryden was a translator of Virgil, including his Eclogues and Georgics, the poems at the roots of English pastoral verse. To compare the 'order' of the poetry to the architecture of a slave-ship offers a sinister new perspective on literary depictions of rural England.

Reading Poets as Pastoral
Valerie Bloom's 1988 introduction to Lemn Sissay's first poetry collection, (*Tender Fingers in a Clenched Fist* (1988)), tentatively describes his poetry as 'almost pastoral'.[169] Now spanning over three decades, Sissay's work easily justifies a more definitive statement. In 'Barley Field' (from *Listener*,

2008), for example, Sissay's speaker stands amidst a ripening crop 'looking for inspiration'. Sissay's way of speaking about his poem parallels Naipaul's own remark that rurality is his 'big subject'. In Sissay's poem an oak tree 'stands, centre page'. As a symbol of ancient England, the oak tree signals Sissay's engagement with the pastoral tradition and asserts his right to participate in it. Ironically, the speaker almost leaves the field without spotting his own initials carved some years earlier into the trunk, a discovery which gives rise to the italicised realisation: '*I had been here before*', an assertion that can be read both literally and figuratively. The speaker's 'inspiration' (sought at the beginning of the poem) derives from his sense of belonging to the countryside and from his consciousness of engaging with the pastoral traditions of English poetry ('centre page'). Yet the pastoral aspect of Sissay's work has yet to register in poetry reviews, which routinely present his work as fundamentally urban, 'songs of the street.'[170]

So, too, Grace Nichols' poetry habitually creates a new pastoral aesthetic. She has composed a number of poems in which the speaker views the landscape from the vantage point of a train, a gesture which has been misinterpreted by Kay, Robinson and Procter as potentially indicating disconnection from rural Britain:

> these poems... often compose place and landscape not from the perspective of a native or settled speaker, but *en route*, on the move, between places. There's a fleeting glimpse of the Angel of the North, or Hull from an InterCity train in the work of Nichols.[171]

As a high-profile poet, Grace Nichols travels the length and breadth of the country to give poetry readings, an experience that Sissay shares. He addresses the issue of extensive travel in his poem 'A Reading in Stansted' (1999), which observes that he has 'travelled two hundred and fifty miles south from his Manchester home'.[172] Given this context, train travel implies more, rather than less, knowledge of the British Isles. It is of course true that viewing the countryside through a train window conveys a sense of movement, one which undoubtedly evokes the idea of migration, and train-bound poems can easily be interpreted as passing through landscapes rather than dwelling in them. However, Larkin's train poems are never interpreted in this way, despite what might sometimes be taken as a misanthropic vision of England.

My view is that Nichols's train poem expresses a greater sense of connection than Kay, Robinson and Procter allow. In 'Opening Your Book' the train window is no distancing device. Dedicated to R.S. Thomas, the poem claims a kinship with a figure seen as one of the few contemporary poets who connects to older traditions of rural poetry. Opening R.S. Thomas's *Laboratories of the Spirit* while on the train, Nichols' speaker enters the countryside through Thomas's poetry:

> Dipping into the well
> of your conversations with God;
> crunching through the communion
> of your Welsh valleys[173]

There is no sense of distance here. The rural tradition is a creative wellspring that sustains her work. Thomas's words spirit her through the landscape. Both train and book transport her to a rural poetic tradition – in both its celebratory and critical guises – with which she identifies. The poem begins:

> Why should departures of the flesh
> still make us weep
> when what we're left holding is
> the bright indestructible spirit?[174]

Her train journey parallels the 'departure' of R.S. Thomas's 'flesh' into death and his book's subsequent arrival into her poetic consciousness. His 'bright indestructible spirit' passes into her hands as she peruses the poetry of a literary forerunner. Her tears of mourning indicate the degree of her affinity with a poetic tradition to which she feels she can belong. Somewhere in this process a third journey takes place: a poetic impulse passes from R.S. Thomas to Nichols, whose own book is then delivered to a new generation of readers. It would be hard to find a more definitive image of continuity with, rather than departure from, British traditions of rural writing. It is important, too, to consider the relationship of both poets to the pastoral tradition. Thomas was a Welsh nationalist. He saw Wales as a country conquered by the English. His poems explore the natural beauty of Wales but rarely shrink from describing the harsh realities of rural life. Nichols was born in Guyana. Like Thomas, her work explores colonial themes in poems like 'Hurricane Hits England', which describes the 'howling ship of the wind' when it makes landfall in her adopted home. The poem references transatlantic slavery and presents the wind as a visitation of Caribbean spirits. Yet the hurricanes, Nichols's opening lines make clear, 'bring her closer / to the landscape'. This sense of continuity from one poet to another is nuanced and relies on a deep knowledge of Britain's literary geography.

There is no sense of alienation in Nichols's poem 'Opening Your Book'. The actual scenery may well be 'glimpsed' through glass and at speed, but the physicality of the imagery and active verbs alike ('dipping'; 'crunching') suggest how vividly she inhabits these spaces, exploring them in 'communion' with a predecessor; they are kindred spirits. In Wordsworthian fashion, nature brings out the speaker's best sense of self: like the speaker of 'Tintern Abbey', she is '[f]illed with an overwhelming sense / of what it means to be human'.[175]

Bernardine Evaristo's verse novel *The Emperor's Babe* (2001) is presented as an urban text about 'a black Roman in Londinium, AD211.'[176] Yet the novel frequently journeys to the countryside and alludes to it. The black Roman, Zuleika, travels with the African Roman emperor Septimus Severus, and he speaks to her about his Roman roads: 'I have only penetrated to Moray Firth, / morale is low, my soldiers hate the cold.'[177] As Evaristo has discussed, the book is founded on Peter's Fryer's mention of Black Romans, which she first came across in *Staying Power: The History of Black People in Britain*.[178] The novel alludes to the African-Roman centurions who were stationed at Hadrian's Wall. Her protagonist Severus recounts this presence, to which Evaristo adds further imaginative details: 'Up North, an Ethiop with legion of Moors / At Hadrian's Wall waved garland / of cypress boughs at me.'[179] The fictional Severus also speaks of his desire to quell rebellions by Scottish 'ginger-heads.'[180] The novel is also under-pinned by rich references to familiar British literary homages to the English landscape, such as Rupert Brooke's First World War poem, 'The Soldier', published in 1915. Brooke's poem imagines the thoughts of an English soldier who anticipates perishing abroad: 'If I should die, think only this of me:/ That there's some corner of a foreign field / That is forever England.'[181] Evaristo's Roman Severus echoes Brooke's opening lines:

> 'If I should die, think only this of me, Zuleika,
> there's a corner somewhere deep
> in Caledonia that is forever Libya.'[182]

Brooke's patriotic poem dwelt on England's unique formative influence: 'Gave [me] once her flowers to love, her ways to roam'.[183] Evaristo's allusion to 'The Soldier' is, by contrast, irreverent. In a tongue-in-cheek reversal, Evaristo's Severus does not cite Brooke, but rather Brooke cites Severus. So in the world of Evaristo's novel, Brooke's eulogy to rural England mimics the words of a Libyan emperor who – in real life – died near York nearly two millennia before Brooke was born.

The Emperor's Babe narrates a journey across now-urbanised areas which were once covered by woods and fields. Travelling alongside Roman soldiers, the protagonist Zuleika retrospectively recreates London as a series of countryside scenes. She passes 'the wild sloping grassland of Mayfair' and 'the wheatfields of Hyde Park' until the army sets up camp at the forests of Fulham.[184] Here, she makes herself comfortable amongst the trees: 'I snapped the stems of forget-me-nots / from the base of a tree, found a raspberry bush, / picked a handful.'[185] Later, she has sex with the emperor in the mud and then they bathe in rainwater: '[I] rinse the mud from your curls, / rain showers us, / you clean my breasts.'[186] In this elemental scene of two black Romans submerged in mud, the novel/poem plays with rural belonging and claims an African enjoyment of the countryside that pre-dates that of the white British. Here, Evaristo indulges in a bout of historical gaming to undermine claims to white, rural belonging which are based on the 'I-was-here-first' principle.

There's another neat reversal in the treatment of Pictish struggles against the Romans. In a chapter called 'Verbosa Orgia', presented as a Roman precursor of contemporary spoken-word nights, a Pictish poet called Hrrathaghervood performs rebellious verses to his Roman audience:

Hrrathaghervood sprang barefoot
onto the rostrum, face dyed blue with woad...

ginger dreadlocks down his back.

There's only three groups of fowk I hate,
De Romans who're trying to tae thief Scotland,
De Celts who've sold oot tae de Romans
An de Christians who didnae wint nae bugger tae enjoy thaimselves... [187]

Like Max Porter's *Lanny, The Emperor's Babe*'s parodic anti-racist performance poetry reminds us that the countryside has long been the site of battles over access and ownership.

There is a different kind of connection made in Maya Chowdhry's poem 'Black Badger Carlin Peas', which links the working-class Lancashire tradition of eating black peas (the historical poverty-diet of country work-houses) and the historical journey that black peas made, by ship, to medieval Britain:

Gutter-slush, the staple of parish workhouses, parched in beef dripping, splashed with rum.
Speckled, Spanish, shipwrecked, washed ashore, curiously sprinkled on a medieval field. [188]

Some writing by Black Britons clearly announces itself as rural and there can be no mistaking it for anything else. Adjoa Parker's poem 'Velvet Dresses' also evokes history to assert her right to belong. The poem is set in Dorset and she writes: 'let its history merge with mine:/talk of Africa and her slaves.' [189] As noted in Chapter Two, Adjoa Parker has spoken publicly about rural racism on the BBC [190] and has explored the history of Dorset in the 'Ethnic Minorities in Lyme Regis' project with Lyme Regis Museum as well as her own 'Black History in Dorset' project, which covered the region's black presence during Britain's four colonial centuries. [191] The verse order of 'Velvet Dresses' is important because it reveals the logic of the speaker's claim that she has a right to enjoy Dorset's countryside, together with others who may be prevented from enjoying it on the grounds of race. The first three stanzas express the speaker's love of the region's hills, fields and fossils. The fourth stanza hints at the region's links to transatlantic slavery and the fifth stanza denounces rural racism:

I want to know it will be fine
for anyone with *not from here* etched
like tribal markings into their skin,
...to walk her beaches, green-velvet fields

with pride, say
I live here, I belong here, she is mine.[192]

In 'Sometimes when I'm making beds' (from the same collection), the countryside's colonial links are explored more precisely. The speaker of this poem reimagines herself as a real historical figure while she does her chores at a Lyme Regis hotel:

> I could be an African servant girl
> brought back two centuries ago
> from Jamaican plantations by a trader,
> my master, his mulatto child in fact.[193]

The poem connects these details of cruelty and powerlessness with the inequalities of modern Britain. 'Little has changed here, up at the big house', she writes, 'pretending I was born for this; / smiling and dusting and cleaning white people's rooms'.[194] Taken together, these poems assert a link between knowing British colonial history and belonging to the countryside. Indeed, Adjoa Parker's solution to the barrier of rural racism is to understand the countryside's colonial past: the enforced transportation of Africans by English, Scottish and Welsh slavers, the rape of enslaved women and the consequent presence of Black and mixed-race people in rural Britain during the 18th century. This deeper history of the countryside allows Adjoa Parker to take possession of it and say *'she is mine.'*[195] Direct statements such as these only provide a partial story of the wider rural turn in writing by black Britons. Adjoa Parker presents a rationale for belonging in her poems, but in some sense this assertion comes after the fact. Taken collectively, her poems convey a rural sensibility, since their metaphors draw from her intimate knowledge of beaches, birds and flowers. One of many such examples is the poem 'Love, Ending', which compares the experience of a relationship break-up to birdwings against the cheek, a rising tide and 'cold water moving over stones.'[196] Adjoa Parker writes: 'Shades of ripening on blackberries tells us when to pick.'[197] Such fine judgements derive from practised experience. This kind of familiarity with the countryside is expressed again and again by poets such as Adjoa Parker, Grace Nichols, Maya Chowdhry and others. Time and time again, their work shows an easy and open engagement with country scenes, settings and creatures. It is surprising that no Black poet is anthologised in Simon Armitage's 2009 book *The Poetry of Birds*, given that so many Black British and Asian British writers have written poems about birds, some of whom are discussed below.

Fauna
Birds are an important migrant metaphor for black British writers because they fly across national borders.[198] One bird, though a poor flyer, is a particularly prominent rural fixture: the pheasant, a feature of a story

I discuss below by Manzu Islam. This bird is habitually represented as native to England's fields, hedgerows and woodlands. It is not known exactly how pheasants arrived on British shores, but it is possible that this Asian bird was brought and bred – to eat – by Romans. It was not popularly referenced as a game bird until the 14th and 15th centuries.[199] As Raymond Williams observes, game birds are important symbols of plenty in country house poems, and pheasants have been incorporated into an aristocratic pastoral aesthetic. In Robert Herrick's 17th-century poem 'The Country Life', a pheasant makes its appearance alongside 'May-poles', the 'Morris-dance' and the 'shearing-feast'. The doomed bird struts through a 'glade' before being hunted and brought to the dining table.[200] The pheasant also symbolises the English past. In John Betjeman's poem about Trebetherick, for example, a pheasant appears in 'the oldest part of Cornwall'.[201] Kipling's poem 'The Land' presents the hunted pheasant as an emblem of bygone rural customs, observing that pheasants have been caught by generations of the Hobden family.[202] More generally, the bird is mentioned in passing by poets as part of an inventory of Englishness. In the poem 'Stephanus Marcus', by Alfred Berggren, a hunting party of lords and knights uses a peregrine to flush out 'ducks, rabbits, pheasants'.[203] Despite its Asian origins, then, the pheasant has become emblematic of Englishness, its indigeneity is taken for granted in pastoral poems past and present.

In colonial-era writing, the killing of a pheasant has been seen as raising the spectre of transatlantic slavery. The critic John Richardson argues that Pope's poem 'Windsor Forest' (1711) communicates a general unease about slave-trading and he connects this to Pope's admiration of the bird's plumage, and his lament for its impending death:[204]

> To what avail his glossy, varying dyes,
> His purple crest, and scarlet-circled eyes
> ...His painted wings, and breast that flames with gold?[205]

The killing of the bird, a bright creature from a warmer climate, echoes the brutality of the slave trade – against the background of the wealth it creates.

In a contemporary poem by Sylvia Plath, 'Pheasant', a plea to a hunter not to slaughter the bird is founded on the assumption that the pheasant is native to the 'elm's hill' on which it roams: 'It is simply in its element' and its rightful presence 'gives it a kingliness'. Plath's use of a regal metaphor naturalises the pheasant's presence by suggesting that it has an age-old right to command the hills on which it lives.[206]

Yet for all this, the pheasant is not native to England, a fact explored in a short story by Manzu Islam, 'Catching Pheasants' (2005),[207] which directly addresses the bird's Asian provenance. The story follows the adventures of two Bangladeshi men who encounter pheasants during a trip to the countryside. One of them, called Dulu, catches one to take home, kill and eat. Creeping thorough a wood after dark, the two friends are chased by men with dogs but escape capture.

From the outset, Islam's story erodes the association between pheasants and Englishness:

> Dulu asked me if I knew that pheasants originally came from the Indian sub-continent...
> – Look how natural they look in this place, he said. Like they've always belonged here.
> – Yes Dulu, I said. That's why people see them as the most English of all birds.[208]

From its beginning, the story establishes parallels between the birds and the men, not merely because they have a common heritage, but because they have each had to establish a relationship to rural places that are historically foreign to them. The pheasants' conspicuous appearance obliges the birds to 'tak[e] cover' in the bushes (p. 41). Feeling similarly out of place, the two men have to conceal themselves in the undergrowth. Their status as intruders is clear: 'We heard a gun go off and the barking of dogs' (p. 42). This threat of violence precipitates an alarming escape. To add to their woes, nature participates in their expulsion: 'the low branches sprang to whiplash us, their thorns cutting into our flesh' (p. 43). The incident recalls Ingrid Pollard's words and her feeling that 'the owners of these fields... want me off their GREEN AND PLEASANT LAND'.[209] The protagonists' status as intruders in Manzu Islam's story is only partly explained by their intention to poach. As the narrator remarks: 'we were carrying neither traps nor guns' (p. 42). The men flee their pursuers simply because they fear their skin colour will mark them as outsiders: 'I imagined the shock of the men as they beamed their torchlight on us: two brown faces in the middle of an English wood.' (p. 43). The narrator writes: '[in] these solitary spaces we felt exposed' (p. 39), a contrast to the populous city in which the two men can pass relatively unremarked. In contrast to the figure of the lone romantic poet, the two men are unable to move peacefully and unobtrusively through the countryside. The romantic stance is unavailable to them.

The pursuit of the two Bangladeshi men by white men with weapons raises both the spectre of colonialism and connects to an older war on English soil. The chase, as well as re-enacting empire's violent past in an English pastoral setting, also links the story's Bangladeshi protagonists to the long war between the landed gentry and their gamekeepers and to poaching by the rural poor. Manzu Islam has almost certainly read his E.P. Thompson on the Black Acts of the 18th century.[209] These resonances lend depth to the men's reflection on pheasants' origins and also link them to alternative, radical histories of rural England. When the narrator warns his companion that they require written permission to catch pheasants, Dulu decisively dismisses his request: '[we] need no licence' (p. 41). He authorises his actions by claiming kinship with the pheasant: 'he's our country brother, isn't he?' (p. 44). By correcting misconceptions of pheasants' Englishness, Islam alters the terms of rural entitlement.

Having provided a postcolonial perspective on this emblematic gamebird, the story re-enacts the rural ritual of pheasant-killing. However, Dulu cannot easily participate in the ritual. Having captured the bird, he takes it home but avoids cutting its throat for several hours. The narrator finds him 'sitting hunched over the pheasant which, I was surprised to see, was still alive' (p. 44). Even after he has killed the bird, Dulu feels a bond with it: '[he] was stroking the pheasant's feathers, their mirrors of rainbow, and he had drifted off into another world' (p. 45). As with Pope's poem, the narrator admires the pheasant's beauty – 'mirrors of rainbow' – but the killing scene also expresses an uncustomary intimacy with the murdered bird since Dulu claims a continental kinship with it. The scene also connects to a particular if minor tradition in rural verse, notably in the work of James Thomson and William Cowper; one which expresses a pained, humanitarian response to the perceived cruelty of hunting.[211]

So 'Catching Pheasants' deploys two established literary tropes – admiration for the pheasant and regret at its slaughter – but reshapes the pastoral by presenting the pheasant as a global, not a local bird. This manoeuvre grants the two friends access to rural England. Observing how the brightly-coloured pheasants 'mov[e] in concord' with their English habitat (p. 41), the men recognise that they can similarly, and rightfully, establish themselves in the same landscape. Given the woodland chase and the bird's cut throat, though, the sense of belonging is perhaps precarious.

As the later chapter on the garden also explores, by establishing parallels between migrating plant species, Black writers are able to interrogate, expand and repurpose common symbols of Englishness in the pastoral tradition.

Rivers

As noted above, transrural visions of the landscape are a feature of the postcolonial pastoral. This can be seen in the anthology *Daughters of A Riverine Land* (2003), edited by Debjani Chatterjee. In her introduction, Chatterjee states that there remains a 'powerful emotional link' between rivers in the Indian subcontinent 'and the rivers of our South Yorkshire homes.'[212] This idea is conveyed by several poems in the collection, including Rashida Islam's 'The River's Name is the Padma' in which 'sitting by the River Don' recalls the Padma in Bangladesh. As Chatterjee observes, 'though they are continents apart, the Don mingles with the

Padma in a single imagined space.' In her own poem, 'An Indian Summer', a series of couplets juxtapose images of Himalayan rivers with a Sheffield canal: 'The dragonfly flits in the Yorkshire afternoon / while Mandakini descends in roaring waters'.[213] Mandakini is a name for the River Ganges in heaven. Such juxtapositions exemplify what the rural studies scholar Kye Askins terms 'transrural imaginaries'.[214] Rivers occur frequently in such transrural imaginings.

In her book, *World City*, Doreen Massey identifies various 'lines that run out' from London: 'trade routes, investments, political and cultural influences'. These lines, Massey argues, represent Britain's 'external geography'.[215] Her concept of Britain's 'external geography' resonates with John McLeod's *Postcolonial London*, which argues that: '[f]ollowing the publication of Paul Gilroy's important study, *The Black Atlantic* (1993), it has become increasingly popular to conceive of diasporic cultures in terms of aquatic metaphors,' and he sees Black Londoners using such metaphors to express a sense of place.[216] Rivers, after all, are lines that run through the British Isles to reach the sea. To combine the insights of Massey and McLeod, then, rivers potently express Britain's past and present connections to the rest of the world.

Rivers, of course, are also an important feature of rural writing. It is significant, then, that Mahendra Solanki's poem 'In A Jar' explores one such river's 'external geography'.[217] In it, a man drives to the River Severn to scatter a relative's ashes (a popular Hindu location for this rite), a custom paralleled in the Caribbean where local rivers were named by Indo-Caribbeans as hyphenations of the Ganges.[218] In Solanki's poem, this ritual is presented as a compulsion. Addressing his dead relative, the speaker states that he is 'driven to discard your remains in running water'. He stands on the riverbank, places offerings in the water and empties out the ashes while praising Rama: '*Om Shantih Shantih Shantih!*'. The ashes disappear from view at the poem's end: 'you go with the river / pulled down into the sea'. 'In A Jar' makes a very personal connection between an internal geography and England's 'external geography'. It explores one of migration's most painful consequences – to be, in the words of Qaisra Shahraz, 'continents away from one's parents' in death.[219] In Solanki's poem, too, geographical distance intensifies the experience of bereavement. Nonetheless, the river ministers to his grief, its 'running water' promising a form of reunion. The Severn's current is strong, 'pull[ing]' the ashes 'down into the sea'. This English river enables and sustains diaspora: the Severn embraces familial bonds by connecting continents.

It is not a comfortable embrace. The man in the poem is self-conscious. He is 'aware of people staring' as he stands 'in socks' on the bank. Logistical challenges intensify his embarrassment. He throws in 'balls of flour' but these become 'landlocked by flowers, rice, cotton threads and god knows what'. He pictures himself as an 'other', conducting an inexplicable ceremony. He declares himself '[w]orried that all this will not move', the phrases 'all this' and 'god knows what' communicating his suspicion that the objects look like litter to passers-by. The idea unbalances him and he 'almost topple[s] into the river'. So, while nature facilitates a sense of communion and belonging, it is not easily attained. The poet's connection with nature is marred by a feeling that he is out of place.

'In A Jar' expresses a transcontinental experience of dwelling in the world. The poet is drawn to the Severn because it represents a line that runs from Britain to another homeland. 'In a Jar' is pastoral but not naive. The poem evokes a rural setting in order to explore grief but the encounter with nature is not romanticised. He arrives by car. The urn is plastic. The offerings are in shopping bags. He stands on the bank in socks. Once again, the idea of 'postcolonial pastoral' is inadequate to the task, since Solanki's encounter with the river is consoling, even if it is awkward at moments. Procter's concept of the 'postcolonial everyday' is perhaps more helpful because a regional river – the Severn – acquires a postcolonial dimension in the poem which expands the pastoral to accommodate the experience of migration and diaspora at all stages of human life.

The same idea occurs in Khadijah Ibrahiim's poem 'When My Time Come' from her collection *Another Crossing* (2014). Spoken in the voice of a grandmother giving instructions for her funeral, the old Jamaican woman, long resident in Britain, insists:

> Mi no waant bury a England,
> mi waant mi ashes spread cross de River
> Thames, make de waves teck
> mi back to which part mi did come from.[220]

The parallel with Solanki's poem is striking. This poem shares a similar imaginative geography. The old woman seems confident that the River Thames will comply with her wishes, helping to convey her body on a transatlantic journey from Britain's old imperial capital to her place of ancestral origin.

Other river poems engage with the pastoral tradition more directly. Rommi Smith's poem 'Night River' contains an epigraph from John Keats's Shakespearean sonnet, 'Bright Star, Would I Were Steadfast As Thou Art' (c.1819).[221] The reference to Keats locates 'Night River' in the romantic tradition, and like Keats, Smith uses night to explore the theme of love. 'Night River' also borrows Keats's form: it is a sonnet which is mostly composed, like 'Bright Star', in a single sentence. Smith's subject is nature, her epigraph and setting are Keatsian, her metre characteristically English, her sonnet Shakespearean. The pastoral tradition and an English river are presented as important poetic sources of inspiration in the parallels Smith creates between nature, composition and reading: 'the field [is] a page of green'; 'the sentence of the stream'; 'the dew of words'; 'the deepening sky is our book'; 'our fingers trace each wave of cloud'. By implying that nature can be read, the poet shows that rural England is knowable, and known, to her as a Black British poet. The intertextual reference to Keats tells us that whilst the poem draws on direct, personal experience, Smith's way of writing about it belongs to a poetic tradition. There is no sense of alienation here. She encounters the countryside by venturing into it and lingering there as darkness falls. Kay, Procter and Robinson claim that many Black and Asian poets do not 'compose place and landscape... from the perspective of the native or settled speaker'. Rommi Smith is a Leeds woman, born and bred, who has known no other landscape so intimately, but she is at home in the landscape of the poem. Keats was hardly a rural poet, but like her a townie who goes out to experience the countryside.

Even so, communion with nature is not without its challenges. Addressing Keats, the speaker of Smith's poem fails to 'find your star'. But she does not falter. Enchanted by the night scene, she is sanguine about the fact that she cannot rely on 'map, or moon, to guide' her through 'the wide unknown'. What is striking about this poem is its untroubled tribute to the romantic tradition of writing about the natural world, and Smith explores nature's benevolence more straightforwardly than Walcott or Naipaul. She fully embraces the spirit of Keats's epigraph about 'moving waters at their priestlike task'. 'Bright Star', her intertext, evokes priests, hermits and ablution to suggest that communion with nature is both sacred and healing, and in 'Night River' Smith's closing couplet likens 'one word' – presumably 'love' – to nature's 'healing' elements, in this case 'soft and tender rain', a romantic reverence for nature's ministrations. Again, 'Night River' contradicts Huggan and Tiffin's suggestion that postcolonial pastoral affords no comfort. Neither is it an anti-pastoral poem.

As this section on river poems demonstrates, the possibilities embedded in aspects of the pastoral tradition have not been rejected. Encounters with rivers are consoling. These are poets immersed in the landscape; they do not merely pass through it. Since, as Matless claims, a sense of Englishness is 'essentially rural', their work both highlights and contradicts the racialised politics of belonging.

Morris Dancing

In a *Guardian* review of John Agard's poetry collection *We Brits* (2006), Jeremy Noel-Todd dismisses the book as 'a safe mix of the cosy and the postcolonial'.[222] This is far too hasty a dismissal. Being playful is not the same as being 'safe'. It is doubtful, for example, that Noel-Todd spots the subversive literary parallels between Agard's 'monocled black Brit in jodhpurs going for a ride' and William Cobbett's 1830 classic, *Rural Rides*. The poems in *We Brits* launch a systematic assault

on countryside symbols and pursuits from John Bull to Morris dancing.
His poem 'Moorish' simply reads:

The more the Morris Dancers strut their knees
And flash their swords, the more the Moors are pleased.[224]

Morris dancing is one of the countryside's most controversial rituals.
Not only is it associated with claims of an essential white indigeneity, but
the face-blackening practised by the dancers has become a potent symbol
of rural racism. Over the centuries, Morris dancing has had a mixed
reception. Stephen D. Courssin observes that Morris dancing was sometimes wrongly believed to derive from primitive sacrificial rituals. Late
nineteenth-and early twentieth-century folkloric writing compared Morris dancing to the 'backward' customs of 'presumed savages'[225] or, in the
work of one folklorist, Percy Manning, to 'crude' Indian (native American)
rituals. Another folklorist, George Laurence Gomme, called Morris dancing a 'primitive institution' in his book *The Village Community* (1890).[226]
Over the years, other writers have tried to rescue the dance's reputation.
Hugh Massingham wrote that 'if anybody labours under the delusion that
Morris dancing is a simple rustic affair, leave the poor thing in his
ignorance! The elaborate foot-work, the swaying of the body, the movement of the arms…the interweaving figures make up an intricate whole.'[227]

Morris dancing is an iconic component of the pastoral tradition. As seen
in Herrick's 17th-century poem 'The Country Life', the dance evokes
village custom and routine. Morris dancing was first mentioned by a writer
in 1438, though the dance itself is far older than that.[228] It is frequently
mentioned in 16th and 17th-century writings which depict it as an innocent rural pastime.[229] From the late 18th-century, literary references to
Morris dancing became tinged with nostalgia. Jane Garry observes that
'antiquaries reported occasional sightings of Morris dancers, and their tone
almost always suggests that they regarded them as an endangered species on
the verge of extinction.'[230] In 1807, Douce's 'Dissertation on the Ancient
English Morris Dance' closed with the words: 'in the course of a short time,
[there will remain] but few vestiges of our popular customs.'[231] Such
sentiments exhibit the same nostalgia for a lost rural past which Williams
identifies as an English trait in *The Country and the City*.

As Agard's poem implies, though Morris dancing is habitually associated with Englishness, its origins have long been pondered. Chambers
Cyclopaedia of 1727 appeals to the etymology of the word 'Morris' to suggest
that Morris dancing has North African roots: 'Moresque dances, vulgarly
called morrice-dances, are those altogether in imitation of the Moors.'[232]
Garry observes that face-blackening is frequently offered as evidence to
support this view. To complicate matters, she notes, the custom got
muddled with Tudor face-blackening, a courtly practice reflecting a fasci-

nation with all things African. Whatever the truth of it, the longstanding literary preoccupation with the connection cannot be denied. A much-quoted example is *Muleaffes The Turk*, in which Morris dancers are depicted as 'coal black Moors dancing their high lavoltas'.[233]

Contemporary academics do not agree on Morris dancing's African link and the connection has never been proven. Agard's perspective on Morris is very likely informed by Peter Fryer's mention of the link in *Staying Power*, which is mentioned in the acknowledgements page of *We Brits*, listing it among 'a number of eye-opening books'. Agard's poem 'Moorish' pays tribute to the dance's unconscious African originators, who are 'pleased' to accept the tribute.

Referencing Agard's previous work, Noel-Todd's *Guardian* review of *We Brits* demands to know 'what happened to the grammatical mash-up?' in this new collection, yet the wordplay in 'Moorish' – 'Moors'; 'more'; 'Moorish' – gives ordinary words colonial resonances and stirs ghosts of Anglo-African encounters. The wordplay is historically apt. As this book's later chapter on moorlands observes, similar linguistic resemblances can be found between *moors* (moorland) and *Moors* (black people). Early descriptions of moorlands were often racialised, as 'black Moorish land'. Making a combined appeal to history and etymology, then, Agard's 'Moorish' finds strains of colonialism in the Morris dance. These strains are present in the practice, literary representation and in contemporary perceptions of the dance.

Morris dancing is radically reimagined by Wilfred Emmanuel-Jones, a farmer of African Caribbean heritage who produces gluten-free sausages for British supermarkets. Emmanuel-Jones dubs himself the 'Black Farmer'. He advocates for a sense of Black rural belonging and he runs, as part of this effort, a work-experience scheme on his farm for urban Black teenagers. In 2016, Emmanuel-Jones released an advert for his sausages. The advert features a specially commissioned poem spoken as a voice-over, which is narrated by Emmanuel-Jones himself. The advert is the industry-standard two minutes long and its most dramatic section features a dancing troupe called the Dartmoor Border Morris.[234] In it, Emmanuel-Jones provides his own postcolonial version of the pastoral. The poem, which is performed in a declarative style, is accompanied by images that consciously play with agriculture, waving wheat and village custom. The advert asserts a Black British right to belong to the countryside, placing this right in the context of rural racism. In the opening scene, Emmanuel-Jones carries a British flag through the fields in the manner of a military standard-bearer. His gesture heralds the occupation of new ground. A declarative tone reinforces his call to arms. He repeatedly proclaims 'I am!' Walking through fields with the Union Jack, he declares 'I am black, red, white and blue. I am an English-man!' These words – and symbols – evoke Gilroy's *There Ain't No Black in the Union Jack*,[235] emphasizing colonial histories of intercultural contact to combat the countryside's presumed whiteness.

Emmanuel-Jones creates a historical atmosphere by dressing in the manner of a nineteenth-century gentleman farmer, complete with wide-brimmed hat and long tailcoat. Perhaps a latterday William Cobbett, posing as the master of all he surveys, he regards his fields from a hilltop. He leads the Dartmoor Border Morris dancing troupe across the fields as the voice-over declares: 'I am freedom!' The troupe do not have blackened faces. Instead, the Black Farmer leads the charge. The effect is to subvert the troubling overtones of face-blackening. The sense of freedom that this affords is encapsulated in his product slogan: 'flavours without frontiers.' There is no terrain, the advert implies, on which a Black man may not tread.

Like Rommi Smith, Emmanuel-Jones consciously presents himself as being at home in the countryside. He poses under a tree, stating 'I am the trees, I am the roots!' Using an organic image, he stresses his closeness to nature. Roots are alive, but they stay put. The image emphasises settlement over movement. Like Naipaul, Sissay and Smith, Emmanuel-Jones dwells in the English landscape. As with *Black Men Walking*, the play discussed in Chapter Five, this use of the roots metaphor contradicts Salman Rushdie's belief that the metaphor is outmoded and should be replaced by images of movement.[236] The history of rural England was, of course, characterised by patterns of movement: itinerant labour, Irish immigrants, Gypsies, urbanisation and emigration to the empire, and farm workers from Eastern Europe. Rural racism is undoubtedly a factor in challenging a Black British sense of rural belonging, but by retaining the idea of roots, Emmanuel-Jones suggests new geographies and terms for a rural presence. Given the advert's historical atmosphere and its reference to reinserting the black into Gilroy's Union Jack, the image also presents Britain as an imperial formation that has been nourished by its former colonies. Emmanuel-Jones takes this one step further by presenting himself as elemental: 'I am the summer breeze, I am the winter chill'. He even invokes the form of a popular creature of pastoral verse: 'I am a blackbird!' – the blackbird being an established feature of British nursery rhymes and the poems of John Clare, Robert Frost and Edward Thomas. The advert repurposes old pastoral symbols – agriculture, morris dancing, blackbirds – to insist on a new sense of Black British rurality.

Conclusion

Black British writers have allied themselves with rural literary tradition more often than they have rejected it. Back in the 1990s, the poet Fred D'Aguiar traced Black engagements with the pastoral tradition back to Phillis Wheatley's late 18th-century *Poems on Various Subjects, Religious and Moral*.[237] Moreover, as D'Aguiar asserted, writing is about place as much as about race:

With the regional loyalties which poets like Jackie Kay or Levi Tafari
carry… the reality is that poets of a particular age, class and locality often
have more in common, in terms of their craft and themes, than poets
of the same race who belong to a different generation and live at opposite
ends of the country.[238]

D'Aguiar terms this spirit of appreciation or collaboration 'compatriotism
in craft.' This compatriotism is most obviously expressed in Nichols's ode
to R.S. Thomas. Yet critics rarely consider Black writers' engagement with
established literary tradition, and this is especially true of the pastoral
tradition. Correspondingly, poems by Black writers are routinely omitted
from poetry anthologies about England's countryside, though there are
exceptions. These exclusions cannot be justified. They are, often unconsciously, informed by the popular view that the countryside has nothing to
do with empire, or indeed with blackness. As my analysis of the pastoral
tradition's relationship to colonialism shows, this is very far from the truth.

Much contemporary British writing about nature is post-pastoral. It
reveres nature but rejects romanticised depictions of the countryside,
especially in the light of environmental destruction. Writing by Black and
Asian Britons does not fit easily into this category, since it does not fully
reject idealising visions of the countryside. On the contrary, rural spaces
inspire almost utopian anti-racist visions of engagement with nature, but
one which is very much aware of rural England's relationship with the
colonial. Initially expressed as a transrural overlaying of local rural scenes
with the landscapes of Africa, the Caribbean or South Asia, work by Black
and Asian British authors that engages with pastoral themes has acquired
new characteristics and sought to renew and expand the pastoral tradition.
Such writing draws from rural Britain's postcolonial dimensions to find a
place for Black and Asian Britons within that space. There is no expression
of bleak disengagement. Black and Asian British authors' rural writing
demonstrates clear emotional and literary investment. So it is necessary to
disagree with Huggan and Tiffin that rural writing which deals with
colonial themes seldom derives comfort from nature. Naipaul takes obvious solace in the countryside during his 'Wordsworthian' wanderings, and
Solanki and Emmanuel-Jones show that to connect with nature is to
embrace diaspora. The writers discussed in this chapter deconstruct enduring symbols such as Morris dancing and 'English' fauna. The effect is to
question the countryside's association with the local, the settled and the
insular as well as to question its 'racial and…cultural virtue'.

These forays into the English pastoral disrupt the customary cultural
politics of belonging to the countryside. As Naipaul intimates in *The
Enigma of Arrival*, to commune with nature is 'an awakening to the natural
world' (p. 105). To embrace pastoral writing is to be accommodated by
nature, to claim it, and to be at home in it.

Endnotes

1. John Siddique, email to the author on February 1ˢᵗ, 2013.
2. David Matless, *Landscape and Englishness* (London: Reaktion Books 1998), p. 25.
3. For an overview see Paul Alpers, *What is Pastoral?* (Chicago: Chicago UP, 1996).
4. See Charles Martindale, 'Green Politics: the Eclogues' in *The Cambridge Companion to Virgil*, ed. Charles Martindale (Cambridge: CUP, 1997), pp. 107-124.
5. See Martin Breaugh, *The Plebeian Experience: A Discontinuous History of Political Freedom* (Columbia UP, 2013), pp. 4-10.
6. Martin Empson, *Kill All the Gentlemen: Class Struggle and Change in the English Countryside* (London: Bookmarks, 2018), pp. 11-64.
7. See Eric Weiskott, 'Manley Hopkins' Copy of Piers Plowman: Medievalism and Historicism', *The Hopkins Quarterly*, vol XLV, Nos. 3-4, 2014, pp. 101-114. This was Hopkins's father's annotated copy.
8. For a discussion of Philip Sidney's *Arcadia* see C.S. Lewis, *English Literature in the Sixteenth Century excluding Drama* (Oxford, Clarendon Press, 1954, 1962), pp. 330-347.
9. See Martin Empson, *Kill All the Gentlemen*, pp. 123-167.
10. See Raymond Williams, *The Country and the City*, p. 22.
11. For a discussion of the pastoral in *As You Like It*, see C.L. Barber, *Shakespeare's Festive Comedy* (Princeton: Princeton UP, 1972), pp. 223-229; and see Juliet Dusinberre, Introduction to *As You Like It* (London: The Bloomsbury Arden, 2006), pp. 46-57.
12. For a discussion of the pastoral in the work of Robert Herrick, John Milton and Andrew Marvell, see Frank Kermode, *English Pastoral Poetry from the Beginnings to Marvell* (London: Harrap, 1952), pp. 11-44, and see Alpers, op cit., pp. 52-66, 93-112, 230-245.
13. On the genre of loco-descriptive or topographical verse see Donna Landry, *The Invention of the Countryside: Hunting, Walking and Ecology in English Literature, 1761-1831* (Houndmills: Palgrave, 2001), pp. 128-132.
14. On the 18th century pastoral and its movement towards the georgic see Karen O'Brien, 'Imperial Georgic', in *The Country and the City Revisited: England and the Politics of Culture, 1550-1850*, ed. McLean, Landry and Ward (Cambridge: Cambridge UP, 1999), pp. 160-179.
15. Robert Herrick, *The Poetical Works of Robert Herrick* ed. L.C. Martin (Oxford: Clarendon Press, 1968), p. 229.
16. Herrick, *op cit.*, p. 230, 231.
17. For a discussion of James Thomson and the global see Suvir Kaul, *Poems of Nation, Anthems of Empire: English Verse in the London Eighteenth Century* (New Delhi: Oxford University Press, 2000), pp. 131-182.

18. On the eighteenth century investment in the georgic see John Chalker, *The English Georgic* (London: Routledge, Keegan & Paul, 1969), pp. 1-65.

19. James Thomson, *The Poems of James Thomson* (London: Oxford UP, 1963), p. 139.

20. Thomson, *op cit.*, p. 5.

21. Thomson, *op cit.*, p. 6.

22. Thomson, *op cit.*, p. 155.

23. Thomson, *op cit.*, p. 89.

24. Thomson, *op cit.*, p. 81.

25. Thomson, *op cit.*, p. 178.

26. Thomson, *op cit.*, p. 202.

27. Oliver Goldsmith, *The Miscellaneous Works of Oliver Goldsmith* (London: Macmillan, 1874), p. 586. For a discussion of this poem see John Montague, 'The Sentimental Prophecy: A Study of the Deserted Village', in *The Art of Oliver Goldsmith*, edited Andrew Swarbrick (London: Vision Press, 1984), pp. 90-106.

28. On enclosure see J.M. Neeson, *Commoners: Common Right, Enclosure and Social Change in England 1730-1820* (Cambridge: Cambridge University Press, 1993).

29. *The Miscellaneous Works of Oliver Goldsmith*, p. 586.

30. *Goldsmith*, p. 582.

31. *Goldsmith,* p. 586, 587.

32. *Goldsmith*, p. 589.

33. For 'Stoklewath; or, the Cumbrian Village' see *Poetical Works of Miss. Susanna Blamire: The Muse of Cumberland* (Edinburgh: John Menzies, 1842, facsimile edition), pp. 1-39. On Blamire, see Christopher Maycock, *A Passionate Poet: Susanna Blamire 1747-1794* (Patten Press, 2003).

34. For 'The Splendid Village' see *The Poetical Works of Ebenezer Elliott* (London: Henry King, 1876: facsimile ed. George Olms Verlag, 1975), pp. 314-342.

35. Susanna Blamires, *op cit.*, p. 3

36. Blamires, *op cit.*, p. 10.

37. Blamires, *op cit.*, p. 4.

38. Blamires, *op cit.*, p. 12.

39. Blamires, *op cit.*, p. 20.

40. Ebenezer Elliot, *op cit.*, p. 319.

41. Elliot, *op cit.*, p. 322.

42. Elliot, *op cit.*, p. 330.

43. Elliot, *op cit.*, p. 342.

44. Raymond Williams, *The Country and the City*, p. 32.

45. Stephen Duck, *The Thresher's Labour: Two Eighteenth Century Poems*

([1730] London: The Merlin Press, 1989), p. 4.

46. *The Thresher's Labour*, p. 6.

47. *The Thresher's Labour*, p. 11-12.

48. *The Thresher's Labour*, p. 8.

49. Mary Collier, *The Woman's Labour: Two Eighteenth Century Poems* ([1739] London: The Merlin Press, 1989), p. 17.

50. Mary Collier, p. 23.

51. George Crabbe, *The Poetical Works* (London: Henry Frowde, 1908), above, p. 34; this p. 36. Raymond Williams, *The Country and the City*, pp. 90-95. For further discussion of Crabbe see Oliver Sigworth, *George Crabbe: Nature's Sternest Painter* (Tucson: University of Arizona Press, 1965); and see M.M. Mahood, *The Poet as Botanist* (Cambridge, Cambridge UP, 2008) pp. 82-111.

52. See Franca Dellarosa, *Talking Revolution: Edward Rushton's Rebellious Poetics 1782-1814,* pp. 7-8.

53. *The Complete Poetical Works of Thomas Chatterton*, Vol. 1, (London: Routledge & Sons, 1906) p. 5.

54. *The Collected Writings of Edward Rushton,* ed. Paul Baines (Liverpool: Liverpool UP, 2014) p. 55. On Edward Rushton see Franca Dellarosa, *Talking Revolution: Edward Rushton's Rebellious Poetics 1782-1814* (Liverpool, Liverpool UP, 2014).

55. *A Tour of the English Lakes with Thomas Gray & Joseph Farington RA*, ed. John Murray (London: Francis Lincoln, 2011), p. 35. On the sublime see Edmund Burke, *A Philosophical Enquiry into the Origin of Our Ideas of the Sublime and Beautiful* ([1756], and see 'The Sublime, The Picturesque, The Beautiful', 2017, published by The Blanton, University of Texas at Austen and produced by Westmoreland Museum of American Art, Greensburg, PA. www. blanton museum.org, accessed 4 July 2018.

56. Victoria Perry, 'Slavery and the Sublime: the Atlantic trade, landscape aesthetics and tourism' in Dresser and Hann ed. *Slavery and the British Country House* (Swindon: English Heritage, 2013), p. 108

57. Perry, *op cit.,* p. 109.

58. Perry, *op cit.,* p. 110, 112

59. James Buzard, *The Beaten Track: European Tourism, Literature and the Ways to 'Culture' 1800-1918* (Oxford: OUP, 1993); and see for a view more sympathetic for what Wordsworth achieves in the poem and its local geographic context, Damian Walford Davies, 'Romantic Hydrography: Tide and Transit in 'Tintern Abbey', in *English Romantic Writers and the West Country,* ed. Nicholas Roe (London: Palgrave Macmillan, 2010), pp. 218-236. For the transformations of rural poetry in the Romantic period see Simon J. White, *Romanticism and the Rural Community* (Houndmills: Palgrave Macmillan, 2013).

60. For an account of Wordsworth's visit to the Wye, see Mary Moorman, *William Wordsworth: A Biography: The Early Years 1770-1803* (Oxford: Clarendon Press, 1957, 1965), pp. 401-407.

61. Legacies of British Slave-Ownership database entry on John Pretor Pinney at ucl.ac.uk/lbs/person/view/2146646281, accessed 5th December 2019. On the Pinney family see Richard Pares, *A West India Fortune* (London: Longman Green & Co., 1950).

62. Stuart Andrews, 'Coleridge, Bristol and Revolution', *Friends of Coleridge,* friendsofcoleridge.com/MembersOnly/andrewsBull7.html, accessed 5th December 2019; and Peter J. Kitson, 'Coleridge's Bristol and West Country Radicalism', *English Romantic Writers and the West Country*, pp. 129-151.

63. Williams, *The Country and the City*, p. 125.

64. See Judith Thompson, *John Thelwall in the Wordsworth Circle: The Silenced Partner* (London: Palgrave Macmillan, 2012).

65. The theme of rural retirement probably begins with Horace (the sixth poem of the second book of satires), and continues through Marvell, Pope and many others. See the discussion of the country house poem in the following chapter.

66. Katherine Sutherland, ed., 'Introduction' to *Mansfield Park*, (London: Penguin, 2007)., p. xiii.

67. *Mansfield Park* (London: OUP, 1988), p. 113.

68. William Wordsworth, *The Prelude* (London: Penguin Books, 1995), p. 262. Quoted in Saree Makdisi, *Romantic Imperialism: Universal Empire and the Culture of Modernity* (Cambridge: Cambridge UP, 1998), pp. 23-44.

69. *The Prelude*, p. 290.

70. Makdisi, *Romantic Imperialism*, pp. 46-47.

71. See Stephen Gill, *William Wordsworth: A Life (Oxford: Oxford UP, 1989), pp 284-286; and see Peter Bicknell's* introduction to *The Illustrated Wordsworth's Guide to the Lakes* (Exeter: Webb & Bower, 1984).

72. On Wordsworth's response to the proposal to build a railway to Windermere see Mary Moorman, *William Wordsworth: A Biography: The Later Years 1803-1850* (Oxford, Clarendon Press, 1965), pp. 561-565. For the quoted words see *Prose Works of William Wordsworth* vol. 2, ed. W. Knight (London: Macmillan, 1898), p. 398.

73. For this period of Wordsworth's writing see David Bromwich, *Disowned by Memory: Wordsworth's Poetry of the 1790s* (Chicago: University of Chicago Press, 1998).

74. George Lamming, *The Pleasures of Exile* (London: Michael Joseph, 1960), pp. 45-46.

75. On Stephen Duck see William J. Christmas, *The Lab'ring Muses: Work, Writing and Social Order in English Plebeian Poetry, 1730-1830*

(Newark: University of Delaware Press, 2001), pp. 63-95. And see E.P. Thompson's introduction to Stephen Duck, *The Thresher's Labour: Two Eighteenth Century Poems, pp. i-viii.*

76. John Clare to Taylor, 21 February, 1822, *The Letters of John Clare*, ed. J.W. and Anne Tibble (London: Routledge, Kegan & Paul, 1951), p. 133.

77. These are the Oxford Works of John Clare in nine volumes that would set you back nearly £3000. The best substitute is *John Clare: Major Works* (Oxford, 2008). The series of individual collections published by Carcanet Press and the Mid Northumberland Arts Group is worth seeking out, mostly now only second hand.

78. For some of the most insightful criticism of John Clare's poetry, see Simon Kovesi, *John Clare: Nature, Criticism, History* (London: Palgrave, 2018); Paul Chirico, *John Clare and the Imagination of the Reader* (London: Palgrave Macmillan, 2007); Tim Chilcott, *A Real World and Doubting Mind: A Critical Study of the Poetry of John Clare* (Hull: Hull UP, 1985); ed. John Goodridge, *The Independent Spirit: John Clare and the Self Taught Tradition* (Helpston: the John Clare Society, 1994).

79. Works inspired by John Clare include Hugh Lupton, *The Ballad of John Clare* (2010), Adam Fould's *The Quickening Maze* (2010), Iain Sinclair, *Edge of the Orison: In the Traces of John Clare's 'Journey out of Essex'* (2006), and David Morley's remarkable sequence, *The Gypsy and the Poet* (2013) which has John Clare in dialogue with Wisdom Smith, Prince of the Gypsies.

80. See for instance Paul Chirico, *John Clare and the Imagination of the Reader*. For the now standard biography of Clare see Jonathan Bate, *John Clare: A Biography* (London: Picador, 2003).

81. 'The Lament of Swordy Well', John Clare: The Oxford Authors, ed. Eric Robinson and David Powell (Oxford: Oxford UP, 1984), pp. 147-152.

82. 'The Village Minstrel', *The Village Minstrel* vol 1. (London: Taylor & Hessey, 1821 [Kessinger Reprint]), p. 49.

83. John Clare, *The Parish*, ed. Eric Robinson (Harmondsworth: Viking, 1985), p. 37.

84. For William's discussion of Cobbett's *Rural Rides,* see *The Country and the City*, pp. 108-113, quote, p, 111.

85. Cobbett, quoted by Williams, 1973, *op cit.,* p. 111.

86. Cobbett, quoted by Williams, 1973, *op cit.,* p. 111.

87. William Cobbett, *Rural Rides*, Volume 1 ([1830], London: Dent Everyman Library, n.d.), p. 104.

88. Laurence Brown, 'Atlantic slavery and classical culture at Marble Hill and Northington Grange', in Dresser and Hann, eds., *Slavery*

and the British Country House (2013), p. 99.

89. William Cobbett, *Rural Rides,* Volume 1, p. 304.

90. Sarah Houghton-Walker, *Representations of the Gypsy in the Romantic Period* (Oxford: Oxford UP, 2014)

91. John Clare, *John Clare By Himself* (Manchester: Carcanet Press, 1996, 2002), p. 83

92. John Clare, *The Shepherd's Calendar* ([1827] Manchester: Carcanet Press, 2006); for the prose account see *John Clare By Himself,* pp. 82-87

93. See the case of Steel v. Houghton, en.wikipedia.org.wiki/ SteelvHoughton.

94. 'The Gypsy Camp', *John Clare: The Oxford Authors*, p. 278.

95. John Barrell, *The Idea of Landscape and the Sense of Place 1730-1840: An Approach to the Poetry of John Clare* (Cambridge: CUP, 1972), and see Paul Chirico, *John Clare and the Imagination of the Reader.*

96. See Timothy Morton, *Ecology without Nature* (Cambridge Mass.: Harvard UP, 2009).

97. Patrick Bresnihan, 'John Clare and the Manifold Commons', *Environmental Humanities*, vol 3. 2013, pp. 71-91.

98. William Wordsworth, 'Gipsies', *William Wordsworth: The Oxford Authors*, ed. Stephen Gill (Oxford: Oxford UP, 1984), p. 332. Wordsworth berates the Gypsies for their presumed idleness because he observes them in the same place all day, whilst he marches off on an energetic walk.

99. Jane Austen, *Emma* ([1816], Oxford: Oxford UP, 1933, 1988), p. 333.

100. *Emma*, p. 334.

101. Houghton-Walker, *op. cit.*, p. 185.

102. John Barrell and John Bull, *The Penguin Book of English Pastoral Verse* (London: Penguin, 1975).

103. On William Barnes see Alan Chedzoy, *The People's Poet: William Barnes of Dorset* (Stroud: The History Press, 2010).

104. 'The Scholar Gypsy', *Matthew Arnold's Poetical Works* (London: Macmillan, 1890), pp. 273-280; 'Thyrsis', pp. 281-288.

105. Michael McCarthy, 'What is the best poem about the British countryside?' *The Independent* 30 August, 2010. www.independent. co.uk/environment/what-is-the-best-poem-about-the-British-countryside-2066110.html, accessed 5 June, 2017.

106. It may be in, for instance, Edmund Stedman, *A Victorian Anthology* (Cambridge, Riverside Press, 1895). The quotations following are from *Aurora Leigh*, ([1857] Oxford: Oxford World Classics, 2008), pp. 12-13, 21-24, 35-37.

107. Hall et al. 2014, *op cit.*, p. 192.

108. Hall et al. 2014, *op cit.*, p. 192.

109. Hall et al. 2014, *op cit.*, p. 194.

110. www.ucl.ac.uk/lbs/project/details/, accessed 14 June 2017.

111. Hall et al. 2014, *op cit.*, p. 196. On Victorian literature and race and empire see Patrick Brantlinger, *Rule of Darkness: British Literature and Imperialism* 1830-1914 (Cornell: Cornell UP, 1988).

112. Laura Fish, *Strange Music* (London: Jonathan Cape, 2008).

113. For a discussion of *The Return of the Native* (1878), see Jean Brooks, *Thomas Hardy: the Poetic Structure* (London: Elek, 1971), pp. 177-195.

114. For a discussion of *Tess of the d'Urbervilles* (1891) see Jean Brooks, *op. cit.*, pp. 223-253.

115. For a discussion of *Jude the Obscure* (1896) see Jean Brooks, *op. cit.*, pp. 254-275.

116. On Richard Jeffries and Edward Thomas see W.J. Keith, *The Rural Tradition* (Hassocks: The Harvester Press, 1975), on A.E. Housman see Peter Parker, *Housman Country: Into the Heart of England* (London: Little Brown, 2016).

117. On the Dymock poets see Keith Clark, *The Muse Colony: Rupert Brook, Edward Thomas, Robert Frost and Friends – Dymock 1914* (Bristol: Redcliffe Press, 1992).

118. *The Muse Colony*, p. 8.

119. 'The Pike' appeared first in Edmund Blunden's *The Wagoner and Other Poems* (London: Sidgwick and Jackson, 1920), and 'The Poor Man's Pig' in *The Shepherd and Other Poems of Peace and War* (London: Cobden Sanderson, 1922), p. 43.

120. Vita Sackville West, *The Land* (London: William Heinemann, 1927). For a biography of Sackville West see Victoria Glendenning, *Vita: The Life of V. Sackville-West* (London: Weidenfield & Nicholson, 1998).

121. Terry Gifford, *Green Voices* (Nottingham: CCCP, 2011), pp. 7-21.

122. Glen Cavaliero, *The Rural Tradition in the English Novel, 1900-1939* (London: Macmillan, 1977), p. 33.

123. Cavaliero, *op. cit.,* p. 47.

124. On Williamson's involvement with fascism see Richard Griffiths. *Fellow Travellers of the Right: British Enthusiasts for Nazi Germany 1933-39* (London: Constable, 1980), pp. 134-137.

125. T.S. Eliot, *The Complete Plays and Poems of T.S. Eliot* (London: Faber, 1969), p. 178.

126. Edmund Blunden, *English Villages* (London: Collins, 1941), p. 8.

127. Robert Macfarlane, 'This Spectred Isle: The Eeriness of the English Countryside' *The Guardian,* 10 April 2015, p. 1.

128. *Ibid.*

129. *Ibid.*

130. Ted Hughes, 'The Rain Horse' in *Wodwo* (London: Faber and Faber, 1967), pp. 45-55. The story was probably most widely read in the anthology, *Modern Short Stories*, ed. Jim Hunter (London: Faber, 1964), was much used in schools.

132. 'The Rain Horse', p. 45.

133. 'The Rain Horse', p. 46.

134. 'The Rain Horse', p. 49.

135. 'The Rain Horse', p. 55.

136. Owen Sheers, ed. *A Poet's Guide to Britain* (London: Penguin, 2009); Samuel Carr and Jo Bell, eds., *Ode to the Countryside. Poems to Celebrate the British Landscape* (Heelis: National Trust Books, 2010).

137. Jo Bell, 'Introduction' to *Ode to the Countryside*, p. 8.

138. Terry Gifford, *Green Voices: Understanding Contemporary Nature Poetry*, pp. 7-8.

139. *Earth Shattering: Eco Poems*, ed. Neil Astley (Newcastle: Bloodaxe, 2007).

140. Max Porter, *Lanny* (London; Faber, 2019), p. 84

141. Lorna Goodison, 'At The Keswick Museum' in Kay, Robinson and Procter, *Out of Bounds: British Black and British Asian Poets* (Tarset: Bloodaxe, 2012), pp. 83-84.

142. *Out of Bounds*, p. 13.

143. Grace Nichols, *Passport to Here and There* (Bloodaxe: Tarset, 2020), p. 40.

144. Adjoa Parker, *How to Wear a Skin.* (Indigo Dreams: Beaworthy, 2019), 'Love, Ending', p. 68.

145. Rob Nixon, *London Calling* (Oxford: OUP, 1992), p. 162.

146. Huggan and Tiffin, 2015, *op cit.*, p. 101.

147. *Out of Bounds,* p. 19.

148. See in particular Derek Walcott, *Another Life* (London: Cape, 1973), pp. 41-45.

149. Stephen Siddall, *Landscape and Literature* (Cambridge: Cambridge University Press, 2009), p. 13.

150. Derek Walcott, 'xxxv', *Midsummer* (New York: Farrar Straus Giroux, 1984), np.

151. Kay, Procter and Robinson, eds. *Out of Bounds,* p. 21.

152. See Kye Askins, 'Crossing Divides: Ethnicity and Rurality', *Journal of Rural Studies* 25, 2009, 365-375; quote, p. 371.

153. V.S. Naipaul, *The Enigma of Arrival* (London: Viking, 1987), p. 59.

154. *The Enigma of Arrival*, p. 43.

155. V.S. Naipaul, 'Preface' *The Enigma of Arrival* (London: Penguin) 2002 [1987], p. vi.

156. Nixon, *London Calling*, p. 162.

157. Ian Baucom, 'Narratives of Postimperial Memory', *Modern Fiction Studies* Vol. 42:2 (Summer 1996) pp. 259-283.

158. See Loh, *The Postcolonial Country*, p. 78.

159. Nixon, *op cit.*, p. 162.

160. *The Enigma of Arrival*, p. 41. Further page references to this novel are given in the text.

161. Huggan and Tiffin, *op cit.,*. p. 131.

162. en.wikipedia.org/wiki/Edward_Tennant,_1st_Baron_Glenconner.

163. Telegraph View, 'The National Trust needs to drop its woke nonsense', 25th September 2020, https://www.telegraph.co.uk/opinion/2020/09/25/national-trust-needs-drop-woke-nonsense/, accessed 15 October, 2020.

164. James Buzard uses the term 'anti-tourism' in his book *The Beaten Track. European Tourism, Literature and the Ways to Culture 1800-1918* (Oxford: Oxford University Press) 1996.

165. Kamau Brathwaite, 'The Namsetoura Papers', *Hambone*, vol 17, 2004, pp 125-173.

166. Huggan and Tiffin, *op. cit.*, p. 98.

167. David Dabydeen, *A Harlot's Progress* ([1999] London: Vintage, 2000).

168. *A Harlot's Progress*, pp. 67-68.

169. Valerie Bloom, Introduction, *Tender Fingers in a Clenched Fist* (London: Bogle L'Ouverture, 1988), p. xi.

170. Kay, Procter and Robinson, *Out of Bounds*, p. 18.

171. *Ibid.*

172. Lemn Sissay, *Morning Breaks in the Elevator* (Edinburgh: Payback Press, 1999).

173. Grace Nichols, *Picasso, I Want My Face Back* (Tarset: Bloodaxe, 2009), p. 33.

174. *Ibid.*

175. *Ibid.*

176. Bernardine Evaristo, *The Emperor's Babe* (London: Penguin, 2001), back cover blurb.

177. *The Emperor's Babe*, p. 148.

178. Peter Fryer, *Staying Power: The History of Black People in Britain* (London: Humanities Press, 1984). Evaristo discusses the importance of this book in 'The Book That Made Me Cry? I'm As Tough As Old Boots', *The Guardian*, 9 November, 2018.

179. *The Emperor's Babe*, p. 149.

180. *The Emperor's Babe*, p. 148.

181. Rupert Brooke, 'The Soldier' in *Rupert Brooke: Collected Poems* ([1915] Cambridge: Oleander Press, 2013), p. 139.

182. *The Emperor's Babe*, p. 217

183. *Ibid.*

184. *The Emperor's Babe*, p. 219.

185. *The Emperor's Babe*, p. 196.

186. *The Emperor's Babe*, p. 228.

187. *The Emperor's Babe*, p. 196.

188. Maya Chowdhry, 'Black Badger Carlin Peas', *Fossil* (Leeds: Peepal Tree Press, 2016), p. 14.

189. Adjoa Parker, 'Velvet Dresses', *How to Wear a Skin*, p. 68.

190. BBC News, 9th July 2020, 'Dorset writer trying to raise awareness of racism', https://www.bbc.co.uk/news/av/uk-england-dorset-53184523, accessed September 17th, 2020.

191. https://www.louisaadjoaparker.com/bame-history, accessed 17th September, 2020.

192. Adjoa Parker, 'Velvet Dresses', *How to Wear a Skin*, p. 69.

193. Adjoa Parker, 'Sometimes when I'm making beds', *How to Wear a Skin*, p. 69.

194. *Ibid.*

195. Adjoa Parker, 'Velvet Dresses', *How to Wear a Skin,* p. 69.

196. Adjoa Parker, 'Love, Ending', *How to Wear a Skin.* p. 56.

197. Maya Chowdhry, 'Relativity', *Fossil* (Leeds: Peepal Tree Press, 2016), p. 13.

198. Elleke Boehmer, *Colonial and Postcolonial Literature. Migrant Metaphors* (Oxford: Oxford University Press, 2005).

199. On the introduction of pheasants, see www.wildlifetrusts.org/wildlife-explorer/birds/grouse-partridge-pheasant-and-quail/pheasant.

200. 'The Country Life', *Herrick Poems* (Oxford: Oxford Standard Authors, 1965), p. 231.

201. John Betjeman, 'Trebetherick', *John Betjeman's Collected Poems* (London: John Murray, 1958), pp. 59-60.

202. Rudyard Kipling, [1917], 'The Land' in *A Diversity of Creatures* (London: Hardpress, 2013).

203. Alfred Berggren, *Stephanus Marcus: Third Christian Crusade, Book 1*, (CreateSpace Independent, 2013).

204. John Richardson, 2001, 'Alexander Pope's Windsor Forest: Its Context and Attitude Toward Slavery', *Eighteenth-Century Studies* 35.1 pp.1-17.

205. Alexander Pope, 'Windsor-Forest', *The Poems of Alexander Pope*, ed. John Butt (London: Methuen, 1963), pp. 195-210, quote p. 199.

206. Sylvia Plath, 'Pheasant' in *Crossing the Water: Collected Poems*, (London: Faber and Faber, 1971).

207. Manzu Islam, 'Catching Pheasants' in Rajeev Balasubrayamam, ed. *Tell Tales. Volume Two. The Short Story Anthology* (London: Tell Tales, 2005).

208. Manzu Islam, 'Catching Pheasants', p. 41. Page references to quotations from this story are given in the text.

209. Ingrid Pollard, *Postcards Home* ([1989] London: Autograph, 2004), p. 29.

210. See E.P. Thompson, *Whigs and Hunters: The Origin of the Black Act* (London: Allen Lane, 1975).

211. See Donna Landry, *The Invention of the English Countryside*, pp. 115-125.
212. Debjani Chatterjee, ed., *Daughters of a Riverine Land* (Sheffield: BWSG, 2003), p. 13.
213. *Daughters of a Riverine Land*, p. 49.
214. See Kye Askins, 'Crossing Divides: Ethnicity and Rurality'.
215. Doreen Massey, *World City* (London: Polity, 20070, p. 8.
216. John McLeod, *Postcolonial London. Rewriting the Metropolis* (London: Routledge 2004), p. 163.
217. Mahendra Solanki, 'In A Jar', *The Redbeck Anthology of British South Asian Poetry* (Bristol, Redbeck Press, 2000), p. 155.
218. For instance, Albion-Ganges. See too, www.scattering-ashes.co.uk/places/scattering-cremated-ashes-over-the-water-of-the-ganges/ accessed 11th August 2017.
219. Qaisra Shahraz, 2010, 'The Escape', *South Asian Review*, 31:3, p. 195.
220. Khadijah Ibrahiim 'When My Time Come', *Another Crossing* (Leeds: Peepal Tree Press, 2014), p. 95.
221. Matless 1998, *op cit.*, p. 25.
222. Matless, *ibid*.
223. Jeremy Noel-Todd 'Rioting Rhymes?' *The Guardian*, Saturday 7 January 2007, accessed 14 February 2014.
224. John Agard, *We Brits* (Newcastle: Bloodaxe, 2006), p. 13.
225. Stephen D. Corssin, 'The Founding of English Ritual Dance Studies Before the First World War: Human Sacrifice in India…and in Oxfordshire?' *Folklore* vol. 115 issue 3 December 2004, pp. 321-331, p. 322.
226. Quoted in Courssin, *op cit.*, p. 326.
227. Massington quoted in Matless 1998, *op cit.*, p. 146.
228. See Jane Garry, 'The Literary History of the English Morris Dance' *Folklore* 94: ii, 1983 pp. 219-228, p. 222.
229. Garry 1983, *op cit.,* p. 219.
230. Douce cited by Garry 1983, *op cit.*, p. 225.
231. Chambers quoted in Garry 1983, *op cit.,* p. 223.
232. Garry 1983, *op cit.*, p. 225.
233. William Atkins, *The Moor: Lives, Landscape, Literature* (London: Faber, 2014), p. 229.
234. The advert is directed by Tony Kaye and lasts for 2 minutes, https://www.youtube.com/watch?v=53twFqvOJ5Q, accessed 10th August, 2017.
235. Paul Gilroy, *There Ain't No Black in the Union Jack: The Cultural Politics of Race and Nation* (London: Hutchinson, 1987).
236. Salman Rushdie, 'Step Across This Line', in *Step Across This Line: Collected Non Fiction 1992-2002* (London: Cape, 2002).
237. Fred D'Aguiar, 'Have You Been Here Long? Black Poetry in Britain', in Hampson and Barry, eds., *New British Poetries: The Scope of the Possible*, (Manchester: MUP, 1993), p. 53.
238. D'Aguiar, 'Have You Been Here Long?', p. 70.

CHAPTER FOUR: COUNTRY HOUSES

The British country house, that symbol of refinement, connoisseurship and civility, has long been regarded... as an iconic signifier of national identity. – Madge Dresser and Andrew Hann, *Slavery and the British Country House*.[1]

In *Slavery and the British Country House*, Madge Dresser and Andrew Hann observe that country houses are 'jewel[s]' in the 'nation's heritage crown.'[2] Country house gardens, libraries and galleries epitomise high culture. They represent England's greenest, most pleasant land.

When heritage organisations violate this symbolism they get into hot water. Journalists from the *Daily Mail*, *Times* and *Telegraph* were scathing about three of the National Trust's national cultural programmes: Prejudice and Pride (2017), Women and Power (2018) and People's Landscapes (2019).[3] They accused the organisation of alienating its core members by telling gay, female and working-class stories. Formal visitor experience evaluation did not bear this out. Prejudice and Pride, which explored the Trust's gay and lesbian histories, was positively received by over 71% of its membership, with a very small proportion of hostile responses.[4] On 22nd September 2020, the organisation published its 'Interim Report on the Connection Between Colonialism and Properties Now in the Care of the National Trust'.[5] The report identifies that just under a third of Trust properties are linked to colonial administration, colonial wealth, transatlantic slavery and the East India Company. The report was condemned by the Culture Secretary, Oliver Dowden, angry because Winston Churchill's house Chartwell was included in the report. The report observes that Churchill was Secretary of State for the Colonies and that he voted against the India Bill in 1935. The British politician Ann Widdecombe announced on air that she was giving up her National Trust membership because, she said, the Trust report connected Churchill with slavery, although it did not. A few days after the report's publication, Jacob Rees-Mogg, Leader of the House of Commons, gave a Parliamentary speech stating, 'an organisation like the National Trust... should remember that its properties were given to it by people who expected them to be custodians of our history, to be proud of our history, and to think well of our great nation, not... feel abashed about the greatness that this nation has enjoyed over so many centuries.' The *Telegraph* later reported that Charity Commission 'regulators approached it [the Trust] earlier this month after members of the public complained about its controversial review into links between its properties and the British empire and slavery.'[6] In response to this last turn of events, the Trust's Director-General, Hilary McGrady, tweeted: 'As the *Telegraph* itself reports, we are not facing an enquiry. Our purpose remains as it always was – to care for nature, beauty and history. If researching the history of National Trust places is wrong, then we've been doing something wrong for 125 years.'[7]

Writing some time earlier, Clive Aslet's article in *The Telegraph* highlights what country houses conventionally provide:

> It's not that [the membership…] is reactionary. These days, most British people have a liberal view of many matters. They just don't feel that the Trust is the platform on which to promote edgy contemporary agendas. We'd like the gardens, houses and open spaces of the Trust to provide a refuge from the insistent drumbeat of… political correctness, not an amplification of it through a search for an historical precedent.[8]

Whether he is conscious of it or not, Aslet's ideas derive from the long tradition of the country house poem, advanced by English poets from Ben Jonson through to Alexander Pope in the 18th century and on to Vita Sackville-West and the fiction of Virginia Woolf in the twentieth. Aslet uses a pastoral vocabulary too: as for previous generations, country houses are a 'refuge' from 'contemporary' life.[9] Albeit in wry tones, Aslet allots stately homes the same function that the country house poem had done for over four centuries. He accuses the National Trust of attempting to 'expunge tradition from the national soul'.[10] These words merely confirm Dresser and Hann's contention that country houses are 'iconic signifier[s] of national identity.'[11] Aslet speaks of a false historical 'precedent', yet his idea has a clear historical and literary pedigree. His wish for a 'refuge' reflects precisely the same sentiments of the builders and purchasers of many country houses, the families whose wealth derived from empire's human and material exploitation. These new capitalist and commercial classes were embracing the ideology of the country house as a bastion of unchanging tradition. With their colonial wealth, estate owners bought into the 'duties' and privileges of old propertied families. The rural location of houses and garden estates placed them at a remove from the port cities and commercial centres and further still from the wider unease about aspects of colonial activity that were believed to threaten national virtue.[12] The irony of that contradiction is one of the key themes of this chapter.

Country houses were not always as celebrated as they have been for the past forty or so years. In the years before and just after the Second World War, the frequent abandonment and demolition of historic country houses became a symbol of collective mourning for a glorious national past, lost colonial status, economic decline and the breakdown of class hierarchies.

This moment is embedded in the collective cultural and literary conscious-ness in influential pre- and postwar works such as Virginia Woolf's *Orlando* (1928), Evelyn Waugh's *Brideshead Revisited: The Sacred and Profane Memories of Captain Charles Ryder* (1945) and in contemporary works including Ian McEwan's *Atonement* (2002) and Julian Fellowes's *Past Imperfect* (2009).[13] But the decline of the country house was halted by the 1937 and 1939 National Trust Acts. These Acts allowed the National Trust to acquire stately homes donated by their owners in lieu of death duties. This is the circumstance to which Jacob Rees-Mogg referred in his parliamentary speech on 25th September, 2020.[14] By the 1980s, visiting the country house had become a national pastime; in 2019, Historic Houses (which repre-sents 1,500 independent historic houses and gardens) reported 26 million visits a year. The National Trust has 5.6 million members. Almost a third of foreign tourists visit one or more country houses during their stay in Britain. A 2013 report by VisitBritain – the official British tourist website – attributes this phenomenon to the popularity of British period dramas.[15]

Because stately homes are a significant leisure phenomenon, the herit-age industry has a clear incentive to capitalise on the curiosity about luxury they clearly arouse. However, data shows that the membership of historic housing associations disproportionately represents white, middle-class Britons. Less than one percent of National Trust members are Black.[16] The irony is that country houses attract nostalgia for an era when Britain, unequivocally 'Great',[17] was connected with colonized countries across the globe. The links of country houses to empire are mostly hard to see because the colonial action took place elsewhere, off stage. Imperial naval battles were fought in distant oceans; sugar wealth was created by enslaved people in the West Indian islands; the East India Company fought on Asian soil. People in Britain saw the signs of repatriated wealth as the end products of colonial ventures. Not until anti-slavery campaigns began in the 1770s did the British public see quite how that wealth was created. Later, British people visited grand imperial exhibitions, such as the Great Exhibition of the Works of Industry of All Nations in 1851, but they learned about the bloody quashing of rebellions at second hand, through newspapers, literary works, tracts and speeches. More conscious British critics of imperial violence had to rely on colonial accounts of resistance and rebellion or more rarely from anti-colonial writings from within the empire.[18]

In her book, *Country Houses and the British Empire 1700-1930* (2014), Stephanie Barczewski documented that up to one in every six country houses – some now demolished – were connected to colonial trade.[19] In the period she covers, 349 houses were purchased or built by colonial mer-chants, 229 by East India Company officials or related traders, 211 by West Indian planters, 259 by military officers with colonial careers.[20] The research in this area is at yet incomplete and Barczewski's is necessarily a conservative estimate. The 2020 National Trust report includes properties which are not listed in her book, such as Hardwick Hall, home to successive generations of colonial investors and administrators from William Cavendish, 1st Earl of Devonshire (1551-1626) – who had investments in the Russia Company, East India Company and North-West Passage Company – to Spencer Compton Cavendish, 8th Duke (1833-1908), who was Secretary of State for India.[21]

As Miranda Kaufmann's English Heritage survey in 2007 found, houses often link to slavery in multiple ways, and across successive generations. Some houses were owned by men who insured slave ships or plantations, or who participated in parliamentary debates on issues which affected their own financial interests, such as East India Company trade.[22] Many dwellings were built or remodelled with slave-produced wealth, or with the compensation that was paid to slave-owners to relinquish their ownership of their human property in c. 1840. The connections between the speeches landowning MPs made in parliament against abolition and their ownership of plantations, shares in the Royal African or South Seas Companies, or their involvement in the production of goods to trade for enslaved people, or their holding of colonial office, have all become clearer in recent historical research.[23] Not all connections are straightforward or clear-cut. The Vernon family at Sudbury Hall, for example, is only distantly connected to Admiral Vernon's victory over the Spanish during the so-called War of Jenkin's Ear. Another branch of the family owned plantations, but the profits of Caribbean sugar only came to the Sudbury Hall family through marriage and inheritance.[24]

The 2020 National Trust report found that 93 of the organisation's 300 historic houses had colonial links.[25] Some houses, like Clevedon Court near Bristol, have substantive links to the British Atlantic world. Abraham Elton bought the house in 1709. Elton was Master of the Merchant Venturers, Bristol Mayor and an MP who lobbied in favour of local slavers. He provided salt and brass from the Clevedon estate to exchange for enslaved Africans. The Elton family's slave-ships sailed from Bristol port.[26] One of these was the *Amazonn*, which departed Bristol in 1712, purchasing and embarking 243 Africans off the Gold Coast and delivering 210 surviving people to Port Royal in Jamaica.[27] Here again there is tension between the property's appeal as a visitor destination and the transatlantic slavery involvement of its former owners. Clevedon Court's property overview describes its '18th century terraced garden... a peaceful paradise to pause and recharge.'[28] In Bristol itself, as David Olusoga showed in his programme *The House Through Time*, fine terraces were created on Guinea Street (the name provides the clue), built on the proceeds of slave trading by sea captains a little lower down the scale.[29] Meanwhile this wealth gradually enhanced the region in ways that are consistent with a general pattern observed by Nicholas Draper and Katie

Donington:[30] the Elton family reinvested this wealth in local schools and hospitals during the 19th century.[31]

Croft Castle, meanwhile, holds stories of the early English colonisation of America, Antiguan plantations worked by enslaved Africans (gained through marriage), East India Company involvement, and financial ruination due to investment in the South Sea Bubble. Another example is Wimpole Hall, which was the home of the pro-slavery lawyer, Philip Yorke (1690-1764), the First Earl of Hardwicke and Lord Chancellor, who gave a casual ruling over dinner in 1729 (known as the Yorke-Talbot opinion) that it was legally permissible to recapture people who had escaped their enslavers on British soil.[32] This ruling was not overturned until 1772, by Dido Belle's great uncle Lord Chief Justice Mansfield's famous Somerset Ruling. As Nigel Pocock and Victoria Cook write, as a consequence of Yorke's judgement, the enslavers of people who then escaped in England were free to advertise rewards for their recapture and specialist gangs were hired to find them,[33] so for fifty years Yorke's ruling had an impact on the lives of enslaved people in England. Before the publication of its 2020 report, the National Trust's overview of Hardwicke simply stated: 'the first Earl of Hardwicke and Lord Chancellor bought Wimpole in 1739. He rebuilt the north and south fronts of the house in red brick with Portland stone dressings.' This description was subsequently changed to incorporate the Yorke-Talbot legal opinion. Before this, the property overview concentrated on aesthetic decorative features: '[i]ntimate rooms contrast with beautiful and unexpected Georgian interiors, including Soane's breathtaking Yellow Drawing Room and wonderful plunge bath.'[35] Such choices characterised the historic house sector's prioritisation of style over substance, emphasising buildings' formal qualities and omitting details about colonial connections.

Empire's influence is more easily discernible in domestic interiors and house collections. Even in houses where no direct connection to empire has yet been established, domestic interiors assumed styles that displayed, for instance, utensils and furniture made from woods of colonial provenance because they were fashionable.[36] Then as now, material objects embody stories of suffering as well as ingenuity. The latter point is easily lost to modern day country house visitors because interior décor reflects curatorial choices about which version of history is present, or reflects staff specialisms. To the trained eye, there are objects everywhere which reveal colonial connections. Mahogany is an important example. In her book *Mahogany* (2012) Jennifer Anderson notes that, from its arrival in Britain and the North American colonies, 'mahogany was associated with emulative consumption, aristocratic patronage, and notions of discovery, mystery, exoticism, modernity and delight'.[37] At Harewood House, built by the slaving, banking and plantation-owning Lascelles family, one of the most obvious displays of imperially-derived wealth was in the proliferation of doors and furniture made from expensive imported mahogany. This exotic wood was already on its way to extinction in Jamaica. The State Dining Room contains a table made by Chippendale, surrounded by a dozen carved chairs. As James Walvin points out, this mahogany 'had been felled by gangs of slaves working in the tropical forests of the Caribbean.'[38] This is why Adam Bowett suggests that mahogany furniture is not just a matter for art historians. Its ubiquity in country houses also reflects Britain's 18th century commercial supremacy and the system of enslavement which enabled it.[39] As a tropical crop, it travelled on the same ships as sugar produced by enslaved people. There are many other stories to tell about items on display in country houses – sugar bowls, punch bowls, tiger rugs, ivory billiard balls, Chinese porcelain, African torchiers, paintings of black servants, Bengali cotton, exotic woods, Indian tea chests and Chinese wallpaper (such as that belonging to Sir Walter Scott which was obtained by his East India Company cousin). Some major colonial figures had priceless ivory furniture shipped to their rural retreats, notably Edward Harrison, the former Governor of Madras, and Warren Hastings, Governor General of India.[40]

Sezincote Manor in Gloucestershire, as another instance, is a Mughal palace built in Cotswold stone, designed to display the Cockerell family's East India Company wealth.[41] More generally, however, neo-classical and gothic styles of architecture obscured the newly gained colonial origins of owners' wealth because of the stigma attached to new money and the growing opposition to slavery – so the design of many houses evoked anything *but* empire.[42] When the origins of wealth were signalled it tended to be in subtle ways. Jill Casid even speculates that the artificial lake and little island at Harewood point towards the house's West Indian origins.[43]

Some of the hothouses, pavilions, orangeries and temple-like structures reflected estate owners' experience of colonial travel, while others simply echoed elite tastes for exotic fruit. There was a culinary impact not only in the globalised dishes recorded in country house recipe books but in quirkier cases, too. From his Berkshire home, Sir Francis Sykes received barrels of mango chutney from the Indian merchant who once kept his books, cash and secrets.[44] Basildon Park, built with East India Company profits, has entrance-gates topped with stone pineapples. Christopher Columbus introduced pineapples to Europe and the fruit subsequently became a popular architectural feature during the colonial period. The Pineapple, so named because of its shape, is a stone summerhouse commissioned by the Scottish Earl of Dunmore, who was Governor of Virginia and the Bahamas between 1776 and 1790. Rather than being mere local places, country houses lay at the centre of an imperial map that extended East, to Company trading, and West, to Caribbean plantations worked by enslaved people.

Margot Finn observes that it was imperial wealth – as much as agrarian and industrial profits – that admitted people into the landed gentry.[45] For men who had made their money in the colonies, country houses were an instrumental means of acquiring power and influence, particularly because, before 1832, almost all parliamentary constituencies were based in the countryside and market towns, and ownership of land (as well as wealth) was the main qualification for becoming an MP. MPs with plantations and colonial investments pursued commercial self-interest when they opposed ending the slave trade and slavery itself. Living as absentees, buying into the perceived gentlemanly ethos of the country house, they aimed to make their defence of wealth respectable.

There were other practical advantages. Land was a good and safe investment and its ownership made marriage into the old aristocracy more possible. For those whose wealth had been gained by the outward thrust to empire and its goods, particularly for the self-made adventurers with no distinguished family trees to boast of, the aura as well as the fact of the country house offered a gentrified self-image that in time they could hope others would accept. This was important, because even outside those who were, as a matter of principle, opponents of slavery and East India Company plunder, there was a widespread feeling that the West Indian Creole or the nabob returned from India were not quite true Englishmen. They were quite frequently figures of satirical alarm, not least because of their propensity for sexual liaisons with enslaved women and women of colour. There was always the threat that the colonies would contaminate England and the country would lose its purity of whiteness.[46] The idea of the country estate as a place of virtuous rural retirement meshed well with the desire for a respectable self-image amongst those absentee proprietors of West Indian sugar estates who employed others to manage and punish enslaved people with their ever-present propensity to revolt. The case of the Hibbert family, involved with the slave economy from the late 17th century until abolition, illustrates this point. Their fortune was linked to slavery, yet their integration into rural life helped to obscure its origins

Katie Donington in *The Bonds of Family: Slavery, Commerce and Culture in the British Atlantic World* (2020) demonstrates that the Hibbert family's progress from being merchants to their investment in country estates secured them an enduring place in the aristocracy and began the process of 'decontaminating' the record. As merchants, the Hibberts first traded in materials used for exchange in the West African slave trade. They provided logistical support for finished cotton (grown by enslaved people) and other goods to be transported to Liverpool warehouses.[47] In Jamaica, the family made money between 1764 and 1774 by purchasing and selling enslaved people who came off sixty-one ships, before acquiring land there.[48] In London, the family financed sugar's commission and supply, investing in the West India Docks on the Isle of Dogs. They publicly defended slavery by means of speeches, pamphlets and letters to newspapers. They received £33,408 for the loss of business in these docks following the abolition of slavery in the Caribbean, compensation for which George Hibbert (1757-1837) had actively campaigned.[49] The Hibberts used their accumulated wealth to move into the countryside around Cheshire, Buckinghamshire and Hertfordshire. They owned Birtles Hall, Chalfont House, East Hyde, Hare Hills, Bilton Grange and Braywick Lodge, among others. Once ensconced in the countryside, the family boosted its social, political and civic standing. Family members secured their legacy by funding local churches, schools, hospitals and alms houses.[50] As noted in Chapter Six, George Hibbert attained a considerable reputation as a botanist, a funder of botanic expeditions, a fellow of the Linnaean Society and introducer of hostas to the British garden. Robert Hibbert (1769-1849), merchant, Jamaican planter and owner of an estate in Bedfordshire was a significant beneficiary of compensation for 852 enslaved people (worth £2.5M in current sterling). Although a Unitarian who came under intense criticism from other members of his church, such as the radical Gilbert Wakefield, he continued to defend slavery as an institution. He became chiefly known as the philanthropic founder of the Hibbert Trust, which awarded scholarships and sustained 'liberal' Christian publishing, annual Hibbert lectures and a journal. With no sense of irony, Katie Donington observes, a leaflet about abolition describes John Hibbert (1811-1888) as a 'local philanthropist'.[51]

Similar strategies were used by returning East India Company nabobs, (a term sometimes also applied to West Indian returnees). Lowri Ann Rees observes that philanthropy helped to combat local suspicions about the unsavoury sources of nabobs' wealth. Three famous Welsh East India Company returnees, John Wynn (1760-1840), Thomas Phillips (1760-1851) and William Paxton (c.1744-1824) spent their money on infrastructural projects, such as canals, and also funded schools and colleges.[52]

Concealing the Connections
I have begun to indicate some of the ways in which the published brochures for country houses tend to focus predominantly on landowners' lives and genealogy, and occasionally on the experiences of servants below stairs. This is accompanied by an art-history approach, characterised by the appreciative display of valuable paintings and artefacts. Whenever empire's role *is* acknowledged, it has usually been presented in restrained or understated terms. Until recently, you could tour Snowshill Manor in Gloucestershire without realising that its 'treasures' were purchased with sugar wealth from estates in St. Kitts. The owner's colonial inheritance was explained in a hyperlink on the Snowshill Manor webpage, but the information was previously unavailable inside the house.[53] You could

have walked through Speke Hall without learning that one of its owners was involved with all aspects of transatlantic slavery, although the website was rightly updated after the publication of the 2020 National Trust report. The official guidebook *does* say that the owner found 'a position on a ship to Jamaica' from whence he returned 'fabulously rich'. However, the celebratory tone ('fabulously') is at odds with the human suffering that underpinned his wealth.[54] As the cases of Snowshill and Speke both suggest, houses' colonial pasts were, for a long time, routinely presented as more peripheral than the history warranted.[55]

Previous generations of curators have left us with euphemistic or freighted language. At Charlecote Park, for example, an 19th century Indian sword was accompanied by the words: '*taken* at the *relief* of Lucknow, 1857. Brought to Charlecote by Captain Paulet Lane who fought in the *Indian Mutiny.*'[57] The term 'taken' has no historical justification. Even the recipient of the sword, Mary Elizabeth Lucy, who received several Indian items from her son-in-law Captain Paulet – refers to the artefacts as 'loot.'[58] The original label was also partisan. Though a military term, the 'relief' of Lucknow was only experienced as such by imperial colonisers. Similarly, the term 'Mutiny' reflects the propagandistic attempt to diminish the political and military significance of the Indian Rebellion. Mutinies are revolts from within against legitimate authority. For the Indians who rebelled, it was the British East India Company presence that was illegitimate. The labelling of the sword raises further questions about its provenance. It is difficult to know what its original significance was, who made it and who its Indian owners were. If an object's significance only begins with the moment it was acquired by the British, the original context of its production and meaning is lost to us. A further example is found in Kedleston Hall's 'Eastern Museum', which houses Asian and Middle-Eastern objects collected by Nathaniel Curzon, the Viceroy of India. The museum labels date to the 1900s. An ivory statue of an elephant is captioned: 'native personage on an elephant with attendants, Murshidabad, Bengal.'[59] Inevitably, the description is a historical label which expresses colonial hierarchies of race as well as alluding (now anachronistically) to pre-partition Bengal.

A number of factors – nostalgia, organisational imperatives, insufficient specialist knowledge and under-explored archives – have shaped country house interpretation. Risk aversion has also played its part. This is unsurprising because attempts to tell country houses' repressed histories are frequently misrepresented as glib quests to attach contemporary values to the past, values, according to such critics, that have no historical basis. This is a contention that deserves evidence-based rebuffs.

Associations who manage historic houses face big challenges in telling the truth about colonialism's legacy, since past attempts to do so have met with press hostility and even government intervention. In his *Telegraph* article, Aslet argues that the National Trust should simply 'let its properties be themselves.'[60] He makes a more radical suggestion than he intends. If we truly let 'properties be themselves', the result will shock, rather than soothe, a British public which has had an underdeveloped sense of such houses' colonial pasts. To let country houses 'be themselves' necessarily takes us beyond English shores to explore Britain's four colonial centuries. Here, to gain the fullest understanding, it is necessary to unite what tend to be two separate strands of research into Britain's colonial legacies: transatlantic slavery and the operations of the East India Company.

Important advances in knowledge of these connections have been made, but the research is far from complete. There remain significant archives which require exploring or re-examining. Speke Hall contains a little-read Jamaican Assembly statute book, which records meetings attended by owner and planter Richard Watt during his Caribbean years. Although the Speke Hall statute book has not yet yielded much new information, other such records exist as yet unexamined in Jamaica, suggesting the need to join archives across the Atlantic.[61] Wightwick Manor, near Wolverhampton, houses unexplored trade records of a global paint and varnish business, founded in 1773 and belonging to the Mander brothers. Examining this archive will provide insights into their dealings with China and India. Other documents are withheld because they are regarded as sensitive family papers which might cause reputational damage. On a larger scale, other evidence of British colonial activity has been hidden or destroyed. The historian Shrabani Basu found that the royal family burned letters between Queen Victoria and her respected servant, Abdul Karim.[62] Official secrets are also an issue. In 2002, the investigative journalist Ian Cobain found that official British colonial records at the National Archives con-flicted with Kenyan accounts of historical atrocities committed by British forces during the suppression of the Mau Mau uprising. Professor David Anderson of Oxford University discovered that the British government was withholding some 1,500 Kenyan files, which proved key to the legal case. These files had been loaded on to a flight on the evening before Kenyan independence and were eventually transported to a secure facility at Hanslope Park. Amongst these files was an account by the colonial attorney general that compared the treatment of Mau Mau suspects by the British to the treatment of prisoners in Nazi Germany.[63] Besides these attempts to conceal official secrets, the feelings of propertied families remain an issue. The current direct descendants of the Lascelles family deserve credit for opening up the business archives of their West Indian sugar estates in 2007 (to commemorate the 200th anniversary of the ending of the trade in enslaved people), especially since some reported comments from family members suggest there was once a desire to play this history down. The Earl of Harewood once said, 'the slave trade is a blot on all our histories and raking through the past is not particularly helpful'.[64] James Walvin observes that, upon the death of the household head, Henry Lascelles, in 1753, he left the modern equivalent of £28M to his family. The family once owned almost 3,000 enslaved people and received £26,000 (equivalent to £2.9M today) in compensation for their human property in 1838.[65] As the research shows, slavery compensation was concentrated in the hands of landed families.[66] In research terms, the contours of Britain's colonial countryside are still emerging from the mists of centuries. But the story of the country house and empire is not solely one of their white builders and buyers.

The Country House and the Black Presence
Inevitably, given the connections between the country house and colonial trade there is also growing evidence of a substantial Black presence in the countryside. Enslaved people and Indian servants were shipped to England to work as servants in country houses. In *Staying Power* (1984) Peter Fryer wrote: 'Sometimes, along with a gaudy parrot or two and other exotic gifts, a rich traveller would bring back a captured Black child as a present for his own children, to be their page and plaything.'[67] 18th-century paintings testify to this presence, depicting Black children as the trophies of aristocratic families. In his study, *Hogarth's Blacks: Images of Blacks in 18th Century English Art* (1987), David Dabydeen discusses the work of William Hogarth, the most active painter and engraver of Black people in 18th-century London, observing that – at the time when he was writing this book – no other books existed on the topic of Black people in English art more generally.[68] Miranda Kaufmann cautions that a Black servant's appearance in a portrait is not definitive evidence of a literal presence: it was also a form of self-fashioning to be painted alongside a Black servant whether or not that servant was part of the household.[69] There is the anecdote of the visit of the early 19th century writer James Hogg to the Edinburgh house of his friend James Lockhart, and his surprise to find he was waited on by six Black servants. The friend confessed he only had one and had borrowed the rest from his neighbours.[70] Nevertheless, Gretchen Gerzina,[71] Kathleen Chater,[72] Caroline Bressey,[73] Madge Dresser,[74] Deborah Cohen,[75] Barbara Willis-Brown, Onyenka[76] and Kaufmann herself have collectively amassed evidence of a black rural presence from Tudor times to the mid-nineteenth century. Kevin Le Gendre's *Don't Stop the Carnival: Black Music in Britain* (2018) tells the story of five hundred years of Black musicians including John Blanke, trumpeter to Henry VIII and the violinist and composer Joseph Antonio Emidy (1775-1835).[77] There is also the important research of community groups such as the Midlands cohort led by Barbara Willis-Brown and David Callaghan, who published a booklet about a 1680 painting

of Captain Lucy with a Black page which currently hangs in the entrance hall of Charlecote Park.[78] The group's research in the Warwickshire office of baptism and burial records revealed that several of the county's stately homes had Black servants,[79] while a tombstone at Oxhill cemetery, inscribed with the words 'Black Girl' and 'Negro Slave', is the subject of my poem 'Myrtilla' in the second part of this book.

As discussed in Chapter Six, there are records of Black gardeners connected to country houses, such as Samson, who worked at Llanforda House near Oswestry in the 17th century[80] and the work of a forgotten mixed-race African botanist, the Reverend Thomas Birch Freeman (1809-1890).

Returnee planters and nabobs also sometimes brought or sent back their mixed-race children to Britain from the Caribbean and India, although such children were only rarely acknowledged as legitimate relatives. Daniel Livesay's *Children of Uncertain Fortune* (2018) examines wills, legal papers and inheritance trials to trace hundreds of children with Black Caribbean mothers and white fathers who travelled from Jamaica to Britain to educate themselves, improve their lives and claim their inheritance.[81] This practice was also common in East India Company circles. Mirroring the significant presence of Scots in advancing the fortunes of empire, quite a number of these children had been fathered by Scots. A recently researched example was Margaret Bruce, the illegitimate daughter of a Company captain named Robert Bruce. Margaret was brought to Edinburgh in 1786; there she married Oniciferous Tyndall and bought a country house, Falkland's Kirk, to cement their social standing. The house cost £30,000 to build and was finished in 1844. It shows little evidence of the Indian connection today.[82]

Literature

Beyond the physical presence of surviving country houses and the body of research that is uncovering their imperial and slavery origins, there is also a rich body of literature, from the past up to the present, that offers an invaluable source of interpretative information about how people have thought about the country house. The genre of poetry known as 'the country house poem',[83] is concerned with eulogising the country house; the genre was at its height from the Elizabethan period until the mid-18th century.

No attempt is made here to retell in any detail the history of the changing themes and genres of country house poetry and fiction, except at the points where it enlarges and deepens the focus of this book – where it helps explain the persistence of hierarchical values; where the tensions between surface forms and hidden realities connect to the present; and where literature catches the country house at points of change and makes explicit its links with colonial wealth. And because, in their beginnings, both the country house and the literature about it are so exclusionary in terms of class and so enmeshed in patriarchy, emphasis on the patrilineal line and masculine pursuits, the writing of women such as Ann Winchelsea and, at the opposite end of the social scale, Mary Leapor, is discussed briefly as a prelude to the work of Black British writers confronting the physical presence and historical reality of the country house and its sources of wealth.

The Country House Poem
There are ideas that run through the classical phases of the genre from Ben Jonson's seminal 'To Penshurst' (1616) to Alexander Pope's 'Epistle IV (To Richard Boyle, Earl of Burlington, Of the Use of Riches [1734])' that are highly pertinent to the ideological motivations for investing colonial wealth in landed estates. The country house poem professed the ideals of modest self-sufficiency, stewardship of the land, retirement from city corruptions, the necessity of hierarchy and its pseudo-feudal duties, the legitimating power of the family tree, and the virtues of hospitality and becoming a centre of cultivation and the arts – in Pope's phrase – on the proper use of riches.[84] In Robert Herrick's 'A Panegyric to Sir Lewis Pemberton', Sir Lewis is praised for redeeming the times with 'ancient honesty', because it is that which will survive the ages, not the buildings:

> Goodness and greatness, not the oaken piles;
>   For these, and marbles, have their whiles
> To last, but not their ever: virtue's hand
>   It is, which builds, 'gainst fate to stand.[85]

These are the ethics at the heart of Jane Austen's *Mansfield Park*, discussed below, but as Alistair Fowler demonstrates in *The Country House Poem* (1994), praise for the virtues of honoured patrons frequently needs taking with a pinch of salt. Moreover, many of the tropes of the genre were already ideologically nostalgic and backward-looking by the time this sequence began. Richard Vaughan, the dedicatee of a poem by Rowland Watkyns (1616-1664) is praised for a heart as 'good as balsom, pure as gold'. Watkyns not only dispossessed his tenants through enclosure, but was forced to retire from his royal posts because he is alleged to have cropped ears and cut the tongues of some of his servants.[86] More generally, the notion of communal hospitality had long disappeared with the increasing privatisation of life, and any remnants of feudal duty disappeared with the commoditisation of land and its rising rentable value. Richard Fanshawe's 'An Ode upon the Occasion of His Majesty's Proclamation in the Year 1630: Commanding the Gentry to Reside upon Their Estates in the Country', recognises this reality when he bewails the fact that the gentry have moved to the towns, a 'growing evil', in a poem that lauds the virtues of rural life as both a pleasure and a necessity.[87]

As Raymond Williams notes, one common trope of the 17th century country house poem was that of a cornucopia of food that presents itself at the table without the intervention of any human labour. Ben Jonson's 'To Penshurst' tells how the 'painted partridge lies in every field / And for thy mess is willing to be killed', while 'Fat, agèd carps, […] run into the net'.[88] Thomas Carew's 'To Saxham' features 'The willing ox, of himself came / Home to the slaughter with the lamb'.[89] One can read this device as both a way of creating a fairytale about where wealth actually came from and of making those who actually did the work to keep the country house going disappear from view – a neat analogy for the image and reality of the sugar estate discussed in the previous chapter. Even the pleasures of the hunt – which was what probably most excited the rural gentry (though whether or not hunting semi-tamed deer in the enclosed deerparks was sporting is another matter) – was rarely mentioned, and then, as in Ben Jonson's 'To Sir Robert Wroth', the flying hare is pursued 'More for exercise than fare'.[90] Though hunting became a target of the later 18th century culture wars, it is only towards the end of the country house poem cycle that it gets explicit mention. Thomas Shipman's 'Pindaric…' dedicated to the Earl of Rutland and Belvoir Castle ends: 'There, there, the hunted buck does go / So swift, that swallows fly more slow'.[91]

There is a frequent disjunction between the imagery and themes of the country house poem and the social and commercial reality it supposedly refers to. As in the case of the pastoral verse discussed in the previous chapter, this quite often has to do with the poem's source in classical Greek and Roman literature. As Alastair Fowler argues, both in imitation of phrases and in thematic shape, much of this poetry derives from Virgil's *Georgics*, and from the poems of Horace and Juvenal which praise a retired rural life. Being able to write in Latin, or at the least quote in the original language of the classics, was another way in which the ideologues of slavery and the sugar estate – such as the historians Edward Long and Bryan Edwards and the doctor-poet James Grainger – could offer a veneer of civility over the brutal realities that they were defending.[92]

But from time to time the country house poem reveals something of its historical backdrop: the opening up of commercial empire. This is sometimes made apparent through denial. The previous chapter provided an example of this in Robert Herrick's poem to Endymion Porter where he praises Porter's retired, country life, congratulating him that, 'Thou never ploughst the ocean's foam / To seek, and bring rough pepper home'. Yet Porter was an investor in Sir William Courteen's colonial ventures, including slave trading and trade in India.[93] In Thomas Carew's 'To My Friend G.N. from Wrest' (1639-1640), the house and garden of Wrest Park in

Bedfordshire are praised for their essential Englishness. The poem depicts a garden of 'native aromatics' which shunned 'foreign gums, nor essence fetched from far', with a lake that is contrasted with the seas of imperial exploration, where 'our Fishes, Swans, our Waterman, and Boat [...] Disport and wander freely where they please / Within the circuit of our narrow seas'. It is a house devoid of 'carvèd marble, touch or porphyry' (all imported stones), yet a plain house built for 'real use' and 'for hospitality'. Carew's vision of stability, in Alistair Fowler's words, 'an island paradise in a sea of threatened disorder' was an illusion: both Carew and its dedicatee, Gilbert North, would be dead within months, and the royalist cause they supported defeated.[94] Other imperial connections surface in poems such as Richard Corbett's (1582-1635) 'Iter Boreale' with its mention of the recent return of Walter Raleigh 'with soe much ore'. Using his own image, Raleigh had set off to take the maidenhead of Guiana's virgin territory.[95] Increasingly though, the trope of the pleasures to be had from staying at home, rather than risking all by seeking wealth on the high seas, becomes self-contradictory. After all, the country house was increasingly celebrated as the repository of admired goods brought from overseas. Mildmay Fane (1602-1666) uses both tropes. In one poem he plays on the 'contracted virtue' of the house, 'Wherein all travellers may truly say / They never saw so much in little way: / And thence conclude their folly that did steer / To seek for that abroad, at home was near / In more perfection'.[96] The fact that what may be admired came from imperial trade, and that its perfection lies in the way it has been tastefully curated becomes clearer in another poem when Fane thanks the owner for loaning him his house by itemising the delights to be seen in it. He writes of the objects that 'Hang trophy-like to represent / The figure of each continent' in a way that matches the excitements experienced by a long list of global explorers.[97] Fane's voyage of exploration *within* the house signals a major shift in its function, as a space for display and connoisseurship, a theme expanded below, and sometimes in discomfort and recoil from what it signified.

The theme of the world paying tribute in goods for display is also picked up in a late (1679) anonymous poem dedicated to the Duke of Rutland and Belvoir Castle, a place full of 'all the boundless stores, / Brought thither from far distant shores:', from 'China... Fair Bantam [Java], Goa and Japan; / The treasure western caverns lend, / Dug by the miserable American. / All the black negro dives for in the deep: Gems...'.[98] If the earliest country house poems stress the idea of English self-sufficiency, later poems embrace the wealth of empire.

Ann Finch, Countess of Winchelsea (1661-1720), was a poet from a powerful landed family in the court of Charles II. She and her husband later retired to Eastwell Manor in Kent. Her poetry recognises the arrival of a new merchant class, which has both town and country seats. She evidently felt their commercial values were at odds with the ethos of the old landed order. Her poem, 'Man's Injustice Towards Providence' (c. 1713), is a satire on ostentation, troubling business morals ('Sometimes I interlope, and slight the Laws', the thriving merchant confesses) and the vainglorious impiety of a class that imagines their industry can outwit God's providence. The word 'interlope' indicates the merchant's business – slave-trading in territories (French, Spanish or Dutch) where this activity was forbidden by international treaties. This business is also indicated by the 'Grinning malottos ... in true Ermin state' who are on display in the merchant's wife's parlour. Of the wife, Finch tells us 'A Dutchess wears not so much Gold and Lace'. In her house is 'The best Japan, and clearest China Ware' – all designed to 'Put down the Court and vex the City-Guest'. This picture of wealth generated by enslaving people is among the earliest to be recorded. Finch's poetry has an unmistakable snobbish tone: 'No Luxury's by either unenjoy'd / Or cost withheld, tho' awkardly employ'd'. In these lines, she regretfully acknowledges that the old landed class has had to make space for new imperial wealth.[99] There's a similar note in James Bramston's (1694-1743) satire, *The Man of Taste* (1733), where amongst an exhaustive list of the newfangled tastes in consumption, he asks, 'Say thou that do'st thy father's table praise / Was there *Mahogena* in former days'.[100] As noted above, the import of mahogany went hand in hand with the trades in slaves and sugar, a connection explored in Dorothea Smartt's long poem, 'Samboo's Grave – Bilal's Grave' in *Shipshape* (2007). Smartt's poem meditates on a young African boy buried on the Lune River estuary of Morecambe Bay, identified only by the racist name of Sambo. The boy was probably brought by a ship's captain and, as supposed by Smartt, intended as a gift for his wife. Smartt reflects on what else travelled on that ship (as well as the sugar for the Lancaster grocers) that, like the grave, survives into the present. This is the now much-prized furniture of a firm called Gillows of Lancaster and London. Robert Gillow (1704-1772) owned a part share in a slaving ship, *Briget*, which he used to bring back mahogany from Jamaica (and later re-export it as furniture). Smartt's poem parallels the fate of the wood and of the enslaved African boy:

Sunderland points to West Indies plantations.
A Samboo, like Gillows' crafted mahogany,
is farmed and forested, torn from root
systems to harden or die,
to be shaped into something new
and of use to Lancaster Town.[101]

The link between enslaved humans and colonial goods has remained a poetic theme across the centuries, even though the two poets' views here are so completely at variance.

Mary Leapor's poem 'Crumble Hall' focuses on the idea of the display of domestic interiors, but in a comically deflating way. Leapor (1722-1746), a child of labouring parents who worked as a kitchen maid, wrote one of the last country house poems, and the first seen from a position below stairs. It is very far from being a mere curiosity of plebeian poetry, but a witty poem that looks in several directions and calls up traditional images of such houses with the purpose of thoroughly undermining them. Leapor recognises that the country house has become an object of fascination for 18th-century connoisseurs who wish to admire the collection of art and cultural artefacts, curated by the often-absent owner. As Adrian Tinniswood and Jocelyn Anderson document, country house tourism and guidebooks for visitors were well established by the middle of the century.[102] Mary Leapor's poetic alter-ego, the servant 'Mira', plays the role of guide to a visiting tourist. The poem is framed by her invitations and questions – 'Then step within', 'Shall we proceed?', 'Will you go further?' The problem is, as Mira reveals, there is nothing to see. The hall is introduced as a gothic pile with a fantasy past of knights and squires, 'the sable Frier, and the russet Clown', whose 'hospitable Door' once fed the 'good old fare' of 'powder'd beef [salted beef], and Warden-Pies' – foods of store and domestic economy rather than plenty. That was then. Now Crumble Hall is a grimy, neglected place, where 'the pleas'd Spider plants her peaceful Loom / Here weaves secure, nor dreads the hated Broom',[103] and 'Safely the Mice through yon dark Passage run' – because, as we discover, the household servants do what any unsupervised servants would do: nothing – except pursue their own interests. As a tourist guide, Mira is deflatingly honest: 'See! yon brown Parlour on the Left appears, / For nothing famous, but its leathern Chairs'. Elsewhere, the Hall is a glory hole of the discarded; these are, significantly, the abandoned remains of an agricultural past:

> These Rooms are furnish'd amiably, and full:
> Old shoes, and Sheep-ticks bred in Stack of Wool;
> Grey Dobbin's Gears, and Drenching-Horns enow;
> Wheel-spokes – the Irons of a tatter'd Plough.[104]

Indeed, the only thing of interest that Mira can show her visitor is 'the Menial Train', the servants going about their mostly idle business. 'Unwieldy Roger' lies snoring on the kitchen table, and Colinettus 'of his oxen dreams', thinks about his 'new-mown Hay [...] 'But Dinner calls with more prevailing Charms'.[105] 'Crumble Hall' looks forward to both the gothic and the territory of Jane Austen in the discourse of the 'improvement of the estate'. The gothic arises from the gloom of the house where 'Along each wall the Stranger blindly feels; / And (trembling) dreads a Spectre at his Heels'.[106] The actual hall on which 'Crumble Hall' was based was the old house on Edgcote estate in Northamptonshire. Mary Leapor was dismissed by its owner, Sir Richard Chauncy, a London merchant and East India Company Chairman. The building was demolished in 1747, the year after Leapor's early death, to make way for the new Edgcote House (built 1747-1752, and still standing). Like Jane Austen, Leapor was suspicious of estate improvement. She alerts the visitor: 'But, hark! what scream the wond'ring Ear invades! / The Dryads howling for their threatn'd Shades'.[107] Whether or not Leapor knew of the actual plans Sir Richard had for the estate, she evidently knew what the new merchant occupiers of the country house tended to do, and asks, rhetorically, of the threatened 'rev'rent Oaks' that have 'known a hundred Springs, / Shall these ignobly from their Roots be torn [...] To clear the Way for Slopes, and modern Whims; / Where banish'd Nature leaves a barren Gloom / And aukward Art supplies the vacant Room?' She ends the poem by commanding: 'Then cease, *Diracto*, stay thy desp'rate Hand; / And let the Grove, if not the Parlour, stand.'[108] She was evidently ignored, since the neighbouring village was later moved to improve the owner's view as part of the estate's enclosure of common land.

If Leapor's poem marks the death of the old ethos and the recognition that the new country house was a commercial reinvention, there were other political and intellectual developments that made the country house poem as a celebration of 'old' England increasingly impossible. There was the growing split, as will be noted in the discussion of Jane Austen's fiction below, between the country house rooted in its agricultural and quasi-community localism, its connections to village and church, and the country house occupied primarily for leisure, either for the display of the picturesque, or for the sport of hunting. For both the latter, agriculture was the increasingly distanced business of tenant farmers. Enclosures had made more extensive cultivation possible and the resulting rent increases provided an income stream that, for some, was as important as imperial trade. One growing complication for the image of the country house was that the emphasis on hunting was being overtaken by an increasing sensitivity to animal suffering. As noted in the previous chapter, James Thomson celebrated the rural world in *The Seasons* (1726-1730), but his lines on hunting show him to have been greatly out of sympathy with many of the class who were his patrons. For Thomson, hunting was a 'falsely cheerful barbarous game of death [...] the thoughtless insolence of power'. His lines 'Poor is the triumph o'er the timid hare'[109] and his description of the stag-hunt with the 'growling pack' that 'Blood-happy, hang at his fair jutting chest, / And mark his beauteous chequered sides with gore'[110] were, as Donna Landry shows in *The Invention of the Countryside* (2001), widely quoted later in the century as the cult of sensibility opened the way towards romanticism. The poetry of William Cowper was signally important here (along with his still-powerful poems on slavery) in educating generations on right feeling. In *The Task* (1785), Cowper described hunting as:

...detested sport;
That owes its pleasure to another's pain,

That feeds upon the sobs and dying shrieks
Of harmless nature, dumb, but yet endued
With eloquence that agonies inspire... [111]

The growing belief that the way to enjoy the countryside was on foot,
observing plants and leaving animals to their own diversions represented a
major shift in thought about the natural world, as Landry reminds us, and one
of its consequences was a corresponding shift in perceptions of the country
house and what it stood for.[112] It is no coincidence that a good many of the
people involved in the campaigns against slavery, particularly women, were
also concerned with animal rights.[113] Tender feelings for both suffering
humanity and for the animal world were matched by feeling's rougher
cousin, the gothic, as noted below, in the assault from within of the country
house by the gothic novel. And whilst by the romantic era there were still
country houses, rich patrons and poor poets, the poems that arise from such
relationships tend to stress a more egalitarian sense of community, as in
William Wordsworth's poems to his friend and patron, Sir George Beaumont,
and his country manor, Coleorton Hall in Leicestershire.[114]

Fiction and the Country House
By the middle of the 18th century, concern with the country house
had shifted from poetry into the novel. This began with Paradise Hall
in Henry Fielding's *Tom Jones* (1749), continued in the territory of the
gothic, and then into the social moralities of Jane Austen. Indeed, as
Austen's satire on the gothic novel in *Northanger Abbey* (1803/1817)
reminds us, Austen knew she was writing in a period when the idea of
the country house was being turned upside down. Horace Walpole's
The Castle of Otranto (1764) had given birth to a whole genre of fiction
in which the country house, far from being a protector of hierarchy
and lineage, and a bastion against social change, had itself become the
enemy. *The Castle of Otranto* begins with the fatal crushing of the heir
by a giant falling helmet.[115] In the novels of Ann Radcliffe, Clara Reeve,
Matthew Gregory Lewis and others, the house itself is a symbol of
disease from within.

In this genre, the desirably rural grand house becomes threateningly
remote. A classic example is the imprisoning castle in Ann Radcliffe's *The
Mysteries of Udolpho*, a text which is playfully parodied in *Northanger Abbey*.
The danger that once came from without and is resisted by the virtue of the
house, becomes the danger from within. The open communal hall becomes the closed and the secret. Cellars, locked rooms and attics feature
regularly. Examples include the room in which Caleb Williams uncovers
Falkland's secret, or the attic where Jane Eyre encounters the Creole wife
locked up in Thornfield Hall. Picturesque tranquillity crumbles and
dilapidates (a metaphor in V.S. Naipaul's postcolonial *The Enigma of*

Arrival). Legitimate long family lines are disturbed by illegitimate and contested heirs.[116] The need to control women's sexuality as a destabilising force becomes a prevalent theme. Female desire is often the subject of literary expressions of anxiety about foreign intrusion into country estates. *The Mysteries of Udolpho* introduces a group of novels that present women's desire for 'experience' with foreign men as a disruptive force, with terrifying consequences for heiresses' fathers.[117] Rich Jews are included in the idea of what is foreign, such as Trollope's character of Augustus Melmotte in *The Way We Live Now* (1875), a novel which expresses unease about the influence of new money. Melmotte is a wealthy Jewish speculator who tries and fails to purchase a country estate.

The attraction of the radical philosopher William Godwin to the gothic suggests his recognition that it was a genre well suited to portraying a society in turmoil. In *Things as They Are; or the Adventures of Caleb Williams* (1794), he dramatised a challenge to the old landed hierarchy and its fierce defence of its position. The loss of the American colonies, the Gordon Riots, the French Revolution and the repression of British radicals by the Pitt administration provided evidence of this turbulence to both conservatives and radicals. The latter were made all too aware of the power that the ruling class still exercised in the treason trials of the 1790s.[118] The conservative polemicist against the influence of the French revolution on British radicals, Edmund Burke (1729-1797), was also the theorist of the 'sublime', the aesthetics of pleasurable terror.[119] The connection between empire and the gothic is similarly clear. It is there in the romantic fascination with obeah in the West Indies,[120] and in the figure of Matthew Gregory Lewis (1775-1818), author of the popular and influential novel, *The Monk* (1796/98), who was later to become the owner of two sugar estates in Jamaica and over 500 enslaved people. *The Monk* injected loathsome horrors into the more suggestive horrors of earlier writers such as Mrs Radcliffe. Though Lewis was heir to Jamaican property at the time he wrote *The Monk*, very little in that novel *directly* suggests the West Indian connection. However, his gothic play, *Castle Spectre* (1798), contains a powerful African character, Hassan, bent on revenge for his own enslavement. Lewis had supported the abolition of the slave trade, and consulted William Wilberforce about how he might emancipate his slaves. However, he concluded that he would try to improve their condition rather than free them. When Lewis came into his inheritance and visited Jamaica in 1815-16 and 1817-18, his account of his visits, *Journal of a West Indian Proprietor* (not published until 1834, sixteen years after his death on the second of the return voyages), makes very clear the connections between the gothic and slavery.[121] Lewis's account of his Jamaican visits provides an important record of an Englishman's interaction with African Caribbean lives. The record is by turns sympathetic, racist, observant, humane and self-deceiving. Ultimately it expresses the idea that slavery could work without the whip. As D.L. Macdonald observes, it is the psychologically revealing poem, 'The Isle of Devils' that Lewis wrote on his first voyage out to Jamaica (which he included in his journal), which shows that the 'Gothic imagination itself, with its recurrent fantasies of domination and revolt, was shaped by the debate over slavery and abolition'.[122] The poem depicts the rape of Irza, a shipwrecked white woman, by an enslaved monster-demon. The poem contains references to Shakespeare's play *The Tempest*, with its allusion to Caliban. The monster is black, has rolling eyes and fathers two children with Irza. The first is a monster child (with 'shaggy limbs and eyes of sable fire'); the second one is 'beautiful' (his skin is smooth and white). The demon slays both children and then commits suicide when Irza is finally rescued. It is impossible not to see 'The Isle of Devils' as an allegory of West Indian slavery, and the terror of interracial sex and rebellion that expressed Lewis's guilty conscience.[123]

Charlotte Smith's novel, *The Story of Henrietta* (volume two of a five volume series, *The Letters of a Solitary Wanderer* (1800), also connects the gothic to the Caribbean. It was the first, but not the last, novel to export the setting of the gothic house to Jamaica. Smith's heroine escapes from her tyrannical father's plantation house there because he wants her to marry a man she hates. In her escape she encounters even greater terrors, a slave rebellion and the workings of obeah.[124]

Jane Austen and the Country House

The background of the gothic novel and what it signifies provide one of the ways in which we can read Jane Austen, the most significant writer on the topic of country houses and empire, not least because her work is still widely read and generates sharply divided views. Here, Alistair Duckworth's influential *The Improvement of the Estate* (1971) provides a useful reading of Austen's novels. He argues for the thematic and ideological centrality of the country house and estate in all of her work until her late novel, *Persuasion* (1818). He also sees that break in *Persuasion* as signalling Austen's awareness that the country house could no longer work as a symbol for the stable, traditional, hierarchical values that her novels implicitly support. Duckworth argues that Austen's novels follow a narrative pattern in which her heroines are threatened with the loss of the security that the possession of a country estate offers, but who (with the exception of Anne Elliot) are restored to that security through marriage. Sir Walter Elliot's renting out of Kellynch Hall in *Persuasion* makes it evident that the country house has become a commodity to be bought, sold and tenanted. As such it can no longer be a refuge for the Austen heroine, as in the earlier novels.[125]

Austen's novel *Mansfield Park* (1814), which features a house financed by

Antiguan sugar wealth, is the target of Edward Said's seminal essay, 'Jane Austen and Empire' (1993),[126] a piercing critique of cultural imperialism. In the essay, Said wrote, 'it is genuinely troubling to see how little Britain's great humanistic ideas... stand in the way of the accelerating imperial process.' He argues that *Mansfield Park* promotes 'a domestic imperialist culture without which Britain's subsequent acquisition of territory would not have been possible.'[127] Said believed that Austen's novel was agnostic about the extent to which slave-produced wealth funded luxurious lifestyles. Much of his argument still holds water, particularly on the parallel he draws between Sir Thomas Bertram's role in keeping order in the colonies and at home.[128] This chapter does not rehearse in any detail the decades-long discussions around 'Jane Austen and Empire', including Gabrielle White's *Jane Austen in the Context of Abolition* (2006), which presents plausible evidence that Austen was much more concerned about the issue than Said allows.[129] Later criticism has shown flaws in Said's argument that *Mansfield Park* shows authorial indifference to slavery. His essay nonetheless remains a touchstone for discussions of the entanglement of country houses with slavery because it was the first sustained and detailed examination of the link. Until it appeared, virtually no critical work on *Mansfield Park* had dealt with the issue, including Alistair Duckworth's otherwise insightful study. Duckworth merely mentions that Sir Thomas returns from the West Indies.

Continued argument over what Austen stands for is evident in the high-profile feminist campaign to put Austen's image on the Bank of England's ten pound note.[130] Julian North argues that the image of Austen used on the resultant banknote emphasises her perceived conservatism. The image displays a 'prettified' portrait of Austen against the background of Godmersham Park in Kent, an estate which was inherited by Austen's brother, Edward Austen Knight. The choice of Godmersham Park, North argues, endorses the 'romantic glow and "heritage" appeal' of Austen's novels, promoting a reading of *Mansfield Park* as:

> a celebration of the ideal of the English country estate as a microcosm of the well-governed society. In practice, the ideal breaks down in this novel... because, as postcolonial readings have pointed out, the wealth of Mansfield Park is founded on the slave trade – as was the case with many English country estates.[131]

The image of a country estate on a British banknote carries further historical ironies. The slave-trade depended on bank credit, and bankers' resultant wealth was increased both by interest and by acquiring properties whose mortgagers had fallen into debt. This money was often used to purchase, build or redesign further estates.[132] The Bank of England's own slavery links are clear. Two of its former Governors, Sir Richard Neave and Beeston Long, chaired the Society of West India Merchants. Another Governor, the pro-slavery campaigner, Alexander Baring MP (1774-1848), purchased and rebuilt the Northington Grange estate in Hampshire with wealth inherited through marriage to Anne Bingham, daughter of the American senator William Bingham. This money came from Caribbean molasses and American tobacco, produced by enslaved people.[133] The Austen banknote provides a potent example of historical amnesia.

Though Alistair Duckworth's book remains startlingly silent over Sir Thomas's occupation, it usefully presents *Mansfield Park* as both wedded to the values of conservatism (through the metaphor of the country house and estate), and critical of slavery as an institution. The attention paid to Austen's own reading in Duckworth's book and in William Deresiewicz's *Jane Austen and the Romantic Poets* (2005) rightly presents Austen as being immersed in the 18th century social conservatism of thinkers such as Edmund Burke. However, Deresiewicz shows she was also influenced by Wordsworth, Coleridge, Scott and Byron in the 19th century.[134] *Mansfield Park* was the work of an author who venerated the abolitionist poet William Cowper and she both read and admired the abolitionist campaigner Thomas Clarkson. At the same time, she was deeply opposed to the novel as a work of propaganda. She disliked the sermonising fiction of the evangelical, anti-slavery writer, Hannah More.[135] Between those two poles it is possible to see that whilst there is, as Said wrote, 'a dead silence' when Fanny asks Sir Thomas about the slave trade, the condemnation of the trade and its representatives is made by implication. Austen invites the reader to juxtapose one discourse with another (though this is not a suggestion that Duckworth makes).[135] Duckworth reads the novel in terms of the motif of the 'improvement of the estate', and the arguments expressed by characters over legitimate improvements (because they refresh and renew) and damaging improvements (because they break the connections with tradition). This distinction expresses the difference between the kind of values associated with the country house poem, and the subjective selfishness of the 'improver' who wants to impose his or her individual taste over historically accumulated materials. In the novel, it is the modernising Crawfords who stand for 'improvement' of the damaging kind. Their tastes are associated with 'extravagance, selfishness, and disregard of use', and with the hubris of reshaping the landscape in an anti-natural way, in a denial of continuity. Mary Crawford, for instance, makes the self- and ideologically revealing declaration that she wishes for the services of a Humphrey Repton who would give her 'as much beauty as he could *for my money*' [my italics], conflating money and beauty as commodities (pp. 56-57).[136] Miss Bertram considers Repton's daily fees affordable, though Mary Crawford thinks he is expensive, charging five guineas a day, almost 250 times what an agricultural labourer would have earned at the time. Duckworth makes the point that Repton's aesthetics can be associated with commerce. His ideologies shape the views of those characters whom Austen clearly most wants us to see as endangering social stability. When her characters visit different sites, Sotherton, for instance, an Elizabethan manor house, the place stands out for the Crawfords as a prime example of what needs improving. The house is not sufficiently prominent in its elevation. It is 'a good spot' for practising fault-finding. When the party visit the Rushworth estate, the owner is complimented for the 'improvements' he has made: he has moved the house away from the church and bypassed the village. The one objection the Crawfords make is not that the village houses have been neglected, but that their dilapidation spoils the drive towards the house. Similarly, Henry Crawford wants to see Edmund's vicarage 'raised into a place' and separated from the farm, which must be cleared away. All these proposals threaten the ideology of organic wholeness and the stability of tradition.[137]

What then of Sir Thomas and his two estates? Men like Sir Thomas were precisely amongst those who had the kind of money to improve their estates in the most conspicuous ways that the Crawfords advocate – enclosing the grounds, adding new wings, or building in the ahistorical gothic styles that were then fashionable. As the keen reader of Cowper and Clarkson, Austen could not have seen the running of plantation slavery as belonging to 'pre-existing structures of morality and religion',[138] to use Duckworth's words. More likely, Austen may want us to see Crawford and Sir Thomas as opposite sides of the same coin. Both are absentee landowners; Crawford hardly ever visits his estate because 'to anything like a permanence of abode [...] Henry Crawford had, unluckily, a great dislike'.[139] Something similar is true of Sir Thomas's Antiguan estates. Both are part of the modern, market-based, cash economy. Duckworth accepts, for instance, that Sir Thomas's views on marriage 'have a mercenary tinge'.[140] If Sir Thomas's education of his own children, in Austen's authorial words, shows 'grievous mismanagement',[141] what are we supposed to think about his responsibility for the enslaved people he owns? It is not incompatible, then, to see Austen not only as an author whose 'deepest impulse was not to subvert but to sustain a social heritage',[142] but also as an author who thought that Sir Thomas's slave-owning threatened that heritage. We do not need to consider Austen as secretly subversive to also think that she regarded slavery as morally wrong. She hints at such, in oblique, unsermonistic ways in the silence that follows Fanny Price's question about slavery, addressed to Sir Thomas. Austen was right in her aesthetic judgements. Her books are still widely read; it is mainly academics who read Hannah More's moralistic fiction now. Ultimately, it is not the grandeur of the estate that matters in the moral economy of the novel, but the small East room that Fanny takes over, unfussy and plain as it is, as a place for quiet contemplation. If the Mansfield estate survives (and it has been under threat from the behaviour within), it is not saved by the heavy hand of Sir Thomas Bertram, but by the moral virtue of Fanny Price.

Such a reading makes more plausible Margaret Doody's argument in *Jane Austen's Names: Riddles, Persons, Places*: that close attention to character and place-names rewards the active reader.[143] Paula Byrne and Margaret Doody both argue that the name 'Mansfield' references Lord Chief Justice Mansfield, who ruled in 1772 that slavery on English soil was unsupported by common law.[144] Margaret Doody contends that the historical link between the 1772 Mansfield ruling and an estate owned by an enslaver is 'too pointed to be accidental'.[145] The name Lascelles – which appears in *Mansfield Park* – is likely a further reference to the known involvement of such families with transatlantic slavery. Hawkins (the name of England's first slave-trader)[146] is the maiden name of Mrs Elton in *Emma*, and her father, the novel hints, was quite probably involved in the slave trade.[147] Mrs Elton's married name is equally potent: Sir Abraham Elton of Clevedon Court was the mayor of Bristol who owned slave-ships and produced goods for exchange in West Africa.[148] The name Norris in *Mansfield Park* almost certainly alludes to the brutal slave captain, John Norris, condemned by the abolitionist Thomas Clarkson, who was favoured by Austen.[149] Her novels reference the names of major players on both sides of the slavery debate, often aligning these characters with good or ill. Mrs Elton, née Hawkins, is a dislikeable snob. Maria Bertram of *Mansfield Park,* who moves into the Lascelles' former residence, is a fickle and selfish young woman. Such naming points to these self-seeking characters as the morally bankrupt offspring of an economic system that relies on colonial cruelty. There are also hints of colonial strife in the depiction of Portsmouth (to which Sir Thomas banishes Fanny Price), in the allusions to *HMS Canopus*, which fought in the 1805-6 Battle of Saint Domingo, and *The Cleopatra*, which recalls the 1798 Battle of the Nile, in which Nelson overcame Napoleon – who wished to impede Britain's access to India.

Despite its satiric demolition in *Northanger Abbey*, gothic fiction enjoyed continued popularity with readers as a means of exploring the anxieties as well as the immense wealth that empire brought to the nation via the merchant and administrative colonial class. In many of these novels the country house, in gothic inversion, continues as an iconic device. In Charlotte Brontë's *Jane Eyre* (1847), Thornfield Hall, where Jane goes to work as a governess, has all the properties of the gothic hall. It is remote, has unused rooms, and there are mysterious and inexplicably malign happenings. In time, these are discovered to be the work of Bertha Mason, the West Indian Creole wife of Edward Rochester, escaped from her imprisonment in the attic when her keeper, Grace Poole (a gothic stock character), gets drunk. In a letter of 1847, Charlotte Brontë expresses regret that in her treatment of Bertha Mason she made the 'horror too predominant', when 'profound pity' should have been the sentiment.[150] As it is, the marriage between Rochester and Bertha plays on British domestic anxieties about the potential corruptions of bringing home racial mixing from the empire. Rochester trades his 'good race' for the vast fortune that comes as Bertha's dowry. She is the daughter of a West Indian planter (English and white) and his Creole wife (pale in appearance but almost certainly of mixed race). Rochester concludes that Bertha with her violent passions and madness is the product both of tropic geography and heredity, her madness passed down through three generations. As *Children of Uncertain Fortune* (2018) documents, three or four generations was the span that the Jamaican Assembly believed it took for children of white and African parentage to become sufficiently white to be treated as such in Jamaica (which never went in for the USA's one-drop theory of racial identity).[151] Bertha's madness, then, points to the threat of racial mixing. It was these elements in the novel that inspired Gayatri Spivak's searing critique of Brontë's Christian feminist imperialism in her essay 'Three Women's Texts and a Critique of Imperialism' (1985).[152] The underlying racism of *Jane Eyre* brought Jean Rhys's anti-colonial riposte in *Wide Sargasso Sea* (1966), a novel that looked forward to V.S. Naipaul's *Guerillas* and *The Enigma of Arrival*, as well as to the novels of David Dabydeen and the consciously postcolonial writing discussed later in this chapter.

The country house as a symbol of decline and shameful secrets is also at the heart of Charles Dickens's *Bleak House* (1853), the dark mansion of Lady Dedlock at Chesney Wold. Dickens undoubtedly had views on imperial issues. As noted, he supported the racist brutality of Governor Eyre in Jamaica, but in *Bleak House* concern with empire is seen as a distraction from the corruption and misery at the nation's heart. The novel connects characters who spin out from the secrets of Chesney Wold to the dread life of the streetsweeper, Jo. The presence of empire is sketched in through the satire on the minor do-gooding character, Mrs Jellyby, who is obsessed with the unfortunates of 'Borrioboola-Gha' on the Niger, but is blind to the dereliction immediately around her in London.

While Austen and Brontë look to the West Indies, and Dickens looks to Africa, Wilkie Collins's novel *The Moonstone* (1868) explores East India Company connections with the country house. A Yorkshire country estate is linked to the theft of a sacred diamond by a corrupt Company colonel during the 'storming of Seringapatam' (in 1799, p.9).[153] In this notorious battle, Tipu Sultan was killed and his belongings *looted* – a Hindu word which became common currency in Britain during the 18th-century.[154] Some of these items are now displayed at Powis Castle in Wales.

In *The Moonstone*, Colonel Herncastle, the soldier/company official gifts the moonstone to his young niece, but meantime, three Indian men are sent to retrieve the jewel, which has sacred significance, at any cost. Their presence in the grounds, disguised as jugglers on the day of Rachel Verinder's birthday, creates a menacing atmosphere, punctuated by the foreboding sound of their drum. After the theft of the jewel, a series of disasters befalls those who were in the house: a housemaid drowns herself, Rachel's mother dies and her relationship with her close friend Franklyn collapses in suspicion over the theft. The depiction of the Indians is Orientalist – they are described as 'tigerish' and the jewel is presented as having religious significance – yet their presence expresses anxiety about the repercussions of violence committed in the name of empire. The moonstone wreaks havoc, and its theft raises the possibility that other furniture in the house, including the 'India cabinet', may have been similarly looted. *The Moonstone* presents karmic misgivings about enjoying the material benefits of empire.

Arthur Conan Doyle's short story 'The Adventure of the Five Orange Pips' (1891) also shares *The Moonstone*'s sense that colonial transgressions will be avenged.[155] A Florida-based planter, Elias Openshaw, purchases a country estate in his native Sussex with profits from plantations worked by enslaved people, but his past crimes against abolitionists and the enslaved ultimately lead to his murder. His body is discovered 'face downward in a little green-scummed pool' without 'any sign of violence'.[156] Conan Doyle had no hesitation about making the unsavoury and violent origins of Openshaw's house the motive of plot in his story.

The connection between the country house and colonialism persists into the twentieth century, as indeed empire did.[157] But, as E.M. Forster's novel *Howards End* (1910) demonstrates, any sense of connection is now inevitably complicated by the fact that empire had both its gradualist and revolutionary enemies inside Britain and in the colonies, and the economic and political power of the old landed classes now had to deal with a Britain where all adults, male and female, had the vote within a decade of this novel's publication. Forster represents all those constituencies in his novel: the Wilcoxes buy Howards End with money that has come from the Imperial and West African Rubber Company. The Schlegel sisters' father is a stern critic of empire as the 'vice of the vulgar mind to be thrilled by bigness'. The character Leonard Bast is a clerk in an insurance company. As the critic Lionel Trilling argues, *Howards End* is about the fate of England, and its plot asks, 'Who shall inherit England'?[158] Forster is clear about the nature of colonial exploitation, though he suggests this metaphorically rather than describing the actual working conditions of forced African labourers in the rubber plantations. Seen through Margaret Schlegel's eyes, the map of Africa in Henry Wilcox's company office makes the continent look 'like a whale marked out for blubber'.[159] What is never in doubt in the novel is that, as a symbol, Howards End is worth inheriting. As H.V. Morton's bestseller, *In Search of England* (1927) suggests, even in decline, England's noble past lies amongst 'rural relics and ruins'.[160] This identification offers a potent challenge to Black British writers.

Black British and British Asian Writing and the Country House

I discussed elements of V.S. Naipaul's novel, *The Enigma of Arrival*, in the previous chapter – on the connections he draws between Trinidad and England and his education in unlearning colonial assumptions about the English countryside – but *The Enigma of Arrival* is also set in the grounds of an actual country house, Wilsford Manor in Wiltshire. The house is described to visitors as 'a quintessential English estate', playing into the idea of the 'real' England.[161] The fact that it was a 20th century creation (built in 1906) is itself a further witness to the power of the idea, but also of its ultimate hopelessness. Just 70 or 80 years after it was built, the manor becomes an icon of physical and moral 'dilapidation' (a frequently occurring word in the novel), a symbol of post-imperial emptiness, an outward sign of its owner's 'accidia' and 'sloth'. The entangling, creeping ivy is the house's most striking image, and the view from the house 'of ivy and forest debris and choked water meadow' merely confirms the owner in his sloth. As Naipaul writes: 'there was nothing in that view which would encourage action in a man already spiritually weakened by personal flaws, disappointments, and above all, his knowledge of his own great security'.[162] The knowledge of a security that discourages action is Naipaul's epitaph on the country house and its traditions. If E.M. Forster concludes that *Howards End* is eminently worth inheriting as an emblem of English possibility, that is very far from the conclusion that *The Enigma of Arrival* leads us to, even if Naipaul, personally, found space for reflection in the manor's grounds. But then, as W.H. Auden and Christopher Isherwood had written in *The Dog Beneath the Skin* (1935):

> The great houses remain but only half are inhabited.
> Dusty the gunrooms and the stable clocks stationary.
> Some have been turned into prep-schools where the diet
>   is in the hands of an experienced matron,
> Others into club-houses for the golf-bore and the top-hole.[163]

Auden and Isherwood's work, with its emphasis on lost splendour, suggests that the golden age of country house literature was at an end. Naipaul revived the tradition but gave it a postcolonial twist. *The Enigma of Arrival* has left writers an important legacy by finding the countryside to be a potential source of 'healing' (p. 56) from empire's aftershocks. A literary lineage of contemporary country-house writing has since emerged in the work of Black British and British Asian playwrights, poets and novelists. Resourced by new historical work, this writing has been increasingly able to draw more precise lines between colonial settings and country houses and estates. In doing so, it is able to dismantle country house mythologies.

Key literary engagements with country houses' colonial histories have come from John Agard, David Dabydeen, Seni Seneviratne, Roger Robinson, Rita Dove, Tanika Gupta, Tyrone Huggins, Jo Baker, Catherine Johnson and Pete Kalu.

David Dabydeen's fiction displays a keen but much more radical take on the pioneering work of V.S. Naipaul, and is undoubtedly foundational in revisioning of the English scene as shaped by empire. His novel *A Harlot's Progress* (1999), noted in the previous chapter, presents country houses as places where colonial goods are delivered and racial abuses happen.[164] At the beginning of the novel, a formerly enslaved man called Mungo sits with a smug abolitionist called Mr Pringle. The abolitionist writes and reshapes Mungo's story, clearing it of 'indelicate or infelicitous expressions' to ensure its suitability for drawing-room audiences. Mungo talks of Captain Thomas Thistlewood, named after a real slave-owner, who brought him to England thirty years previously as a boy and sold him to Lord Montague, whom he served in the family's country house. Here, he is treated as a 'perfumed pet', a description that alludes to Peter Fryer's phrasing in *Staying Power* (1984), noted above.

Whilst Austen's *Mansfield Park* refers to slavery in the Caribbean, Dabydeen brings it home to the English country house. The novel's historical setting parallels that of Austen's text, which is itself an historical novel. This correspondence of dates places Dabydeen's novel within the Austen tradition. Like Austen, Dabydeen resists diatribe and he does not romanticise the enslaved. The difference is that he does not avert his eyes from slavery's brutality. In so doing, he explores history's complexity and no doubt aims to change the way that we remember Britain's involvement with transatlantic slavery.[165] In the novel, the portrait of Mr Pringle, a self-serving abolitionist, is designed to undermine the self-congratulatory British representation of anti-slavery campaigners as moral heroes. Waiting with pen poised to record Mungo's 'first person narrative', Mr Pringle plans to convert 'the droolings of a decrepit nigger'[166] into 'a book purporting to be a record of the Negro's own words' (p. 3). As the 'young Secretary' for the 'Committee for the Abolition of Slavery… Mr Pringle would of course be universally applauded for his dedication and achievement in recording the Progress of the oldest African inhabitant of London' (p. 3). The capitalisation of the word 'Progress' draws attention to the process of converting the stories of enslaved people into mediated accounts of the past. The text is Christianised and standardised in accordance with the conventions of 'slave narratives' of the time. In his mind, Mr Pringle re-plots Mungo's narrative using numbered points, beginning with '1. Africa' through to '5. Service in the Household of Lord Montague' and ending with '9. Redemption of Mungo by the Committee for the Abolition of Slavery' (p. 6). This irreverent parody of white abolitionism is accompanied by deliberate and obvious historical inaccuracies throughout the novel. As Abigail Ward observes, Captain Thistlewood was indeed a real historical character, but the novel amalgamates the man's actual actions with those of other colonial figures. The novel concentrates on *how* history is written. Rather than being bound by fidelity to facts that went unrecorded, Dabydeen focuses on the question of historicity itself.[167]

A Harlot's Progress connects country estates with the British Atlantic world and it makes this link very clearly. Captain Thistlewood commits horrible acts in the Caribbean and he himself observes how the money he makes through slavery translates into rural property: 'by these reasonable deeds he presided over several successful ventures, accumulating a fortune for himself which he properly invested in the purchase of an estate in Hampstead'. But Thistlewood's estate reflects the owner's moral corruption. It is 'a veritable jungle, the gardens grown wild, the house strangled by vines' (p. 112-113). The line is reminiscent of Naipaul's description of the choking ivy of Wilsden estate.

Dabydeen's novel draws on the distinction that Austen and her contemporaries made between old and new money. The Montagues represent old money; Thistlewood is newly wealthy. Lady Montague works hard to 'honour...her husband's ancient title and lineage' (p. 186) whilst Lord Montague is 'contemptuous of the world of commerce, particularly the West Indian merchants whose manners were as unbecoming as their traffic in human bodies' (p. 188). The unconscious irony of these musings, of course, is that Montague has purchased Mungo as a gift for his wife. In Montague's mind, the child helps to complete the house's possessions, '[i]n all his years of collecting, Lord Montague had never sought to possess African artefacts, preferring the lightness and delicacy of things Chinese' (p. 200). Not only do these musings reduce a human being to the status of property – a step away from considering people as cargo – but it reminds the reader that the collections in country houses are often colonial in nature.

Mungo is taken to the Montagues' estate in the country, but nature's bliss is not for him. As one of the house's global ornaments, he is not free to explore the Montagues' version of rural paradise. Slavery abroad becomes slavery at home. Mungo recalls that Lady Montague 'put a chain on my silver collar and take me for afternoon walks in the grounds of the house' (p. 240). If this is not punishment enough, Mungo is hated for supposedly being out of place. He reflects, 'a simple nigger like me was deemed to be the undoing of England, darkening its bright historical fabric: black moth, black adder, black beetle, blackfly, black bryony, infecting and strangling and poisoning and blighting England's heritage' (p. 242). Blackness is aligned in English minds with nature's shadowy side, killing blooms and producing poisonous berries (black bryony) that must not be eaten. Mungo represents an invader species that destroys, not enjoys, England's idyll. Nonetheless, as Abigail Ward rightly argues, Dabydeen's novel draws from slave narratives to remind readers that men like Mungo existed, and his fictional but historically real Black presence refutes the notion that white people alone inhabited rural England.[167]

In Mungo's mind, Lady Montague embodies colonial exploitation. Her mere physical appearance conjures up past traumas at the hands of slavers. Her blue dress is 'ruffled like waves of the sea, little nips here and there like the beaks of fish, Captain Thistlewood's care of all living creatures making him empty us overboard as meal.' (p. 184). Feeding fish with African bodies foregrounds the irony of Thistlewood's self-fashioning as nature's guardian. Such horrifying acts present pastoral aesthetics as serving the purpose of soothing profoundly troubled consciences. Dabydeen presents country houses and propertied families in this light. The description of Lady Montague invites this reading: 'Imagine skin of bleached sugar, bales of cotton her breasts, veins of gold running along her arms, her lap a mine of inexhaustible ores, and yet all the cargoes of Empire but a trifle compared to the effort that went into her creation, the centuries and centuries of constant progress, the harbouring of the seed to ensure purity of race and lineage, the gradual accumulation of riches and reputation, like a stately ship starts from rude forest, a mansion from rude stone' (p. 185). The passage connects ships, colonial profit and racial hierarchies to the chiselled 'stone' of 'mansion' houses. Strikingly, the metaphors describing Lady Montague's body both evoke and reverse Rider Haggard's imperialist depiction of 'Africa as a prone female body' to be discovered and exploited in 'The Legend of King Solomon's Mines' (1885).[168] Lady Montague is clothed with material from the colony and her household's demand for luxury goods drives the transatlantic slavery system and leaches the earth of its natural resources. But Lady Montague's consumption of colonial goods ends up consuming her. She sickens. The doctor is called for. He prescribes 'purges and vomit pills' and a toxic stench emanates from her body: 'all the servants run about opening windows to let out fumes like offal boiled in horse-manure' (p. 237). Having ingested the products of cruelty and mistreated Mungo, Lady Montague's body becomes the prone body of England. If Africa's body is exploited, England's bloated body malfunctions and tries to rid itself of empire's corruption: 'she vent and puke and squirt from every available hole like the legions of demons cast out by Our Lord' (p. 238). Confirming this interpretation, the doctor connects Lady Montague's sickness with the afflictions of enslaved people, 'From the moment he set eyes on me', Mungo remembers, 'he seemed to have known that the true patient was not my Lady but myself' (p. 254). Focusing on metaphor and historicity, then, Dabydeen brings to the surface and explores Austen's submerged critique of slavery.

John Agard is another influential re-interpreter of British rural traditions whose poetry engages with the writings of Austen's generation. Like
Dabydeen, Agard is informed by recent historical and literary debates.
Agard's poem 'Mansfield Park Revisited', for instance, references Said's
essay:

> The air is civil with cakes
> and marriage proposals,
> for overseas possessions
> are best kept overseas
> and slave revolts not
> right for polite conversation
> or what's considered good taste.
> Here even history knows its place.[169]

Here, as well as addressing the silence in Austen's novel ('slave revolts'
are considered 'not right for conversation'), the poem targets the modern
practice of marketing country houses as sites of leisure. For visitors,
the pleasure of 'afternoon teas' takes precedence over public knowledge
of 'overseas possessions', and the poem snipes at country houses' 'great
day out' philosophy.

In addition to historical research and the rereading of classic fiction, the
paintings of Black servants in country houses have also provided a rich
source of inspiration. Seni Seneviratne's poem 'Sitting With the Mistress'
(from *Creative Freedom: The F Words Anthology*, 2007) was inspired by a
painting by Pierre Mignard in the National Gallery of a Black girl seated
beside the Duchess of Portsmouth. Seneviratne was commissioned to
respond to this late 17th-century painting as part of the bi-centenary of
Abolition commemorations in 2007. Imagining the girl's perceptions of
the situation, Seneviratne writes that she has been compelled to sit still by
a 'nip' from her mistress and strict exhortations from the painter: 'Tilt your
chin up! Look at the mistress, not me!' The only comfort for the child is
nature itself, which soothes her, the peaceful sky – to be seen in the portrait
– making her sleepy: 'clouds... drifting in a painted sky'.[170] Seneviratne also
wrote a commissioned piece for the 'Colonial Countryside' project in
which she depicts Black sitters in portraits that are owned by historic
houses. Her poem begins unequivocally:

> Less status than the lapdogs, whose coats
> They combed daily, they were curiosities...[171]

As well as imagining the trauma of the children whose experiences
are in most cases lost to us, Seneviratne envisions the details and ironies
of their daily experience. The theme of the Black page is explored in
Seneviratne's poem 'They Have Named Me Page', which puns on the
resonant meanings of the word: 'a word they use for the flimsy things
inside / the leather bindings they call books', and the poem imagines

the experience of encountering a foreign country, the English language feeling 'like stones falling / on my head'. For this child, silence is a form of resistance and not merely an experience of victimhood: 'I will not let my tongue curl / around the sound of them [English words]'. 'This Page', he declares, 'is silent.'[172] Whilst the Black children who served in country houses are their most vulnerable colonial subjects, Seneviratne refuses to victimise them, instead depicting them in resistant acts. In 'Sitting With the Mistress', the girl in the portrait watches a blackbird and envisages herself flying back to her mother over the seas.

Roger Robinson's poem 'A Young Girl With a Dog and a Page' (from *A Portable Paradise*, 2019) similarly draws attention to the Black child as 'a darkness in the background, / a dark and ghostly presence / searing through history', but is moved to reimagine the painting by reversing its visual priorities. He will:

> put you in fine blue linen,
> place her unlit behind the dog,
> an animal collar around her alabaster neck.
> You're in a fine hat with a peacock feather,
> and I'll have her look at you, in awe.[173]

Through this reversal, Roger Robinson highlights the racist conventions of the classic portrait-with-black-servant, but lovingly reconfigures the painted scene in ways that cherish the child and punish the white sitter.

The music performed in country houses also provides inspiration, as in Rita Dove's *Sonata Mulattica* (2010), which explores the experiences and sensibilities of a virtuoso black violinist as he journeys through Europe, playing in palaces and historic houses. The collection's preface foregrounds its relationship to research:

> Although this… is a work of literature, any resemblance to actual people, events, or locales is deliberate. No names have been changed; the identities of the not-so-innocent are verifiable'.[174]

The statement expresses a wish to leverage history's authority in order to rewrite the past, to correct acts of omission. Dove's poems commemorate the life of George Polgreen Bridgetower, to whom Beethoven originally dedicated his most famous violin sonata (although Beethoven subsequently scribbled out this dedication, and Bridgetower was temporarily lost to history). The collection recuperates and disseminates Bridgetower's story.

The collection ends with a detailed chronology. This timeline indicates that the poems are founded on verifiable historical events, the kind conventionally associated with established historical figures, but Dove's chronology begins with Bridgetower's birth in 1780 and ends shortly after his death. This reinstates him among iconic composers such as Beethoven and Haydn.[175] The historical anchorage of Dove's collection is further suggested by the notes that accompany individual poems, pointing to their origins in diaries, letters and other writings, calendars and actual artefacts.

Sonata Mulattica's early action takes place in country houses, and the poems emphasise empire's influence on material culture. Section Two is entitled 'Bread and Butter, Turbans and Chinoiserie', juxtaposing mundane local life (bread and butter) with material evidence of Britain's global expansion (turbans and Chinoiserie). The result conveys the daily, proximate presence of empire. Several poems in the collection – 'Black Billy Waters at His Pitch' (p. 67),[176] 'Ode on a Negress Head Clock, with Eight Tunes' (p. 81), 'Staffordshire Figurine, 1825' (p. 215) and 'Moor With Emeralds' (p. 176) – depict sculptures as well as popular curios, suggesting empire's ubiquitous presence. The poems also show that empire affected all social strata, building up a picture of colonialism's influence on both royal fashions and customs for dressing servants. Queen Charlotte's wardrobe assistant wears expensive 'yellow Indian muslin'[177] while Black Georgian servants are obliged to wear exotic and bizarre clothes that have nothing to do with their cultural origins. In 'Janissary Rap', as Dove's notes explain, African musicians wear 'the lavish garb of an imaginary Levant'[178] and Bridgetower's father laments the oddly amalgamated apparel because it obscures his cultural identity. These 'strange adornments' include a 'quilted turban', 'Caesar's cape' and 'gaily layered robes'.[179] People at court 'lust' over black figures, who are perceived as 'thing[s]' more than people, leaving Bridgetower's father morally compromised.[180] His violin-playing son receives similar treatment. During 'The Undressing', the son removes a 'peacock blue' sash, 'tasselled' shoes, 'satin pantaloons' and his 'Monkey Jacket'.[181]

Dove's collection is attuned to recent research into empire's influence on architectural design and domestic culture. She situates Windsor Castle in a larger colonial geography. The Castle's long path is viewed transrurally by Bridgetower:

> It makes me think of ships,
> Of travel: a line slicing the soft green,
> God's whiplash straight down
> The heaving back of England... [182]

Dove's consciousness of England's colonial history imbues Bridgetower's vision of England's 'soft green' land with a consciousness of enslavement and plantation violence.

Sonata Mulattica is the work of a distinguished African American poet. Other works discussed below are by British writers with a closer eye for a British readership. Tanika Gupta's play *The Empress* (2013)[183] is set in the final years of Queen Victoria's rule. The play, later followed by a film, features Abdul Karim, an Indian servant who rises in the queen's esteem, later becoming her 'munshi', who teaches the aged queen Hindi and enchants her with stories about the country of which she is empress, but which she has never visited.[184]

Tyrone Huggins' play, *The Honey Man* (2015), explores the hidden black history of a country house, indicated by an overlooked black presence in a painting, while Catherine Johnson's *The Curious Tale of the Lady Caraboo* (2015) is about the real Mary Willcox, who persuaded the occupants of Knole Park that she was a kidnapped princess. Like Bernardine Evaristo's novel *The Emperor's Babe* (2002), Baker's and Johnson's stories help to further debunk the notion that Black Britishness only originated in 1948, when the *Empire Windrush* arrived in Tilbury Docks. Johnson's novel focuses on Bristol as a port and hub of global trade and intercultural encounter.

Jo Baker's *Longbourn* (2013) implicitly responds to Said's criticism of *Mansfield Park* in retelling *Pride and Prejudice* from the perspective of the servants, particularly a Black footman based at Netherfield Hall. His presence reflects the author's familiarity with recent research into Austen's world, including one of Austen's letters which refers to her neighbours' Black footman. Baker had also read Ben Wilson's book *Decency and Disorder: The Age of Cant, 1789–1837*, on vernacular culture in Austen's day, which documents the 18th century Black presence.[185] Further, the author's undergraduate history degree made her aware that Lancaster, her home for many years, was an old slave port. The resurgence of popular interest in ancestry also played its role in the making of Baker's Black protagonist; she had seen a television documentary about a white Scottish family who traced their ancestry to a Black servant in Paisley.[186] Armed with this information, and following the logic of Austen's plot, Baker deduced that the Bingley family could have made their money from sugar and were correspondingly likely to have had a Black servant. Baker reported that she 'just knew that the background would not be as uniformly white as […we see in Austen] adaptations, and that Austen and her readers would have known this too – whereas modern readers might need it noticing for them.'[187] Baker's novel, particularly as a bestseller that was also made into a film, was a milestone in reconceptualising the country house, hopefully raising wider public awareness of a pre-twentieth-century Black presence.[188]

There is a clear sense of occasion when the Black footman, Ptolemy Bingley, first appears in Chapter Four of *Longbourn*. The chapter's epigraph quotes Austen, using ellipses to linger on her phrase: '…the entrance of the footman…'.[189] In *Pride and Prejudice*, this phrase refers to Mr Bennet's manservant; here the footman's surname, Bingley, confirms the slavery connection, which Ptolemy makes fully clear, saying 'If you are off his estate, that's your name, that's how it works' (p. 123).

From the outset, the novel offers a below-stairs perspective. As the maid says of Miss Bennet's countryside walks, 'If Elizabeth Bennet had the washing of her own petticoats… she would be more careful not to tramp through muddy fields.' (p. 16). In this way, Ptolemy's presence is connected to a rural realism that undermines heritage films' nostalgia about country life. Though there is no explicit statement that Bingley's money comes from sugar wealth, sugar's absent presence is conveyed by a servant's naive fantasy that Netherfield has floors of 'polished toffee' and 'barley-sugar columns' (p. 73). His fellow servant Sarah overturns this fantasy: '[t]he columns are just the local stone, I am sorry to inform you' (p. 73), an exchange that can be read as reminding *Longbourn*'s readers that colonial links are not immediately evident. Even so, the novel shows how conscious Sarah is of other climes: 'the sun would be shining on other places still, on the Barbadoes [sic] and Antigua and Jamaica where the dark men worked half-naked and the Indians wore almost no clothes at all' (p. 14). Sarah's 'knowledge' is filtered through the ignorant gaze of popular culture as well as through the literary imagination, but *Longbourn* also makes numerous references to abolitionist pictures and writings. When Sarah searches the stable quarters of her fellow servant, James, she finds: '*A Letter on the Abolition of the Slave Trade*. A cheap volume, well worn, by one William Wilberforce' (p. 93). Here, Baker would seem to be endorsing the view that Austen had abolitionist sympathies; James is the hero of *Longbourn* just as Fanny Price, who questions her uncle about slavery, is the hero of *Mansfield Park*.

Baker is less concerned with developing the connections of country houses to sugar wealth and slavery than in establishing the figure of Ptolemy. He reflects late twentieth-century knowledge of Britain's early Black presence, his name probably deriving from Peter Fryer's discussion of the naming practices affecting enslaved people in *Staying Power*,[190] and in particular the biography of Ignatius Sancho, the real-life 18th-century Black Londoner. Like Sancho, Ptolemy visits the Vauxhall Pleasure Gardens and aspires to own his own shop.[191] Ptolemy's depiction is, of course, circumscribed by the plot of *Pride and Prejudice* in that he must follow Bingley, who owns a residence in London but merely rents Netherfield. Inevitably, then, the novel aligns Ptolemy with the city. Like the African American character Jack Ross in *Downton Abbey*, Ptolemy's association with the English countryside appears more anomalous than history suggests it might have been – feasible but temporary and unusual. Like Jack Ross, Ptolemy's representation is shaped by modern multiculturalism: he represents the impending demographic and social change following mass immigration one century ahead: 'Things were cut adrift, and shifting, and nothing could continue as it had been' (p. 124). This narrative echoes the Dowager's comments in *Downton Abbey* as Jack Ross sings to the family: 'Things can happen at Downton that no one imagined even a few years ago.'[192] In both texts, Black figures are seen as solitary pioneers and harbingers of social change, rather than as integral to Britain's story.

As well as revisioning the fiction of the past, other contemporary work in film and fiction has responded to the visual evidence of paintings of the past, as Seneviratne and Robinson have done. Both the film *Belle* (2013) and Catherine Johnson's young adult novel, *The Curious Tale of Lady Caraboo,* draw their inspirations from paintings. *Belle* references the painting of *Dido Elizabeth Belle and her cousin Lady Elizabeth Murray*, which was completed in 1779 by David Martin in the style of Zoffany, whilst Johnson looks to William Bird's 1817 portrait of *Princess Caraboo*. Both young women are painted in turbans topped with peacock feathers. Peacocks were markers of prestige, brought to Europe from the Middle East and greatly treasured in elite settings.[193]

The Curious Tale of Lady Caraboo[194] is based on the actual case of Mary Willcox (or Willcocks), the daughter of a Devonshire cobbler, who presented herself as 'Princess Caraboo' to Mrs Worrall of Gloucestershire's Knole Park, dressed in pseudo-oriental costume. At first the girl is seen as a vagrant, but when a Portuguese sailor mistakenly identifies her as coming from the East Indies, the Worralls take her into their home, and the 'Princess' becomes a celebrity and has her portrait painted (which can still be seen). However, after a period of fascinated observation and attestations of authenticity, Willcox was exposed in 1817 and the incident widely reported by the press. Rather than blaming Mary Willcox, however, Johnson's novel depicts her fantasies as being shaped by the colonial myth-making of the time.

Set just after *Mansfield Park*'s publication, Johnson's novel also connects country house grandeur to sugar wealth and to the novels of Austen. Knole Park 'glitte[rs] like a...sugar palace' in Johnson's novel.[195] Like *Longbourn*, the novel depicts Austen's world as being imbued in the colonial but, showing an awareness of the work of contemporary historians, it sets country houses even more squarely in the context of empire, imperial textuality and the historical Black presence. Throughout, the novel is preoccupied with material culture, in its passing allusions to the numerous colonial commodities that defined elite British life in the early 19th century. The Worralls display these as part of a domestic, cosmopolitan aesthetic to enhance their social status. They employ a steward, who they believe speaks Persian, though his roots are actually in Turkey and Alexandria (p. 83). A naval captain, who also turns out to be an impostor, drinks Jamaican rum, which is said to be 'straight off the boat' (p. 87), while the barman jokes that the captain will 'drink the West Indies dry' (p. 239). In keeping with upper-class love of Chinoiserie, Mrs Worrall creates a 'dainty Chinese drawing room' (p. 11), though Mr Worrall resents paying 'a sultan's ransom' for its decoration (p. 43). All this is in keeping with what heritage professionals such as the National Trust historian Emile de Brujin have told us about the fashions of the time.[196] Mrs Worrall fetishises this room further by inviting friends to dress in Chinese clothes to celebrate its opening (p. 30). The daughter, Cassandra Worrall, has a 'new Indian print' dress and gives Princess Caraboo one of her 'cast-off Indian muslins' (p. 53).

Many of the novel's major events and realisations happen on the house's roof, visits which Caraboo initiates as a habit the household follows. Her rooftop position affords her an elevated perspective, suggesting her inter- pretative role as an outsider. She has the clearest perspective on the house's relationship with the outside world, and shares this viewpoint with the Worralls' son, Fred. Sitting among the roof-tiles, he is offered a revelation about British society: 'we are all liars, in one way or another' (p. 237). From the roof's vantage-point, Fred is also offered 'a most excellent view all the way down to the Bristol Channel, and even the docks – he could just see a small forest of masts, so far away they could have been toothpicks – and the blue of the water stretching away to the west' (p. 67). Here, the novel obviously alludes to Bristol's slave port and its visiting vessels, connecting the house to maritime history and commercial trade.

Johnson makes the point that the early nineteenth-century world was populated with people from elsewhere. 'Caraboo' sees 'lascars…Turks [and] Africans' (p. 178) in the docks. There are passing references to Romany camps (p. 47), 'Negro beggars' (p. 46), "octaroons" (p. 62), praying 'Mussulmen' (p. 70), maharajah's sons (p. 244), and 'dar[k]-skinned girls two a penny' (p. 89). In this way, the novel emphasises older contexts of immigration without being naively celebratory. Racism is rife. Fred comes to regret having made 'a misery' of an Indian schoolboy's life because he worshipped Ganesh (p. 244). Meanwhile, 'Caraboo' is subjected to gruel- ling 'cranial exploration[s]' by phrenologists (p. 79), a reminder of the pseudo-scientific racism which came to inspire eugenics in the Nazi era. Robert Youngs once wrote: 'theories of race are also theories of desire'[197] and colonial desire looms large in Johnson's novel. Mrs Worrall and her associates wish to study Princess Caraboo 'at close quarters' (p. 45) because she is an object of fascination whom they wish to categorise and dominate. This fascination combines with the phrenological incident to suggest, as Youngs does, that colonial desire is frequently sadistic;[198] or as Elleke Boehmer observes, '[e]mpire was itself, at least in part, a textual exercise', and its mythologies were disseminated in a range of fictional and non- fictional literary forms.[199] The lies told by the historical Mary Willcox are linked to colonial storytelling, a brand of myth-making also represented by the fraudulent captain, who keeps the family in thrall with tales of Indian tigers (p. 99). Liar though she is, Mary Willcox possesses a critical distance from such tales. She sees that tall tales are a feature of colonialism: '[the captain] was as big a liar as she was' (p. 100). She inhabits a fantasy world inspired by explorer narratives and colonial adventure tales. She shoots and eats pigeons with arrows and dresses in 'suitable warrior princess mode…

fabric wound around her head as a turban, a strip tied around her waist as
a belt, with a small sharp knife... tucked into it' (p. 53). The novel diagnoses
the gullibility of the household's women as stemming from boredom and
a lack of fulfilment, from which the colonial world enables a form of
escapism. The mother holds meetings about 'the habits of... whatever
group of happy, carefree woodland peoples were to be discussed [that...]
month' (p. 8). She lingers over 'engravings of semi-naked American
Indians' (p. 15), an objectifying gaze very easily turned upon Caraboo. Such
colonial texts play a leading part in confirming that Caraboo is genuine. The
daughter, Cassandra, thinks Caraboo's turban resembles those worn by
'people in India... in Mama's books' (p. 21). These proto-anthropological
books in Mrs Worrall's library attract Mary Willcox herself, because they
are in 'full colour' and lift her 'into another world' (p. 72). Caraboo comes
into being because 'the lady of the house... wanted her to be real – one of
those books in the library come to life, a walking, talking, breathing native
for her to study' (p. 48). The novel leads to the inexorable conclusion that
the seeds of Mary's imagination are scattered over fertile soil. When, before
her exposure, Mary looks at her portrait, the painting is seen to unite both
her own fantasies and those of her hosts:

> The girl in the picture, regal in her turban, looked as if she had been
> painted on the distant shore of some kingdom she ruled, only now brought
> back to England... she had become the Princess they all desired her to
> be. The soul of the Princess was there, in this painting of the odd girl
> with the dark skin and the strange hair curling out from under her turban.
> (p. 176).

Mary Willcox's transformation into 'Caraboo' is made possible by
existing artistic conventions, with which other characters 'all desired' her
to conform (p. 176). Their colonial fantasies have been projected on to the
canvas of Mary's imagination. These collective fantasies allow the novel to
channel the 'soul[s]' of historical figures like Dido through Mary Willcox,
who mediates between real and imagined worlds.

Richmal Crompton's William Brown story, 'The Native Protégé' (1923)[200]
looks forward to Princess Caraboo and is a good example of the ways in which
children's literature has long reverberated with stories that reflect the
elsewhere of empire. William, inspired by *Boy's Own* adventure stories and
a school play about Christopher Columbus, daubs himself in brown grease
paint and sets off on a countryside ramble. As he scampers through woodlands he imagines himself to be 'dancing on bare brown feet in a savage land'
(p. 126). He arrives on the vicar's lawn, where an audience has coincidentally
assembled. William is mistaken for a boy from Borneo, who is due to arrive
at that very moment, and he takes advantage of the situation, scoffing the
currant buns that are offered to him. He rises to the occasion, speaking an
imaginary language ('Blinkely men ong', p. 132), which the vicar's wife

becomes increasingly sure is 'Hindustani' (p. 133). She interprets his utterances to rapt attention. The incident corresponds with a scene in Johnson's novel when the fraudulent captain assumes the role of interpreter:

> The captain had a book in his hand, and Caraboo saw it was the same as Mrs Worrall's, about the islands of the East Indian Ocean, Batavia and Malaya. He flipped the pages, and pointed to a picture of some fruit.
> "*Ananas!*" Caraboo exclaimed.
> "My, my," Mrs Worrall said, "isn't that French for pineapple?"
> "It's Eastern originally", Captain Palmer said... "Proves again – and without a doubt, I might say – that what we're dealing with here is a Malay."[201]

Both the vicar's wife and the captain mask their actual ignorance, either by appealing to some relatives' experience in the colonies (as does the vicar's wife) or by resorting to imperialist writings (as does the captain). It is therefore important to situate Catherine Johnson's writing within the literary tradition of both Austen and the long-running literary explorations of colonial encounter.

The remaining writer discussed here was commissioned by the 'Colonial Countryside' project to reimagine the histories of specific country houses. The story discussed below, by Peter Kalu, was supported by leading historians of empire to re-examine the archive and it has a historical awareness not always available to Black writers of the 1980s.

Kalu's story, 'Richard Watt I, Merchantt, of Speke Hall (Intimations of Immortality)', fed by historical research, imagines the dying memories of Richard Watt I (1724-1796), a Liverpool merchant who came from relatively humble beginnings but made the modern equivalent of millions through slave-trading, managing other landowners' Jamaican plantations and exporting slave-produced goods to England.[202] Watt bought Speke Hall in Liverpool in 1795, and it was inherited later by his great nephew, Richard Watt III, who was also bequeathed his great-uncle's Jamaican estate together with 200 enslaved people.[203]

Speke Hall encapsulates the concept of the colonial countryside: its umbilical connection to empire is vital yet hidden. Visitors to the timbered house can see Richard Watt I's silhouette in the morning room and reproductions of his great-nephew's estate plans. There is also information about the last Watt, Adelaide, and her approach to estate management.[204] Even today, visitor information highlights architectural features such as the courtyard and 19th-century gothic revivalism, leisure pursuits and priest holes created during the repression of Catholicism.[205] Nonetheless, the Hall's connection to colonialism cannot be denied, since its purchase, preservation and even the National Trust's ownership of Speke are both direct – and indirect – consequences of wealth produced by enslaved people. The profits of slavery funded the Hall's restoration and Adelaide

Watt, the last of the family line, bequeathed the house to trustees who eventually left the house to the Trust and thus ensured its preservation. Although Richard Watt I bought the property just before he died, Speke conferred social status on his inheritors and gave them a country lifestyle which appeared far removed from Jamaica.[206]

A 2017 article on Watt by Anthony Tibbles provides a historical foundation for Kalu's short story, which announces the origins of Watt's fortune in its opening sentence; the protagonist is introduced as 'West India merchant Richard Watt I'.[207] When Watt's doctor tells him to get well, he says: 'Liverpool, nay England herself, has need of men of your scope and judgement; it is your patriotic duty to recuperate and return swift to the fray of life.'[208] The doctor's statement makes historical sense. It suggests that Watt's Jamaican enterprises were once commonly known – though they have since been forgotten (partly by design). The doctor's accolade, 'men of your scope' expresses admiration for the imperial reach of Watt's ambition and his patriotism; his use of the plural 'men' shows how Watt's profiteering fits into a national pattern of wealth-creation by planters. Like other planters of his generation,[209] Watt established and invested in local business through his shipping company and made philanthropic donations, founding the Bluecoat School and co-founding the Old Swan Charity School.[210] The story contains two further references to slavery's legacy. The architectural legacy is suggested in the story's opening sentence, which depicts Speke in a state of disrepair – 'the crumbling casement windows' – a significant detail because his heir subsequently restored it with money derived from slavery.[211] Slavery's industrial and political legacy is also suggested by the name of Watt's companion in Jamaica, John Arkwright. The name has specific connotations. There was a John Arkwright (1872-1954), a Conservative politician, but the name also references Richard Arkwright (1732-1792), who was Watt's contemporary, the inventor/industrialist, whose mechanical cotton-spinning machinery was linked with cotton grown by enslaved people in the USA, and the connection between slavery and industrial capitalism that was first documented by Eric Williams in *Capitalism and Slavery* (1944).[212] By appropriating the name of John Arkwright, the story hints at the larger historical point that plantation owners often became MPs and held sway over parliamentary decisions. The Society of West India Planters and Merchants increased its parliamentary representation to over 40 MPs by the 1760s, during Watt's most productive business years.[213] And the two Arkwrights are connected. John Arkwright's real-life great-great-grandfather was Richard Arkwright. 'Arkwright' has regional connotations too: Richard Arkwright established factories in the Northern towns of Cromford, Bakewell and Wirksworth, employing factory workers to create luxurious cotton fabric from buds picked by enslaved people in North America, so the name Arkwright

emphasises slavery's material contribution to Northern industrial development. The story alludes directly to cotton when Watt's doctor admires
his patient's clothing:

> "It is English cotton, that hose. The finest."
> "Indeed, it is," the doctor concurred, "and so soft to the touch."

This exchange illustrates that consumer demand – not merely for cotton
but for rum, coffee and sugar – drove the colonial project of profit-
seeking and extraction. 80% of the nation's cotton was produced by
enslaved people in America's Deep South.[214] Cotton, of course, was
not just regionally important; it accounted for 40% of Britain's exports.
So, while the story deviates from strict historical fact by associating
Watt with the Arkwright family, it zooms out from Speke's story to
tell verifiable truths about slavery, British industrialisation and exploitative
economic growth.

Many other details in the story are consciously faithful to the research
findings of Anthony Tibbles. In Kalu's story, as in life, Watt suffers from
gout. His illness is mentioned in his obituary.[215] The story also refers to
some (actual) glazed windows in the Oak Drawing Room at Speke, which
inspires the protagonist Watt to plan his own 'heraldic glass' for posterity.
Watt indeed had a coat of arms designed and the stained glass family crests
can still be seen at Speke. One design shows three Moors' heads – a gesture
towards the source of Watt's wealth.[216] The three heads also appear on
Watt's commemorative monument.

Kalu also explores Watt's attitude to plantation management. His disap-
proval of brutal punishments to enslaved people is alluded to in the story:
'His estate never lost any slaves to beatings. He has run his plantation with
good judgement.'[217] In reality, this 'good judgement' is more pragmatic
than humanitarian, and the story follows Tibbles's conjecture that Watt's
approach made good business sense.[218] After the hurricane that destroys the
estate, Watt laments the loss of human life, but as part of the financial costs
of the destruction: 'A running total of costs extended through Richard
Watt's mind as he swept across George's Plains'. Enslaved people were
invariably the most valuable asset of a sugar estate.[219] Watt's struggle with
his wayward nephew is also incorporated into the story's plot. In Kalu's
piece, Watt tells his doctor about their fraught relationship: 'I told my
nephew, "let the buyer beware, or empty will be both your pockets and
mine." And did he listen?' Watt's actual letters reprimand his nephew for
showing poor business sense: 'Why', he asks, 'my dear nephew do you not
attend to my letters?' In adhering to these details, and in the fidelity to the
fundamental facts of Watt's life, Kalu's story expresses the purpose of the
commission.

Yet Kalu also imaginatively embellishes facts for strategic reasons. His treatment of hurricanes is a case in point. Watt's actual letters reveal that a hurricane wrecked his estate at George's Plain. Here is Kalu's rendering of it: 'The West Indies knew better than England how to do storms, and two of hurricane force had been sent across Westmoreland, one quick on the heels of the other'. As Kalu's story suggests – and as Watt's letters show – there were two hurricanes, in 1780 and 1781. Watt's Jamaican estate was damaged by the first of these, and he wrote that almost 1,200 enslaved people were drowned. Kalu personalises these deaths. His fictional Watt discovers only 'the bodies of drowned slaves by the log store.' Here the scene of death – 'by the log store' – recalls the offensive term 'n- in the woodpile', a phrase used by Conservative MP, Anne Marie Morris, in 2017, who was suspended from the party for using it.[220] By conjuring up this phrase, the story juxtaposes contemporary and historical racism and identifies colonialism as the source of both. The phrase carries further ironies since it traditionally refers to suspicious acts of concealment. This allows Kalu to imply that slavery's legacies have likewise been kept hidden from view. Those who profited from slavery had every reason to tamper with the historical record. Speke Hall, Kalu's protagonist declares, 'will be my monument'.[221] This invented sentiment opens up a new understanding of Speke Hall as a building that commemorates Watt in a misleading way, that raises the question: how is it possible to visit houses like Speke Hall and not know about the miserable lives of those who made its purchase and restoration possible? Watt was immersed in the British Atlantic world but philanthropy and a country house gradually eclipsed the way in which he earned his money. So, though Speke Hall is materially linked to slavery, it is the house – ironically – which distances the family from this association, since succeeding generations of the Watt family established themselves in rural society and fashioned themselves as country dwellers. It is no coincidence, then, that gothic revivalism – such a feature of Speke – appealed to Richard Watt V, who inherited the house in 1855 and was responsible for its restoration. Gothic decorative fashions were favoured by families with relatively new money. The fact that the gothic novel inverted the traditional meanings of the country house is a further irony, but then the original builders were not literary critics. Gothic revivalism was used as a ploy by planters, and as Joley Baker observed, such symbols were a way of falsely suggesting that the family had been present in rural England since medieval times.[222] Richard Watt V is said to have 'entered into the antiquarian spirit with enthusiasm, filling the restored interiors with large quantities of exuberantly carved oak furniture – suitably "ancient" in style',[223] décor as decoy. Richard Watt's actual monument can be found in Standish Parish Church, where the commemorative marble plaque does not refer to the Jamaican source of his wealth, but only to his involvement with commerce.[224]

Though posing big contemporary questions, Kalu's story keeps within the parameters of the social attitudes and practices which prevailed at the time of its setting. For instance, Kalu embellishes a story about the nephew, telling it as a tall-tale at the local inn:

> That nephew. I was on the ship, it cannot be denied. He recruited double crew and each crew on double rations. In Bonny, he took on two Nile crocodiles, placed them in the hold. The crocs ate three slaves a week…[t]he hull when that ship finally docked at Kingston Port was awash with blood, half the slaves bleeding or gobbled to death, but two fat, healthy crocs proudly delivered.

Yet even this wild, invented story is in keeping with the known excesses of Jamaica planters such as Thomas Thistlewood, who appears fictively in Dabydeen's novel, *A Harlot's Progress*. He was a contemporary of Watt, whose diary records his own sadistic acts of punishment and rape. The point of Kalu's crocodile tale is to highlight the fact that slavery gave permission for extravagant acts of cruelty, and the crocodile serves as a bizarre but powerful metaphor for the Middle Passage and its jaws of death.

The story's second flight of fancy concerns rumours, overheard in the same inn, that Watt has a 'Sambo mistress'.[225] In real life Watt never married and there are no children on record. The story presents this as a deliberate deception. For Watt to have had a Black mistress together with mixed-race descendants (and Speke Hall's true inheritors) is historically plausible. As Watt's friend Arkwright declares: 'There is no sin or shame in bedding a slave. And you, sir, are a blockhead to think it.'[226] The story goes further into the plausible imaginary, hinting that Watt's mixed-race child was brought back to England and educated at Eton. Such stories of Black family connections have many real historical precedents. Nathaniel Wells, the son of the Welsh planter – born of a Black mother towards the end of Watt's life – was educated in Britain and bought Piecefield Estate, while Dido Belle, the niece of Lord Chief Justice Mansfield and resident at Kenwood House, is another now prominent example.[227] As noted above, scores more examples are recorded in *Children of Uncertain Fortune*.[228] Kalu's story is thus written with an eye on what we know about slave-ownership more generally.

While commemorating the hidden suffering of the enslaved people whose labour created Watt's wealth and bought Speke Hall, Kalu's story also promotes some human understanding of Watt himself by exploring his inner feelings. Speke Hall's peaceful waterside location is contrasted with life aboard Watt's ships in scenes that replay in the protagonist's mind as he drifts in and out of reverie:

> The thrill of water was across there, in the threading glimmer that was the River Mersey. He told all his captains, board efficiently, check all lists, set sail, tack carefully, then swing out for the Irish Sea, head fast through the Bay of Biscay and strike for the Atlantic Ocean. There, the captain should let his vessel rip. A fourteen-gun brig in full sail was a

sight to behold, skimming fathomless depths, the howl of wood racing on water, the creak of stretching ropes, the joyful song of aching canvas, the deep murmuring of cargo in the hold, the chase of birds above.[229]

Here, everything above deck communicates excitement, freedom and movement: 'skimming', 'racing', 'the chase of birds'. Below deck, however, there is confinement and protest. This wording captures the protagonist's perspective on his cargo's monetary importance. We recall the 1781 *Zong* insurance case (featured in the film *Belle*), in which it was claimed that 130 enslaved people – drowned by crew members who threw them overboard – were 'cargo'. As with the rest of his story, Kalu's choice of the word 'cargo' is historically informed.

Conclusion

The authors of *Legacies of British Slave-Ownership* have declared their wish to reunite modes of writing which have become unproductively disconnected from one another. They observe that historians have been increasingly dispersed to the apparently separate sub-fields of culture, economics, politics and society. By specialising in these ways, historians have too often presented Britain's 'global' and national histories as separate spheres. Pushing against this trend, their materialist focus on slave-ownership unites these distinctive modes of history writing in which Britain figures as an 'imperial political formation'.[230]

Historians rarely recognise literary innovation. Yet the literary works discussed in this chapter, and the critical discussion of them, clearly parallel – and sometimes precede – historians' attempts to integrate Britain's national and global histories. There is the continuing importance of the writing of Jane Austen as both an icon of comfortable heritage, but also as the subject of continuing efforts to get to the heart of her often richly elusive meaning. As historical details of country houses' global connections continue to emerge, Said's criticism of *Mansfield Park* remains foundational. If his reading of *Mansfield Park* does not fully stand the test of time, his work encouraged further investigations of Austen's relationship to empire, and the revisioning of her work by contemporary novelists and poets. The rural turn in writing by Black Britons is progressively questioning some of the nation's most entrenched values, creating parallels between country houses and Britain's moral landscape. Poems such as Agard's 'Mansfield Park Revisited' subvert country houses' state-of-the-nation status, as does a novel such as *Longbourn,* which draws attention to the hidden colonial aspects of Austen's world. Such work extends the urban focus of earlier novels (like Evaristo's *The Emperor's Babe*) to rural settings by establishing historically-nuanced, material connections between empire and country estate, architectural expression and domestic sensibility. Works such as *Sonata Mulattica, The Empress, The Honey Man* and *The Curious Tale of The*

Lady Caraboo variously focus on empire's imprint on clothing, decorative styles, ornaments and spices, a focus on material culture that they share with today's historians of empire.

Historic houses and country estates have had their fortunes revived in recent decades. Visitor numbers are at an all-time high, and nostalgic heritage productions are alive and well. This trend exposes a powerful tension between deepening historical knowledge of houses' global histories and a continuing tendency to gloss over them in productions such as *The Duchess* and *Downton Abbey*. Even when television viewers and cinema goers are acquainted with historical Black figures in films such as *Belle,* they are commonly perceived as historical anomalies, exceptions to the norm. Though the Black and Asian presence has been registered in English literature for more than three centuries, notions of exceptionality stubbornly persist. Evidence is evidently not all.

Growing awareness of country houses' association with empire has provoked Black British and British Asian writers to revisit and reclaim them as built on ancestral labour, and to challenge such houses' persistent representation as seats of refinement or guardians of nationhood. Amassing evidence to the contrary, writers have seen country houses as a lens through which to contest rurality's construction as uncomplicatedly English. Johnson and Dove, in particular, place country houses on a global map which extends both East and West to India and the Caribbean as well as to China. All these writers give a clear sense of the global cartography of the houses that feature in their work.

Writers are now well-resourced by recent historical research to unite imagination and an evidence-based approach to the country house's colonial links. It has been estimated that there are more than 300 paintings in Britain which show Black sitters,[231] a visual documentation of a presence that has provided writers with an intellectual basis for challenging the countryside's presumed whiteness and to contest the idea that Black and Asian people are foreign to country estates. Even so, the interpretation of the country house still revolves around the lives and habits of their propertied families, and only occasionally of their servants. As the pastoral chapter observed, the history of the landed gentry tells only part of England's rural history. Yet country houses are powerfully symbolic heritage sites. Speaking about such houses' connections to empire presents an opportunity to produce more expansive views of the countryside and represent a collective, symbolic return to one of Britain's most zealously guarded sites of national belonging. By including painful memories of colonial violence, writers provide a truthful basis for a healing return to an inclusive vision of our country estates.

Endnotes
1. Dresser and Hann, eds. *Slavery and the British Country House* (2013), p. xiii.
2. Dresser and Hann, *ibid*.
3. Prejudice and Pride told us the gay and lesbian histories of houses and People's Landscapes was about working-class histories. In 2018, the National Trust marked the centenary of the 1918 act with a National Cultural Programme called 'Women and Power: The Struggle for Suffrage'. See Sophie Duncan and Rachael Lennon, *Women and Power. The Struggle for Suffrage* (Swindon: The National Trust, 2018).
4. Prejudice and Pride evaluation, National Trust, 2018.
5. Sally-Anne Huxtable, Corinne Fowler, Christo Kefalus and Emma Slocombe, 'Interim Report on the Connections between Colonialism and Properties now in the Care of the National Trust, Including Links with Historic Slavery' (Swindon: National Trust, 2020).
6. Christopher Hope, 'National Trust could face enquiry into its purpose', *The Daily Telegraph*, 23rd October 2020. A Freedom of Information request found that there had, in fact, been just 3 complaints. See Stephen Delahunty, 'Regulator received just three complaints about National Trust Slavery Links Report, Third Sector, 23 Nov. 2020. www.thirdsector.co.uk, accessed 30 Nov 2020.
7. *The Daily Telegraph*, 23rd October 2020.
8. Clive Aslet, 'The National Trust should spare us the dad-dancing attempts to be hip', *The Daily Telegraph*, 18th January, 2019. https://www.telegraph.co.uk/news/2019/01/18/national-trust-should-spare-us-dad-dancing-efforts-hip/, accessed 26 February, 2019.
9. A phrase used by Raymond Williams in *The Country and The City* (1973).
10. Aslet, 26 Feb. 2019.
11. Dresser and Hann, *op cit.*, p. 3.
12. See Katie Donington, 'Transforming Capital: Slavery, Family, Commerce and the Making of the Hibbert Family' in Catherine Hall, et al, *Legacies of British Slave-Ownership. Colonial Slavery and the Formation of Victorian Britain* (Cambridge: CUP, 2014), pp. 203-249.
13. These literary examples were cited by Urszula Terentowicz-Fotyga, 'The Country House as False Home in the Contemporary Novel', paper given at 'The Country House in Britain, 1914-2014' conference, Newcastle University, UK, 6-8 June 2014.
14. Dresser and Hann, *op cit.* p.xiii.
15. See www.historichouses.org/about/policy-work/facts-figures.html and www.visitbritain.org/visitors-flock-england-historic-properties.

16. Business Live, 2008, 'National Trust bringing history to everyone', published 28th November 2008, www.business-live.co.uk/lifestyle/national-trust-bringing-history-to-everyone-3953788, accessed 27 August 2019.
17. Aslet, 26 Feb. 2019.
18. Priyamvada Gopal, *Insurgent Empire: Anticolonial Resistance and British Dissent*, 'Introduction' (London: Verso, 2019), p. 33.
19. Barczewski, *Country Houses and the British Empire* (2014), p.122.
20. Barczewski *op cit.*, pp.19-122.
21. Interim Report on the Connections between Colonialism and Properties now in the Care of the National Trust, Including Links with Historic Slavery', p. 84.
22. Miranda Kaufmann, email correspondence, 16th November, 2015.
23. Dresser and Hann (2013), *op cit.*, p. 12.
24. Cherry Ann Knott, *George Vernon 1636-1702: 'Who Built This House?' Sudbury Hall, Derbyshire* (Tun House Publishing, 2010).
25. This survey was conducted in 2020 by surveying existing curatorial knowledge, mapping known links through a literature search, conducting a database search and reviewing National Trust commissioned reports into the topic.
26. Thanks to Laurence Westgaph for pointing me towards the possibility of trade links here. Thanks also to David Blundell for his additional research into slave-ships owned by Abraham Elton. The reference to salt and brass comes from Dresser and Hann, *op cit.*, p. 23.
27. https://www.slavevoyages.org/voyage/database, accessed 5 May 2020.
28. National Trust Clevedon Court website, https://www.nationaltrust.org.uk/clevedon-court, accessed 5 May 2020.
29. 'A Brief History of Clevedon Court', www.nationaltrust.org.uk/clevedon-court/features/a-brief-history-of-clevedon-court-, accessed 5 May 2020.
30. Nick Draper, *The Price of Emancipation. Slave-Ownership, Compensation and British Society at the End of Slavery* (Cambridge: CUP, 2010), p. 4 and Donington (2014), *op cit.*, p. 206.
31. Francis Greenacre, 1995, 'Obituary: Margaret Ann Elton', published 7 June 1995, https://www.independent.co.uk/news/people/obituary-margaret-ann-elton-1585283.html, accessed 5 May 2020.
32. Croft Castle 'Property Overview', https://www.nationaltrust.org.uk/croft-castle-and-parkland, accessed 5 May 2020.
34. Thanks are again due to Laurence Westgaph for directing me to the details of this legal opinion. And see Nigel Pocock and Victoria Smith, 2017, 'The Legal Business of Slavery', 2 February 2017, http://www.bbc.co.uk/history/british/abolition/slavery_business_gallery_04. shtml, accessed 5 May 2020.

35. Wimpole Estate, 'Property Overview', https://www.nationaltrust. org.uk/wimpole-estate, accessed 5 May 2020.
36. National Trust Collections online, www.nationaltrustcollections. org.uk/object/624132, accessed 6 May 2020.
37. Jennifer Anderson, *Mahogany* (Cambridge: Harvard UP, 2012), p. 29.
38. James Walvin, *Slavery in Small Things. Slavery and Modern Cultural Habits*, (London: Wiley, 2017), p. 83.
39. Adam Bowett, 'The English Mahogany Trade, 1700-1793: A Commercial History', unpublished thesis, Brunel University, November 1996.
40. Kate Smith and Margot Finn, 'Introduction', *The East India Company At Home, 1757-1857*, p. 8.
41. Smith and Finn, *op cit.*, p. 8.
42. Joley Baker, 'The British Slave Trade and its relationship to country-house neo-Palladian architectural style', Unpublished dissertation, University of Leicester 2018.
43. Jill Casid, *Sowing Empire: Landscape and Colonization* (Minneapolis: Minnesota UP, 2005), p. 55.
44. John Sykes, 'The Indian Seal of Sir Frances Sykes. A Tale of Two Families' in Smith and Finn, eds., 2018, *op cit.,* p. 418.
45. See Smith and Finn, *op cit.*, p. 8.
46. For negative views of the Creole and the Nabob see, Jack P. Greene, *Evaluating Empire and Confronting Colonialism in Eighteenth-Century Britain* (Cambridge: Cambridge UP, 2013).
47. Katie Donington, 'Transforming capital: slavery, family, commerce and the making of the Hibbert family' in Hall, Draper, McClelland, Donington and Lang, 2014, p. 203.
48. Donington, 2014, *op cit.*, p. 207.
49. Donington, 2014, *op cit.*, p. 211.
50. Donington, 2014, *op cit.*, p. 204.
51. Donington, 2014, *op cit.*, p. 226.
52. Lowri Ann Rees, 'Welsh sojourners to India: the East India Company, networks and patronage c. 1760-1840', *Journal of Imperial and Commonwealth History*, 45: 2, 2017, pp. 165-187.
53. Legacies of British Slave Ownership database, https://www.ucl.ac.uk/ lbs/person/view/26074, accessed 26th February 2019. The National Trust website now acknowledges the Caribbean sugar wealth which funded the art collection of Charles Wade https://www.national trust.org.uk/snowshill-manor-and-garden/features/who-was-charles-wade, accessed 26 February 2019.
54. Anthony Tibbles, '"My interest be your guide": Richard Watt (1724–1796), Merchant of Liverpool and Kingston, Jamaica', *Transactions of the Historic Society of Lancashire and Cheshire*, 166 (2017), pp. 25–44.

55. Richard Dean, 'The Rise of the Watt Family' in *Speke Hall*, (Swindon: The National Trust, 2017), p. 12.
56. Caroline Bressey observes that country houses' colonial connections are often unapparent to visitors, or else narrated in a fragmented fashion. Above all, she argues, curators fail to present such connections as integral to British history rather than as appendages to it. Bressey, 2013, *op cit.,* p. 121.
57. Italics mine. National Trust object 532261.1, also found online at http://www.nationaltrustcollections.org.uk/object/532361.1, accessed 11 March 2019.
58. Lady Mary Elizabeth Lucy (1803-1889), *Mistress of Charlecote: The Memories of Mary Elizabeth Lucy.* Thanks to Katie Donington who located references to this book and drew my attention to the story. By the time this book has gone to publication, there are plans to change the label.
59. National Trust Collection, item 107841. Also accessible online at: http://www.nationaltrustcollections.org.uk/object/107841, accessed 11 March 2019.
60. Aslet, 26 Feb. 2019.
61. With thanks to my student Joley Baker, who conducted a survey of National Trust properties for the Colonial Countryside project in 2017.
62. Shrabani Basu, 2010, *Victoria and Abdul. The Extraordinary Trust Story of the Queen's Closest Confidant*, (Stroud: The History Press, 2010), p. 294.
63. Ian Cobain, *The History Thieves*, (London: Portobello, 2016), p. 111.
64. Interviewed by Grace Newton, 'Yorkshire was built with the profits of slavery', *Yorkshire Post*, 7 May 2019.
65. James Walvin, 2011, 'Slavery and the Building of Britain', BBC History website, http://www.bbc.co.uk/history/british/abolition/building_ britain_gallery_03.shtml, accessed 5th November, 2020.
66. See Nicholas Draper, *The Price of Emancipation*, p. 12.
67. Peter Fryer, *Staying Power* (1984), p. 21.
68. David Dabydeen, *Hogarth's Blacks: Images of Blacks in Eighteenth-Century Art* (Manchester: MUP, 1987), p. 9.
69. Thanks to Miranda Kaufmann for drawing my attention to this point. See also Miranda Kaufmann, 2019, 'English Heritage 1600-1830 and Slavery Connections', http://www.mirandakaufmann.com/ehslavery connections.html, accessed 31 January 2019.
70. Quoted from Hogg's *Autobiography* in Eva Beatrice Dykes, *The Negro in English Romantic Thought* (Washington D.C.: Associated Publishers, 1942), p. 6.

71. Gretchen Gerzina, *Black England. Life Before Emancipation* (London: John Murray, 1995).
72. Kathleen Chater, *Untold Histories: Black People in England and Wales During the Period of the Slave Trade c. 1660-1807* (Manchester: Manchester UP, 2011).
73. Caroline Bressey, 'Cultural Archaeology and Historical Geographies of the Black Presence in Rural England', *Journal of Rural Studies* 25, 2009, 386-395.
74. Madge Dresser, *Slavery Obscured: The Social History of the Slave Trade in an English Provincial Port c. 1698-1833* (London: Continuum Books, 2001).
75. Deborah Cohen, *Family Secrets: The Things We Tried to Hide*, (London: Penguin, 2013).
76. Onyenka, *Blackamoores. Africans in Tudor England, Their Presence, Status and Origins* (London: Narrative Eye, 2013).
77. Kevin Le Gendre, *Don't Stop the Carnival. Black Music in Britain* (Leeds: Peepal Tree Press, 2018).
78. This child may or may not have been the boy who served Lady Lucy with hot chocolate. The story was researched by the University of Birmingham and their project, entitled Whose Story? was featured in the *Birmingham Post*, 'National Trust Bringing History to Everyone', 28th November, 2008, www.birminghampost.co.uk/lifestyle/national-trust-bringing-history-everyone-3953788, accessed 13 May, 2019.
79. David Callaghan and Barbara Willis-Brown, *A Day in the Life. A Black Heritage Trail of the West Midlands* (Birmingham: SCAWDI, 2011), p. 2.
80. Callaghan and Willis-Brown (2011), *op cit.*, p. 2.
81. Daniel Livesay, *Children of Uncertain Fortune: Mixed-Race Jamaicans in Britain and the Atlantic Family, 1733-1833*, (North Carolina: The University of North Carolina Press, 2018).
82. Cohen, *Family Secrets* (2014), p. 43.
83. See William Alexander McClung, *The Country House in English Renaissance Poetry* (Berkeley: University of California Press, 1977), and for the invaluable anthology and notes of Alistair Fowler, *The Country House Poem* (Edinburgh: Edinburgh UP, 1994).
84. *Herrick: Poems*, ed. L.C. Martins (Oxford: Oxford Standard Authors, 1965, 1971), pp. 146-149, and anthologised in Fowler, *op cit.*, p. 108.
85. Herrick
86. Fowler, p. 157.
87. Fowler, p. 123-128.
88. Fowler, p. 55.
89. Fowler, p. 86.
90. Fowler, p. 64.

91. Fowler, p. 360.
92. For Grainger see John Gilmore, *The Poetics of Empire: A Study of James Grainger's The Sugar Cane (1764)* (London: The Athlone Press, 2000); for Edward Long see *Jill Casid, Sowing Empire: Landscape and Colonization* (2005), pp. 13-21. Bryan Edwards, negrophobe and ardent supporter of slavery, wrote a collection of poems, *Poems, written chiefly in the West-Indies* (Kingston, Jamaica: 1792), which includes sentimental verses on African deaths, topographical poems in the picturesque mode about Jamaica, and a translation of Horace.
93. Fowler, pp. 113-117.
94. Fowler, pp. 89-93.
95. Richard Corbett, 'Iter Boreale' (1647), *The Poems of Richard Corbett*, ed. J.Bennett & H. Trevor-Roper (Oxford: Clarendon Press,1955), p. 49. Quoted in Fowler, *op. cit.*, pp. 80-81.
96. Fowler, p. 227 ('A Peppercorn or Small Rent').
97. Fowler, pp. 235-245.
98. Fowler, p. 364.
99. *The Poems of Anne, Countess of Winchilsea, From the Original Edition of 1713 and from Unpublished Manuscripts*, Ed. Myra Reynolds (Chicago: University of Chicago Press, 1903), pp. 196-197.
100. James Bramston, *The Man of Taste* (Augustan Reprint Society, William Andrews Clark Memorial Library, University of California, [1733] 1975), Project Gutenberg e-book.
101. Dorothea Smartt, *ShipShape* (Leeds: Peepal Tree Press, 2008), p. 41.
102. See Adrian Tinniswood, *The Polite Tourist: A History of Country House Visiting* (London: The National Trust, 1998) and Jocelyn Anderson, *Touring and Publicising England's Country Houses in the Long Eighteenth Century* (London: Bloomsbury Academic, 2018).
103. Mary Leapor, *Poems Upon Several Occasions*, vol. 2 (London: Printed and sold by J. Roberts, 1751), pp. 111-122, quote, p. 113.
104. Leapor, p. 117.
105. Leapor, p. 118.
106. Leapor, p. 114.
107. Leapor, p. 120.
108. Leapor, p. 121.
109. *The Poems of James Thomson* (London: Oxford University Press, 1963), p. 147.
110. Thomson, p. 149.
111. 'The Task Book 3', *The Poems of William Cowper Vol II, 1782-1785* (Oxford: Clarendon Press, 1995), p. 171.
112. For this observation see Donna Landry, *The Invention of the Countryside: Hunting, Walking and Ecology in English Literature, 1671-1831* (Basingstoke: Palgrave, 2001). p. 229.

113. See Moira Ferguson, *Animal Advocacy and Englishwomen, 1780-1900: Patriots, Nation and Empire* (Ann Arbor, University of Michigan Press, 1998).

114. See Felicity Owen & David Blayney Brown, *Collector of Genius: A Life of Sir George Beaumont* (Newhaven: Yale University Press, 1988), pp. 126-142.

115. Horace Walpole, *The Castle of Otranto* (Penguin Classics, 2002), p. .

116. For an overview, see *The Cambridge Companion to Gothic Fiction*, ed. Jerrold E. Hogle (Cambridge: Cambridge UP, 2002).

117. See James Buzard, *The Beaten Track: European Tourism, Literature and the Ways to "Culture" 1800-1918* (Oxford: OUP, 1993), pp.147-148.

118. See John Bugg, *Five Long Winters: The Trials of British Romanticism* (Stanford: Stanford UP, 2014).

119. See Edmund Burke, *Reflections on the Revolution in France* ([1790] Oxford World Classics, 1999) and *A Philosophical Enquiry into the Origin of Our Ideas of the Sublime and Beautiful* ([1757] Oxford World Classics 2008).

120. For the gothic interest in the Caribbean see Alan Richardson, 'Romantic Voodoo: Obeah and British Culture 1797-1807', in *Sacred Possessions: Vodou, Santeria, Obeah and the Caribbean*, Ed. M.F. Olmos and L. Paravisini-Gebert (New Brunswick: Rutgers UP, 1997), pp. 171-194.

121. See Judith Terry's introduction to Matthew Lewis, *Journal of a West Indian Proprietor* ([1834] Oxford World Classics, 1999).

122. D.L. McDonald, 'The Isle of Devils: The Jamaica Journal of M.G. Lewis', *Romanticism and Colonialism: Writing and Europe 1780-1830*, Ed. Tim Fulford and Peter J. Kitson (Cambridge: Cambridge UP, 1998), pp. 189-205.

123. See Matthew Lewis, *Journal of a West Indian Proprietor*, pp. 160-183.

124. See *The Story of Henrietta* ([1797] Virginia: Valancourt Classics, 2012).

125. See Alistair M. Duckworth, *The Improvement of the Estate: A Study of Jane Austen's Novels* (Baltimore: Johns Hopkins, 1971), pp. 2-34.

126. Edward Said, 'Jane Austen and Empire' in *Culture and Imperialism* (New York: Knopf, 1993), pp. 80-96.

127. Said, *op cit.*, p. 97.

128. Said, *op cit.*, p. 114.

129. Gabrielle White, *Jane Austen in the Context of Abolition* (London: Palgrave Macmillan, 2006).

130. In 2013, the Bank of England announced that Jane Austen's image was to appear on its £10 banknotes from 2017. The decision followed

a campaign led by Caroline Criado-Perez, who threatened to take the Bank of England to court for the consistent under-representation of women in its historical figures series, begun in 1970.

131. Julian North, 'Austen on the £10 note – genuine victory for equality?', *University of Leicester home page,* www.le.ac.uk/north/austen-10-pound-note accessed 14 March 2014.

132. Dresser and Hann, 2013, *op. cit.*

133. Laurence Brown, 'The Slavery Connections of Marble Hill House,file:///D:/1.%20Publications/1.%20PEEPAL%20TREE%20Green% 20Unpleasant%20Land/2.%20INDIVIDUAL%20CHAPTERS/ 5.%20PART%20THREE.%20RURAL%20SETTINGS/Country%20Houses /Chapter%20planning%20and%20journal%20articles/ Secondary%20reading/Laurence%20Brown%20Marble%20Hill%20 House%20notes.pdf, accessed 10 May, 2019.

134. William Deresiewicz, *Jane Austen and the Romantic Poets* (Columbia University Press, 2005); and see Roger Nunn, 'Empire and Austen: A Contrapuntal Reading', *Studies in English Literature* (1999), pp. 1-27.

135. See Duckworth, *The Improvement of the Estate,* pp. 1-34.

136. See Duckworth, p. 75.

137. See Duckworth, pp. 35-80 passim.

138. See Duckworth, p. 57.

139. Austen, *Mansfield Park* (Oxford: Oxford Illustrated Edition, 1923, 1988), p. 41.

140. See Duckworth, p. 76.

141. Austen, *Mansfield Park*, p. 463.

142. Duckworth, p. 80

143. Margaret Doody, *Jane Austen's Names: Riddles, Persons, Places* (Chicago: University of Chicago Press, 2015), p. 336

144. Ed. Sandy Byrne, *Jane Austen. Mansfield Park* (London: Palgrave Macmillan, 2004) p. 205.

145. Doody, *op cit.*, p. 337.

146. John Hawkins was the cousin of Sir Francis Drake, who accompanied Hawkins on his third slave-trading expedition, each sailing in ships provided by Queen Elizabeth I. See Todd Gray, *Devon and the Slave Trade. Documents on African enslavement, abolition and emancipation from 1562 to 1867,* (Exeter: The Mint Press, 2007), p.17.

147. Byrne, 2014, *op cit.*, p. 245.

148. Dresser and Hann, 2013, *op cit.,* p. 23.

149. Byrne, 2014, *op cit.,* p. 249.

150. Letter to W.S. Williams, 28 October, 1847, quoted in Rowena English, Introduces Jane Eyre, online https://library.leeds.ac.uk/special-collections/view/1260.

151. Daniel Livesay, *Children of Uncertain Fortune*, p. 39.

152. Gayatri Chakravorty Spivak, 'Three Women's Texts and a Critique of Imperialism', *Critical Inquiry* Vol. 12, No. 1, "Race," *Writing, and Difference* (Autumn, 1985), pp. 243-261.

153. See Sandra Kemp, Introduction, Wilkie Collins, *The Moonstone* ([1868] London: Penguin, 1998).

154. William Dalrymple, 'The East India Company: the original corporate raiders', *The Guardian*, 4th March 2015. And see William Dalyrymple, *The Anarchy. The Relentless Rise of the East India Company* (London: Bloomsbury, 2019), p.xxix.

155. Sandra Kemp's introduction to *The Moonstone* confirms that Conan Doyle was inspired by Collins's novel. See Kemp's 1998 edited introduction to *The Moonstone. Edited and With An Introduction by Sandra Kemp* (London: Penguin), p. i.

156. A. Conan Doyle, *Sherlock Homes: the Complete Short Stories* (London: John Murray, 1928), p. 109.

157. See Richard Gill, *Happy Rural Seat: The English Country House and the Literary Imagination* (Newhaven: Yale UP, 1972), which focuses on early 20th Century fiction from Henry James to Evelyn Waugh.

158. Quoted in *Happy Rural Seat*, p. 97.

159. E.M. Forster, *Howards End* ([1910] Penguin Books, 1941), p. 147.

160. H.V. Morton, *In Search of England* ([1929] London: Folio Society, 2002).

161. 'About the Estate', http://www.wilsfordmanor.co.uk/the-estate/, accessed 9 November 2020.

162. Naipaul, *The Enigma of Arrival*, pp. 185-186.

163. W.H. Auden and Christopher Isherwood, *The Dog Beneath the Skin* [1935] London: Faber, 1968), p. 12.

164. David Dabydeen, *A Harlot's Progress* (London: Jonathan Cape, 1999), pp. 173-245, when Mungo is brought into the household of Lord and Lady Montague.

166. *A Harlot's Progress*, p. 6. Subsequent quotations from this novel are given in the text.

165. David Dabydeen, *Hogarth's Blacks: Images of Blacks in Eighteenth Century English Art* (Aarhus: Dangeroo Press, 1983).

166. See Abigail Ward, *Caryl Phillips, David Dabydeen and Fred D'Aguiar. Representations of Slavery* (Manchester: MUP, 2011), p .2.

167. Abigail Ward, *op cit.*, p. 2.

168. Abigail Ward, *op cit.*, pp. 114-115. And see Elleke Boehmer, ed., *Empire Writing* (Oxford: OUP, 2009), p. 86.

169. John Agard, 'Mansfield Park Revisited', *We Brits* (Tarset: Bloodaxe Books, 2006), p. 46.

170. Seni Seneviratne, 'Sitting with the Mistress', *Creative Freedom: The F Words Anthology* (Leeds: Peepal Tree Press, 2007), p. 38.

171. To be published in *Colonial Countryside: National Trust Houses Reinterpreted* (Leeds: Peepal Tree Press, forthcoming 2021).
172. *Ibid.*
173. Roger Robinson, 'A Young Girl with a Dog and a Page', *A Portable Paradise* (Leeds: Peepal Tree Press, 2019), p. 58.
174. Rita Dove, *Sonata Mulattica* (New York: Norton, 2014), p. 14.
175. David Hunter, 'The Use of the Profits of Slavery to Support Musical Activity in Eighteenth-Century Britain and its Colonies', paper given at 'What's Happening in Black British History VIII' conference, 10 May 2018.
176. Black Billy Waters was an actual street performer. See Kevin Le Gendre, *op. cit.* p. 23.
177. Dove, 2010, p. 32.
178. Dove, 2010, p. 212.
179. Dove, 2010, p. 160.
180. Dove, 2010, p. 73.
181. Dove, 2010, p. 80.
182. Dove, 2010, p. 40.
183. Tanika Gupta, *The Empress,* (London: Oberon, 2013), p. 41.
184. The play is based on research by Shrabani Basu, who later published *Victoria and Abdul: The Extraordinary True Story of the Queen's Closest Confidant* (London: The History Press, 2017).
185. Ben Wilson, *Decency and Disorder: The Age of Cant, 1789–1837* (London: Faber and Faber, 2008).
186. At the first meeting of 'What's Happening in Black British History', the assembled historians broadly agreed that widespread interest in ancestry has led to important new recoveries of figures from forgotten historical archives.
187. Email from Jo Baker, 18 November, 2015.
188. *Longbourn* was broadcast on *The Book At Bedtime* on BBC R4 in May, 2014.
189. Jo Baker, *Longbourne* (London: Knopf, 2013), p. 37. Subsequent quotations from this novel are given in the text.
190. Fryer, 1987, *op cit.,* p. 139. Fryer quotes from Ptolemy's second century writings about African sexuality.
191. Fryer, 1987, *op cit.,* pp. 93-98.
192. *Downton Abbey*, series 4, episode 3.
193. Christine E. Jackson, *Peacock* (London: Reaktion Books, 2006), p. 256.
194. Catherine Johnson, *The Curious Tale of the Lady Caraboo* (London: Corgi, 2015).
195. *The Curious Tale of the Lady Caraboo*, p. 134. Subsequent quotations from this novel are given in the text.

196. For more information about Chinese wallpapers, see Emile de Bruijn, Andrew Bush and Helen Clifford's *Chinese Wallpaper in National Trust Houses* (2015), available from The National Trust.

197. Robert Youngs, *Colonial Desire. Hybridity in Theory, Culture and Race* (London and New York: Routledge, 1995), p. 9.

198. Youngs, 1998, *op cit.,* p.108.

199. Elleke Boehmer, 1995. *op cit.,* pp. 12-13.

200. Richmal Crompton, *Just William* (London: Macmillan, 1923); and see Christopher Ringrose, 2006. 'Lying in Children's Fiction: Morality and the Imagination'. *Children's Literature in Education,* Volume 37, pp. 229-336.

201. *The Curious Tale of the Lady Caraboo,* p. 101.

202. Anthony Tibbles, 2017, *op cit.,* p. 166.

203. Tibbles, 2017, *op cit.,* p. 41. An 1814 list of enslaved people that Richard Watt III inherited from his great-uncle can be viewed at the International Slavery Museum in Liverpool.

204. Richard Dean, 2017, *op cit.,* p. 3.

205. Tibbles, 2017, *op cit.,* p. 44.

206. Peter Kalu, 'Richard Watt I, Merchantt of Speke Hall (Imitations of Immortality)', in *Colonial Countryside: National Trust Houses Reinterpreted* (Leeds: Peepal Tree Press, forthcoming 2021).

207. Kalu, *ibid.*

208. See Katie Donington in Hall et al, 2017, *op cit.*

209. Tibbles, 2017, *op cit.,* p. 40.

210. Dean, 2017, *op cit.,* p. 3.

211. Eric Williams, *Capitalism and Slavery* (North Carolina: University of North Carolina Press, 1944).

212. Hall, Draper and McClelland, 2014, *op cit.,* p. 56.

213. Henry Louis Gates, Jr. 'Why Was Cotton King?' published at www.pbs.org/wnet/african-americans-many-rivers-to-cross/history/why-was-cotton-king/, accessed 1 April 2019.

214. Tibbles, 2017, *op cit.,* p. 33.

215. Dean, 2017, *op cit.,* p. 13.

216. Kalu, 2020, *op cit.*

217. Tibbles, 2017, *op cit.,* p. 42.

218. Kalu, 2020, *op cit.*

219. Rowena Mason, 2017, 'May orders Anne Marie Morris MP to be suspended after using the N-word', *The Guardian* newspaper, Tuesday 11 July.

220. Richard Watt quoted by Tibbles, (2017) *op cit.,* p. 34.

221. See the database on Legacies of British Slave-ownership and Nicholas Draper, *The Price of Emancipation* (2010), for how the value of enslaved people as property was calculated as a unit of profit-producing labour.

Youth, artisanal skills and location came into it. For instance, enslaved people in British Guiana were reckoned more value as capital than in St Kitts, because of the greater fertility of the soil in the former.

222. Baker, 2014, *op cit.*

223. Tibbles, *op cit.*, p. 36. This incident is related in Kalu's story.

224. Donington in Hall et al, 2017, *op cit.*, p. 225. And see Joley Baker's discussion of David Crouch, 'The Historian, Lineage and Heraldry 1050-1250,' in *Heraldry, Pageantry and Social Display in Medieval England* ed. by Peter R. Cross and Maurice Hugh Keen (Woodridge: The Boydell Press, 2002), pp. 17-38, quote, p. 17.

225. Kalu, 2020, *op cit.*

226. Kalu, 2020, *op cit.*

227. Byrne, 2014, *op cit.*

228. Livesay, 2018, *op cit.*

229. Kalu, 2020, *op cit.*

230. Hall, Draper and McClelland, 2014, *op cit.*, p. 5.

231. Miranda Kaufmann commissioned a survey of black sitters in historic houses and her research assistant, Jennifer Cooper, compiled a list of these paintings in 2017.

CHAPTER FIVE: MOORLANDS

'[O]ld topographers use…the word "black" to describe the moors – "black desart", "black-a-more" – was n[o] metaphor: black it is, and the place names, too: Blackpits, Blackford, Blackland.' William Atkins, *The Moor. Lives, Landscape, Literature* (2014), p. 28.

Becks Boil in Empire's Cauldron

British moors are the stuff of folklore and legend. For hundreds of years, they have been depicted as untameable and hostile, desolate and uncultivated. They are – in the words of William Atkins – Britain's 'badlands'. Moorland may be mostly green but it is often not pleasant.[1] As *King Lear* illustrates, moors are commonly depicted as wilderness and wasteland and are far-removed from the domesticated landscapes of pastoral poetry.[2] Moors provide the sinister setting for Macbeth's encounter with the three witches,[3] and many writers produce faintly Shakespearean descriptions of them, conjuring up sinister heathland hags with phrases like 'blasted heath' and 'fog's cauldron'.[4] There is a longstanding tradition of linking moors with the devil, particularly Exmoor's Tarr Steps (Satan's sunbathing spot) and Dartmoor's Brent Tor (the film setting for *Jamaica Inn* where the evil vicar roamed).[5] Moors are places where beggars, wayfarers, itinerant workers, disabled soldiers and vagrants of all kinds are to be found in Wordsworth's poetry.

Moors exude danger: famous literary protagonists lose their bearings on them or are sucked into bogs and, as Atkins notes, villains come to sticky ends in three iconic texts: Richard Blackmore's *Lorna Doone* (1869), Arthur Conan Doyle's *The Hound of the Baskervilles* (1902) and Daphne Du Maurier's *Jamaica Inn* (1936). In a parodic replay of such scenes, Atkins recounts a boyhood memory of sinking waist-deep into a morass.[6]

Moors' transcendent quality lives on in twentieth-century works such as John Buchan's *The Thirty-Nine Steps* (1915), *Tarka the Otter* (1927) by Henry Williamson and several of T.F. Powys's short stories, such as 'Lie Thee Down, Oddity!',[7] which contrasts tamed, cultivated grass with the wild moor, between: 'the soft pelt of a smooth lawn, which was indeed like the skin of a tamed beast' and the heath, separated only by a fence, which is 'a wild, fierce, untutored mother'. This contrast pulls Mr Cronch, the gardener, across the railings of Mr Bullman's comfortable Eden into the hazards of the world beyond the garden. Moorland can also be found in cosier form in popular twentieth-century writing, such as the Yorkshire

Dales scenes of James Herriot's veterinary memoirs (1970-1992), and in the form of enlivening wilderness in the more questioning, post-millennial works of landscape writers like Robert Macfarlane.[8]

Oliver Rackham's meticulous account of landscape history, in *The History of the Countryside* (1986), shows just why moors should have attracted such a range of complicated feelings. In the historic past (the Bronze Age) moors showed evidence of extensive human settlement that, over time, fell back into the valleys. Some moors were areas of land that were once extensively wooded, with later historians unsure of how much of that loss was the result of human or natural activity. Rackham shows that the answer was both – but not necessarily together, the spread of acid peat bog occurring without human intervention.[9] Moorland has always been ambivalent terrain, resistant to human intentions.

Although their ecosystems are almost unique to the British isles, moorlands' physical geographies locate them globally; they are composed of geological materials from elsewhere. William Atkins describes them as 'tectonic' because they remind us that the world's continents were once joined.[10] Adam Hopkins observes that some moorlands once lay under tropical oceans before being buried in sediment. Ecologically, too, moors are connected to the world's waterways. Hopkins's book contains a photograph of a man fishing for eels that swim from the Sargasso Sea to the River Parrett which runs through Dorset and Somerset.[11]

Like all discourses about the countryside, attitudes to moorland show distinct historical shifts. Defoe's disgust with moorland is recorded in his 1726 *A Tour Thro' the Whole Isle of Great Britain*. Here, he describes the Peak District as 'a waste and houling wilderness', a 'comfortless, barren and... endless moor'. The observation stems from his perception that uncultivated and probably uncultivatable land cannot be absorbed into a capitalist economy of agrarian improvement.[12] Similarly, Dr Johnson in his *Journal to the Western Isles* (1775) is horrified by the blanket bogs and flat expanses of the Hebrides, which he views as poverty-stricken, desolate and ugly.[13] But by the later 18th century, for the poets Thomas Gray and later for Wordsworth, the moorland landscape exists as an emotional, subjective experience that enters into their being.[14] Moorland and mountain have become powerful symbols of personal freedom, to be treasured precisely because they are untameable. For romantic novelists and poets, moors represent relief from the new industrial cities, as modernity's resistant otherness.

Moors' association with freedom also derives from historical struggles over who owns or belongs to them. As Raymond Williams observes, in the 18th and 19th centuries, poets and writers such as George Crabbe, William Cobbett and John Clare wrote resentfully about landlords' enclosure of common land, some of which was heath and moorland. Whilst moorlands did come under the parliamentary enclosure acts, Ian Whyte's research shows that they were rarely fenced off in the way that lowland commons were because it was too expensive.[15] Even so, the commodification of land, including uplands, is at the heart of Wordsworth's pastoral narrative, 'Michael'. John Clare's poem 'The Mores', is quite specifically about the consequences of enclosure. His landscape is evidently more lowland and heathland than the high acid moorlands of the north, but it nevertheless shares those open qualities that shifted the emotional evaluation of such lands by the turn of the 19th century. 'The Mores' presents uplands as former 'paths to freedom', but now 'A board sticks up to notice "no road here"'.[16] Clare's moorland has never 'felt the rage of blundering plough,

Nor fence of ownership crept in between
To hide the prospect of the following eye
Its only bondage was the circling sky
One mighty flat undwarfed by bush and tree
Spread its faint shadow of immensity...[17]

For the early 19th century radicals campaigning for electoral reform and trade union rights, moorland was frequently the only space where they were able to congregate in the years after the 1819 Peterloo massacre. The government's repressive Six Acts had shut down the right to mass dissent and the local elites prevented working people from meeting in the buildings and squares of towns and cities. These they controlled through the power of the magistracy, backed up by military force. As Katrina Navickas records in *Protest and the Politics of Space and Place, 1789-1848* (2016), moors such as Crooks Moor, Hunslet Moor, Kersal Moor, Skircoat Moor, and many others in Lancashire and Yorkshire, were regular places for mass meetings of the Chartists. In 1846, 30,000 people processed up Blackstone Edge, near Rochdale and not far from Saddleworth Moor (in part the setting of Caryl Phillips's novel *The Lost Child*, discussed later in the chapter), an event commemorated in Ernest Jones's militant hymn, 'But waved the wind on Blackstone height', which ends with the rousing conclusion: 'Loud swelled the nation's battle prayer / Of – death to class monopoly!'. Blackstone Edge was safe territory; it was not suited to charges by sabre-slashing cavalry as St Peter's Fields had been. In some places, the most militant Chartists engaged in quasi-military 'drilling'. This was conducted well out of sight of the authorities. If 'drillers' were caught, transportation to one of Australia's penal colonies was the most regular punishment. Navickas also records that amongst these same radicals, moorland on the edge of industrial towns was also a place for recreation, including picking wild flowers, but that organisers such as Samuel Bamford used this knowledge of moorland footpaths to evade the authorities hunting out illegal meetings.[18]

Our contemporary appreciation of moorlands' open spaces contains traces of this history. The modern 'sense of enclosure' that Robert Macfarlane describes does not merely refer to the experience of urban confinement but also has a political charge which reflects conservationists' present-day struggles against property developments and roads which encroach on our surviving wilds. Along with many of his contemporaries, Macfarlane links moors to relatively recent struggles over the right to roam, as documented in Guy Shrubsole's *Who Owns England?* (2019) and Nick Hayes's *The Book of Trespass* (2020). Like them, Macfarlane is fully aware that ownership of moorland is concentrated in very few hands and, for people like him and others, the communist-led Kinder Scout mass trespass of 1932 has a heroic status in taking on these vested interests. Macfarlane and others, such as Simon Armitage (whose work is discussed below) and William Atkins, all endorse this right, enshrined by the Property Law Act of 1925 and enforced by the 2000 Countryside and Rights of Way Act.[19] Over the last two centuries, then, the desire of some of the romantics to escape from the dehumanising modernity of industrialisation has evolved into present-day concerns with protecting the ecology of moorland, the 'other' of the metropolis.

Moorland has also been at the heart of debates about its ecology and use, particularly by the heavily subsidised grouse-shooting industry, worth £67M a year. Conservationists express concerns about the industry's destruction of endangered raptors and mountain hares through poisoning. Other practices include swaling (burning old heather to encourage the new shoots that grouse feed off) and introducing artificial drainage channels to run water downhill, practices seen as causing moorland to become ecologically monocultural, and to lose the capacity of peat bog to act as a natural sponge to hold water. The result is flooding in neighbouring valleys. These charges are, predictably, denied by the Moorland Association.[20] As this book was going to press, the Scottish government announced measures to control the activities of the Scottish grouse-shooting industry, since it could not be relied on to regulate itself.

The moors discussed in this chapter – Bodmin, Dartmoor, Exmoor, the Pennines, and the Yorkshire Dales – are prized by the heritage and tourist industries. Tourism to these places again reflects the importance of literary cultures to modern-day life. These industries focus predominantly on the Brontë sisters and 'Herriot Country' (the Dales), Henry Williamson (Exmoor), Conan Doyle (Dartmoor) and Daphne Du Maurier (Bodmin), but not the little known work of two romantic period poets Sophie Dixon (?-1855) and Ann Batten Cristall (1769-1848) (both Dartmoor).[21]

By contrast with such packaging, many who venture out on to the moors would like to feel that true moorland represents the opportunity to reconnect with unfettered nature, accompanied by the energising agency of moorland birds. In Emily Brontë's poem 'Loud Without the Wind Was Roaring' (1846), the song of skylarks and linnets reawakens the speaker's love of the wild, 'wintery brae'. In her poem, barren hillsides outweigh the pastoral appeal of 'corn-fields all waving'.[22] As Nancy Armstrong contends, moorland life often acts as a foil to educated, urban sensibilities.[23] Above all, moors have allowed generations of writers to escape city life. Macfarlane in his book *The Wild Places*, writes vividly about moors' ability to console reluctant city-dwellers: 'Living constantly among streets and houses induces a sense of enclosure. The spaces of moors...counteract this' (p. 76). Such spaces, Macfarlane suggests, sustain the intergenerational experience of life in the open wilds.[24]

But beyond the historical shifts in sensibility and literary expression there are constants: any account of writing about moorland inevitably records swings between images of open freedom and images of danger – and sometimes the delight to be had in contemplating such terrors.

Generations of writers have associated moors with 'deep time'.[25] This claim has geological dimensions: bog and peat preserve things. As Atkins observes, peat contains no oxygen, which is why bodies can be dug up intact and age-old vegetation extracted for laboratory analysis.[26] Few writers can resist the symbolic implications of such an ecology. In *The Wild Places*, Macfarlane quotes from Thomas Hardy's novel, *The Return of the Native* (1878), which describes Egdon Heath as land which: 'underneath had been from prehistoric times as unaltered as the stars overhead' (p. 77). Moors do not belong to the realm of the future, and Christina Hardyment argues that writers use moorlands to 'look into history, rather than forward towards progress'.[27] This is often the 'prehistoric' past, as Hardy puts it, rather than the recent past, so moors are often depicted as primordial, with poems, novels and plays presenting them as museums of primitive society. Henry Williamson, the author of *Tarka the Otter*, writes in the same vein: '[t]he heather here was the same heather of a thousand years ago...[t]he leaves and stalks were gone into the peat, which nourished the present plants...There was no age on the moor; there was no change'.[28]

Ted Hughes goes back to such a past in the title poem of *Wodwo* (1967), a collection steeped in moorland images from around Heptonstall, to the mythical wild, half-human creatures of woods and wilderness encountered in the medieval poem, *Sir Gawain and the Green Knight* (c. 1390). Hughes's Wodwo wonders who or what he / she is, 'I seem to have been given the freedom / of this place what am I then?'[29] More recently, the moorland writing of Simon Armitage reflects this literary preoccupation with ancient barbarism. In *Walking Home* (2012), he describes how walking the Pennine Way, '[I saw] small cairns at regular intervals, like relics of a primitive religion of ritualistic practice'.[30] The humour arises from our sense that this is only just an exaggeration.

Part of moors' threat comes from actual histories of Britain's ancient, savage ways. Donna Landry, writing about 19th century Dartmoor, notes that tin miners 'had long been a law unto themselves' because they could not be tried 'by the county courts for any crimes except wounding and murder'. They had their own local 'Stannary court' or tinners' parliament for dealing with other crimes.[31] In historical fact and later fiction, the moors and moorland villages were quite often occupied by people in refuge from the state. A prominent example is the career of the Cragg Vale coiners led by King David Hartley of Heptonstall, leader of a gang who fought a mutually brutal war against government representatives and potential witnesses (1769-70). Eventually Hartley and other gang members were caught, tried and executed. The coiners' exploits are celebrated in fiction and song, including Phyllis Bentley's children's novel, *Gold Pieces* (1968), Peter Kershaw's graphic novel, *The Last Coiner* (2006), and the definitive novel on the subject, Benjamin Myers's *The Gallows Pole* (2018). There is also Chumbawamba's song, 'Snip, Snip, Snip.'[32]

Moors have also been associated with the most socially traumatic kinds of crime.[33] Nowhere is this more clearly expressed than in accounts of the moorland murders of children, now over 60 years ago, but still resonant in public memory. As the work of both Simon Armitage and Caryl Phillips attests, Saddleworth Moor is uniquely tainted by the Moors Murders committed by Ian Brady and Myra Hindley. In an interview with Matthew Sweet, Phillips recalls that: 'any child... brought up in the North of England during the 1960s was very aware of the names Ian Brady and Myra Hindley. It cast a very big shadow over family life... the idea that children were being taken and were being tortured and killed on the moors... [which were] a foreign, strange place' to children brought up in Leeds. To Phillips's contemporaries, moorland was 'a place to be avoided'.[34] In 1983, The Smiths wrote a song about the murders, called 'Suffer Little Children', which names Hindley in a repeated refrain.[35] Such moors are places where people get lost forever. As Armitage wrote: 'We always knew that beyond the immediate horizon, even beyond Saddleworth Moor which Myra Hindley and Ian Brady turned into a macabre children's cemetery, there was a more foreboding and forbidden place... people go there and don't come back.'[36] Aligning *The Lost Child*, discussed further below, with the 'northern hardscrabble' of 1960s writing, Phillips observes that the setting of his novel is far removed from 'Arcadian picnics on sun-kissed grassy river banks with cream cakes and lashings of ginger beer.'[37]

Moors and Blackamoors

Inevitably, moors' established literary associations tend to stress their Englishness and this overshadows the histories of their relationship with travel, empire and migration.

Adam Hopkins observes that the Yorkshire Dales have 'experienced every wave of immigration in the formative centuries after the Romans left.'[38] The Dales make harsh dwelling places and have historically been used to graze livestock. Settling or farming there has generally been a temporary measure for newcomers; the Romans did not linger on them. However, the Celts did, and subsequent generations of settlers left their mark on local place names. The Angles gave the suffix 'ley' to place-names (Ilkley and Shipley) and 'ton' (Grassington, Skipton). The Danes brought 'thorpe' (Ainthorpe; Copmanthorpe) and 'by' (Baldersby; Ormesby), while Norse people gave 'thwaite' (Carlton Husthwaite; Langthwaite); and 'sett' (Appersett).[39] Southern moors are associated with the Normans, who used Dartmoor as a hunting ground. Cistercian monks arrived in 1128 and, appreciating moorlands' remoteness, founded monasteries at their margins, notably Buckfast Abbey (Dartmoor), Cleeve Abbey (Exmoor), Bodmin Priory (Bodmin) and Yorkshire's Rievaulx Abbey.[40]

Similarly, moors' geological naming tells an age-old story of human settlement. The limestone pavements, known as *clints* in Northern English dialect, reveal a Scandinavian influence: *klint* is Danish for 'cliff' and Swedish for 'hill'. The term *escarpment* derives from French, Italian and Old Norse.[41] Such terms, and many more like them, remind us of ancient movements of people in Britain's uplands.[42] A further complication is that, as Rackham reminds us, the word 'moors' describes two distinct terrains: as well as the uplands discussed so far, it is used to describe low-lying wetlands such Sedgemoor in Somerset.[43]

The Black Death, itself a consequence of international trade, had a major impact on patterns of moorland habitation. The fourteenth-century plague emptied population from the relatively fertile but difficult land at moorlands' fringes. Moors became more isolated than ever as people abandoned them to till more fertile soil.[44] In the early 19th century, between 1808 and 1816, Napoleonic soldiers were imprisoned on Dartmoor. As Atkins notes, the prison was then populated with 'Malays, Dutch, Chinese, Poles, Danes, Swedes [and] Australians'. Due to unsanitary conditions, at least 1,478 men died there and were buried in mass graves on the moor.[45]

In general, though, such presences are barely perceptible to moorland visitors today. This is especially true of sites like Haworth which has only recently ceased to be seen as primarily a heritage site of the English novel, but now one that records an immigrant experience. Caryl Phillips's novel *The Lost Child* complicated Haworth's 'English literature' brand by reminding readers that the Brontës were Irish immigrants. In an interview, Phillips told how: 'Patrick Brontë… changed his name [from Brunty]. A classic migrant move'.[46] Patrick Brontë appears as a character in Phillips's *The Lost Child*, in which people laugh at his 'attempts to scour the Irish brogue from his tongue' (p. 99).[47] Phillips is not alone in emphasising this aspect of the Brontë's biography. Sally Wainwright's film *To Walk Invisible: The Brontë Sisters* (2016) lends further weight to Phillips's reassessment of the Haworth legacy by foregrounding the reverend's poor, rural Irish upbringing.[48]

Irish people – of a different social class to Patrick Brontë – were associated with moors in the 19th century. Irish navvies built railways on tracts of the Peak District and Yorkshire Dales. These labourers lived in rough moorland encampments while they constructed the Cromford and High Peak Railway.[49] 83,000 Irish people worked on the Settle to Carlisle line.[50] At Ribbleshead Viaduct there is a memorial to the over one hundred men who lost their lives in its construction. At least another hundred men, women and children from the encampments – prone to outbreaks of smallpox – were buried in the churchyard at Chapel-le-Dale. Well over 2,000 employed men, often with their families, lived in navvy shanty-town settlements at the viaduct's base. Similar evidence of construction villages can be seen at the Scar House reservoir in Nidderdale. Many other Irish migrants were driven out by the Great Famine (1845-52) and arrived on British shores with few possessions. There are records of Irish basket-weavers who sold their wares on Yorkshire's moors at one end of the country, and others who sought work in Bodmin's tin mines, which have an Irish-born patron saint.[51]

An intriguing recent example of moorland settlement is that of Polish World War II refugees who lived at camps on Blackshaw Moor in Staffordshire. Many of these Poles worked in local coalmines, mills and in the building industry. Initially outcasts, their moorland camp was isolated from the local community in nearby Leek; by today, four generations of Poles have lived in the area.[52]

But beyond these mainly European migratory presences, there is the issue of a Black presence. This goes beyond the curious linguistic resemblance between *moors* and *Moors*, the catch-all sixteenth-century term for Black people. Linguistically speaking, the resemblance is coincidental. Before Old English, the two words would not have sounded identical; this came about because of a sound change from the Latin /au/ to the French /o:/. From Middle English onwards, the two words would have sounded the same, or almost the same.[53]

But African 'Moors' have had a historic presence in moorland regions. An African, recorded as 'John Moore – blacke', lived in seventeenth-century Yorkshire. This connection is hinted at in Testament's play *Black Men Walking*, which features three Black friends walking on the Yorkshire moors. They discover the story of 'John Moore. "BLACK"'[54] and the reference to his prior presence allows the characters in the play to 'claim this land', the moors through which they walk, declaring: 'We have always been here!'[55] Meanwhile, advances in genetic research are reshaping popular perceptions of people's origins in the region. In 2009, Turi King linked men's Y chromosome to rare surnames, revealing, in one case, a genetic relationship between an African man who lived in Northern England in the

1780s and 18 'white' Yorkshire men who were unaware of their ancestry.[56] As David Olusoga asserts in *Black and British: A Forgotten History*, many Britons who see themselves as white may have Black ancestry. He provides the example of Cedric Barber, a man who is white in appearance and yet who is the great, great grandson of the Black Georgian, Francis Barber, Dr Johnson's servant and companion.[57]

The linguistic resemblance between moors and Moors resonates with these immigration histories, which may be familiar to locals but is rarely widely known. One example is Staffordshire's Biddulph Moor, home to the Bailey family, known locally as the black men of Biddulph. Legend states that they are descended from Saracens, and the family still believe this today, pointing to their physical traits (dark skin and red hair) and the area's unproven historical connections with the Middle East, (though historical accounts do claim that Saracen stonemasons were brought to the area by a local Crusader named Orm.) The first printed reference to this appears in Sleigh's *A History of the Ancient Parish of Leek* (1862), which states that 'a Knight Crusader…is reputed to have brought over… from the Holy Land a Paynim whom he made Bailiff on his estate, and from whose marriage with an English woman the present race of "Biddle Moor men" is traditionally said to have sprung.'[58] Possible evidence of this Middle-Eastern connection is found at St. Chad's church in Stafford, which has some claimed Islamic architectural features. A local historian has also observed further hints of the connection among the tombs of St. Lawrence's parish church of Biddulph.[59]

The Bailey claim has not gone uncontested. In a crowded meeting of the Biddulph & District Genealogy & Historical Society in 2005, a researcher argued that the Bailey family were probably related to Gypsies and hinted that they might have cultural reasons for preferring their ancestors to be Saracens rather than Romanis. The former provides a more romantic explanation for physical features which have fascinated generations of local commentators. Genetic tests on the Baileys have proved inconclusive.

Neither science nor history can confirm or deny Staffordshire's tenacious Saracen legend. The idea has gripped locals precisely because it is possible, inspiring a self-published tale entitled *The Dark Men of Biddulph Moor* by Bill Siviter. The tale is a fictitious account of the Bailey family's Saracen ancestor during the Third Crusade.[60] It fuses Arthurian legend with elements drawn from the children's book, *The Weirdstone of Brisingamen* (1960) by Alan Garner, which is set in Alderley Edge. In Siviter's story, the Saracen delivers the Holy Grail to a cave-dwelling wizard at Alderley Edge. This intertextual device allows Siviter to place the Middle East at England's geographical and mythical heart. Siviter's Saracen is completely at home in his adopted moorlands. As bailiff, he 'often spends time alone on Biddulph

Moor, hunting wolves and tending the land' (p. 33). When the wizard comments that he is 'far from home', the Saracen replies that it is 'not that far from Biddulph Moor' (p. 27). In this conversation between the 12th and 21st centuries, Garner's wizard politely identifies the Saracen as an interloper and Siviter's Saracen corrects this impression by staking his own claim to the moor and expressing his attachment to it.

Siviter's tale can be read as making parallels between the Crusades and the 21st-century War on Terror, though the book largely resists the 'clash of civilizations' thesis, in which cultural and religious differences are held to be insurmountable.[61] Siviter's Saracen is actually presented as a faithful guardian of English tradition, destined to rise up and defend England alongside other sleeping knights. The book's Islamic characters swear allegiance to Britain. On one level, this is a fantasy of interfaith harmony which ignores the wounds inflicted by international conflict, and assumes a world in which British Muslims are apolitical believers who practise their religion in discreet privacy. More positively, the novel rejects modern-day British Islamophobia by harking back to older, intertwined histories of settlement and mingled bloodlines.

By evoking the legend of sleeping knights, Siviter's story harnesses the romantic power of Arthurian legend to uphold the Bailey claim to Saracen rather than Romani ancestry. The novel's ending reflects the Bailey family's preoccupation with genetics by alluding to their physical appearance in rather old-fashioned terms: 'swarthy men with the surname Bailey' (p. 44). In its last few chapters, the book addresses recent Syrian immigration to Staffordshire and neighbouring Cheshire. A Syrian refugee boy called Shariff discovers that he is distantly related to the original Saracen bailiff. This bloodline becomes a lifeline allowing Siviter to present Shariff's arrival as a form of homecoming. The Saracen magically protects his young relative from racist assailants when Shariff seeks refuge in the local woods and caves. In Siviter's novel, the Biddulph Moor legend has evolved into an alternative, geographically expansive version of the nation's rural story. Whether or not the Bailey legend is true, it is not so outlandish to link moors with Moors.

Moors and sugar wealth
In his famous book *The Making of the English Landscape* (1955), the landscape historian W.G. Hoskins demonstrates that the countryside is not as natural as it appears.[62] His book focuses predominantly on the activities and impact of the Romans, the Danes and Cistercian monks, noted above, but overlooks the connections and impact of slavery-related wealth on rural landscapes.[63] For instance, the demand for copper goods on the African Gold Coast gave the commercial impetus to extractive mining, principally from the Cornish and Devonshire moorlands but also from

Llangyfelach and Flintshire in Wales.[64] There is scope, then, for extending Hoskins's work to consider how empire shaped moorland settings, and the writing that these inspire.

Though current historical work on the countryside's colonial connections has focused predominantly on country houses and their estates, research on a landscape improvement scheme on Exmoor National Park proves an exception. It was the brainchild of Sir John Knight of Wolverley Hall, the son of an industrialist who married the daughter of a West Indies planter, or 'sugar baron', as William Atkins calls him.[65] Knight bought thousands of acres on Exmoor in 1818. He enclosed Exmoor forest with a thirty-mile wall, and planted beech woods with his son, and also built twenty-two miles of metalled road.[66] This infrastructure, part-financed by sugar plantation profits, gave tourists access to Exmoor and allowed them to disseminate images and ideas about it. It is ironic, as Saree Makdisi points out in *Romantic Imperialism* (1998), that novels that celebrate the otherness of 'wild landscapes' were written under the influence of the modernising (capitalist and global) 'improving' processes that Knight was undertaking.[67] Henry Kingsley (*Ravenshoe*, 1851) and R.D. Blackmore (*Lorna Doone*, 1869) both travelled these same roads and produced works of literature that feature Exmoor's improved landscape. Knight's scheme involved damming the River Barle to create Pinkery Pond, the setting for Henry Williamson's conservationist novel, *Tarka The Otter* (1927), beloved by the poet Ted Hughes[68] and the nature writer, Roger Deakin.[69] Knight is remembered for the improvement scheme he financed rather than for his money's origins. Literary celebrations of 'wild' Exmoor rarely acknowledge the West Indies connection or disturb the idea that its landscapes are wholly natural.[70]

But if there is an approach towards imperial connections it sometimes occurs in both seemingly unconscious and historically uninformed ways. For Simon Armitage on the Yorkshire moors, 'Cross Fell is a truly terrible place… some abhorrent strain of that particular fell species, the Caliban version, illegitimate and monstrous'.[71] Armitage's phrase points to how writing about moors frequently acquires an imperial flavour. It is there in the colonial turn of phrase used by W.G. Hoskins when he writes about the futility of planting things on moorlands, stating that: 'the frontier of cultivation was… pushed higher up the hillsides' during the thirteenth century.[72] 'Cultivation' readily becomes 'civilization'. In fact, many early descriptions of moorlands are racialised. In 1607, the topographer William Camden borrows the term *Blackamoor* from the ornithologist Thomas Hudson Nelson to describe uplands as 'black Moorish land'.[73] It is an image that connects to Leo Mellor's description of wildernesses as 'unknowable' places of exile from God, home to beasts and demons,[74] like the places of banishment of Old Testament prophets and scapegoats, or the narrative of

Christ's sojourn in the wilderness before the crucifixion. It is easy to see how such images of moorland's demonic blackness morph into the blackness of the 'savage'. This is consistent with a wider trait of 19th-century writing, which, as Ian Ward observes, frequently uses colonial analogies to explore 'humanity in its starkest, most troubling form'.[75] Moors, as Simon Armitage writes, are the Caliban of the English landscape.

In Walter Scott's *Waverley* (1814), as Saree Makdisi points out, the Highland landscape is seen as wilderness and the highlanders are compared to the 'natives of Africa and America, India and the Orient'.[76] Even when moors are not stalked by 'savages', they are overlaid with colonial landscapes and represented in a transrural, transglobal way.[77] In *The Thirty-Nine Steps* (1915), the protagonist's boyhood in colonial South Africa makes him compare 'a little place… in the heart of the bog' with 'one of those forgotten little stations in the Karoo' (p. 32).[78] It is his 'veldcraft' skills, acquired in the colony, that allow Richard Hannay to outwit his ruthless pursuers (p. 24). Transrural representations are also found in non-fiction. Atkins notes in his book, *Moorland*, how the Reverend R.S. Hawker wrote of Fowey Moor, that its 'vast and uncultured surface… is suggestive of the bleak steppes of Tartary or the far wilds of Australia'.[79]

In moorland mythology, savagery is presented as both internal and external to constructions of British culture. Nancy Armstrong links Emily Brontë's novel *Wuthering Heights* to the work of Victorian folklorists and photographers who rendered rural Britons as 'quaint and primitive' and tended to view peasant cultures 'nostalgically'. Armstrong and Ian Krielcamp both argue that Emily Brontë's character Mr Lockwood views the inhabitants of the Heights as living remnants of Britain's past.[80] This attitude is evident in the anthropological style of Lockwood's narrative. When he finds Catherine's diary, he tries to 'decypher her faded hieroglyphics' (p. 20), an image that connects Catherine's handwriting with ancient Egypt. Lockwood identifies her as a source of fascination, even while he consigns her to the distant past by suggesting that she – and her society – are foreign to civilized English life. Also in anthropological mode, he explains to readers that 'Wuthering' is 'a provincial adjective' for houses in exposed locations (p. 4). This is not to suggest that Brontë's novel endorses Lockwood's view. Armstrong argues convincingly that the novel parodies Lockwood's self-appointed role as an educated interpreter of Yorkshire's 'arcane' customs.[81]

Having established that Yorkshire's moorland people – to Mr Lockwood at least – exhibit savagery, the critic Nancy Armstrong places her analysis squarely in the realm of postcolonial criticism. She connects Victorians' 'internal colonialism'[82] with the British empire and argues: 'this class of educated people were… beginning to reclassify… the urban poor and the peoples of Asia and Africa in much the same way.'[83] She observes that

Britain's 'primitive' rural dwellers were often depicted as dark-skinned people whose physical appearance contrasted with that of their city-dwelling counterparts.[84] Brontë creates Heathcliff as a kind of Shakespearean Caliban, because people of the moors have long been represented as extrinsic to Englishness. It is in *this* sense that moors are associated with Blackamoors, in the broadest, sixteenth-century sense of the word. Heathcliff's uncertain parentage reactivates the traditional connection between those who dwell at Britain's rural fringes, and those who live at the edge of empire.

Traces of this colonial connection remain in contemporary writing. In Atkins's *The Moor*, the colour black dominates the descriptive palette. He describes a peat cutting as having a 'black face' (p. 155), while Exmoor bogs are 'black as death' (p. 27). He depicts 'dark heather, with its dark roots, and beneath the dark roots the dark earth' (p. 150) and writes that '[e]ven the footpath puddles were black' (p. 150). Like Hoskins' colonially-freighted sense of cultivation's retreating 'frontier',[85] Atkins states that 'the moors had advanced from the margins to the centre' (p. 116) and describes how his walk leads 'from cultivation to the barbarism of the moors' (p. 128). The practice of juxtaposing ideas of urban civility and moorland barbarity[86] is found in Charlotte Brontë's introduction to *Wuthering Heights* where she compares the novel to a giant chiselled out of a moorland crag. It is 'savage, swart, sinister'.[87] Here again, Charlotte Brontë hints at the colonial connotations of *Wuthering Heights*. There is a scene when Nelly calls Catherine and Heathcliff 'rude as savages' (p. 46), and describes Cathy as 'a hatless little savage' (p. 53). In this light, the name *Yorkshire Dales* becomes oxymoronic: symbolising the foreign and the indigenous at the same time. When Nelly says, 'We don't in general take to foreigners here' (p. 46), she is not simply referring to people from another town, but also suggesting that educated, urban Britons are alien to the world in which she lives. Her words suggest that this brutal moorland society is both separate and locked into itself, yet part of Britain's ancient core. Lockwood, on the other hand, takes the locals' inward-looking sensibility as further evidence of *their* foreignness, their remote otherness from the civilized, reading public.

Moors are fascinating psychological landscapes. From the 18th-century to the present, they have been the focus for all sorts of anxieties about modernity: freedom and confinement, civility and barbarity, indigeneity and foreignness, empire and immigration. As contemporary cultural production suggests, moors provide irresistible settings for writers and filmmakers who wish to complicate or trouble established perceptions of them. Consequently, moorlands have become the stage for some significant challenges to received versions of England's rural past.

In the rest of this chapter, I focus on more recent English cultural production as it has become increasingly informed by historical work on moorlands' connection to slave-produced wealth and newly arrived peoples: Andrea Arnold's film version of *Wuthering Heights* (2011), Caryl Phillips's novel *The Lost Child* (2014), Bernardine Evaristo's short story 'Yoruba Man Walking' (2015), Jade Montserrat's film *Burial* (2015) and Stephen Thompson's drama series, *Jericho* (2016). The British empire meets the anti-pastoral in these works, which variously challenge and revise established perceptions of moorland.

The Black Heathcliff

Haworth is at the epicentre of "Brontë country". Jonathan Rutherford observes that the village has been constructed as 'a caricature of olde England',[88] epitomizing the ways in which 'heritage... commodif[ies] the past and... denies' social change.[89] Academic work has, by contrast, drawn attention to some underexposed aspects of such changes. James Procter reminds us that Bradford was once the 'worsted textile capital of the world', receiving immigrants from both Central and Eastern Europe.[90] Such presences register in the Yorkshire writer J.B. Priestley's *English Journey* (1933), which describes how: a 'dash of the Rhine and the Oder found its way into...t'mucky beck. Bradford was determinedly Yorkshire and provincial, yet some of its suburbs reached as far as Frankfurt and Leipzig'.[91] In addition to the Brontës themselves, Rutherford also points out that Haworth's surrounding urban developments have been shaped by immigration. Nearby Daubhill was home to Polish and Irish migrants, later joined by people from South Asia, whose mosque now stands alongside the old Catholic church.[92]

Although Haworth lies near the city of Bradford, it has long been constructed as remote from British cosmopolitanism. Making no mention of her sister's Irish heritage, Charlotte Brontë constructs Emily as 'a native... of the moors' in her introduction to *Wuthering Heights*, representing the Brontës as cultural insiders.[93] In this respect, Charlotte Brontë echoes Nelly's words: 'We don't in general take much to foreigners here' (p. 46).

James Procter argues that the historical tendency to present the region as culturally isolated was re-inscribed during the Rushdie Affair, when in 1989 a group of Muslim Mirpuri men burned a copy of *The Satanic Verses* on Bradford's streets. As Procter observes, this image was screened around the world. An international incident, the Rushdie Affair, gave the local tourism industry a marketing headache. The response, Procter argues, was for Bradford 'to reinvent itself [...as a] distilled village landscape built upon the racialised rhetoric of the pastoral.'[94] One might query the term 'pastoral', but his point stands, insofar as he demonstrates that, in the 1990s, local tourist advertising appealed to the neighbouring countryside's presumed whiteness. Procter examines a tourist poster that substitutes Bradford's streets with images of the scenery around Haworth, thereby presenting Yorkshire as far-removed from the national story of immigration.[95] Procter also examines a

book by a local politician called Tom Clinton, and suggests that Clinton's
Laugh? I Nearly Went to Bradford (1991) executes a similar manoeuvre, drawing
on established moorland iconography to create a 'purified, provincial setting'
featuring: '"wild" weather, "craggy" landscape, "a dry stone wall" […and] "a
curlew"'.[96] Both the poster and the book evoke 'an older, whiter Bradford'
which 'actively forg[ets]' local Muslims.[97]

This amnesia is challenged by Daniel Wolfe's film, *Catch Me Daddy*
(2013), set in 'Brontë country'. Its protagonists are Aaron and Leila, lovers
trying to escape from the racially intolerant towns and villages nearby. As
they hide in a caravan on the moors, Leila's male relatives drive through the
Yorkshire Dales in search of her. They are tailed by two white hitmen,
commissioned by the family to kill Aaron and return Leila to her father for
punishment. The film's preoccupation with barbarity is made clear from
the outset. Ted Hughes's poem 'Heptonstall Old Church' is recited over
shots of the Dales in the film's opening sequence. The poem, which
portrays Heptonstall church as a bird perched at the edge of the wilderness,
and whose death symbolises the church's decline, communicates Hughes's
sense that moors exude a primordial life force that resists domestication. In
the poem, Christianity's influence recedes when the moors repel its
advance because their ancient savagery precedes and succeeds it, mocking
the idea you can 'put a harness on the moors':

A great bird landed here.
Its song drew men out of rock
Living men out of bog and heather.[98]

The opening scenes of *Catch Me Daddy* focus on a mosque, drawing Islam
into a connection with Hughes's vision. In spirit, if not by birth, the angry
Muslim men in Wolfe's film are akin to Hughes's moorland dwellers,
described in his poem as '[l]iving men' who emerge from the vegetation like
Neanderthals. The film presents the mosque as an integral feature of
moorland life, with uncivilized men occupying uncivilized terrain. The
film's fascination with Muslim brutality is in many ways analogous to
Victorian folkloric fascination with the primitive. In *Catch Me Daddy*, furious
Muslims and paid hitmen epitomize a degree of pathological violence which
is supposedly alien to English civilization. They are modern incarnations of
the insular, ancient moorland society at the nation's fringes.

In expanding the global geographies of moorland space, something
similar is going on in Stephen Thompson's ITV drama series, *Jericho*
(2016), which is set on a navvy encampment on the Yorkshire moors in the
1870s.[99] *Jericho* opens up the region's global geographies, embodied in the
figure of Ralph Coates, an African-American foreman who runs the navvy
encampment. Based on a real-life person, Coates has thirty years' experience of building railways. Cinematically, the figure of Coates resonates
with that of Solomon Northup in *Twelve Years A Slave* (2013) by the Black

British film director Steve McQueen. Like Northup on his journey from Louisiana to NewYork, Coates is mistaken for a runaway slave and has had to flee his oppressors in the USA. *Jericho* joins a growing constellation of productions focused on Britain's 18th and 19th-century Black presence, including *Belle* (2013), discussed in earlier chapters. Like *Belle*, *Jericho* complicates the portrayal of Black people's social status in Britain during this period, presenting such figures in more nuanced ways. Like Dido Belle, Coates is a relatively autonomous character whose professional experience and personal tenacity allow him to occupy a position of some authority. *Jericho* also shows a geographically dispersed picture of the historical Black presence in a wide array of settings: cotton mills, shops, mines, moorland and ports.

Jericho's screenwriter, Thompson, compared the series to the Hollywood Western, *Shane* (1958), which featured settlers in frontier towns.[100] Thompson drew on Yorkshire's history of itinerant navvies and expanded the settler genre's geographical reach. Clarke Peters, the actor who plays Coates, saw English moorland as under-utilized creative territory that could enrich the Western genre: 'As you see in *Jericho*, you do have the land for it, the vastness… You have gorgeous, gorgeous landscapes in England, they are just not as exploited as America did on their films.' Peters also emphasises *Jericho*'s genuine historical foundations: 'If you… put a frontier town or pioneer town, you have got exactly the same thing [as a Western] and you do have a history for it here.'[101] Here, Peters refers to the historical fact of the encampment and the figure of Ralph Coates.[102] The series also included two other Black characters who work in the Blackwood household. Their inclusion is not merely an inventive contemporary twist on moorland life, but is based on a clear historical rationale for Black servants' presence on the moor. The viaduct is funded by Charles Blackwood, whose family wealth comes from Caribbean sugar plantations. The very name Blackwood suggests a Caribbean connection, indicating both the origins of the family's wealth in slave labour and alluding to Harewood House, which has the most notorious slavery connections of any stately home in Yorkshire.[103] Characters in *Jericho* repeatedly refer to the Blackwoods' sugar money. In this way, *Jericho* foregrounds the region's colonial connections and offers a geographically devolved, Yorkshire-based portrayal of Black England.

But both *Catch Me Daddy* and *Jericho* were striking exceptions to the norm. As Rutherford and Procter argue, Haworth and Yorkshire are more generally portrayed as white, English spaces, particularly as they have been experienced by Black visitors. A poem by the Grenadian poet Merle Collins, 'Visiting Yorkshire – Again' (1992), describes her uncomfortable literary pilgrimage to the Brontë parsonage:

> …people stared at a

> Black
> woman
> walking the cobbled streets.[104]

The separate verse lines for 'Black' and 'woman' demonstrate the speaker's consciousness that her skin-colour is seen before anything else. Disturbed by 'the glances, the stares', her defence strategy is to invoke her father's memory of fighting for Britain in World War II. Her retreat to a relatively recent period of history illustrates how thoroughly Yorkshire's older global connections have been erased.

Perhaps inevitably, Emily Brontë's *Wuthering Heights* has been the text through which much traffic, critical and creative, has passed; perhaps equally inevitably much of the focus has been on the character of Heathcliff and whether he is Black. Much of this discussion centres on the Dales' relationship to Liverpool, a world centre for slave-trading during the period in which the novel is set. Discussion also focuses on the way in which Heathcliff is portrayed – his representation conforming to moorlands' traditional association with uncivilized regions at home and abroad. Heathcliff is quintessentially uncivilized. As Cameron Dodworth observes, in *Wuthering Heights* Heathcliff is said to have 'howled, not like a man, but like a savage beast'.[105] His foreignness is both internal to the moors and external with respect to his presumed origins, though in the novel it is the former that is explicit, the latter a matter for conjecture. Elizabeth Gaskell called the local people a 'race' apart[106] and the Victorian reviewer G.W. Peck suggested that the novel 'shows boldly the dark side of our depraved nature'.[107] Lockwood's view that moorland people are ignorant rustics is shown to be apiece with his frequent cultural blunders and errors of interpretation.[108] Nonetheless, Heathcliff is clearly seen as peripheral to civilized society.

Historicised readings of the novel suggest that Heathcliff's foreignness is not merely internal to the moors. The novel is set in 1801, by which time Liverpool had overtaken cities such as Bristol to become Britain's slave-trading capital. By then these activities were visible in the 'busts of blackamoors and elephants, emblematical of the African trade' in the city's town hall, as the 1887 letters of historian Gomer Williams recorded.[109] Humphrey Gawthrop, writing about the Brontës, notes that: 'Wilberforce's colleague, Thomas Clarkson… saw in the windows of a Liverpool shop leg-shackles, hand-cuffs, thumb-screws, and mouth-openers for force-feeding used on board the slavers.'[110] The historian Laurence Westgaph has amassed evidence of a significant and continuous historical Black presence in Liverpool.

If Heathcliff was not Black (and we have to accept that Emily Brontë chose to be unspecific about his past or his ethnicity), historians have demonstrated that he very easily might have been. So while many critics are asking: 'Is he Black?', the wealth of new historical research on Yorkshire's

Black histories makes it more pertinent to ask: 'Why was he *not* depicted as Black until 2012?'[111] After all, Latin American television adaptations of *Wuthering Heights* – entitled *Cumbres Borrascosas* – were portraying Heathcliff as the mixed-race son of Mr Earnshaw as early as the late 1970s.[112] The 1976 Venezuelan *Cumbres Borrascosas* shows Mr Earnshaw bringing home a *mestizo* boy; his wife berates him for sleeping with a Black woman. Slavery's geographic proximity to Venezuela (just across the Main from Trinidad) may have made Heathcliff's blackness self-evident, an act of cultural translation likely to have made perfect sense to Latin American audiences. Maryse Condé's Caribbean homage to Brontë's novel, *Windward Heights* (1995), presents Heathcliff (Razye in her novel) in the following way: 'His skin was too black, that shiny black they call Ashanti, and his hair hung in curls like those of an Indian half-caste, the Bata-Zindien' (p. 8). This description of a highly mixed heritage is not only in keeping with the ethnic diversity of the Caribbean, but also with the spirit of the novel, since Brontë's Heathcliff is of uncertain ethnic origin. It is this uncertainty that V.S. Naipaul picks on in his intertextual references to *Wuthering Heights* in his novel *Guerrillas* (1975). Naipaul's murderous and self-destructive character, Jimmy Ahmed, a man of many ethnicities, is based upon the real-life figure of Michael De Freitas, a mixed-race Caribbean man with a previous career as a pimp and agent for an infamous rack-renting landlord who preyed on Black people. De Freitas reinvented himself as the very black Michael X. His fictional counterpart, Jimmy Ahmed, 'runs' a hopelessly incompetent agricultural commune that he has named Thrushcross Grange, after the house in *Wuthering Heights*. In Naipaul's version of the *Wuthering Heights* narrative, his 'Cathy' – Jane in the novel – is murdered at the behest of his Heathcliff, Ahmed, on the commune, a drought-stricken place where tomatoes wither on the vine. Ahmed is portrayed by the Brahmin Indian-Trinidadian novelist as a man utterly confused about his sexuality and his love-hate relationship to whiteness, precisely because, like Heathcliff, knowledge of his true identity has been stolen.[113]

What was obvious to Caribbean novelists like Condé and Naipaul was not so obvious to generations of Anglophone literary critics who have overlooked the influence of the transatlantic slavery economy on Yorkshire and in particular its moorlands. Terry Eagleton states that 'Heathcliff disturbs the Heights because he... has no defined place within its... economic system', a statement which flies in the face of evidence of the region's umbilical links to the British Atlantic world.[114] It was left to Caryl Phillips's recent novel *The Lost Child* (and Phillips undoubtedly knows V.S. Naipaul's fiction well) to locate what Cassandra Phybus calls 'the submerged social history at the heart of [*Wuthering Heights*,] one of England's most famous novels',[115] in Yorkshire territory itself.

Phillips, interviewed in Adam Low's documentary *A Regular Black* (2009), points out that when gentlemen like Mr Earnshaw went to Liverpool on business, such business predominantly concerned imports of sugar, tobacco, coffee, and slaving.[116] Low's documentary also highlights the significance of Heathcliff's name; most enslaved people had only one name, which served as forename and surname. As the documentary explores, historians and local researchers have made discoveries about the region's slavery connections. Some critics argue, for instance, that *Wuthering Heights* depicts the Yorkshire Dales rather than the moors close to Haworth, noting that the Brontë sisters' school was just a few miles from the Dentdale home of a notorious family called the Sills who, it is argued, were the models for the Earnshaw family. The Sills family worked enslaved Africans on the grounds of their Yorkshire estate, and the Sills' barn in Dentdale was modelled on the sugar factory in Providence, their West Indies plantation.[117] The Sills family history is recounted in Howard Howitt's *The Rural Life of England* (1838), which Emily Brontë had read. Howitt's book recounts a Sills family story which has striking resonances with the plot of *Wuthering Heights*: the mistreated orphan boy Richard Sutton, who was probably Black, falls in love with the daughter of the house, never marrying her but eventually inheriting the property.[118]

Christopher Heywood has also detailed the relationship between *Wuthering Heights* and the area's hidden slavery history. He discovered that Emily Brontë supplemented her reading of Howitt's *The Rural Life of England* with an array of 'story materials from the Dales around Cowan Bridge', where she attended school.[119] Heywood believes that the character of Hindley is an amalgam of the three Sills brothers from Dent, who all died prematurely and left their sister Ann (with whom Richard Sutton was in love) to inherit the family's Jamaican estates. He argues that Cathy is based on the sister, Ann Sill, a view shared by other local historians.[120] The Legacies of British Slave Ownership database confirms that the Sills family owned a large number of enslaved people on Jamaican estates. The database shows that Ann Sill was posthumously compensated with £3,783 in 1836 for the loss of 174 enslaved people from the family's Providence Estate.[121]

Heywood further details the ways in which the Dales were shaped by the 'plantation economy', with well-known local families making their money from the slave-trade and goods produced by enslaved people, and also lobbying Parliament against abolition. His work concentrates on the Sills and the Masons, who – he argues – 'appear in *Jane Eyre* as the Masons and the Rochesters, and in *Wuthering Heights* as the Lintons and the Earnshaws'.[121] He also examines Branwell Brontë's unfinished novel, *And The Weary Are At Rest*, which features a dark-skinned, slave-owning banker based on a well-known local figure called John Bolton, of Storrs Hall. Branwell Brontë's novel contributes to Heywood's sense of the Dales' close links with slavery and its related business activities. A subplot of Branwell Brontë's novel focuses on people who counsel against slavery but actually profit from the trade, like the real-life John Bolton.[122]

All the evidence suggests that the region's slavery connections were readily apparent to the Brontë family. The Cowan Bridge school was situated opposite Leck Hall, which was bought and improved with money earned by the Welch family's business in slaveships.[123] Charlotte was governess to children whose relatives (the Staniforths) were slavers connected to Storrs Hall, the home of John Bolton.[124] Patrick Brontë knew William Wilberforce, who paid for him to attend St. John's College in Cambridge.[125] Wilberforce, a Yorkshire MP who visited the area frequently, was also patron of the Brontë sisters' school at Cowan Bridge. It is not known if Patrick Brontë attended Wilberforce's Keighley talk in 1827, but the family had firm abolitionist sympathies and Patrick had read Wilberforce's *Letter on the Abolition of the Slave Trade Addressed to the Freeholders and other Inhabitants of Yorkshire* (1807).[126] Branwell went to Liverpool and returned with a drawing of two Black boxers, one of them in chains.[127] Furthermore, the region's Black presence is also attested to by 19th-century photographs, which show Black village children in the streets.[128]

Gawthrop observes that both *Wuthering Heights* and *Jane Eyre* display anxieties about slavery. He argues: 'Even where a direct West Indian or African connection is absent, slavery-related themes such as brutality, exploitation and deprivation are present... [b]oth novels... impeach systems that allowed...male domination of female, and adult domination of the child.'[129] Several commentators argue that embedded in *Wuthering Heights* is a critique of slavery as a moral failing. Maria-Lisa Von Sneidern notes that at the time the novel is set, '[a]lthough slavery put sugar in their tea, coffee in their cups, cotton on their backs and pounds sterling in their bank accounts, the institution made English blood run cold.'[130] She connects this anxiety with nationally significant events which parallel the plot of *Wuthering Heights*: 'According to C.P. Sanger's chronology of *Wuthering Heights*, Mr Earnshaw's walk to Liverpool occurs at the 'beginning of harvest' in 1771, [on] the eve of the Somerset case and the Mansfield decision.'[131] At that hearing, it was argued that slavery 'corrupts the morals of the master, by freeing him from those restraints... so necessary for control [sic] of the human passions'.[132] Von Sneidern sees *Wuthering Heights* as forensically exploring the ways in which slavery corrupted both slave-owners and the enslaved. She suggests that the novel shows 'the tyranny and oppression that has twisted Heathcliff and [later...] threatens' other characters such as Hareton.[133] Given the novel's ambivalence towards the mainstream values of Lockwood and Nelly, the critic Donna K. Reid seems justified in arguing that the novel on some level questions the nature of 'civilization itself.'[134]

While close examination of the novel does not provide any definitive evidence that Heathcliff was Black, he is repeatedly referred to as 'it' and made to sleep outside the house.[135] Phybus also observes that Mr Earnshaw says that 'he "inquired for its owner" and found nobody who "knew to whom it belonged"'. Mr Linton', she suggests, 'instantly recognises the boy as chattel.'[136] A number of critics have observed that, in the novel, Nelly says Heathcliff is not 'a regular black'.[137] Quoting frequently from *Wuthering Heights*, Von Sneidern provides a succinct summary of the literary evidence gathered by critics:

> Heathcliff's racial otherness cannot be a matter of dispute; Brontë makes that explicit. From the first and frequently thereafter he is termed a 'gypsy'; Mr Linton recognises him as 'that... little Lascar, or an American or Spanish castaway'; Nelly encourages Heathcliff to 'frame high notions of [his] birth' because his father might have been the 'Emperor of China' and his mother 'an Indian queen'. Heathcliff may not be a "regular black", and Nelly cannot 'image some fit parentage' for 'the dark little thing', but his bloodline is unambiguously tainted by colour. In effect, he is an irregular black, a mongrel, a source of great anxiety for the mid-19th-century Victorian.[138]

The terms *gypsy* and *lascar* have proved something of a red herring. As Cassandra Phybus observes, the term *gypsy* was then used generically to denote a 'dark complexion' or foreign-seeming face. *Lascar* was also a general description for foreign sailors.[139] Nelly's sense of his mixed origins – possibly Chinese, possibly Indian – also suggest that Phybus is right to suppose that 'Nelly Dean is wiser in the matter of Heathcliff's racial identity than her use of the term gypsy implies'.[140] Phybus also notes that, as a boy, Heathcliff is said to speak 'some gibberish that no one could understand'.[141] Seeming to work against this evidence, however, Heathcliff turns 'breathless and white' when struck by Hindley (p. 39), although the reference to blanching is not conclusive evidence either, since at the least he is of mixed race, an amalgam of everything foreign. Edward Said rightly explains such confusion as reflecting widespread ignorance about 'foreign' people's cultural and geographical origins and demonstrating an imprecise sense of Britain's colonial networks.[142] Whatever Heathcliff's origins, the speaker of Merle Collins's poem 'Visiting Yorkshire – Again' might have felt that her sense of exclusion was a double one, being both deeply rooted in the novel and its times, as well as in the present.

Emily Brontë's novel was published in 1847. She wrote it in the shadow of international political events that alarmed the British public. In particular this included the 1830-31 Baptist wars in Jamaica led by Deacon Sam Sharpe, when enslaved Creole Africans sustained a quasi-military revolt lasting for several months.[143] Enslaved Africans knew that the British parliament was debating emancipation and some believed that the slaveowners in Jamaica were denying them freedom granted by the British monarch. These events were widely reported in Britain after hundreds of Africans were executed and white Jamaica engaged in a brutal campaign of intimidation against the white Baptist missionaries who they believed, wrongly, had supported the uprising. Emily Brontë was thirteen at the time, had access to all the reading matter in the house, and was just embarking with her sister, Anne, on the series of stories and poems about Gondal, an imaginary island in the North Pacific, and its neighbour, a southern island with a more tropical climate. There were civil wars and assassinations. These may or may not have been echoes of the news from Jamaica.

In the 1830s and up to the 1840s there were the debates around compensation for slave owners; these were reported in Yorkshire newspapers such as *The Sheffield Gazette* and the *Hull Advertiser*.[144] As with the educated readership of Austen's *Mansfield Park*, many of Brontë's readers would have known about the impact of emancipation and the decline of the plantation economy. Heathcliff's violent actions clearly parallel cases of anti-colonial resistance, and Eagleton's phrase describing Heathcliff's 'insurrectionary energy' is, albeit unconsciously, well chosen.[145] The novel's physical and symbolic geography invites such readings. Von Sneidern believes that Thrushcross Grange resembles a plantation estate, divided from the Heights as though – quoting from the novel – by 'the Atlantic'.[146] As she suggestively observes, '[a]s a slave, Heathcliff is… capable of vicious rebellion. Only Cathy's will… prevents him from tearing Hindley's "heart out" and drinking "his blood".'[147] This was a stereotyped feature of negrophobic reportage that arose in the work of racist historians such as Edward Long with reference to what was known as Tacky's War (1760) and the Haitian revolution (1791-1804).[148] Von Sneidern also argues that Heathcliff's mind is gradually decolonised during the novel: '[w]here once Heathcliff wished he "had light hair and fair skin"… he is [later…] repulsed by…those features' and even stares at Isabella 'as one might do at a… centipede from the Indies'.[149] Directed as it is at whiteness, the prejudiced and racialised gaze of colonialists is here reversed. At the very least, the novel's geographical imaginary – its reference to the Atlantic and the Indies – creates resonant colonial parallels. Phybus endorses this view. She asserts that the fear of enslaved people's vengeance is 'captured in the image of Hindley and Isabella locking the door against Heathcliff, with his black countenance and "sharp cannibal teeth"'.[150]

In 2011, Andrea Arnold released her film of *Wuthering Heights*, in which the role of the boy and adult Heathcliff are played by Black actors. In Arnold's film the Yorkshire Dales provide the backdrop for Hindley's racist assaults on the Black Heathcliff. Hindley calls Heathcliff a 'Nigger' and makes him sleep with livestock. When he whips Heathcliff, the scars resemble those Heathcliff received as an enslaved boy.

The film was well-received. Nonetheless, reviewers found it hard to countenance any genuine connection between British moorland and Black experience. Overwhelmingly, they failed to consider the possibility that

Arnold's Black Heathcliff might be historically justified. Instead, Arnold was widely praised for reinvigorating Brontë's work with an inventive new take on racism for multicultural metropolitan audiences. Leslie Felperin praised Arnold's 'boldness' in converting Brontë's Gypsy Heathcliff into the figure of an enslaved person.[151] Val Kermode declared that Arnold's cultural manoeuvre heightens the novel's 'contemporary resonance', not its transatlantic resonance.[152] Writing in *The Guardian*, Philip French stated that Brontë's Heathcliff is described as 'black-eyed with a dark complexion and possibly of gypsy stock', *whereas* Arnold's film depicts him as 'black, and scorned as a "nigger"'.[153] In his review, French alludes to Francis Barber, Samuel Johnson's Black servant, whose journey from Jamaican slavery to London's literary world was researched by Michael Bundock, but then French's discussion of Black history fizzles out.[154] For French, Arnold's vision of a Black Heathcliff makes pleasing use of artistic licence, but nothing more, and he concludes that this depiction is rather 'a puzzle'. Robbie Collins writes that Arnold's film presents Heathcliff as 'a black child with slave markings on his back *instead of* Brontë's "gypsy-like… aspect"'.[155] Jenny McCartney's review for *Seven Magazine* makes no reference to British Atlantic world history but instead attributes the choice of a Black actor to Arnold's desire to emphasise his physical difference from the Earnshaw family.[156] In one respect, she is correct. Arnold does not herself challenge the idea that Heathcliff is not really Black. Instead she alludes to 'five or six clear descriptions of him in the novel' as a lascar, as 'Chinese-Indian' and as a Gypsy. Without referring to Yorkshire's slavery connections, she simply says, 'I wanted to honour… his difference'.[157] In Arnold's film interpretation, then, Heathcliff's blackness is intended as a synonym for 'otherness'.

By contrast, Caryl Phillips's novel *The Lost Child* (2015) makes the historical location of early 19th century Black lives impossible to duck. The historian Ray Costello observes that orphaned Black children were 'a common sight' in late-18th and early-19th-century Liverpool. One such child was found by William Lindsay Windus, who painted him as 'The Black Boy' three years before *Wuthering Heights* was published. As Costello points out, scores of Britons are today unaware of their family origins in slavery. He argues that today's lost children often 'pass' as white and are ignorant of their 'ancestral lines'.[158]

As its title suggests, *The Lost Child* shares a theme of parental abandonment with Emily Brontë's *Wuthering Heights* and it employs moorland imagery to engage critically with heritage tourism and with the region's histories of immigration and slave-produced wealth. As noted above, in the references to the Moors murders of the 1960s, inhospitable moorland is symbolically apt for exploring the lives of lost and neglected children, an idea captured by the term 'unmoored' that Phillips used in an interview to

suggest that moorland is an apt metaphor for the psychological state of
those who are historically and genealogically dispossessed.[159] Here, the
novel's theme of orphaned children assumes a larger dimension, hinting at
the idea of unclaimed heritage by creating parallels between Emily Brontë's
and his own version of Heathcliff in the 19th century and two abandoned
brothers in the twentieth.

As J.M. Coetzee observed, Phillips's fiction 'remembers what the West
would like to forget',[160] exploiting moorland's traditional association with
crime to explore an unacknowledged colonial offence: profiting from
slavery in England's north-west. Phillips's novel achieves this by establishing parallels between the real-life murders on Saddleworth Moor and the
murder on those moors of the fictional boy, Tommy. These worlds –
historical and contemporary, actual and fictive – are joined by the device of
the name Hindley: Hindley Earnshaw in Brontë's *Wuthering Heights* and the
moors murderer, Myra Hindley. Informed by insights into Black British
history, *The Lost Child* explores the colonial resonance of these two acts of
violence – the murders and slavery – placing the fictional body of Tommy
beside the real bodies of murdered children. In interviews about the book,
Phillips frequently raised the topic of the 1960s moors murders, describing
them as an 'unspeakably malevolent episode'.[161] By linking the real and
fictional murders and *The Lost Child* to *Wuthering Heights* (and its connection to the region's involvement in the plantation economy of the West
Indies), *The Lost Child* compares the wickedness of Brady and Hindley to
the wickedness of Yorkshire's plantocracy.

In *The Lost Child*, Tommy's brother Ben drives on to the moors some
years after his brother's death. He senses his brother's uncanny presence
there: 'I could feel the moors closing in on me, and for the first time in ages
I began to feel close to my brother' (p. 189). Echoing Heathcliff's shout,
'"Cathy, do come!"' (p. 28), Ben shouts '"Tommy!... Tommy!"' (p. 189).
This grief-stricken cry unites novels, centuries and histories, and fits
Macfarlane's description of the eerie, 'traumatised pastoral' of much
contemporary writing about the countryside.[162] Yet Ben's lonely sojourn
on the moor is also one of a series of homecomings in the novel, homecomings that stake historically-informed new claims to the landscape. Phillips's
Heathcliff embodies the region's slavery connection. His first walk across
the moors is presented as a return, rather than a straightforward arrival.
Ben's spiritual reunion with his brother parallels Heathcliff's experience,
a form of compatriotism that is not merely about bloodlines but about a
shared history of colonialism. When Ben comes home to the moors, he is
not merely reunited with his brother, but with his hidden heritage.

Phillips is well aware that Yorkshire's slavery history registers in *Wuthering
Heights* even when this is not apparent to all readers. This can be seen in his
description of how he came to write *The Lost Child*:

Soon there were four Post-Its on my desk, each containing a single word. Yorkshire. Moor. Lost. Child. And as I continued to write, another Post-it eventually fell... into place with a fifth word on it, Literature, a word which spoke to the presence of Emily Brontë as one entryway into my book.[163]

So Phillips supplies the historical details that Emily Brontë's novel omits, pointing to Brontë's restricted view of the colonial world. In *The Lost Child,* the fictive Emily Brontë, mortally sick, dreaming, thinking about the dead Branwell, a lost boy, and her own fictive character, Heathcliff, can intuit the boy's presence, but cannot place him historically: '[S]he knows she will find the boy. A life reduced to one small window. This one view' (p. 110). In other words, Emily Brontë's tiny window on the world only affords glimpses of the Caribbean associations with the landscapes she inhabits. By opening, as it does, on the Liverpool docks, Phillips's novel identifies the city's port as the origin and precondition for both *Wuthering Heights* and *The Lost Child*. Phillips consolidates this impression by focusing on Black servants and material culture to indicate how far slavery penetrated Yorkshire's domestic realm in Brontë's day. His Heathcliff's Congolese mother resists an aristocrat's attempts to take her son into service. This detail is derived from historical research such as Peter Fryer's observation in *Staying Power* (1984) that wealthy travellers often gifted their wives or children with black children.[164] Phillips draws on this history:

> Their foolish tongues used to ask: "Can the boy speak English? Can he dress hair? Is he... fit to wait upon a gentleman? But no, no, no. She has seen the other boys, ornately attired in silks, with silver collars and satin turbans, walking behind fair ladies so that they might attend to their mistresses' trains, or quickly administer smelling salts, or take charge of their fans. But other boys, not her child.[165]

As my chapter on 'Country Houses' explores, there is extensive visual and documentary evidence of Black children who were kept as servants or pageboys to enhance the status of aristocratic families. Phillips's passage draws on the iconography of such paintings, which typically depict such children in the kind of exotic clothing so detested by Heathcliff's mother.

While Mr Earnshaw's connection to slavery is merely a possibility in Brontë's *Wuthering Heights*, Phillip's novel makes it crystal clear. The reader is left in no doubt how he makes his money when a colleague asks Earnshaw, "'Your ship is in Antigua isn't it? Are there problems at your sugarworks?'" (p. 243). The naming of Antigua obviously references Jane Austen's *Mansfield Park*. Phillips extends Said's critique of that novel to *Wuthering Heights* by foregrounding the colonial context of Brontë's novel. In *The Lost Child*, Heathcliff's mother is a formerly-enslaved woman, Mr Earnshaw owns plantations and Heathcliff is his unacknowledged son.

During Mr Earnshaw's visit to the Kingston Coffee House in Liverpool,[166] the conversation turns to 'the fluctuating prices of sugar, rum, and slaves' (p. 250). The fictive Charlotte Brontë's clothes are connected to empire and the East India Company when they 'make a tremendous noise. Silk on cotton. Cotton on silk' (p. 95), an image that also links these clothes to the cotton looms on which Heathcliff's mother can no longer work. The minutiae of empire's material culture accumulates throughout Phillips's novel, amplifying what are veiled intimations in *Wuthering Heights*; like Charlotte's dress, they begin to 'make a tremendous noise' (p. 95).

Phillips's novel also elaborates on and deepens the half-voiced concerns about slavery's morally contaminating effects implicitly expressed in *Wuthering Heights*. Von Sneidern notes how Emily Brontë hints at such anxieties when Edgar Linton identifies Heathcliff's presence as a 'moral poison', the idea that the wrongs of slavery had come back to punish them in acts of revenge.[167] In Phillips's novel, Earnshaw is troubled by his source of income and he feels as stained by slavery as his clothes are 'unmistakably blotched and bog spattered' (p. 243). The bog symbolises a moral morass, but he excuses himself by thinking: '[he] had little choice but to conduct dealings in Liverpool with men whose hearts were hard like stone' (p. 243).

Phillips draws on representations of moors in canonical literature as hostile and ageless, but reframes them as postcolonial spaces. In *The Lost Child*, Mr Earnshaw's journey across the Dales with his unacknowledged son takes place in atrocious weather, and a bystander wonders if 'the connection between the two had been forged in the adversity of this calamitous unrest' (p. 256). The awful weather manifests the historical and literary forces that connect Earnshaw and Heathcliff, Yorkshire and Antigua, *Wuthering Heights* and *The Lost Child*. The pair's moorland walk is imbued with a suitable sense of occasion, its global and temporal dimensions warrant the term an 'odyssey' (p. 259). Founded on the trope of ageless moors, this 'odyssey' emphasises the co-existence of past and present – Brontë's Heathcliff and Phillips's Heathcliff exist in parallel – as well as allowing Phillips to trace confluences between historical periods.[168] As Phillips stated in an interview, '[i]f you were to plonk those characters from the 19th century into that landscape they would recognise it.'[169]

Above all, these literary parallels provide alternative perspectives on who belongs to the moors and who does not. The Brontës have been seen as unquestioningly belonging to Haworth, and although Charlotte Brontë calls her sister 'a native... of the moors', *The Lost Child* complicates such notions of cultural indigeneity by focusing on Emily Brontë's Irish hair, which is said to look 'as though unfamiliar with the scrutiny of a comb' (p. 104). This image associates her symbolically with Heathcliff's 'thick, uncombed hair' (p. 54), which in turn is connected to the appearance of Ben and Tommy, whose guardian complains: '"What am I supposed to do with this hair of yours? Can you run a comb through it?'" (p. 124). The image connects generations of immigrants to the moors, from Emily to Heathcliff, to children like Tommy and his brother, who have become 'unmoored' from their own history and heritage, to borrow Phillips's phrase. In this way, *The Lost Child* widens the circle of belonging to include those who are conventionally viewed as foreign to the moors: Heathcliff, Ben, Tommy and, ultimately, Black Britons.

I noted above the difficulties reviewers had with the historical foundations of Andrea Arnold's Black Heathcliff. Reviews of Phillips's *The Lost Child* were similarly uninformed. Lucasta Millar erroneously asserts that Phillips's Black Heathcliff follows a trend started by Andrea Arnold's 2011 film,[170] a view that overlooks Phillips's longstanding interest in the subject, such as what he had to say in *A Regular Black* in 2009. While other reviewers do not voice this assumption, the influence of Arnold's *Wuthering Heights* is implied, because stills from the film were printed above the *Independent* and *TLS* reviews of Phillips's novel.[171] Comments about Phillips's Black Heathcliff were, though, largely supportive. *The Boston Globe* presented it as a form of strategic modernisation, stating that the author 'takes as a given the speculation of *Wuthering Heights* scholars that Heathcliff is Mr Earnshaw's illegitimate son and refashions the black-haired gypsy boy described by Brontë into an interracial by-product of Liverpool's bustling slave trade.'[172] The premise that Heathcliff is a 'gypsy' in Brontë's novel is presented as fact. Meanwhile, a reviewer for *The Sunday Herald* accuses Phillips of 'an irritation of authorial vagueness' about Heathcliff's origins.[173] This is puzzling, since Heathcliff is mothered by a Congolese former slave and fathered by Mr Earnshaw. The *Sunday Herald* also suggests that Phillips's novel is 'actually about Black people's "intrusion" into Britain, a statement which reinstates the assumption that Britain's Black presence is a recent phenomenon. Once again, Phillips's Black Heathcliff is taken to say more about present-day Britain than its past, as suggested by a curious claim that Phillips's inventive historical analogy helps us to understand the 2011 London riots.[174]

As such reviews suggest, the idea persists that the Black rural presence in the past (and present) were and are exceptions to the norm. Even in Robert Macfarlane's insightful work this historical dimension is lacking. His article, 'This Spectred Isle: The Eeriness of the English Countryside', as noted in Chapter Three, provides an inventory of contemporary literature, film and music that he thinks epitomise anti-pastoral depictions of rural England, works that are eerie and uncanny, showing a tendency to 'conjure violent pasts into visible being'.[175] His list of films, novels and poems includes the influential work of just one Black artist, the photographer Ingrid Pollard, acknowledging her anti-racist response to Wordsworthian scenes and settings. He also praises the Wolfe brothers'

film debut *Catch Me Daddy* (2014) for telling its tale of 'honour killing' in
the Dales. In much of this, then, Macfarlane is correct. His article does not
mention Phillips's *The Lost Child,* though in fairness, this was published
only a month before Macfarlane's article. Phillips's novel undoubtedly
matches Macfarlane's description of anti-pastoral depictions of the countryside because it 'conjur[es] violent pasts into being'. What could be more
eerie than a boy's call to his murdered brother buried beneath the moor?

But Macfarlane's list of concerns that animate contemporary anti-
pastoral cultural production could also have referenced more work by
Black British writers, such as Vahni Capildeo's poem, 'Winter, February'
(2009), which depicts the hair-raising pursuit of the poem's speaker by
dogs across moorland which actively seek to devour her.[176] In this poem,
moors are a space of whiteness, emphasised by 'the snow that lay thirsting'
on them. The section called 'Howl Moor' simultaneously evokes Conan
Doyle's *The Hound of the Baskervilles* and raises the spectre of rural racism as
she is chased off the moors. Such works expand the scope of anti-pastoral
writing and deserve to be incorporated into wider discussions about eerie
representations of the British countryside.

Capildeo's poem expresses both alarm and a sense of possession – of the
tradition of moorland writing, at least. In both Arnold's and Phillips's work
that sense of uncomfortable belonging is taken further. Both explore rural
belonging and rural racism in the same framework.

In Arnold's film, Heathcliff is portrayed as a rain-drenched waif, peering
into windows from his moorland vantage point. Yet, as in Brontë's novel,
the moors are also his element. They absorb and accommodate him, a
process which begins when Catherine gives him the vocabulary to describe
them. It is the language of belonging as much as love. 'Lapwing' is the first
English word that Catherine teaches Heathcliff – an invented scene in
Arnold's film which has no parallel in the novel. In pronouncing the word,
he names a romantic icon of moorland revivification. Throughout the film,
lapwing feathers are collected by him, or fly through the air. These feathers
connect him to Cathy. But they also represent moors as egalitarian, treating
him like any other man.

Arnold's 'muddy hem' version of *Wuthering Heights* communicates the
idea that soil is the grimy substance of belonging. It presents the Dales as
a place where filthy farmyard animals roam and the protagonists romp
through peat and vegetation. McCartney states that Arnold 'drag[s]' Brontë's
novel 'shuddering through the mid-nineteenth-century mire'.[177] Roger
Ebert observes that Arnold grounds Brontë's story in 'Yorkshire
earth...pr[ying] down into the muck and undergrowth'.[178] Arnold's Heathcliff
frequently stands in ditches digging into the bog. He rolls in the peat with
Cathy, lying astride her, blackening their clothes. He sits shivering in the rain
on numerous occasions, even lying in the heather as the drops splash on to

his upturned face. When he digs up Cathy's coffin, his sleeves and hands are covered in soil. These scenes combine to present the Black Heathcliff as being both in and of the landscape. He is immersed in it and he blends into it. As Jonathan Murray observes, the camera almost always shows the moors from Heathcliff's perspective.[179] The opening sequence shows his child's-eye view through blades of grass. The result is to emphasise Heathcliff's sensual encounter with moorland vegetation, showing his rural sensibility and suggesting that he is interior to the landscape.

In *The Lost Child*, Heathcliff's floundering first encounter with moorland is actually alleviated by close contact with it. His feet are 'soiled' by the bog (p. 257). Miserable though the journey is, being submerged in bog-water is presented as a form of initiation. Such physical connections with the landscape are central to Phillips's novel, and in this respect both his novel and Arnold's film connect with the urging of nature writers such as W. G. Sebald, Roger Deakin, and his mentee Robert Macfarlane, for their readers to fuse with the landscape through 'tactile' experience, to explore vegetation viscerally.[180] In *The Wild Places*, Macfarlane advocates walking barefoot, even across rough terrain.

When Phillips's Heathcliff encounters the moors in the closing section of *The Lost Child*, entitled 'Going Home', his 'arrival' is presented as an ambivalent and traumatic homecoming to the heartlands of those who have enslaved his kin. With his mother recently dead, he is cast off from his bloodline and Mr Earnshaw cannot honour the child's request to 'take him to his mother' (p. 259). He literally cannot 'go back to where he came from'. Yet, his arrival is also presented as a return, a possibility confirmed by the novel's final lines, spoken by Mr Earnshaw: 'There's a good lad. We're nearly home' (p. 260). The collective 'we' underscores the relationship between them and identifies that they are each, in their own ways, native to the moors: Mr Earnshaw by birth, and Heathcliff through his father's bloodline and because the region has profited from his enslaved ancestors. In this respect, *The Lost Child* overturns Eagleton's assertion that Heathcliff 'has no defined place within [...the region's] economic system'.[181] Phillips's novel presents Heathcliff's arrival as a return precisely because the profits of slavery are central both to Mr Earnshaw and, more broadly, to the region's economy. This homecoming is simultaneously literary: a Caribbean-born novelist, raised in northern England, stakes his claim both to Brontë's writing and to the landscapes which she loved. For Heathcliff, this return is unmistakably grim, a 'long ordeal' (p. 260). Yet his rain-soaked trudge is rewarded with an uplifting literary gesture towards romanticism when the sky clears to reveal 'silver stars' (p. 259). Ben's spiritual reunion with his brother is equally redemptive. Heathcliff, Ben and, through them, Black Britons, are reconciled with their lost heritage.

Phillips's novel is not alone in exploring the literary and cultural implications of Black people's encounters with moors. Bernardine Evaristo explores precisely this in her short story, 'Yoruba Man Walking',[182] published in the Peepal Tree anthology *Closure. Contemporary Black British Short Stories* (2015), edited by Jacob Ross. In Evaristo's story, a sailor called Lawani arrives at a Cornish port and decides to stay. He settles on Bodmin moor and marries a local woman but dies in a mining accident before his child is born. An afterword by Evaristo confirms that her work is founded on research into British history, stating that Lawani is modelled on a man who actually existed. He is based on 'an African, [who was] buried in one of the worst mine disasters of the 1880s'.[183]

The portrayal of Lawani's encounter with the moor is visceral and uplifting without in any sense being naive. Rural racism is tackled head-on in the story: 'When he came upon remote hamlets and villages, children would sometimes chase him, throw stones, call names and scamper' (p. 258). He is cast 'out in the wilderness' (p. 258). As Donna Landry records, the moorland areas of Cornwall, particularly the tin-mining areas, were laws unto themselves, hostile to and little visited by outsiders and fiercely protective of their independence.[184] Like a romantic exile, Lawani finds himself on Bodmin moor (p. 262) and it is his spirit of independence that opens a place for him amongst such people. In her story, Evaristo builds on and revivifies one legacy of romanticism, Wordsworth's gallery of moorland figures, the wanderers, pedlars, displaced persons, maimed soldiers and characters like his leech-gatherer. Indeed, Lawani is an undoubtedly iconic figure of 'Resolution and Independence', and like early Wordsworth, Evaristo does not gild the tragic insecurity of such lives. As noted, Lawani is killed and buried in a mining accident. The story promotes a metatextual understanding of his subterranean death, which represents his disappearance from historical memory, until his reappearance in this story.

Lawani's walk into the wilds is an important addition to the rural turn that is a significant strand of postmillennial writing by Black Britons and their interrogation of history. Strolling away from the Cornish port where he disembarks, Lawani 'noticed a dirt slope between two houses and beyond that, woods' (p. 257). 'Turn[ing] his back' to the town, he 'came upon a wide open space that did not move between his feet' (p. 257). Combining romantic and popular cultural imagery, Lawani is presented as an heroic wanderer: 'he was a caped crusader as the blanket billowed behind him, drying out' (p. 258). The sense of 'wide open space' is revivifying. As the dampened blanket suggests, Lawani's rural encounter is also visceral and elemental. And barefoot. Lawani 'took off his boots and tied them to his knapsack. He stripped down to his waist and felt his feet make contact with earth, pebble, grass.' (p. 257). History meets nature writing and the romantic legacy in Lawani's naked-chested encounter with the moor. At the heart of the description is the sheer physicality of walking, what Anne

D. Wallace in her book, *Walking, Literature and English Culture: the Origins and Uses of the Peripatetic in the Nineteenth Century* (1993) terms the 'peripatetic'. She argues there is a shift from the poetry of the 18th century where all the focus is on the destination, or the picturesque view as seen from above, towards a poetry of walking that emphasises process and the contact with the ground. This concerns not only the bodily engagement in walking and its connection with perception and thought, but the engagement with the path being trodden, and its making through mingled natural and human processes – a revolution in poetics that Wallace sees as having Wordsworth at its centre.[185] In Evaristo's story, the bog baptises Lawani: his 'boots squelched as he walked because he had sunk knee-deep into a marsh' (p. 259). Literally immersed in the landscape, his moorland walk inaugurates his relationship with the earth in which his corpse will eventually be buried. Like the Heathcliff of Brontë, Arnold and Phillips's works, Lawani is in his element, and his element is eternally the moor. He lives on it, procreates on it and is interred beneath it.

Lawani's physical encounter with the moor does not merely inaugurate his relationship with landscape, but gives rise to his geographically expansive perspectives on it, connecting Cornish moors with the world beyond: 'When the wind blew he imagined he was sailing between continents' (p. 266). This transnational view of moorland is reinforced by several other details in the story. Lawani's presence on Bodmin is presented as nothing new. A local farmer remembers other 'men who looked like this one' (p. 259). The same farmer grows red wheat from Turkey (p. 259), reminding readers that England's 'traditional' wheat-fields are not native at all.[186] The story's cosmopolitan perspective challenges any idea that moors are constant and unchanging. Instead, Bodmin is presented as a place where people come and go. The mine manager, Mr Yelland, is all too aware of this: 'His men had been migrating in droves to the silver mines of Mexico and the copper mines of Tasmania. He told Lawani he'd been a supervisor at a diamond mine in Kimberley in the Cape Colony until his wife insisted they raise their children in God's Own Country and not some hellhole a million miles from civilization' (p. 261). Even though Mr Yelland's wife implies that rural England preserves the nation's soul, Evaristo suggests that travel and empire have shaped the nation's wild places: the Cornish mine is only made possible by the owner's previous experience in the mines of colonial South Africa.

Black history brings environmentalists' calls for earthly union into a whole new dimension. One further production takes on the theme of communing with nature and explores it very literally. Jade Montserrat's short film, *Burial* (2014), is a tribute to Emily Brontë's *Wuthering Heights*. The film's black protagonist stands in a trench at the edge of the Dales and smears her naked body with mud.[187] It is a rite like baptism. But this baptism is far from genteel, since it is mud that blesses her communion. As the film progresses, her entire body is painted with mud. Montserrat, the film-maker, observes that England's wild landscapes are 'scarred by borders'. In evoking the trenches of World War I, the setting of her film establishes an association with warfare, reflecting historic struggles over moors' owner-ship and belonging as well as the participation of Commonwealth troops in that war. Montserrat observes that Brontë's Heathcliff 'comes to own land', taking possession of it in ways that goaded her to 'own the land' in the film.[188] However, taking possession of the moor entails real risk: the protagonist's mud-smearing is presented as a form of defensive camou-flage. Yet this act also immerses her in the landscape and stakes her claim to it. A second, unnamed, video shot near Scarborough shows the same woman walking barefoot through long grass and peat-water, which runs over her toes, again suggesting baptism by the elements.[189]

The work of Arnold, Phillips, Evaristo and Montserrat demonstrates that moors are the focus of new, postcolonial renderings of England's wildest, anti-pastoral terrain that place moorlands in new historical and global perspectives. Wanting to feel close to the earth is not, of course, unique. But, in the face of rural racism and exclusion, it acquires a powerful symbolism. In a country where immigration is almost automatically associated with urban settings, communing with nature profoundly dis-turbs England's dominant cultural politics of belonging.

Conclusion
Moors are foundational sites of English culture. As Cathy declares in *Wuthering Heights,* they are 'like the eternal rocks beneath' (p. 82). Symbolically as well as geologically, moors link past and present.

Perceptions of British moorlands are enduringly influenced by writers from Defoe, Coleridge, Emily Brontë, Blackmore, Buchan, Du Maurier and Hughes through to Phillips and Evaristo. These writers inform our sense that moors are ancient and brooding, thrilling and threatening, wild and uncivi-lized. But, as I have argued, moors also occupy an important place in the colonial imagination. Uncultivated uplands represent uncivilized mentali-ties. Right up to the present, moors are metaphorically linked with Moors, in the broad, sixteenth-century sense of the word. As noted above, Atkins writes that moors' blackness is 'no metaphor' (p. 28), but he also records how moors' very names symbolise blackness: 'Blackpits, Blackford, Blackland'.

I have traced how writers and filmmakers have responded to such symbolism to explore moors' colonial and immigration histories, incorpo-rating the experiences of Saracens, Caribbean servants, European textile workers, Irish navvies and miners, Polish refugees and South Asian Mus-lims. Even when depictions of moorland immigrants are speculative, they can engage in dialogue with the history that emphasises moorlands' historical connections with colonial goods and long-forgotten intercultural encounters. Contemporary depictions of a rural migrant presence overturn lingering notions that the countryside is now and has always been unvaryingly populated by white people.

For almost all the writers discussed in this chapter, moorland raises the issues of freedom of access. Simon Armitage's *Walking Home* exemplifies this when he writes:

> Born out of the "right to roam" movement, public disquiet after the great depression and the subsequent mass trespass on Kinder Scout in 1932, it [the Pennine Way] was, in its conception, as much a political statement as a leisure activity, and no doubt there are members of the landed gentry with double-barrelled shotguns who would still like to ban the common people from wandering across certain tracts of open moorland. (p. 3).

Landowners' guns may have stopped smoking, yet, for many Black Britons, there are enduring psychological barriers to the countryside. These barriers are decisively challenged by *The Lost Child* and 'Yoruba Man Walking', both of which offer historicised responses to the kinds of anxieties about moorlands' whiteness that are so vividly expressed in Merle Collins's poem 'Visiting Yorkshire – Again'. For Phillips and Evaristo, the moors are no longer off-limits for Black British writers. Armed with new historical discoveries, Black authors assert their right to roam across a landscape beloved by canonical writers.

This chapter set out to show how travel and empire shaped moorland settings, but also how such influences have been concealed. But like the Iron Age corpses of Heaney's bog poems in *North*,[190] though layers of peat conceal, they also preserve and reveal, in time, the past. Creative work by Black writers adds disturbing new resonances to the final sentence of Brontë's *Wuthering Heights*:

> I lingered round them, under that benign sky, watched the moths fluttering upon the heath, and hare-bells; listened to the soft wind breathing through the grass; and wondered how anyone could ever imagine unquiet slumbers, for the sleepers in that quiet earth. (p. 337).

End Notes

1. William Atkins, *The Moor. Lives, Landscape, Literature* (London: Faber and Faber, 2014), p. xx.
2. Leo Mellor, 'The Lure of Wilderness' in Louise Westling, ed., *The Cambridge Companion to Literature and the Environment* (Cambridge: CUP, 2014), p. 104.
3. William Shakespeare, *Macbeth*, ([c.1606] London: Penguin Classics, 2015), Act 1, scene 3, line 39.
4. Atkins, 2014, *op cit.,* p. xx and p. 29.
5. Adam Hopkins, *The Moorlands of England* (Toronto: Key Porter Books, 1995), p. 92.
6. Atkins, 2014, *op cit.,* p. 76.
7. T.F. Powys, 'Lie Thee Down, Oddity!', in *Captain Patch* (Hamburg: The Albatross, 1935), pp. 17-30.
8. Robert Macfarlane has written *Mountains of the Mind* (London: Granta, 2003), *The Wild Places* (London: Granta, 2007), *The Old Ways. A Journey on Foot* (London: Granta, 2012) and *Landmarks* (London: Granta, 2015).
9. Oliver Rackham, *The History of the Countryside* (London: Dent, 1986), pp. 305-327.
10. Atkins, *op cit.*, p. 76.
11. Hopkins, *op. cit.*, p. 13.
12. Daniel Defoe, *A Tour through the Whole Island of Great Britain* (London: Dent, Everyman Library, 1962), vol. 2, p. 177.
13. Quoted in Hopkins, *op cit.*, p. 130.
14. See Cecilia Powell and Stephen Hebron, *Savage Grandeur and Noblest Thoughts: Discovering the Lake District 1750-1820* (Grasmere: Wordsworth Trust, 2010), pp. 1-34.
15. Ian Whyte, 'Parliamentary enclosure and changes in landownership in an upland environment: Westmoreland, c.1770-1860', in *Agricultural History Review*, 2003.
16. John Clare, 'The Mores', *John Clare: The Oxford Authors* (Oxford: OUP, 1984), pp. 167-169.
17. *Ibid.*, p. 169.
18. Katrina Naviskas, *Protest and the Politics of Space and Place, 1789-1848* (Manchester: Manchester UP, 2016), pp. 88-90, 223-247.
19. Macfarlane, *The Wild Places*, p. 78.
20. See Dieter Helm, *Green and Prosperous Land: A Blueprint for Rescuing the British Countryside* (London: Collins, 2019), pp. 113-126.
21. For fuller lists of moorlands' literary depictions, see Adam Hopkins, *The Moorlands of England* (St. Albans: Key Porter Books, Ltd., 1995), p. 105 and Christina Hardyment's *Writing Britain: Wastelands to*

Wonderlands (2012), published by the British Library. For the poetry of Ann Batten Cristall (*Poetical Sketches*, 1795) and Sophie Dixon (*Castalian Hours*, 1829) see Donna Landry, *The Invention of the Countryside: Hunting, Walking and Ecology in English Literature 1671-1831* (London: Palgrave Macmillan, 2001).

22. Emily Brontë, 1846, , 'Loud Without The Wind Was Roaring' quoted in Owen Sheers, *A Poet's Guide to Britain* (2009), p. 121.

23. Nancy Armstrong, 1992. 'Emily's Ghost. The Cultural Politics of Victorian Fiction, Folklore and Photography' *Novel: A Forum on Fiction* 25:3, pp. 245-267, p. 524.

24. Hopkins, *op cit.*, p. 13.

25. Atkins, *op cit.*, p. 114.

26. Christina Hardyment, *Writing Britain. Wastelands to Wonderlands* (2012), p. 92.

27. Williamson quoted in Atkins, op. cit., p. 115.

28. Ted Hughes, 'Wodwo' in *Wodwo* (London: Faber, 1967), p. 183.

29. Simon Armitage, *Walking Home* (London: Faber, 2013), p. 166.

30. See Donna Landry on the Stannaries in *The Invention of the Countryside*, pp. 235-236.

31. Phyllis Bentley, *Gold Pieces* (London: Macdonald, 1968); Peter Kershaw, *The Last Coiner* (Dutchy Parade Films, 1968); and Benjamin Myers, *The Gallows Pole* (Hebden Bridge: Bluemoose Books, 2018).

32. Hopkins, *op cit.,* p. 88.

33. Phillips in interview with Matthew Sweet on Radio 3's 'Free Thinking', 23 April 2015.

34. The Smiths, 'Suffer Little Children', released by Rough Trade on 20th February 1983 and produced by John Porter. Thanks to Martin Halliwell for drawing my attention to this song.

35. Simon Armitage, *Walking Home*, p. 2.

36. Phillips, 'Works in Progress' essay about *The Lost Child: www.fsgworkinprogress.com/2015/05/finding-the-lost-child/*, accessed 11 January 2016.

37. Robert Macfarlane, 'This Spectered Isle: The Eeriness of the English Countryside' *The Guardian*, 10 April, 2015.

38. Adam Hopkins *op cit.*, p. 50.

39. Hopkins, *op cit.,* pp. 50-54, 55.

40. See W.G. Hoskins, *The Making of the English Landscape* ([1955] Toller Fratram: Little Toller, 2013), p. 110.

41. Dominic Tyler, *Uncommon Ground. A Word-Lover's Guide to the British Landscape* (London: Guardian and Faber, 2015), p. 101. I am grateful to Dr. Philip Shaw at the University of Leicester for providing a critical opinion on the likely stories of settlement implied by the linguistic roots of geological terms.

42. Oliver Rackham, *The History of the Countryside* (Moorland, pp. 305-327).

43. See Rackham, *The History of the Countryside*, p. 305.

44. W.G. Hoskins, *op. cit.*, p. 110.

45. Atkins, *op. cit.*, p. 84.

46. Phillips in interview with Matthew Sweet on Radio 3's 'Free Thinking', 23 April 2015.

47. This detail is reminiscent of Phillips's own experience at Oxford, where his Leeds accent made him stand out.

48. 'BBC to Dramatise the Lives of the Brontë Sisters', *The Telegraph*, 18 May, 2015, http://www.telegraph.co.uk/culture/tvandradio/11612791/BBC-to-dramatise-the-lives-of-the-Bronte-sisters.html, accessed 5 February, 2016.

49. David Hey, *A History of The Peak District Moors* (Barnsley: Pen and Sword, 2015), p. 115.

50. Terry Coleman, 1981. *The Railway Navvies. A History of the Men Who Made the Railways* (London: Penguin), p. 114.

51. Atkins, *op. cit.*, p. 139.

52. Pauline Elkes, 'The Polish Community in Staffordshire Moorlands. A History' www.bbc.co.uk/stoke/features/polish/polish_community.shtml, 2 April 2003. Accessed 7 January, 2016.

53. Thanks are due to Dr. Philip Shaw at the University of Leicester, who provided an erudite linguistic explanation for this resemblance.

54. Testament, *Black Men Walking* (London: Oberon Books, 2018), p. 27-28.

55. Testament *Black Men Walking*, pp. 1, 3. Even hostile works – such as 'The Blackamoor in the wood', in which a black servant murders 'a gallant lord and virtuous lady' testify to this presence. 'The Blackamoor in the wood: Or, a lamentable ballad on a tragical end of a gallant lord and virtuous lady; together with the...death of their two children wickedly performed by a heathenish and bloodthirsty villain their servant. The like of which cruelty was never before heard of', English Broadside Ballad Archive, ebba.english.ucsb.edu/ballad/20261, accessed 31 July 2019.

56. Roger Highfield, 'Yorkshire Name Reveals Roots in Africa' *The Telegraph* 24th January 2007, https://www.telegraph.co.uk/news/science/science-news/3350677/Yorkshire-name-reveals-roots-in-Africa.html, accessed 12 April 2018. The news was also reported in *The Yorkshire Post* on 29 January 2007.

57. David Olusoga, 'Black and British: A Forgotten History', BBC2 episode one, broadcast on Wednesday 9 November 2017.

58. Anonymous blog, 'The Saracens of Biddulph Moor', https://ludchurchmyblog.wordpress.com/places-of-other-local-interest/the-

saracens-of-biddulph-moor/, accessed 7 January 2016.

59. The architectural evidence is explained in a video called 'The Curiosities of Staffordshire', which can be accessed on Youtube at www.youtube.com/watch?v=bH6PuOqJgLM, accessed 7 January 2016.

60. Bill Siviter, *The Dark Men of Biddulph Moor* (self-published, n.d.). The tale is largely set between the years 1189-1192.

61. I refer here to Samuel P. Huntington's 'clash of civilizations' thesis, in which he suggests that much present day conflict is due to irreconcilable cultural and religious differences between people belonging to different nations. See Samuel P. Huntingdon, *The Clash of Civilizations and the Remaking of World Order,* (New York: Simon and Schuster, 2002).

62. W.G. Hoskins, *op cit.*, p. 14.

63. Marian Gwyn has researched this history for 25 years and a summary of her research can be found here: www.nationaltrust.org.uk/penrhyn-castle/features/penrhyn-castle-and-the-transatlantic-slave-trade, accessed 6 May 2020.

64. Chris Evans, *Slave Wales: The Welsh and Atlantic Slavery 1660-1850* (Cardiff: University of Wales Press, 2010), p. 17.

65. William Atkins, *The Moor,* p. 31.

66. Hopkins, *The Moorlands of England*, p. 78.

67. Makdisi, *Romantic Imperialism* (Cambridge UP, 1998), pp. 45-69.

68. Exmoor is the subject of Hughes's poem 'Crow Hill' (*Lupercal*, Faber, 1960, p. 14). This views Sir John Knight's old, crumbled wall as a symbol of failed attempts to tame the moor. Hughes declared that *Tarka The Otter* 'gave shape and words to my world' (Hughes in Atkins, *The Moor*, p. 96).

69. Roger Deakin gave Williamson's eulogy at his funeral in 1977.

70. This observation is taken from Katie Donington's discussion of philanthropy in Catherine Hall, Nicholas Draper, Keith McClelland, Katie Donington and Rachel Lang, *op cit.*, 'Transforming capital: slavery, family, commerce and the making of the Hibbert family', pp. 203-249.

71. Armitage, *Walking Home*, p. 114.

72. Hoskins, *op cit.,* p. 99.

73. Atkins, *op cit.,* p. 229.

74. Leo Mellor, 'The Lure of the Wilderness', *The Cambridge Companion to Literature and the Environment* (Cambridge: CUP, 2014), p. 104.

75. Ian Ward, 'Emily Brontë" and the Terrorist Imagination' *English Studies* Vol. 89, No. 5, October 2008, 524–551, p. 524.

76. Saree Makdisi, *Romantic Imperialism*, pp. 70-99.

77. Kye Askins first conceptualised the 'transrural imaginary', whereby

migrants project the landscapes of elsewhere on to the British countryside (Askins, 2009, *ibid.*, p. 372).

78. Askins, *op. cit.*, p. 11.
79. Ian Krielcamp, 'Petted Things: *Wuthering Heights* and the Animal.' *The Yale Journal of Criticism* 18.1 (2005) 87-110, p. 97.
80. Nancy Armstrong, 'Emily's Ghost. The Cultural Politics of Victorian Fiction, Folklore and Photography' *Novel: A Forum on Fiction* 25:3, p. 524.
81. Armstrong, *op. cit.*, p. 251.
82. Armstrong, *op. cit.*, p. 259.
83. Armstrong, *op. cit.*, p. 245-267.
84. Armstrong, *op cit.*, p. 262 and 259.
85. Hoskins, *op. cit.*, p. 110.
86. Askins *op. cit.*, p. 373.
87. Charlotte Bronte, 1850. 'Editor's Preface to the New Edition of *Wuthering Heights*' in Emily Bronte, 1995 [1847] *Wuthering Heights*, edited by Lucasta Miller (London: Penguin), p. liv.
88. Jonathan Rutherford, 'Ghosts: Heritage and the Shape of Things to Come', Jo Littler and Roshi Naidoo, eds. *The Politics of Heritage. The Legacies of "Race"* (London: Routledge, 2005), p. 82.
89. *Rutherford, op cit.*, p. 83.
90. Procter, *Dwelling Places,* p. 175.
91. J.B. Priestley in Procter, 2003, *op cit.*, p. 175.
92. Rutherford, *op cit.*, p. 83.
93. Bronte, 1850 'Introduction', *ibid.*, p. li.
94. Procter, *op cit.*, p. 109.
95. Procter, *op cit.*, p. 109.
96. Tom Clinton's book, *Laugh? I Nearly Went to Bradford,* cited in Procter *op cit.*, p. 170.
97. Procter, *op cit.*, p. 172.
98. Ted Hughes, 'Heptonstall Old Church', *The Remains of Elmet* (London: Faber, 1979).
99. Steve Thompson, *Jericho*, (London: ITV). In this drama, the navvies are employed to build a viaduct called Culverdale, based on Ribblehead Viaduct. Paul Revoir, 2016, 'Cowboys of the Dales: Is ITV drama *Jericho* Britain's First Western?', *The Radio Times* 2-8 January, p.16-17.
100. Thompson observes that the Western genre encompasses many styles, themes and varies in its degree of violence (Thompson cited by Revoir, *op cit.*, p. 12).
101. Clarke Peters in Revoir, 'Cowboys of the Dales', 2015, p. 17.
102. The influence of Quentin Tarantino's updated take on the Western, *Django Unchained* (2012, Columbia Pictures/A Band Apart), is felt

in *Jericho*. Like Tarantino's film, *Jericho* expands the genre to incorporate black characters. The comparison stops here, however. *Jericho* is undoubtedly a Western, but it lies at the opposite end of the violence spectrum.

103. Dresser and Hann, 2013. *op cit.*, p. 12.

104. Merle Collins, 2013 [1992]. 'Visiting Yorkshire – Again' in Kay, Procter and Robinson, *op cit.*, p. 105.

105. These last observations are made by Cameron Dodworth in his essay 'The Mystery of the Moors. Purgatory and the Absence/Presence of Evil in *Wuthering Heights*'. Brontë Studies. 37:2, April, 2012. pp. 125-137.

106. Cited in Ian Ward, *op cit.*, p. 544.

107. Ward, *op cit.*, p. 545.

108. In the opening chapters, Lockwood wrongly guesses the relationship between the characters and misunderstands the status of each.

109. Maria-Lisa Von Sneidern, 1995. '*Wuthering Heights* and the Liverpool Slave Trade'. *ELH* 62.1, pp. 171-196, p. 171.

110. Humphrey Gawthrop, 'Slavery: Idée Fixe of Emily and Charlotte Brontë'. *Brontë Studies*, Vol. 38 No. 4, November 2013, 281–89, p. 287.

111. I am grateful to Professor Jairo Lugo at Qatar University for suggesting this question.

112. In this Venezuelan series, the face of actor Jose Bardina was darkened to suggest that he is mestiza.

113. V.S. Naipaul, *Guerrillas* (London: Andre Deutch, 1975).

114. Eagleton, cited by Dodworth, 2012, *op cit.*, p. 127.

115. Cassandra Phybus, 'Tense and Tender Ties: Reactions on Lives Recovered from the Intimate Frontier of Empire and Slavery.' *Life Writing* 8:11, 2011, pp. 4-17, p. 17.

116. Caryl Phillips, interviewed in Adam Low, director, 2009, *A Regular Black. The Hidden* Wuthering Heights (Lonestar Productions).

117. Kim Lyon in Low, 2009, *ibid.*

118. Christopher Heywood, 'The Brontës at work on novels by Eugene Sue,' *Bronte Studies,* 37:1, 2012, pp. 30-43, p. 41.

119. Heywood, 2012, *op cit.*, p. 41.

120. Kim Lyon and Melinder Elder corroborate this view in Low's film *A Regular Black.*

121. https://www.ucl.ac.uk/lbs/claim/view/24026, accessed 8 January 2016. The money was awarded to the Rev. Adam Sedgewick, trustee and Canon of Norwich and President of the Royal Geological Society.

122. Heywood, 1998, *op cit.*, p. 17.

123. Heywood, 2012, *op cit.*, p. 39.

124. David Richardson, Suzanne Schwartz and Anthony Tibbles, *Liverpool*

and Transatlantic Slavery, (Liverpool: Liverpool University Press, 2007), p. 132.

125. Gawthrop, 2013, *op cit.,* p. 283.

126. Gawthrop, 2013, *op cit.,* p. 282.

127. Gawthrop, 2013, *op cit.,* p. 284.

128. Gawthrop, 2013, *op cit.,* p. 289.

129. Low, 2009, *ibid.*

130. Gawthrop, 2013, *op cit.,* p. 281.

131. See Low, 2009, *op cit.*

132. Von Sneidern, 1995, *op cit.,* p. 173.

133. Von Sneidern, 1995, *op cit.,* p. 171. It was widely held that Lord Mansfield's Somerset ruling effectively outlawed slavery on British soil.

134. Mr Hargrave cited by Von Sneidern 1995, *op cit.,* p. 183.

135. Donna K. Reed. 1989, 'The Discontents of Civilization in *Wuthering Heights* and *Buddenbrooks*', *Comparative Literature,* vol. 41:3, p. 228.

136. Phybus, interviewed in Low, 2009, *ibid.*

137. Phybus, 2011, *op cit.,* pp. 15-16.

138. Low, 2009, *ibid.*

139. Von Sneidern, 1995, *op cit.,* p. 172.

140. Phybus, 2011, *op cit.,* p. 17.

141. Phybus, 2011, *op cit.,* p. 41.

142. Said, 1993. *op cit.,* p. 103. In his essay 'Jane Austen and Empire', he claims that Austen and her contemporaries were only 'vaguely aware' of the workings of empire, p. 103.

143. See Mary Reckord, 'The Jamaican Slave Rebellion of 1831', *Past and Present,* No. 40, pp. 108-125.

144. See Thomas R. Day, *Jamaican Revolts in British Press and Politics, 1760-1865,* masters thesis, Virginia Commonwealth University, online.

145. Terry Eagleton cited by Ward, 2008, *op cit.,* p. 526.

146. Von Sneidern, *op cit.,* p. 143.

147. Von Sneidern, *op cit.,* p. 143.

148. Edward Long, *History of Jamaica* (London: T. Lowndes, 1774) Book III, Chapter III, p. 479.

149. Von Sneidern, *op cit.,* p. 181.

150. Phybus, 2011, *op cit.,* p. 172.

151. Leslie Felperin, *Variety* review of *Wuthering Heights,* September 26th, 2011.

152. Val Kermode, Review, *An Eye For Film,* http://www.eyeforfilm.co.uk/review/wuthering-heights-film-review-by-val-kermode 11th November, 2011, accessed 11 January 2016.

153. Peter Bradshaw, '*Wuthering Heights* – Review', *The Guardian,* 11th November, 2011 and Phillip French, '*Wuthering Heights* – Review',

The Guardian 13th November, 2011.

154. French, 2015, *ibid*, and see Michael Bundock, *The Fortunes of Samuel Barber. The True Story of the Jamaican Slave Who Became Samuel Johnson's Heir* (New York: Yale University Press, 2015).

155. Robbie Collin, 2011, '*Wuthering Heights:* Review', *The Telegraph*, 10 November, italics mine.

156. Jenny McCartney, *Seven Magazine* review, 10 November, 2011.

157. Andrea Arnold, 'I don't do easy rides', *The Guardian* interview, http://www.theguardian.com/film/2011/oct/31/andrea-arnold-wuthering-heights-interview, accessed 11 January 2016.

158. Ray Costello, 2015. 'The Real Lost Children. The Fate of Some Children of African Descent in Late 18th and 19th Century Liverpool', unpublished paper given at 'Lost Children: The Black Atlantic and Northern Britain' conference, UCLAN on 30 April, 2015. The painting by Windus still hangs in Liverpool's Slavery Museum.

159. Caryl Phillips interview, 'Lost Child: I needed to know where I came from', National Public Radio, 31st March, 2015, https://www.npr.org/2015/03/21/394127475/lost-child-author-caryl-phillips-i-needed-to-know-where-i-came-from?t=1557748150812, accessed 13 May, 2019. And see Caryl Phillips in interview with Mariella Frostrup for BBC Radio 4's *Open Book*, 15 March 2015.

160. J.M. Coetzee, cited by Jeffery Renard Allen, 'Sunday Book Review. *The Lost Child* by Caryl Phillips', *New York Times,* 8 May, 2015.

161. Caryl Phillips 2015, interview for National Public Radio.

162. Robert Macfarlane, 'This Spectered Isle: The Eeriness of the English Countryside', *The Guardian*, 10 April, 2015.

163. Phillips, 'Works in Progress' essay about *The Lost Child: www.fsgworkinprogress.com/2015/05/finding-the-lost-child/,* accessed 11 January 2016.

164. Fryer, 1984, *ibid.,* p. 21.

165. *The Lost Child* (London: Oneworld Publications, 2015), p. 6. Subsequent quotations from this novel are given in the text.

166. Caryl Phillips details Liverpool's association with slave-produced goods in Low's documentary (2009). An oral history account of this coffee house can be seen in the Liverpool Museum of Slavery: /www.liverpoolmuseums.org.uk/maritime/research/mappingmemory/themes/memories/memory-69.html, accessed 12 January 2016.

167. Von Sneidern, *op cit.,* pp. 180 and 185.

168. Thanks are due to Dr. Lucy Evans, who suggested that I link moors' timelessness with Phillips's technique of linking past and present, not merely of history but of literature.

169. Phillips cited by Francesca Wade, 'Book Review.' *The Telegraph* 16 March, 2015.

170. Lucasta Millar, 'The Lost Child by Caryl Phillips review – from Heathcliff to the 1960s.' The Guardian, Saturday 18 April 2015.

171. Gerard Woodward, 'The Lost Child by Caryl Phillips. Book in review. Wuthering Heights Relived in Postwar Britain', The Independent, 26th March; Kathryn Sutherland, 'Reading Well With Caryl Phillips's The Lost Child', Times Literary Supplement, 22nd April, 2015.

172. Wendy Smith, 'Book Review. The Lost Child by Caryl Phillips. The Boston Globe, March 21st, 2015.

173. OneWorld, 'Caryl Phillips: The Lost Child, Sunday Herald, Saturday 25th April, 2015.

174. Jonathan Murray, 2012. Review of 'Wuthering Heights', Cineaste 2012, p. 57.

175. Macfarlane, 2015, op cit., p. 1.

176. Vahni Capildeo, The Undraining Sea (London: Eggbox, 2009).

177. McCartney, 2011, op cit.

178. Roger Ebert, 2012. Wuthering Heights review, November 28, 2012. www. rogerebert.com/reviews/wuthering-heights-2012, accessed 13 January, 2016.

179. Murray, 2012, op cit., p. 1.

180. Macfarlane, Wild Places, pp. 73-83.

181. Terry Eagleton cited by Ward, op cit., p. 526.

182. Bernardine Evaristo, 'Yoruba Man Walking' in Closure: Contemporary Black British Short Stories ed. Jacob Ross (Leeds: Peepal Tree Press, 2015).

183. Evaristo, op cit., p. 268.

184. Landry, The Invention of the Countryside, p. 235.

185. Anne D. Wallace, Walking, Literature and English Culture: the Origins and Uses of the Peripatetic in the Nineteenth Century (Oxford: Clarendon Press, 1993), pp. 119-165.

186. Red wheat originates in Turkey.

187. The film is no longer available on the internet.

188. Montserrat, unpublished paper given at 'Lost Children: The Black Atlantic and Northern Britain' conference, UCLAN on 30 April, 2015.

189. img_2035-0.jpg, on vimeo.

190. Seamus Heaney, 'Bog Queen', 'The Grauballe Man', 'Punishment' and 'Strange Fruit', North (London: Faber and Faber, 1975), pp. 32-39.

CHAPTER SIX
PLANTS, GARDENS AND EMPIRE

'Why must people insist that the garden is a place of rest and repose, a place to forget the cares of the world?' Jamaica Kincaid, 'Sowers and Reapers', *The New Yorker,* January 15th, 2001.

Introduction
Plants and gardens are deeply connected with the themes of this book. Whether grand country house gardens, the cottage gardens of the rural working class, the provision grounds of enslaved people, the allotments of the rural and industrial working class, municipal public parks, or suburban gardens, they all engage with history, with economics and social justice, with ideas about culture, with psychological needs – and with literature.

The framing contexts of this chapter are those of class and colonialism as narratives of power, exploitation and resistance. Within that frame, the migration of people and plants – trees, flowers and vegetables – explains what grows in British gardens and the plants we use inside our homes. Knowledge about gardens and plants, in particular botany, has had deep colonial resonances and the scientific categorisation of plants has at times engaged in the same hierarchies of 'race' that justified empire and slavery.[1] This chapter traces the plants' journeys from colonial activities to domestic wealth. It uses such examples as the travels of rhododendrons from the Himalayas into our shrubberies in parks and gardens.

People and plants belong to the same colonial story. This is especially true of African (and South Asian) people's movement to the Caribbean and then to Britain. Here, the chapter traces a counter-narrative to that of imperial power – the massive contribution made by enslaved Africans (and indentured Indians and Chinese) to the migration of food stuffs to the Atlantic world, to the shaping of Caribbean garden cultures and culinary styles, and the subsequent migration of people, foods and gardening culture across the Atlantic to Britain. (The story of the gardens of South Asian peoples who came directly to Britain is beyond the scope of this book.)

One of the ironies of garden history is that though gardens provide a space where people can feel most to be themselves and least alienated from the demands of waged work, gardens have been inescapably shaped by capitalism from the late 17th century onwards. This includes the activities of the landscape gardeners who redesigned the estates of wealthy landowners and of the nurserymen who, as Roderick Floud shows in his *An Economic History of the English Garden* (2019) comprised one of the most dynamic sectors of the 18th century domestic economy. These nurserymen supplied the wealthy with the new plant species that were part of the imperial flows of goods, labour and capital. In 2017, ornamental horticulture and landscaping industries made a contribution of an estimated £24.2 billion to GDP and supported over half a million jobs in the UK, many low paid.[2] By contrast, the total income from farming in 2014 was only £5.38 billion. Inevitably, then, gardens are matters of class and privilege – a reminder of which came with the Covid-19 lockdown and the sharp inequalities of access to garden space it revealed.

Yet while the academic study of gardens makes a distinction between the elite and the vernacular – and such distinctions are real – the two have permeable boundaries. Influence mostly moves from 'high' to 'low', when what was once prized becomes commonplace. From the 19th century onwards, though, the influence sometimes moved the other way. For instance, the promiscuous profusion of the rural cottage garden led to the gentrified pretensions of the 'cottage ornée'.[3] The science of botany has mostly been seen as an elite occupation, even before it became professionalised. But botanic interests spread to working people, such as the poet John Clare. His passion for plants, wild and cultivated, is discussed below. In our own time, there is, on the evidence of gardening magazines and television programmes, an interest in creating gardens of a tropical appearance. On one level this returns us to the desire for exotic plants collected by plant hunters in the eighteenth century. On another level it signals the cultural diversity of the 21st century British garden, not least because some of its creators are of Caribbean and South Asian heritage.

Gardens are matters of politics as well as aesthetics. At the grand scale of formal gardens owned by the landed elites they raise the issues of decolonisation and restitutional justice. Gardens are also unavoidably enmeshed in campaigns to rescue our environment, whether through pursuing the goal of carbon neutrality or creating safe havens for wildlife. Few gardeners are unaware of issues around the use of plastics and peat or declining hedgehog populations. Meanwhile, there has been a lack of ethnic and cultural diversity in access to public media. Only very recently have broadcasting institutions such as the BBC discovered, after the Black Lives Matter protests of 2020, that there are Black British gardeners and experts in horticulture who could feature in their programmes.

One goal of this book is to contribute to anticolonial history, including that of grand private gardens. This chapter also embraces the contribution to the general good of small suburban and urban gardens, public parks and allotments, limited though they are in size and availability, with access to their benefits still unequal. In addition, this chapter acknowledges the work of others in recognising that gardens are gendered spaces. To this last point it adds the awareness that Britain's Black and Asian population has been disproportionately excluded from garden-based pleasures. Even so, gardens have always provided the most personalisable and widely distributed access to both the natural world and to forms of self-expression that cross classes, ethnicities and educational divides.

Gardens' personal meanings are important. These transfer from actually creating gardens to writing about them. No account can ignore the contribution of fiction and poetry to our pleasure and understanding (and drama – remembering Graham Greene's play *The Potting Shed*). Indeed, Roy Campbell's long poem, *The Georgiad* (1931), complains about the poetic confusion between gardening and writing in works by his rivals:

> Write with your spade, and garden with your pen,
> Shovel your couplets to their long repose
> And type your turnips down the field in rows,
> Equal your skill, no matter which is which,
> To dig an ode, or to indite a ditch.[4]

Another famous example is 'Digging' by Seamus Heaney. Watching his father dig potatoes, he humbly hopes to see his writing accepted as a kind of substitute:

> But I've no spade to follow men like them.

> Between my finger and thumb
> The squat pen rests.
> I'll dig with it.[5]

As with the literature of the countryside discussed in Chapter Three, writing about the garden engages with the genres of both the pastoral (with its image of the leisured rural idyll) and the georgic (with its ideas about work and self-sufficiency – sometimes through stern necessity – and the sheer physical labour involved in gardening). Gardens are located in both camps, depending, of course, on who does the gardening, and who the relaxing.[6] There is no attempt to survey the whole range of writing about the garden, from the biblical Eden, through Milton's *Paradise Lost* and onwards. Instead this chapter concentrates on writing that throws light on plants and gardens as shaped by empire and provides a reference point for discussing contemporary writing about gardens by Black Britons. Some of these writers draw parallels between plant and human migration. Some deconstruct ideas about native and indigenous flora in iconic sites, such as the English cottage garden. But no less than any other writers, Black British authors have taken solace in their gardens. An important variant of such domestic gardening activity is the growing of food in allotments and community gardens. The chapter ends by exploring the connections between historic slavery and concepts of food justice promoted by a Black organisation in Britain today.

Empire, Slavery and the Growth of Botany as a Science
While the potential profits from slavery and colonial goods drove commerce, settlement and forced labour migration, the desire to know about the plant life of conquered and colonial territories followed. Plants were brought to Europe by explorers such as Christopher Columbus from the Americas and by Vasco da Gama from India. The growing knowledge of global plant species is recorded in *Historia Plantarum Generalis* (1686) by the English naturalist John Ray (1627-1705), which lists 17,000 specimens.[7] Ray's encyclopaedic work marks the beginnings of botany as a science based on accurate observation, experiment and the development of taxonomies of classification, rather than on myth and fable. While Ray's work was principally based on specimens gathered across Europe, the work of his friend and sometimes competitor, Sir Hans Sloane (1660-1753), was truly global in its ambition. As noted in a previous chapter, Hans Sloane went to Jamaica in 1687 as a doctor whose duties were to examine enslaved people for profitability of purchase and fitness for work. However, his principal interests lay in collecting specimens of Jamaican flora and fauna, which he wanted to bring back with him to London. The flora fared better, since it could be dried, labelled and preserved for later meticulous drawing. The fauna, including a snake, an iguana and an alligator, fared less well. All died on the return crossing, with the alligator agonisingly close to land.[8]

The purposes of collecting were mixed. The pursuit of scientific knowledge, sheer curiosity and commercial utility all had their place, though there were some in London who thought that Sloane was a mere collector. One of the commercial possibilities that he pursued was to do with the medicinal properties of plants. Later in his life he made possible the construction of the Chelsea Physic Garden, which in time became the 'central seed market of the British Empire',[9] both with respect to the drugs that enabled Europeans to survive in Africa, and the supply of cotton seeds to the colonial state of Georgia. The latter supported two centuries of African American slavery and sharecropping misery. Sloane's own discovery of the Jamaican use of cacao led to a new elite fad in the coffee houses of London.

James Delbourgo's biography, *Collecting the World: The Life and Curiosity of Hans Sloane* (2017), suggests that Sloane might have discovered more about the medicinal and sometimes hallucinogenic properties of the plants he collected had he respected better the knowledge of enslaved Africans in Jamaica. He did admit that Africans knew of the effects of 'Jesuit's bark' (cinchona), which contained quinine. It is likely that Sloane visited the Sunday markets (where enslaved people sold and exchanged surpluses from their provision grounds), in order to collect herbal specimens. He may also have used enslaved people to collect specimens for him. But even though his long-term correspondent, a Jamaican resident, Henry Barham, supplied him with information about the African use of herbal plants, this is not acknowledged in Sloane's *A Voyage to the Islands, Madera, Barbados, Nieves, S. Christophers and Jamaica* (1707 and 1725). Barham was unusual because most of his compatriots were more interested in bringing England to Jamaica, like Captain Harrison whose garden in Liguanea impressed Sloane as being 'the best furnished of any in the island with European garden plants'.[10]

By contrast, attempts to acclimatise West Indian plants in Britain were much less successful. This was because they depended on the heavy use of glasshouses and stoves. Even so, Sloane's friend Arthur Rawdon brought over 400 plants from Jamaica to his gardens in Moira, County Down, and managed to grow many of them, including cacao, in his glasshouses.[11] But generally, while absentee planters in Britain used their Caribbean wealth to create gardens and botanical collections, they did so in ways that tended not to reflect the Caribbean origins of that wealth.[12]

Despite his negrophobia, Sloane does provide an early account of the provision grounds of the enslaved, 'small plantations... wherein they took care to preserve and propagate such vegetables as grew in their own countries, to use them as they saw occasion'. He also recognised that the Africans provided a link to earlier Taino and Spanish knowledge of plant species. Sloane's Jamaican specimens included Guinea corn (sorghum), okra, lima beans and bell peppers – the former two from Africa, the latter two from the Tainos. It is also clear that Sloane recognised that the flora of Jamaica had already been much changed by Taino arrival from the mainland and by later Spanish, African and British colonisation.[13]

Back in Britain, Sloane remained wholly committed to the institution of slavery as essential to colonial commerce. His wife was an heiress of West Indian plantations and he invested in the Royal African Company and the South Sea Company, both primarily engaged in slave-trading.

We think of Britain and the Caribbean as quite separate entities, but in the 18th and early 19th centuries this was not the case. People, ideas and capital moved within a common political order, even though communications were difficult and much delayed. Jill H. Casid observes that ideas about the picturesque, which dominated elite gardens for the best part of a century, coincided with commercial expansion 'into the East and West Indies, Africa, North America, and finally the Pacific.'[14] As a result, such ideas were embraced on both sides of the Atlantic. The slave-owner and colonial administrator Edward Long evokes the picturesque in his *History of Jamaica* (1774) to attract English planters to Jamaica. He discusses growing English vegetables[15] and describes 'romantic hills and woods... exhibiting a very picturesque and beautiful appearance' with 'clumps of trees' which closely resemble Capability Brown's aesthetics.[16] Artists invariably either excluded the presence of enslaved workers from view, or showed them, improbably, taking their leisure.[17] William Beckford in *A Descriptive Account of the Island of Jamaica ... Chiefly Considered in a Picturesque Point of View* (1790), describes hours spent in 'complacency and pleasure' admiring the landscape. He rhapsodises:

> How delightful it is, when the soul appears to be detached from the body, and the cognitive powers are awake, to contemplate the sublime and the obvious wonders of creation in her more splendid as well as humble ornaments...[18]

There is, too, the troubling connection between the aesthetic pleasures of gardening and the gross sexual power made possible by slavery that is found in the obsessively detailed diaries of Thomas Thistlewood (1721-1786). As overseer, then slave-owner, he recorded how he indulged his sadistic fantasies on women, men and underage children alike – as with 3,852 rapes of 138 different women.[19] As Douglas Hall records, the same diary contains an equally detailed record of his exploits as a keen, experimental, and proficient gardener, who grew plants that were both European and tropical. 'I have now a white narcissus in flower,' he wrote, '...probably the first that flowered in this island.' It is evident that Thistlewood worked in the garden alongside 'his Negroes' and gave the vegetables they grew (including asparagus) to free and enslaved alike.[20] The images of Thistlewood as sexual exploiter and companionable gardener are difficult to reconcile because they challenge our view of gardening as a humanising activity.

Most of those who made their fortunes from slavery enjoyed the aesthetic fruits of that money more comfortably on this side of the Atlantic, and Casid argues that the greatest desire of most West Indian planters and East India Company nabobs was to return from the colonies and settle in the English countryside.[21] Thistlewood never made it back to England, and Beckford was in prison in London for debt when he wrote his picturesque account; but those who returned from the colonies with their wealth considerably stimulated British appetites for plants brought from around the globe.

Katie Donington provides a striking illustration of this phenomenon in her study of the Hibbert family.[22] As previously discussed, intergenerational Caribbean wealth reached the absentee owner and MP George Hibbert (1757-1837); he was both a leading pro-slavery advocate in Parliament and a serious and well-informed botanist. He commissioned plant collectors to find Jamaican specimens; one botanist remarked that Hibbert's garden in Clapham had an impressive and global collection of flowers.[23] Plant cultivation met a range of expressive and ideological needs for the elites. There was pleasure to be had in the elegance of gardens, but these floral havens also showcased sophisticated botanical knowledge. As Donington observes, introducing and propagating new plants presented an image of colonial figures as improvers of gardens at home and of colonies abroad.[24] Their wealth stimulated the commercial economy. It enabled them to employ the most fashionable landscapers and botanists, whose activities created the gardens that are celebrated today. As Roderick Floud shows, the newest, most desirable imports from the North American colonies and from Asia were astronomically expensive. A Benjamin tree cost the equivalent of £223, a prize rhododendron from India £1142, and a 25ft tulip tree sold for £38,000.[25] George Hibbert's specialism was in collecting heaths, Banksias, roses from China and plants from Botany Bay and the Cape of Good Hope.

Other examples of slavery connections to horticulture include Sir Rose Price (1768-1834), who gained his wealth from inherited sugar plantations in Jamaica. He used this money to develop a walled garden in a picturesque style in Trengwainton in Cornwall, near Penzance, where it can still be visited.[26] Michael Craton and James Walvin, in their study of Price's Worthy Park estate in Jamaica, describe the 'magnificent gardens' of Trengwainton as 'crammed with every sub-tropical tree, shrub and flower it is possible to grow in England'.[27] Price was able to invest in this beautiful garden by expanding production at Worthy Park, increasing its enslaved workforce to over 500 people. The Cornish connection with Jamaica was expressed in the name given to the house cook: Penzance. Price had two children with an enslaved girl named Lizette, and though these children were later educated in England,[28] he remained an ardent opponent of slave emancipation. He wrote a pamphlet claiming that the life of an enslaved person was preferable to that of an English labourer. After emancipation his family received just over £5,000 in compensation, worth around £4M today. This was actually a small amount for a large estate, but the compensation board discovered that many of the enslaved people he had claimed for were owned by others.[29]

Colonial Expansion, Plant Prospecting and the Consumer Economy
These possessors of colonial wealth sought the new skills of the landscape designer. They also depended heavily on the activities of others such as freelancing plant prospectors, quasi-state enterprises like Kew Gardens and private nursery businesses, which saw a huge growth in the 18th and 19th centuries.

Jill H. Casid notes that Lancelot 'Capability' Brown (c1716-1783), the principal landscape architect of his time, was popular precisely because his landscapes blended transplanted specimens with the English countryside.

Brownian landscapes clumped foreign trees together to make them look natural, like old English copses.[30] Brown designed the grounds owned by Robert Clive, at Claremont, and by George Anson, at Moor Park, when they returned from India and the Caribbean respectively. Brown also designed the 1,800 acre parkland at Harewood House.[31] As well as the lake, small islands and mahogany doors noted in previous chapters, the Harewood grounds also contained a grotto decorated with shells that were, like those on Hatfield Forest's Shell House, cowries shipped by the East India Company and also transported as commodities of exchange on the slave coast of West Africa.[32] Other gardens displayed military features such as bastions, no doubt to signal the military prowess of families involved in European and colonial wars. Such was the case with Thomas Goldney II, who bought Goldney Hall in 1705 and whose ironworks supplied goods – including manillas [copper money] – to exchange for enslaved people on the African West Coast.[33]

Both the garden historian Advolly Richmond and Jill H. Casid conclude that trees and shrubs from the North American colonies were probably the most common garden imports in the 18th century. In 1732, the cloth merchant Peter Collinson employed a botanist and plant collector, John Bartram, to send over more than 200 American specimens, which Collinson then supplied to rich subscribers and nurserymen. Advolly Richmond notes that this helped to popularise North American plants. She also notes that the gothic novelist and collector William Beckford had an American plantation at Fonthill Abbey.[34]

Banksias were flowering plants that originated in Australia. Their collecting by George Hibbert points to the activities of Joseph Banks (1743-1820) who, a couple of generations later, followed Hans Sloane's footsteps in taking botany in a more scientific and commercial direction.

Banks first came to attention when he led a team of naturalists and artists on the *Endeavour* (1768-1771), the ship commanded by Captain Cook on the first voyage to Australia and the South Pacific. Banks was then just twenty-five. He was a meticulous recorder of what he saw and it was this attention to detail that revealed that, like Sloane, his Eurocentric prejudices prevented him from understanding what he observed. Banks wrote in his diary about his first sight of cultivation in Tahiti. He saw the groves of coconut and breadfruit trees and other vegetables as the result of nature's bounty. He did not understand that they had been created by the agricultural skills of the Polynesian islanders. He believed he had found 'the truest picture of an arcadia of which *we were going to be kings* that the imagination can form' [my italics]. Beth Fowkes Tobin writes: 'Before Banks had laid eyes on Tahiti, he already knew what he was going to see.'[35] His view of the place as an arcadia derived from the 18th century European belief in idle and unknowing natives who simply consumed nature's plenty rather than engaging in any actual work. By contrast, Europeans had to struggle with a less bountiful climate which taught them the habits of industry and the need for the scientific knowledge that would make them masters of the world. Banks's phrase 'of which we were going to be kings' betrayed the European idea that these virtues gave them the right to take possession of such uncultivated lands (and teach idle natives the virtue of work). Banks failed to see that the Tahitians had created an agricultural system which balanced ecological and human needs. His misinterpretation forecasts the colonial destruction of such agricultural systems, misconceived as natural Edens, around the imperial world, not least in the North American colonies. This misconception had serious consequences for colonised people because it provided the crucial evidence used to prove the British legal basis for the stealing land and dispossessing its former occupants. This rested on John Locke's argument that where no agriculture was practised land was waste and could be occupied.[36]

In Tahiti, however, Banks saw the potential of the breadfruit tree as a cheap means of feeding enslaved people in the Caribbean. Importing food from the North American colonies was expensive, and the practice on some islands of allocating garden plots to enslaved people both took time away from cane cultivation and risked encouraging greater independence on the part of the enslaved. Banks's first attempt to have breadfruit trees shipped to Jamaica fell foul of the mutiny on the *Bounty*. But by 1793, 333 breadfruit trees had been delivered to the botanic gardens in St Vincent, and 346 to Jamaica. These trees were swiftly distributed to estates across the island (including to George Hibbert's brother). They grew well but there was a problem: the enslaved people would not eat them and fed them only to their pigs.[37] Generations of historians put this down to ignorant culinary conservatism, but B.W. Higman's *Jamaican Food: History, Biology, Culture* (2008) sees the refusal to eat breadfruit as 'a vehicle of resistance to the will of the slave-owning class'.[38] Breadfruit was 'slave food', promoted by the estate owners and managers, whereas the yams and plantains they grew in their gardens were vegetables that had come from Africa. After slavery ended, the breadfruit in time became a staple of the Jamaican diet.

Banks's reputation evidently suffered no great setback because of the breadfruit débâcle. By 1772 he had become the unofficial director (royal advisor) of the Royal Gardens at Kew. By 1778 he was elected president of the Royal Society, both of which positions he held for the next four decades. Under Banks, Kew Gardens became an influential place for knowledge-exchange, plant propagation and garden visits by the public.[39] This put Kew at the heart of 'botanical imperialism', a position it held well into the twentieth century. Like Sloane, Banks was an advocate of slavery, because of the economic contribution it made to British expansion.[40] Banks also proposed Botany Bay as a penal colony in 'New Holland' where judges could deport those Britons who fell foul of the increasingly harsh laws designed to protect private property.[41]

Kew, Plant Collectors and Changing Landscapes
By the 1840s, Kew's attention, now under the dynasty of the Hookers – William Jackson Hooker and his sons William Dalton Hooker and Joseph Dalton Hooker – was turning eastward. The Hookers' most far-reaching contribution to empire was the 'hub and spokes' system they established by setting up botanical gardens in India, Jamaica, Sri Lanka, St Vincent and Trinidad. Kew was at the centre, supplying trained horticulturalists, but also, over time, training local men too. The main goal of the Hookers was to trial new varieties of plants to increase the profitability of the mainly British-owned plantations in the colonies. In two crucial instances they wanted to extract plants from zones outside the empire and establish them within it.[42] One goal was transporting tea, grown principally at that time in China, to British-owned tea plantations in India, Assam in particular. After some setbacks, this became commercially successful. Even so, China remained an important source of British tea imports and the ruthlessness of empire is revealed in two opium wars (1839-42 and 1856-60). These were fought to force China to allow the import of opium from India as a British export commodity to balance the import costs of tea, for which China was until then demanding payment in silver.[43]

Another significant action of the Hookers at Kew was their instigation of the illegal extraction of seeds and saplings of the cinchona tree from Peru and other Andean areas. Known variously as Peruvian bark or Jesuit's bark, because Jesuit missionaries had observed indigenous Peruvians using it as a febrifuge, the bark, containing quinine, was the only effective treatment of malaria. Taking seeds and saplings from Peru to India not only damaged the local Peruvian industry but made possible the scramble for Africa (till then the graveyard of Europeans) and the establishment of the Raj when the wives and children of white officials felt able to join their husbands and fathers in India. Cinchona plantations were established in all parts of the tropical empire where it would grow – Burma, Fiji, Mauritius, Jamaica, Trinidad – places where Britain had organised the export of indentured labour from India to work on sugar and rubber plantations. Malaria was endemic amongst these workers, who were malnourished and lived in insanitary conditions. This not only affected their productivity but shortened their lives. Using the cheaper and less effective compound of sulphate of quinine, plantation managers kept more of their imported labour force at work.[44]

Supporting commercial plantation activities was at the heart of Kew's role in expanding the empire, but there were some notable aesthetic by-products in both the colonies and in Britain. Many of the botanical gardens that Kew helped to establish in the Caribbean still exist, and whilst in the colonial period only a small minority of West Indian people gained access to botanical knowledge as defined by Western science, many more urban West Indians of all classes began to visit these gardens to enjoy local and naturalised flora.[45] No accounts of the plots of enslaved people discussed below mention the growing of flowers, and Jack Goody in *The Culture of Flowers* (1993) asserts that he could find no evidence of flower-growing in West African culture,[46] yet the mixed growing of vegetables and ornamental flowers has been a common feature of vernacular West Indian gardens for at least the past century. Perhaps it is possible to see such gardens as having two parents: one being the botanical gardens of the elites, the other being the provision plots of the enslaved. One was about display, the other about survival. Combined, this gardening style came with Caribbean people to Britain.

The activities of Robert Fortune (1812-1880) illustrate other by-products of Kew's activities. Fortune was initially employed by the East India Company to take tea plants (illegally) from China to India. As an avid plant-hunter and botanist, Fortune is also credited with having brought back around 250 ornamental plants from China and Japan, for which there was already a commercial market in Britain (and the USA). These are plants that became staples of the British nursery business and suburban garden: bamboos, euonymus, hostas, mahonia, jasmine, weigela, Japanese anemones, Chinese honeysuckles.[47]

The same was true of rhododendrons which became such a feature of designed landscapes, their surrounding woodlands, public parks and garden shrubberies (and to some extent an invasive weed). Joseph Hooker describes their collection in *The Rhododendrons of Sikkim-Himalaya* (1851): 'The splendour of the Rhododendrons is marvellous: there are 10 kinds on this hill: scarlet, white, lilac, yellow, pink, marroon [sic]: the cliff actually blooms with them.' Yet this trip itself was charged with colonial implications. The Rajah of Sikkim had only allowed Hooker north of Darjeeling on the understanding that he did not stray into Tibet. He was afraid that Hooker's party might provoke the ire of China. But when the Rajah placed Hooker under house arrest, he was forced to relent under threat of a British invasion.[48]

Plants brought from around the world for sale to wealthier gardeners and botanists chimed with a new global imagination. Through the new art of the nursery catalogue, produced by the shrewd businessmen who by 1808 ran 49 sizeable nurseries in London, buyers were made aware of plants' rarity value; plant catalogues exaggerated their exotic appearance. The nurserymen knew buyers enjoyed engaging in shows of one-upmanship.[49] Theresa M. Kelley provides an example of this exaggeration in a letter from the botanist R.K. Greville in 1831. Having spotted a *Phaca Astragalina* in the Scottish Highlands, he said it was 'like seeing a new species of Elephant or a Palm tree in Nepal.'[50] Kelley observes that many Scottish botanists were East India Company officials or employees. Sir William Jones (1746-1794) became an amateur botanist whilst working on legal matters for the East India Company and the British government. His later publications on Indian plants and Sanskrit literature convey a genuine fascination with India's ancient culture, but also express a strong sense of contemporary colonial superiority.[51]

But gathering and describing specimens relied on collaboration with Indians, including the painting of specimens, because the plants themselves might not make the difficult journey back to Britain. For this reason volumes of botanical illustrations were produced by Indian artists for use by Company employees and consumers back in Britain. Such illustrations became an invaluable part of the wider taxonomic effort. Theresa Kelley argues that the sophisticated images produced were at odds with British assumptions about the inferiority of Indian art and culture. The scientific business of classifying plants was supposedly a British endeavour, but the history of botany in India gives a different picture: 'British botanists relied on Indian gardeners, pandits and artists' and lavish books of paintings by the latter were of genuine commodity value.[52] The East India Company employee William Roxburgh respected Indians' botanical knowledge, acknowledging, for instance, his own inability to extract dye from the chay, or madder root, as Indians did. In his 1778 volume, *Plants of the Coast of Coromandel*, Roxburgh provides the Indian names for plants, sometimes in Sanskrit, Hindi, Telegu and Tamil.[53] The scores of Indian artists who produced botanical paintings for British botanists are named in the archives, but there is little more to go on except their brief appearance in these records. When Joseph Banks praised their artistry to East India Company directors, Kelley speculates that this was in order to gain funding for Roxburgh's *Plants of the Coast of Coromandel*.[54] As Kelley concludes, British support for and appreciation of Indian botanical artists complicates the expected story of colonial domination and subjection.[55] What Kelley discovered in British attitudes to Indian colonial subjects differs quite sharply from attitudes towards enslaved Africans in the Caribbean, an instance of the kind of hierarchy of races espoused in the discourse of pseudo-scientific racism.

Slavery, Imperialism and the Landscape Garden in Literature
According to several works of eighteenth-century fiction and in a number of poems, returnees from the West Indies and India changed the appearance of rural England for ever. Tobias Smollett's *The Expedition of Humphry Clinker* (1771), Henry Mackenzie's *The Man of Feeling* (1771) and Joseph Cradock's *Village Memoirs* (1765, 1776) all blame enclosure and landscape redevelopment on returning nabobs.[56] Detailing these cautionary tales of ruined landscapes and displaced villagers, Jill H. Casid detects 'anxiety that the contact zone of colonial plantation would dangerously and irrevocably implant itself in the emblematic heart of the metropole, the countryside, displacing the familiar and familial'.[57] The minor clerical

poet, Rev. James Cawthorn (1719-1761) in his poem, 'Of Taste: An Essay' complains about the unwelcome incursion of the foreign into the English garden, designs set to match 'the boasted villas of Pekin' and the absurdity of estates where 'choice exotics to the breeze exhale' and where 'In Tartar huts our cows and horses lie, / Our hogs are fatted in an Indian stye'.[58] Such fears connect with William Cobbett's later complaint about the Baring family's ostentatious trees and alien-seeming 'plantations', discussed in Chapter Four. But views on these alterations to rural England were not all negative. Horace Walpole's *History of the Modern Taste in Gardening* (1771) thought that '[t]he introduction of foreign trees and plants... contributed essentially to the richness and colouring so peculiar to our modern landscape.' Walpole admired the 'mixture of the various greens, the contrast of forms between our forest trees and the northern and West-Indian firs and pines'.[59]

At the more intimate level of small-scale gardening, the poet William Cowper took pleasure in the flowers, fruits and vegetables of empire. He embraced the diversity of plant origins as a metaphor for a kind of human commonwealth united in its difference, but he also stressed the necessity of imperial power. He does this in the metaphor of the controlling gardener who brings this plenitude together and commands its order. There is no question that Cowper was sincere in his hatred of slavery; he consistently opposed it. Nonetheless his lines in *The Task* (1785) fail to recognise that slavery and the tropical flowers of empire he enjoyed were so intimately connected. In Book Three of *The Task*, 'The Garden', Cowper writes in the georgic tradition of giving practical horticultural advice (how to make a hotbed with straw and dung to raise cucumbers, for instance), and he promotes the garden as a space for modest human happiness, suited to the gentle pursuits of someone who abhors bloodsports. Then he turns to the desirability of gardening under glass. He writes: 'Who loves a garden, loves a green-house too':

> There blooms exotic beauty, warm and snug,
> While the winds whistle and the snows descend [...]
> The ruddier orange and the paler lime
> Peep through their polished foliage at the storm,...

He lists amomum, geranium, ficoides, ausonia and jessamine and their countries of origin:

> ...foreigners from many lands
> They form one social shade, as if convened
> By magic summons of th' Orphean lyre.
> Yet just arrangement, rarely brought to pass
> But by a master's hand, disposing well
> The gay diversities of leaf and flow'r.[60]

Though the 'master's hand' nods to the divine as well as to the gentleman gardener, it also points to the British imperial state that lies behind this gathering in of global flora. Kindly soul though Cowper evidently was, he is also clear about the necessity for power and hierarchy. It is the learned gentleman who must control, 'conscious how much the hand / Of lubbard labor needs his watchful eye, / Oft loitr'ing lazily if not o'e'rseen' (p. 173).[61] Writing about two-hundred years later, Douglas Dunn, perhaps with an eye on Andrew Marvell's 17th century poem, 'The Mower against Gardens', wittily counterblasts such ideas in his poem, 'Gardeners'. The poem speaks up for the silenced voices of centuries of labouring gardeners performing under the arrogant humiliations of generations of lordly commands, and imagining the revenge:

> Townsmen will wonder, when your house was burned,
> We did not burn your gardens and undo
> What likes of us did for the likes of you;
> We did not raze the gardens that we made,
> Although we hanged you somewhere in the shade.[62]

Botanising and the Poets

Gardening is still a class-divided occupation. This was all the more true in the 18th, 19th and early 20th centuries when labour was cheap and mostly deferential and the costs of new foreign varieties put them beyond the means of all but the rich. But even before botany became a professional occupation, the passion for studying and understanding the distinctions and relationships between different families of plants, their identification and ecology, was not limited to the gentry and those possessors of colonial wealth. Peering at plants was not just the preserve of wealthy amateurs. What engaged poets such as Erasmus Darwin, George Crabbe and John Clare was, in their different ways, more than the kind of enthusiasm for the beauty of flowers that we tend to associate with the romantic movement. In her excellent book, *The Poet as Botanist* (2008), Molly Mahood notes Dorothy Wordsworth writing in her journal in 1800, 'Oh! that we had a book of botany'.[63] The Wordsworths later equipped themselves with the four volumes of William Withering's *Arrangement of British Plants according to the latest Improvements of the Linnean System and an Introduction to the Study of Botany* (1796), and though they were keen garden-makers at both Dove Cottage in Grasmere and later at Rydal Mount,[64] the way William Wordsworth wrote about primroses, daisies, lesser celandines and daffodils tends to express an emotional and spiritual response rather than a focus on the specific characteristics of the flowers themselves. This was not the way of the true botanist. Erasmus Darwin (1731-1802), radical, abolitionist and supporter of women's right to education, brought a genuine scientific curiosity to the revelations of the Swiss botanist, Carl Linnaeus (1707-1778), that the best way of classifying plants was by their sexual organs (the number of stamens flowers had). But even Darwin was drawn to seeing the human analogies of plants in his *The Loves of the Plants* (1789), the first part of his trilogy of educative poems, *The Botanic Garden* (1792). Mahood quotes his lines on the helianthus:

> Great Helianthus guides o'er twilight plains
> In gay solemnity his dervish-trains;
> Marshalled in *fives* each gaudy band proceeds,
> Each gaudy band a plumèd lady leads...[64]

By contrast the activities and poetry of both Crabbe and Clare is based on closely observing plants as part of the natural order quite separate from human beings. Both are aware of plant uses – Crabbe began training as a herbalist; Clare worked for a time as a gardener at Burghley House in Lincolnshire – but their botanising is focused on observing variation and how this related to ecology – aspect, soil, climate and other forms of animal life. Crabbe was drawn to witness the difficult environment of the East Anglian coast, to find interest in what others dismissed as mere weeds. In his long poem, *The Village*, noted in Chapter Three, he writes of the competition for space in cultivated fields:

> There the blue bugloss paints the sterile soil;
> Hardy and high, above the slender sheaf,
> The slimy mallow waves her silky leaf;
> O'er the young shoot the charlock throws a shade,
> And clasping tares cling round the sickly blade...[65]

As a gardener (both for himself and the noble Cecil family), a villager who at times had to work as an agricultural labourer, and an avid botanist ('I took a walk today to botanize'), auto-didact and poet, John Clare shows just how far the passion for botanising had spread from the elite to the agricultural and later to the industrial working classes. Donna Landry notes that Elizabeth Gaskell's novel *Mary Barton* (1848) describes how among 'the handloom weavers of Oldham ... were botanists "equally familiar with the Linnaean or the Natural system, who knew the name and habitat of every plant within a day's walk from their dwellings..."'.[66] John Clare had problems with the Linnaean system of taxonomy, not because he couldn't understand it but because its latinate formality offended his belief that 'the vulgar are always the best glossary', though he also acknowledged that in his village community there were flowers that had no name. It was to older encyclopaedic works that Clare turned, such as that of John Ray. For Clare, after reading Linnaeus, such works were like 'meeting the fresh air and balmy summer of a dewy morning after the troubled dreams of a nightmare'.[67] In his poetry and serious attempts to write a prose work on local wild flowers (he wanted to follow in the footsteps of Gilbert White's *The Natural History and Antiquities of Selborne*

(1789) for his own local Helpston), Clare stayed with such regional names as hernshaw, lambtoes, totter grass, eyebright, horse blobs and the like. Those were the terms that connected these plants with local places and local knowledge.[68] As I discussed in the pastoral chapter, Clare used close observation as a weapon against the permanently impoverishing experience of enclosure as experienced by ordinary country people.[69] 'Vulgar 'glossaries' were a claim to rights of access. His descriptions of flowers and trees detailed what was being destroyed by the '[a]ccursed wealth' that was laying waste to the countryside, including the 'woods [that] bow down to clear a way' for landowners.[70] A good example of his plant-knowledge can be found in his poem 'Wild Flowers', which ranges over various habitats – pastures, lakes and meadows – to observe how flowers bloom wherever the conditions are right without regard for artificial boundaries, 'where herd cows meet the showers' or 'in the wood'.[71] Clare had a reputation for spotting flowers that no one else could match and his detailed observations extended to the wildlife around him.[72] Mahood estimates that there are 370 plants named by Clare in his poetry and prose, but as she notes with regard to the class-divided world in which Clare existed, there were times when he 'was in dire need of guidance through this Babel of local, popular, horticultural, scientific and poetic names'.[73]

But it would be wrong to think that there was no connection between Clare and the more genteel world of botany found in country estates and rural parsonages. There was a close and mutually enriching friendship between Clare and two senior members of the staff at the nearby Milton Hall in Northamptonshire – Edmund Artis, the steward and Joseph Henderson, the head gardener, who had published papers on ferns and other cryptogams. There were visits, exchanges of letters, gifts of plants and loans of books from the Milton Hall library. Clare also acknowledged Henderson's help in lifting him out of one of his depressions: 'We talked about books and flowers and butterflies'.[74] Clare's interests spanned easily across from his botanising walks to cultivating his own garden, where he was just as keen on growing the new flowers of fashion, probably given to him by Henderson, as on bringing wild flowers into it. He notes in his journal in 1825, 'Made a new frame for my auriculas'.[75] This was likely an auricula theatre, a kind of open-air bookcase for displaying pots of these intensely variegated flowers. If so, it creates some historical precedence for one of the first appearances of a Black British gardener on the television programme, *Gardener's World,* in May 2020. In this programme, the garden historian, Advolly Richmond, talked about auricula theatres.[76]

Allotments: Discipline or Opportunity for Working People?
With the exception of the account of John Clare's botanising, the dominant narrative of gardens and plants has so far been one of wealth, inequality,

empire, enclosure and the capitalization of land. Very little has been said about the lives of those whose labour, on either side of the Atlantic, made the wealth possible. For them, the growth of allotments and public parks in the 19th century made minor but real differences to the quality of their lives. Even so, the development of such facilities remained closely connected to the economic forces described above.[77]

We tend to associate allotments with cloth-capped old men, though currently more women than men rent them. Demand for them (many with waiting lists of up to five years) has also spread to young professionals, as suburban gardens have shrunk.[78] But in their origins in the later 18th and early 19th centuries, allotments were the response of the landed elites to a mix of rebelliousness and rising poverty amongst the rural working class.[79] These had been caused, in part, by the acceleration of enclosures between 1760 and 1845. The motivations behind the provision of allotments were complex. They undoubtedly met a need for survival that otherwise had to be found from poor relief, with the consequence of higher rates levied on local landowners and others. Another of the promptings, particularly in the south and midlands of England, were the Swing Riots of 1831. These struck terror in the minds of landowners and the bigger farmers; their threshing machines were destroyed and their farms were at risk of arson and mass invasions by labourers armed with agricultural implements.[80] Supporters of allotments boasted that in areas where there was adequate provision, labourers had not joined the Swing campaigns. Another strand in the elite case was the value of allotments as a means of social engineering – to civilise agricultural workers and keep them from the alehouse. Enthusiasts for allotments reported miraculous improvements of behaviour – including pride in appearance, neat homes, and the conversion of the previously ungodly to observing the sabbath.[81] How much of this was true, how much propaganda is hard to determine, but it is evident that allotment renters were under strict discipline enforced by landowners, such as not, for instance, being allowed to keep pigs. There was also the constant threat of eviction for any breach of the prohibitions against catching game in the surrounding fields.[82]

Whatever the motivation, for many rural workers allotments made a significant contribution to survival. In the 1830s the average agricultural worker earned between £12 and £21 a year, depending on local soil quality and the supply and demand for labour. Allotments could produce a profit (in goods at least) of between £3-4 pounds a year.[83]

Though there was a debate about the utility of allotments amongst the landed elite as well as the bigger tenant farmers and would-be improvers of the lives of the agricultural poor, those with most economic power won the argument. The debate was over size. Allotments had to be big enough to keep workers' families from having to turn to poor law doles, but landowners did not want to give up any more land than they had to, nor see the emergence of an independent peasantry that had no need of wage labour. As Steve Poole observes of that debate, landowners thought that if the allotments were too big, it would put agricultural labourers 'above the necessity of labour, and would render them idle, insolent and immoral'.[84] This was precisely the argument made by plantation owners in the West Indies against a minority of more enlightened colonial officials in the decades after emancipation, who saw the desirability of a self-sustaining African Caribbean peasantry, which could also produce for the market.[85] Both in Britain and the Caribbean, those who owned land made sure this never happened. When the ruling Victorian agricultural and industrial classes referred to 'labour', they meant only the discipline of wage labour and the control of workers' lives. As a consequence, as Poole notes, by the 1830s, 30,000 agricultural workers were leaving the countryside every year. This was unsurprising when a railway worker could earn wages three times that of a farm labourer.

The attempt to introduce the breadfruit as cheap food to feed enslaved people in the Caribbean has its parallel in British agricultural history with another 'exotic' vegetable, the potato from South America. The staples of the rural diet had traditionally been beer and bread, the products of wheat and barley. However, by the 1750s the price of both had risen as farmers and merchants exported the best quality grains. In the 1790s there was a series of disastrous harvests. Worse still, the French wars and Napoleonic blockade of imports doubled prices. Food riots resulted and angry working people attacked the king in London. The potato was seen as a panacea. While in some parts of the country allotment holders had enough land to grow wheat, the potato needed far less space to feed families and, as already mentioned, those with land wanted to restrict the size of allotments. Though radical campaigners such as William Cobbett complained bitterly about the poor quality of the labourers' diet, the need was so great that, unlike in the West Indies where enslaved people rejected the breadfruit, English agricultural labourers embraced the potato to such an extent that many allotments became the 'potato patch'. Enthusiasm for the potato was, though, dampened by potato blight in 1846 – which also decreased the demand for allotments.[86]

Land issues surfaced again in the last decades of the nineteenth century when agricultural workers briefly found a political leader in Joseph Arch, the founder of the Agricultural Labourers Union in 1872, who led the farm labourers' strike in 1874. This, though, was defeated by the bigger farmers with a mass lockout. Having allotments became a matter of survival, and the threat of being evicted from them pressured workers to abandon both the union and the strike.[87]

There was a brief period in the midst of the long agricultural slump in the later decades of the 19th century, during William Gladstone's Liberal government of 1880-1885, when the issue of land reform surfaced on the national agenda. 'Three acres and a cow' became the rallying cry of the campaigns for the extension of smallholdings (to between one and fifty acres). Though successive acts between 1882 and 1926 enabled some expansion of smallholdings known as 'county farms', these did not last. In 1977, county farms comprised less than 2% of agricultural land; by 2018 this was less than 1%.[88]

From the twentieth century onwards, the demand and provision of allotments became primarily an urban matter. Thereafter, with the exception of the two periods of world war, and the Dig for Victory campaign of 1939-45 when there were 1.75 million tenancies, allotments have increasingly been seen as spaces for leisure and exercise. Even in the period after 1945, when there were acute shortages of fresh vegetables, tenancy of allotments declined sharply, and further plummeted from the 1960s onwards as supermarkets started to supply cheap, continentally-grown vegetables. Allotments were looked on as old-fashioned. There has been something of a revival from the 250,000 or so renters in England in 1999, to around 300,000 in recent times with 100,000 on waiting lists. This partial revival of the allotment movement followed the Thorpe Report (1969), which advocated plots for city-dwellers without gardens. In the 1980s, the Thorpe Report was used by a Friends of the Earth campaign to encourage domestic food-growing for environmental reasons.[89]

In his otherwise highly informative history (from which this brief account is drawn), Steve Poole's *Allotment Chronicles: A Social History of Allotment Gardening* (2006), there is, though, a mix of the patronising and disapproving in the coverage of the access of Black British and British Asian people to allotments. Poole notes how West Indian tenants took up allotment gardening in the 1960s, and how such tenants grew sweetcorn, peppers, pumpkins, and chillis' but 'largely took a casual attitude to allotment gardening, and placed little emphasis on tidiness'.[90] By this he probably meant that they did not favour the strict segregation of vegetables and the methodical planting in rows favoured until recently by generations of British gardeners. As the later discussion of West Indian gardening practices inherited from Africa sets out to show, mixed plantings were rooted in African gardening practices, and, as more recent expertise in raised-bed gardening has shown, these help to avoid insect-borne and other plant diseases.

The Public Park

From the Restoration period onwards, particularly in London, there were parks open to the public. One such park was immortalised in John Wilmot's scandalous 'A Ramble in St James's Park', where beneath the park's trees at night:

Are buggeries, rapes and incests made.
Unto this all-sin-sheltering grove
Whores of the bulk and the alcove,
Great ladies, chambermaids and drudges,
The ragpicker and heiress trudges.
Carmen, divines, great lords, and tailors,
Prentices, poets, pimps and jailers,
Footmen, fine fops do here arrive,
And here promiscuously they swive... [91]

Here, Wilmot, the Earl of Rochester (1647-1680), sees parks as places
where the grand social mixing that the serious-minded social improvers
of the 1830s set their hearts on, actually took place – though for rather
less wholesome purposes. The improvers sought to bring morally
enlightening and healthful recreation to the urban working class in
cities throughout Britain. Indeed, the history of parks reflects a constant
struggle between users seeking their self-defined pleasures and the
municipal and other would-be circumscribers of behaviour in parks –
such as the sabbatarians or the officials who persecuted 'verminous'
park users (the homeless). Park users have always had a sense of their
rights. In her study, *Public Parks* (1996), Hazel Conway records that,
in the 1720s, Queen Caroline wanted to close St. James's Park to the
public, and asked Sir Robert Walpole how much this would cost. 'Only
a crown, madam' was Walpole's supposed reply.[92] In later times, parks
have been places for political demonstrations and debate, as in London's
Hyde Park. It is also clear that parks have always been a territory for
sexual encounters of all kinds, and equally as grounds for moral panics.
A 1995 Demos report on public parks noted that they have always been
places where rules were subverted, as well as and spaces for oppressed
social groups.[93] It mentions, for instance, Isaac Julien's film *Young Soul
Rebels* (1991), with key scenes set in a public park where young people
of different classes, races and sexualities clash, interact and sometimes
find points of contact.[94] As signs of the official desire for control, over
the years, children have been banned from ball games in small green
spaces in the most deprived areas. More recently, during the Covid-
19 pandemic, people were locked out of parks, and police officers were
sent to reprimand sunbathers and bench-sitters. In their history, there
were always tensions between those who saw public parks as continuations
of 18th century pleasure gardens, with a focus on 'attractions', displays
and entertainments, and those who saw parks as places for the improvement
of the working class through the quiet contemplation of trees, shrubs
and flowering plants, and observing wildlife in ponds and lakes.[95]

Before their later municipalisation, parks' colonial connections were
strong. Travis Elborough notes that on his return from India where he had
made his money working as Commissioner-General, the Tory MP Joseph

Hume (1777-1855) sought and gained royal approval for an East London park, near Bonner's Fields. This became known to locals as Botany Bay, because people hid there to escape from being forcibly transported to Australia.'[96] In Liverpool, the park known as Allerton Towers was the home of the plantation owner Hardman Earle (1792-1877), the descendant of three generations of slave-traders. Earle received over £19,000 in compensation for lost slave-labour in 1834 and employed a fashionable architect to design his Allerton home. Earl's orangery can still be visited.[97]

In her as yet unpublished work on London public parks, Katrina Navickas observes that the shape, arrangement, plantings, provision of utilities (such as toilets, drinking fountains, and cafés) that we know today, were all established in the 19th century. This began from the 1830s onwards (though parks were only gradually accessible to the poorest).[98] But by 1900 almost all the 27,000 parks and green spaces that currently exist in the UK had been established. Navickas shows that the establishment of parks was a shrewd partnership between those who saw their social necessity, such as the House of Commons select committee of 1833 (who warned that unless parks were provided, 'great mischief must arise'),[99] and landowners and house-builders who saw the potential for raising land values by building houses around park borders. The provision of road, rail and bridge infrastructure around and into parks was another means of increasing land values. Some speculators made high profits from selling land for parks. Others so inflated the asking price that some parks were much smaller than originally intended. By the mid 1840s there was a government body charged with the oversight of parks (Her Majesty's Commissioners of Woods and Forests, later the Commission of Works). By the mid 19th century, most English cities had begun the process of establishing the parks still present today.

Navickas's history of Battersea Park illustrates some of the phases through which parks across the nation passed, although London's 3,000 parks across 35,000 acres have always been the location of much higher investment than elsewhere in the country. They were part of the project of national and imperial display to impress visitors and out-compete continental rivals. As Nan Hesse Dreher shows in her doctoral thesis, *Public Parks in Urban Britain, 1870-1920: Creating a New Public Culture* (1993), parks were intended to stimulate a composite national identity that competed against radical political and trade union voices. Park planners installed 'Shakespeare gardens', full of the plants named in the plays, erected war memorials for the victims of the Napoleonic, Crimean and Boer wars, flew the flag, installed military bandstands, designed imitation Khyber passes,[100] planted commemorative trees and held royal jubilees. In London, the botanical and zoological gardens displayed plant and animal life from all quarters of the empire. Dreher suggests that provincial parks were less nationally and imperially focused, with more emphasis on local civic pride.[101]

Navickas's history shows Battersea Park's beginnings as a place of landscaping, tree-planting, and the establishment of shrubberies and borders on a vast scale. Though John Gibson, who was appointed to manage the park, was instructed to plant at as low a cost as possible, it was a bonanza for the London nurseries who supplied over 2000 trees and larger shrubs (including the newly fashionable rhododendrons) and many more flowering and ornamental plants. Gibson himself was a veteran of Indian plant-hunting expeditions and he planted hardy banana plants he himself had grown. Thereafter it seems that the emphasis was chiefly on creating visitor attractions: sports facilities, bandstands, refreshment rooms, boating lakes, putting greens, cycling circuits (by the 1890s) and sculpture exhibitions – the goal being to bring culture to the masses. Much less attention was paid to Battersea park as a natural place of trees, shrubs and plants. By 2000, Navickas reports: 'the few remaining features of the gardens had deteriorated almost beyond recognition'. Fortunately, the Heritage Lottery fund enabled the local council (Wandsworth) to invest in 'perhaps as much work [as] was done on the site as when it was first laid out in the 1850s and early 1860s'.[102]

A similar crisis brought about by decreasing financial investment in parks prompted reports by the House of Commons Communities and Local Government Committee and by Heritage England in 2016-2017. Both reports showed that while there was little decrease in demand for access to parks, there were major inequalities in provision and that decades of government budget cuts to local authorities had led to a deterioration of the condition of parks and their facilities. Local authorities have no statutory duty to maintain parks, so, cash-strapped, they cut staff and maintenance to the point where the state of paths, trees, children's playgrounds, ponds and toilet facilities raised serious health and safety concerns. As a result many parks suffered littering and increased vandalism. Investment through the Heritage Lottery Fund has mitigated some of these problems, but since Heritage funding was dependent on councils having the budget to maintain restored or new facilities, many councils were unable to apply for funds. Other threats to the future of parks lay in the pressure on local authorities to sell off parts of parks (and playing fields) for housing to ease budget constraints, or hand over the management of parks to private, profit-making concerns, without democratic accountability.[103]

One of the major findings of both reports were the structural inequalities of park provision and, often as a result, of their use. Research found that the 20% of the most affluent wards in council areas had on average five times more green space than the 10% of most deprived areas.[104] Again, though Black and minority ethnic households used parks in general more frequently than white users (71% visited at least once a month, against 56%), in areas where Black people accounted for 40% of the population, the provision of park space was poorest. The Commons report quoted a study that showed that 'the quality of, access to, and use of green urban space was a significant predictor of general health for people of African Caribbean, Bangladeshi, Pakistani origin and other BME groups, who were also those with the poorest health'.[105]

But, as the Covid-19 pandemic has shown, many urban Britons (37 million or 57% of the population) regularly use parks as places to bring young children to play, for sport and exercise (park runs for example), for quiet contemplation, for disabled access (the countryside is often inaccessible), and meeting friends (particularly important for school age children). Parks are also used as safe routes to walk or cycle to work, for community events, family picnics, dog-walking, feeding ducks, taking photographs, or observing nature.

The poet Grace Nichols expresses a Black British enjoyment of parks, because they are places where nature expresses the interconnectedness of continents, peoples and histories. Her poem 'In the Shade of a London Plane Tree' closely observes the tree's aesthetic characteristics – its 'spiked fruit balls' and 'maple-like / leaves' – but also its lesson for modern Britons. She is inspired by its 'hybrid heart' which combines 'a merging of Oriental plane / and American sycamore' expressing 'green and breathing tolerance.'[106]

The suburban garden

Historic England notes that, while 8 out of 10 people live in suburban areas, Office of National Statistics data shows that 1 in 8 people in England have no access to a private or a shared garden, and that people of colour are 2.4 times more likely than white people not to have a garden.[107] Again, the notion of the suburban garden must be recognised as an incredibly wide one. It ranges from those of the large detached houses often built in the first phase of suburbia with half-acre gardens (just over 2000 square metres), to the much smaller 4 million semi-detached houses built in the interwar period with an estimated average garden size of between 200 and 250 sq metres (the 80 ft long x 25 ft wide plot of 0.06 acres). The garden size of many recently built houses is even smaller. The minimum garden size recommended by local planning authorities can vary from between 70 and 100 sq. metres, where families have to choose between minimal play areas for children or growing plants.[108] Land-hoarding and land-speculation, as discussed in Chapter Two, has driven up the price of land.

Though we may consider the suburban garden a democratic space, it is no less shaped by class and inequality than the landed estate. As working people moved into the industrial and commercial cities of England in the 19th century, the newly rich middle and professional classes moved out to escape increasing overcrowding and insanitary conditions. Initially this was a movement of a rich minority, but as railways, omnibus routes and underground systems expanded, particularly around London, it became possible for a much wider segment of the population to move and commute into the city to work. This phase of suburbanisation was at its height from the 1860s to the turn of the century. Another important phase was the idea of the garden suburb, the planned approach to building mixed communities in open land theorised by Ebenezer Howard in his *Garden Cities of Tomorrow* (1902).[109] His ideas are still being revisited. The garden city movement initially distinguished itself from the paternalist activities of earlier nineteenth century philanthropist industrialists such as Sir Titus Salt, Joseph Rowntree and George Cadbury, who thought that workers would be more productive and loyal if better housed.[110] But as Standish Meacham argues in his book, *Regaining Paradise: Englishness and the Early Garden Movement* (1999), the movement dropped the more radical calls for land reform and became a culturally conservative programme for maintaining the established order. Meacham argues that Letchworth and Hampstead village were seen as places where the middle classes would civilize the lower orders, after the fashion of the village squirearchy.[111]

The housing boom of the interwar years saw over 4 million private and council houses built. This was probably the phase when the greatest number of Britons gained access to gardens. Council tenants were bound by their tenancy agreements to keep their gardens tidy (no pigeons). For private householders 'a neat garden was an essential hallmark of respectability'.[112] For both private and council tenants there was often the problem that work involved long commutes and the nearest shops, libraries, schools, churches, cinemas and pubs were sometimes distant. Wives, more usually working in the home than outside during this period, often felt isolated and housebound. These were George Orwell's prisons 'with the cells all in a row... semi-detached torture chambers'[113] Other stereotypes followed of car-washing, gnomes, the 'tudorbethans of metroland',[114] and of materialistic aspirations. Perhaps more seriously, suburbia took the form of ribbon development eating into the countryside and making car ownership essential.

Yet, for many millions of people, suburban garden spaces are as good as it gets. As many wildlife trusts have shown, the suburban garden is an important space for protecting bio-diversity – providing gardens are not paved or concreted over. Black British and British Asian writers, as discussed below, have written about them as places that provide access to the natural world and promote self-expression.

From Africa to the New World: a Counter-Movement within the Empire
So far I have discussed the relationship between gardens and colonial figures who brought plants back home. There is a counterstory. This

concerns the movement of people, plants, skills and cultural styles from Africa to the New World, and then from the Caribbean to the heart of empire in Britain and to the process of redefining the garden's essential Englishness.

The contribution of the indigenous peoples of the Americas to the global food variety is discussed in books such as Alfred W. Crosby's *The Columbian Exchange* (1972). Crosby showed just how many important foodstuffs were cultivated by indigenous peoples and brought back to Europe to become staples. These include the potato, sweetcorn, tomato, and chilli peppers among many others.[115] What Crosby's first book did not recognise was the degree to which African foodstuffs diversified food staples in the Americas and the Caribbean. This omission was corrected by Judith A. Carney and Richard Rosomoff's *In the Shadow of Slavery: Africa's Botanical Legacy in the Atlantic World* (2009). This is an important study of cultural transmission and of African agency in the transatlantic world. As the authors argue, the past failure to recognise the African contribution was part of an array of negative stereotypes about Africa. Carney and Rosomoff observe that the long, three-month voyages endured by enslaved Africans from Africa's west coast to the North American and the West Indian colonies could not have taken place without a well-developed system of food production on the West African coast that produced a surplus for selling to slave-trading ships. Individual ship's records show, for instance, 8 tons of rice and 1000 plantains and high quantities of other foodstuffs being taken aboard for a single voyage.[116] Carney and Rosomoff indicate that West Africa had developed sophisticated systems of cultivation of plant staples such as the cereals sorghum, millet and African rice, many varieties of green vegetables including okra and pigeon peas and the domestication of animals (such as n'dama cattle and woolless sheep, goats and guinea fowl) that were suited to the local environment. Africans had evolved methods of horticulture using one type of plant to shelter another (multi-storey garden plots) and inter and multi-cropping to avoid the kind of diseases and insect depredations that came with mono-crop cultivation. Areas of erosion from heavy rainfall and limited natural soil fertility were counteracted by interaction between specialist groups of herders and agriculturalists, with dung as the herders' gift. This was not a closed system. West African farmers were cultivating crops brought by longstanding trading relationships with India, including the ancient arrival of plantains and bananas to Africa, and sorghum, millet and okra went from Africa to India. West African farmers were also quick to utilise plants that fitted into seasonal gaps, such as maize, sweet potato and manioc (cassava) that Portuguese slave traders brought from Brazil.[117]

But this was not a free movement of people and plants. It was driven by transatlantic chattel slavery. Maize was important because of the keeping

qualities of its flour. As Carney and Rosomoff write, maize flourished
because 'its cultivation and preparation made the cereal ideally suited to the
trade in human beings'.[118] But while the plants travelled on the ships of
European slavers as sustenance for the long voyage, how these plants became
embedded in Caribbean systems of cultivation is very much an African story.
It is clear that at the Caribbean end, Europeans rarely knew what the foods
were, or how to grow them. In both historical probability and stories handed
down the generations, Africans saw in the transfer of foodstuffs one of the
few ways to sustain a connection with their homeland. These stories mostly
centred on the agency of an African woman who hid seeds and grains of rice
in her hair, or in her children's hair. Such narratives have been found, as
Carney and Rosomoff record, amongst Maroon communities in Suriname,
Cayenne and in Brazil. The Brazilian version has a white man running his
hands through the hair of children disembarking from a slave ship, discovering red-husked rice grains, then asking what they were. The point of the
story was that it was African knowledge that effected the transfer.[119] The
British-born Jamaican-American poet, Marcia Douglas has a seven part
poem, 'Wild Rice' in her collection *Electricity Comes to Cocoa Bottom* (1999)
that pursues this connection:

I
Before she stole away,
Mama Pansa braided grains of rice into her hair;
tying it with a red cloth.
Later, in the dark hills safe from barking dogs,
she loosened her plaits,
seeds falling like soft rain
into the cupped palms of her children. [...]

III

Here is your coat of arms:
two and a half cups of rice
one cup of red beans
a dry coconut, a little garlic, a little thyme,
quarter teaspoon black pepper, a few pinches of salt.
No instructions needed. [...]

VII
In this small zinc house,
we go to bed with bellies fluffed full of white rice
and we all know that the patter of the rain against our window
is really the swollen finger tips of the forgotten dead
longing
        to come in.[120]

More generally, however, prejudices about Africans meant that credit
for making the plant transfer was habitually attributed to Europeans.
Hans Sloane credited the transfer of the African palm oil tree (a key

ingredient in skin preparations) in this way, writing that the tree was 'brought over with some others from Guinea in Tubs water'd by the Way, and then planted by Colonel Collbeck in his Plantation now belonging to Mr Bernard.'[121] Katie Donington notes that a botanist named Thomas Dancer credited a significant seed transfer to George Hibbert's slave-ships: 'Amomum Gr. Paradisi Grains of paradise or Guiney Pepper. Introduced by Mr Hibbert from Africa'. But Dancer also noted that 'Aka Africana', the modern day staple, ackee, was 'introduced by Negroes in some of Mr Hibbert's ships'.[122] Text-based historical knowledge of what was achieved on the provision grounds of enslaved Africans largely depends on the records kept by plantation owners and managers and white visitors whose estimate of the abilities of Africans was shaped by the need to justify enslavement. For instance, in 1687, Hans Sloane wrote that he saw enslaved people growing Angola peas on their plots: 'This shrub is frequently cultivated by the negroes, because it is a perennial, and does not require so much care... The seeds are much used among the poorer sort of people, and reckoned a hearty wholesome pulse.'[123] As previously noted, the one unquestionably European food import to support slavery, the breadfruit tree, was a failure.

What ensured the survival of African foodstuffs (and of enslaved people's sense of their origins) was the predicament of the plantation owners. They needed to keep their investments alive, with sufficient nutrition in order to slave hard 'in the burning sun' as Israel Vibration sang in 'So Far Away'.[124] Barry Higman has calculated that enslaved people worked for an average of 4000 hours a year against the 2900 hours of British factory workers in 1830. This did not include work on their own plots. (Such figures contradict the claims of slavery's supporters – and some contemporary historians – that British factory workers were treated as badly, if not worse, than slaves.)[125] The owner's predicament was that, on the one hand, at the height of sugar's profitability, any sacrifice of productive plantation land and enslaved people's labour was anathema; on the other, the turn to the North American colonies to supply commodities such as salt fish, salt beef and salt pork was a growing cost of production, particularly after American independence.

The solution of the more astute estate owners was to put the onus for survival on the Africans themselves. This was a further exploitation since enslaved people had to labour on their food plots in their scant free time (usually on a Sunday) in order to feed themselves or starve. Estate managers also thought that giving enslaved people access to provision plots would make them less liable to run away and abandon their own produce. But because many of the bigger provision plots were on difficult terrain unsuitable for sugar cultivation (at some distance away from the central parts of estate lands), this distance provided rare moments away from constant observation and harsh labour discipline. Carney and Rosomoff suggest that work on what they term 'the botanical gardens of the dispossessed' helped to form social and family bonds.[126] Enslaved people often had much smaller 'dooryard gardens' by their huts for medicinal herbs and green vegetables. Their plots also sometimes generated a surplus and the phenomena of the previously mentioned Sunday markets, where goods (foodstuffs, pottery, housewares, clothing, alcohol, tobacco) were sold or exchanged. As Roderick A. McDonald documents in *The Economy and Material Culture of Slaves* (1993) this helped to develop an alternative cash economy in Jamaica and other sugar islands.[127]

The tradition of provision growing amongst enslaved Africans also went back to the earliest days of slavery; one of the principal achievements of these growers, who for a time overlapped with the dwindling Amerindian populations, was to create a Caribbean gardening culture that fused Amerindian and African staple foods. As the Amerindians ceased to survive on islands such as Jamaica, Africans became the main repository of the Amerindian food heritage. Food plants to be found on these plots included egg plants (guinea squash), okra, taro, cassava, several varieties of yam, plantains, gourds, pigeon peas, black-eyed peas, sesame, sorrel, amaranth (callaloo) and others. Okra, for instance, was a good source of vitamins and folate, whilst pulses contained proteins. Without this food culture (and the provision of such plots was not a universal feature of the slave world), basic calorie, mineral and vitamin deficiencies led to many illnesses and early deaths.[128] As Vincent Brown writes in *The Reapers Garden: Death and Power in the World of Atlantic Slavery* (2008), the owners of sugar estates were utterly dependent on fresh importations of enslaved people to maintain stable numbers, and new arrivals were most vulnerable to death during their first years in the colony.[129]

It was not just the seeds or roots that Africans brought to the Caribbean but the knowledge of how to grow them on, for instance, hilly terrain, or in seasons of drought or flood. African gardeners knew how, for instance, to use taller plants with resistance to fierce sun as a means of shading smaller, less heat-tolerant plants. Such cultivation techniques have been studied in the Caribbean right up to the 21st century in islands such as mountainous, volcanic Montserrat, where Lydia M. Pulsipher records the persistence of such methods.[130] Richard Westmacott similarly finds evidence of this African heritage in his book, *African-American Gardens and Yards in the South* (1992). He found this both in the kinds of plants grown, in the spatial arrangements of gardens and in the social and spiritual values that owners associated with their plots. Sustainability and working with nature appeared to be key values.[131]

Modern Caribbean food culture reflects this history. The cuisines of the islands and Guyanas reflect different histories of contact – including the culinary influence of Spanish, French, Dutch and British conquerors. But it is on an African (and submerged Amerindian) base that the region's food culture rests. Added to that, there is the culinary influence of the more than a quarter of a million ex-indentured Indian and Chinese people whose descendants settled in the region. Indeed, to see Caribbean cuisine through the lens of conquest and domination, or even through African, Indian and Chinese settlement, underplays the importance of longstanding culinary creativity which has fused styles and combined ingredients to create creolised Caribbean dishes that differ significantly from their African, Indian, Chinese and European origins.[132]

When emancipated Africans were at last free to leave the plantations and sugar prices fell in the 1840s, there was an opportunity to allow the development of an independent peasantry based on the skills Africans had sustained on their provision grounds, but on a larger scale. However, as in 19th century Britain where there was also a campaign to encourage smallholdings, the landowning class in both Britain and the colonies continued to control land-use, keen to hold down wages by maintaining a labour surplus.[133] With the exception of Guyana where a self-generated Indo-Guyanese rice-farming peasantry emerged – until it was decimated by the statist policies of the Burnham government from the 1970s to the 1980s – Caribbean agricultural smallholdings have in general been too small and too starved of any kind of national priority to achieve more than mere subsistence. Farms of less than two hectares comprise almost 90% of all the agricultural sector in countries in the Caribbean community of 15 nations (CARICOM).[134] The low status of agriculture has undoubtedly been a driver of mass emigration, but as this chapter shows, people of Caribbean heritage have brought their vegetables, foodways, and gardening styles to Britain.

The presence of Black gardeners in Britain is by no means only a post-Windrush phenomenon. For instance, gardening historians such as Jeffrey Green, Jan Marsh and Advolly Richmond researched Thomas Birch Freeman, born in Hampshire in 1809, from among the network of plant experts during the Victorian period. He had an African father and was employed as a gardener at Orwell Park, near Ipswich, by Sir Robert Harland. Freeman ended his days on the Gold Coast of West Africa, where he was a Methodist Christian missionary, but continued to correspond on botanical matters (using Latin nomenclature) with William Hooker at Kew Gardens.[135] In addition, the Garden Museum owns a full-length portrait of a barefooted Black gardener painted around 1905 by the socialist painter Harold Gilman. The subject's dignified posture depicts gardening as a noble occupation.[136] Jeffrey Green discovered that in 1888, Newcastle's Green Park employed a Black park-keeper, but that the locals disliked him on account of his race. The *Newcastle Weekly Courant* commented that 'it is very improbable that the coloured gentleman will be re-engaged.'[137] Another Black gardener, George Makippe, who was known as Watteau, worked at Chislehurst, in Kent. He married, had three sons and died in 1931.[138]

Currently, there are a number of Black British and British Asian gardeners with national profiles. As noted above, Advolly Richmond, a Trustee of Welsh Historic Gardens, has presented on *Gardener's World*. So has Arit Anderson, a landscape designer. Juliet Sargeant is another high-profile Black British landscape and garden designer.

Migratory Plants and Migratory People

Richard Mabey has published many influential books, beginning with *Food for Free* (1972), an attempt to revive the old custom of wild foraging. Like John Clare, he regrets how in the countryside '[e]very road and path seemed to lead straight to a "Private" sign.'[139] His later books, such as *Flora Britannica* (1996), took botanic knowledge back to the meanings that flowers have in social rituals, reminding us that 'From the outside, it must look as if we are botanical aboriginals, still in thrall to the spirits of vegetation'. He observes that there is nothing constrained about the way that plants behave, noting 'exotic species constantly escaping into the wild', and of the 'two-way traffic of wild and cultivated plants over the garden wall'.[140] The psycho-geographer Iain Sinclair has praised Mabey for showing how 'wild nature... obliterates the laminated notice boards of unsanctioned history'.[141] Mabey observed that we look for nature in the usual places but fail to notice it everywhere around us. He wrote that our 'attitude towards nature is a contradictory blend of romanticism and gloom... If we are looking for wildlife we turn automatically towards the official countryside, towards the great set-pieces of forest and moor.'[142] His early book *The Unofficial Countryside* (1973) practised a form of postcolonial botany in its examination of a landfill site. He noted that imported canary seed ended up in landfill, and then sprouted colourfully on the hillsides. He saw kitchen waste as an incidental introducer of species, 'the remains of bottles of oriental spice... can turn into flowers that are an astonishment to find blooming in a down-and-out English field ... On a tip, a local firm's latest import line can introduce seeds from halfway across the world, caught up in the packaging materials.'[143] He recorded that liverworts arrived from the Mediterranean in Roman times, orange balsam from the Americas in 1822 and that giant hogweed was 'introduced ...as an exotic curiosity for Victorian gardens.'[144] Meanwhile, in the rural outlands of Essex, birdseed bloomed: 'Here, the sunflowers... outshone everything else... there were the deep purple cascades of love-lies-bleeding; countless breeds of millet and canary grass from Australia, Morocco and South America: niger from India, yellow safflowers, blue flaxes, and, most curious of all, a shoofly plant from Peru, with pale lilac flowers tightly closed in the gloom and Chinese lantern fruit cases.'[145] Mabey remains ever-conscious of global plant migration and nature's transforming power.

Jackie Kay's poem 'Extinction' makes this connection even more direct and obvious. The poem begins 'We closed the borders, folks, we nailed it. / No trees, no plants, no immigrants.'[146] Kay uses an exaggerated pararhyme – 'plants…immigrants' to ridicule the idea that nature or people can be so easily confined.

But just as plants are important metaphors of migration and diaspora, they are equally vital to the politics of settling. In *Dwelling Places* (2003), James Procter observed that the time had come to balance the habitual focus of diaspora scholars on dispersal (like seeds) and nostalgia for a homeland by emphasising the importance of planting and settlement.[147] Maya Chowdhry's poem 'Forest Garden' perfectly illustrates this theme. The poem begins with a statement of the speaker's grand design, to plant a forest:

> I remember acorns collected, stratified through winter
> germinating into Spring saplings, nursed for five years
> while we dreamt of birthing a forest.[148]

The poem conveys the experience of collecting and planting and a sense of intervening in nature's design. There are images of nurture – 'birthing' the forest and 'nursing' the saplings – but also of belonging when Chowdhry draws on the metaphor of roots. The speaker's long shadow resembles a tree, 'a three-metre solstice shadow of me'[149] – a celebration of the experience of being settled, of dwelling within green spaces.

What Chowdhry says is important, because even now the language we use to talk about the migration of plants has lingering colonial connotations. New nature writers, whilst wary of romantic nostalgia and on the surface aware of the persistence of colonial discourse, sometimes allow the latter to creep in. The language of conservation, in particular, readily acquires imperialist overtones when its vocabularies centre on a dichotomy between native (good indigenous) plants, and alien (harmful) ones. In a recent tract entitled 'The Threat to England's Trees', the (then) MP Zac Goldsmith worried about the threat 'from invasive Non-Native Species' to 'iconic English oaks' and 'London's plane trees.' Given the origins of the plane tree and the wide distribution of oak trees across the Northern hemisphere, Goldsmith's complaint is unintentionally ironic. As Richard Mabey counters:

> botanists… turn up their noses at these alien plants… They aren't British, they say… They flourish one year and clear out the next. I think these purists tend to forget that much of our flora is recently arrived, and that even flowers as apparently solidly English as the poppy are immigrants introduced by early colonists.[150]

Mabey cites David McClintock's 1966 *Companion to Flowers*, which argues that there is little historical evidence to justify the label 'indigenous' species. Linking the classification practices of conservationists to human history, McClintock argues that 'sycamores are invariably, even after two-thirds of a millennium, branded as aliens. Yet what would these same people say if I retorted that they were not English because their ancestors had only come over with [William] the Conqueror?'[151] Maggie Campbell-Culver's *The Origin of Plants* (2001) draws on more recent research to support that point.[152] Yet, George Monbiot's book *Feral* repeatedly uses such phrases as 'our native ecosystem' and subtly imbues ancient forest trees with what is described as British colouring ('great ginger branches'), creating an unfortunate parallel between immigration and non-British moss:

> It was as if an enamellist with a fine brush had crept up the mountainside, ornamenting them minutely with a shocking deep orange. We stepped over the crimson plush cushions of sphagnum moss, like the upholstery in an Indian restaurant.[153]

The garishness of the moss with its 'shocking' Indian restaurant colour highlights its alien properties. His aim of regenerating old forests in place of 'exotic trees – Sitka, spruce, lodgepole, pine' – is accompanied by a reflection on the identity of Scotland's landowners: 'most of the north of Scotland [is] in the hands of a tiny number of landowners... most of whom are not Scottish.'[154] Monbiot is a radical, anti-racist thinker who worries about the creeping privatisation of land, and yet his words juxtapose the desire for 'a contiguous native forest' with a reflection on the unScottishness of the local landowners. The complaint echoes that of the earlier, but sometimes xenophobic, radical, William Cobbett, who in *Rural Rides*, expresses disdain for incomers who plant overly large trees because they lack the locals' understanding of the landscape.[155] As Kylie Mirmohamadi writes in her essay 'Wog Plants Go Home', 'the discourses of botany and race have been interwoven from colonial times to the present through... war and the challenges of postwar immigration and multiculturalism.'[156]

Black British and British Asian Writers, the Garden and the Reconstruction of Englishness

When as radical a writer as Monbiot can appear to imply a 'deep' sense of botanical nationhood, David Dabydeen's novel *Disappearance* (1993) is an important work of deconstruction. Dabydeen's narrator is an Afro-Guyanese engineer, employed to shore up the crumbling cliffs of rural Kent. Like Naipaul in *The Enigma of Arrival*, Dabydeen's protagonist dwells in the countryside for an extended period. At first, he too shares Naipaul's initial but corrected belief that the countryside is the place where 'rituals of nationhood' are most potently 'enacted'. He identifies the cottage garden as one such symbol: 'as soon as you caught sight of it, you thought you were in the presence of a venerable England'.[157] As the word 'thought' indicates, the notion is retrospectively discredited and the narrator comes to recognise 'the mythic power of the garden' (p. 68) for encouraging false ideas. He writes: 'I remarked naively that the names of flowers seemed... essentially English in their evocation of the lyrical – Lady's bedstraw, Lady's tresses, Queen Anne's lace, Dame's violet' (p. 66). This naivety is mocked by the cottage's owner, Mrs Rutherford, with her experience of a colonial service that has led her to become a fierce critic of empire. To her, his perspective betrays 'a colonial's sense of this place' (p. 66), and she challenges him to look beneath the surface, encouraging him to see, as Naipaul does in *The Enigma of Arrival*, the naive falsity of such ideas.

Here, Dabydeen joins Naipaul's quest to disturb the countryside's association with 'racial, and historical, and cultural virtue' (p. 221) when the 'anti-patriotic' Mrs Rutherford assists the engineer to shed his illusions: 'England is more than maidens dancing around maypoles, which is the kind of image we gave the Africans while our men were pilfering their treasury' (p. 66). She provides an anti-pastoral account of botanical history, pointing out that 'devil's-bit scabious' was once used 'to prevent plague spreading over medieval England' (p. 67). The flower, she suggests, shows England to be 'every bit as dark and diseased' as the colonisers' representation of Africa (p. 67). To Mrs Rutherford, flower-names like 'Dane's Blood' do not attest to Englishness but to the Viking invasion and intercultural contact, whilst flowers like 'Turk's cap' provide 'echoes of sultans everywhere in England' (p. 68), and she provides a suggestive description of the flower's growth patterns: 'once upon a time [it] used to turn the woodland around here into gay Islamic territory' (p. 68). She extends this historical analogy by remarking that rosebuds resemble 'Turkish domes' (p. 68). Her lecture on nomenclature speaks to wider horticultural naming practices. More extreme examples of racist names – still in current usage – include 'Niggerhead', 'Niggerfinger', 'Nigger-toes', 'Jew Bush' and 'Kaffir Plums'.[158] As Teresa M. Kelley observes, botanical names carry the traces of colonial hierarchies of race.[159]

Grace Nichols's poem 'Wild About Her Back Garden' turns the kind of deconstruction practised by Mrs Rutherford into a positive virtue when she creates an analogy between floral communities and multicultural society. Emphasising the global migration of plants, Nichols expands customary ideals of rural community by suggesting that the English cottage garden is an international affair:

Grapevine sneaking
     between Bay leaves
Buddleia nestling

    against Bamboo.
      Climbing Rose
      in the arms of Cherry.

The flowers and shrubs described here reflect centuries of human travel and exploration, often involving violence together with painful consequences for the victims of colonialism. Nichols had explored this history in collections such as *I is a Long-Memoried Woman* (1984). Yet these plants peacefully co-exist, 'sneaking / between' and 'nestling / against' one another, despite their diverse origins. The theme of intimacy continues:

    African Violet...
    revealing her mauveness
    under Fern's spreading armpit[160]

Nichols's plants thrive in cohabitation, offsetting each other's best qualities: the fern's greenness enhancing the purple violet's 'mauveness'. She invites human parallels by personifying the plants with armpits and wearing 'trousseaux'. The classic cottage garden allegorises Englishness but Nichols turns the analogy on its head to present a convivial vision of multicultural England. It is a vision that perhaps William Cowper, in his lines on the greenhouse noted above, would have endorsed – if he could have been persuaded to adopt a more egalitarian position.

In her recent poetry collection *Passport to Here and There* (2020), Nichols affirms her love of English gardens and expands on how she sees them with an international eye. As a schoolgirl in Guyana she had the vicarious experience of daffodils, through Wordsworth's famous poem; as a woman in England, she decided the daffodil was 'my favourite English flower'.[161] The poem itself makes no direct reference to the Caribbean, but in the collection's preface she details her colonial education in Guyana – 'Shakespeare, Keats, Wordsworth, Jane Austen'[162] – and her familiarity (at a distance) with English flowers. Nichols is also taking on a much repeated trope of anti-colonial complaint – of having Wordsworth's daffodils 'stuffed down one's throat' as a schoolchild, whereas Caribbean flowers were rarely to be found in poems taught at school. V.S. Naipaul's story, 'B. Wordsworth' (i.e. Black Wordsworth) in *Miguel Street* (1959) satirically explores some of those cultural tensions.[163] One suspects that Nichols is well aware that the rejection of all Wordsworthian connections is slightly disingenuous since so much Caribbean poetry has come through the autobiographical narratives of Wordsworth's 'egotistical sublime' as John Keats described them.[164] Nichols's title, 'Ode', used here in an unironic way, communicates a connection with, rather than a break from, English nature poetry, alluding also to iconic romantic poems such as Shelley's 'Ode to the West Wind' and Keats's 'Ode to a Nightingale'. Nichols's poem celebrates the daffodil, calling it a 'yellow-headed swan' and 'a small chandelier'.[165] At the same time, the poem explores her cross-geographic, cross-chronological encounter with daffodils – one literary, one in her English garden. She explores the same phenomenon in her poem 'Robin Redbreast', first seen in Guyana in the 'Christmas cards of my snowless childhood' and then again in England, 'at my frosty garden door'.[166]

Black British writers have been no less entranced by the combined pastoral and georgic possibilities of the small domestic garden than generations of gardeners and poets before them. The garden as solace, as fulfilling psychological needs (and sometimes reflecting psychological despair) is a prominent theme. Poems in *Salt, Sweat and Tears*,[167] by Louisa Adjoa Parker, depict gardens as a place of comfort against the backdrop of an unhappy childhood home. Holidaying at her grandparents' home offered escape:

> Safer than any houses, this white house in Devon
> with its garden roses, circled with red earth.
> At the back an apple orchard lined our path
> to see the trains.[168]

In this poem, the garden both encloses and expands horizons. The red earth circles and the trees 'lined our path', marking out a route outwards to safe adventure, worlds away from the poet's tumultuous home life. Other images – the suspended garden sail, the frozen kite and the subjunctive tense of 'as though' – hint at the temporariness and fragility of the refuge:

> Above our heads a green triangle hangs suspended in the sky,
>   like a frozen kite. It's called a garden sail, as though this quiet
> happy space – all plants and colour, light-dappled wood,
>   Children who are kept close by – a ship this family sails on...[169]

Parker revises the idylls of pastoral verse because her poem addresses, rather than obscures, the violence from which the countryside affords an escape.

A similar psychological acuteness is present in Degna Stone's poem 'Allotment' from her collection *Handling Stolen Goods* (2019), which observes:

> We listen to Mum and Dad pick over
> last night's rows as they tease
> out the bindweed creeping over the plot,
> strangling this year's crops.
>
> Mum watches us carry our harvest
> to the stand pipe, rinse off dust and grubs;
> our hands stop berries tumbling over the edge
> as we pour sunlit water back into the earth.
> We sit in the shade of the shed and eat.[170]

Whilst the blackberries offer an ambivalent image of a productive nature (but with dust and grubs), the pun on 'rows' and the bindweed strangling this year's crops creates a gardening metaphor for what is going on between the child's parents. It echoes the kind of perception the 'Traveller' makes in Wordsworth's 'The Ruined Cottage' (later included in *The Excursion*) when he reports how the abandoned wife's despair is signalled in what has happened to her previously well-tended garden, which has 'lost / Its pride of neatness':

> The cumbrous bind-weed, with its wreaths and bells,
> Had twined about her two small rows of peas,
> And dragged them to the earth.[171]

Further subverting the pastoral garden is Roger Robinson's 'Brixton Flora', from *The Butterfly Hotel* (2013) where the flower has become a drug metaphor of death:

> There are petals of blood
> still blooming in the syringe
> stuck in the stem of your vein,
> a hummingbird sucking
> nectar, a stinging bee... [172]

A more comfortable relationship to the garden is contained in Shanta Acharya's poem, 'Aspects of Westonbirt Arboretum'.[173] This cherishes the signature plants of spring: 'primroses', 'bluebells' and 'wild garlic'. From there, it moves reverently through the English seasons, suggesting repeated visits to the arboretum. This familiarity allows the poet to speak authoritatively about the arboretum's many '[a]spects'. She positions herself as a cultural insider with intimate knowledge of a local rural space. Immersed in nature, her postures communicate an easy sense of belonging as she 'rest[s] in the venerable oak's dappled shade' and lies on 'a mattress of leaves'.[174] Here, nature is a benevolent force that unquestioningly accommodates her presence.

Throughout Seni Seneviratne's three collections, plants and gardens make regular appearances. They are the scene of ordinary pleasures, as in 'Remembered Raspberries', of childhood's 'foraging through / the jungle of bushes halfway down our garden. / Six eyes searched the tangled green for flash of red.'[175] But most often garden in her poetry mark moments in time, as in 'Returners' where a personal moment of coming to rest ('I plant clematis in a new garden / to mark the end of my nomad days') echoes the remembered return of her father from war when he 'planted / in a new garden, to mark the end / of his rootless days', but whose attempt to create some place of rest was cruelly ended by cancer.[176] This sense of the garden as a marker of time that underscores human impermanence is also there in the poem 'Dandelion Clocks' where the seedhead carries multiple and conflicting images – of fragility, of returning seasons, of dispersal, of persistent new growth – that take on moving resonances as they surround the playing child:

In my garden, she crawls small
amongst tall grass, dandelion clocks
like fluffy moons above her head.
She blows and silky plumes
stick to her lips, hover in her chuckle,
dappled wishes, heartbeats of delight,
before the clutter of words.[177]

Democratisation and Access to the Garden

In the section on allotments I noted one historian's rather critical allusion to the presence of Caribbean-heritage allotment renters. More recently there have been calls to create better access to allotments for Black Britons. In 2020, Wilfred Emmanuel-Jones – the founder of the Black Farmer food brand mentioned in Chapter Three – called on the government, Ministry of Defence, Church of England and landowners who 'all own vast swathes of land' to do something to encourage allotments in multicultural Britain. He wrote that '[they] could be doing a lot more to welcome people from diverse urban cultures – but particularly black people – into allotments and ultimately into the countryside.' Emmanuel-Jones remembers tending his father's Birmingham allotment as a boy and, from this experience, he decided to become a farmer. He remembered the allotment as 'an oasis and an opportunity to escape from the cramped two-up, two-down terraced house I shared with my family of 11.' He also links tending land to his Caribbean roots: 'as a child of the Windrush generation, it means something to own and tend land'.[178] This kind of memory is found in Khadijah Ibrahiim's poem, '56 Cowper Street' about her grandparents' house, in her collection, *Another Crossing* (2014):

Grandma grew roses and dahlias
in the front garden, picked gooseberries
to make jam and wine; Grandad dug tuff dirt
in the back yard, planted potatoes and cabbage.[179]

A related development is the inner-city community garden movement which reclaims and repurposes wasteland for public benefit. This grass-roots movement highlighted the benefits of producing food communally to reduce crime, improve wellbeing, improve skills and provide safe areas for children to run around.[180] *The Voice* newspaper reported on an impressive range of Caribbean foods grown in one such project in Tottenham, known as 'Harmony Gardens', in which the Jamaican-born horticulturalist Robbie Samuda grows cho-cho, coco yam, red maize and Scotch bonnet peppers. The West Midlands-based gardener, Eunice McGhie-Belgrave runs a community gardening project called Shades of Black. She grows food with local schoolchildren but also cultivates Caribbean produce at Ryton Organic Gardens in Coventry.[181] There are initiatives of this nature across British cities and the use of Caribbean plants has evidently spread beyond Caribbean heritage communities. Suttons Seeds offers at least a dozen different chilli pepper plants to its customers, as well as amaranth (callaloo) seeds.

A knowledge of colonial history and a commitment to decolonise lies behind new landownership and food-growing initiatives that have emerged from the community garden movement. Land In Our Names (LION) is a Black-led grassroots collective which aims to secure green spaces for Black communities and change the narrative about Blackness, food-growing and green spaces. A co-founder of LION, Josina Calliste argues that land should be 'a common treasury'. She defines food justice as the right to access locally-grown produce but her polemic also reaches into both food and landowning history to show that reconnecting with the land is about putting historical injustice to rights. She argues that 'our ancestors did not farm here [in Britain], but they farmed *for* here.' LION's co-founder, Olá Ayòrindé similarly observes that 'British colonialism... did not occur on this land. We were forced here [to Britain] through displacement.'[182] Accordingly, the movement advocates reparative justice for the wrongs of transatlantic slavery through a return to common land ownership, a programme that revives the goals of the Chartist Co-operative Land Plan, the writings of the late 18th and early 19th century radical Thomas Spence, and before him the communitarian Digger movement of the English Civil War.[183] Josina Calliste directly connects transatlantic slavery to rural British struggles over enclosure of the commons in British history. She observes that the discussion about to whom land truly should belong has been part of British debate since those days. This is how LION connects colonial history with the idea of food justice: 'There are vast amounts of land that are unused or poorly managed and we need to join up these issues and grow healthy food and have sustainable farming.'[184] The movement emphasises Black land stewardship in a non-exploitative relationship between people and the soil. Drawing on the cultural history of African and Caribbean food-growing, its members advocate drawing from ancestral practices of husbandry and plant-knowledge.[185] Olá Ayòrindé explains how the movement addresses any cultural 'stigma' attached to working on the land, a stigma inherited from the history of enslavement, by making connections between the food culture of Black Britons and the growing of its distinctive ingredients.

That connection between cuisine and gardening is caught in Malika Booker's poem 'Brixton Market' from *Pepper Seed* (2013) about the way her mother 'would test the okra, / bending their tips, placing only / the ones that snapped into a brown paper bag'. These days the connection between food and the garden lies in memory (elsewhere in the collection the gardens are all Caribbean ones), but the connection is real:

I would learn that this is how my grandmother
taught her, kneeling in the bush uprooting dasheen
on the family land. She, too, hawk-eyed,
tested each provision to know
what was ripe, ready and good to cook.[186]

Louisa Adjoa Parker's poetry puts flesh on the bones of the argument advanced by Olá Ayòrindé. Her poem 'Mulatto Girl' in *Salt, Sweat and Tears*, which begins: 'See the mulatto girl walking / down country lanes', reflects upon her historical relationship with the land:

she is not the first
to walk this green and pleasant
countryside, she has history stirring within her limbs.

The title evokes the context of transatlantic slavery even before it is mentioned in the poem. The term 'mulatto' reaches back to the early days of slave-trading by the Portuguese and Spanish, who brought the word into use. Her 'DNA', she reflects, is 'a... mix of gene pools / scattered across continents.' Crucially, the woman's presence in the countryside both illuminates Britain's slaving past and claims her inheritance:

She shows Africa in a way the English hide.
She shows an eighteenth-century master's love for slaves.
She shows a slave's contempt.[187]

Her awareness of the link between British enslavers and rural England – her deeper, broader knowledge of it – provides an historical rationale for belonging to it: 'see her smile, see her sway, as she walks'. From beginning to end, the poem knowingly resists any idea that she does not naturally belong to the countryside. The word 'see' in the first line – 'See the mulatto girl walking' – signals awareness that a brown woman is visibly different to white Britons in the countryside. The end of the poem offers a final retort: her greater knowledge of English history explains her presence there and this insight makes her proud to walk through it. She moves along the country lane 'with her head held high.'[188] In an article called 'Decolonising the Countryside', Louisa Adjoa Parker has argued that 'Black and Asian people have a right to connect with nature, although historically our relationship with the land has been denied (by white people and by ourselves).'[189] Her words resonate strongly with the premises of the co-founders of LION that Black people's access to green spaces connects with historical atrocities that took place on the other side of the globe, out of sight of the British public.

Conclusion

This chapter has shown that colonialism transformed English gardens and landscapes. Colonial profits were spent on transporting, introducing and commercialising plants from various parts of the empire. Parallels between transplanted plants and migrating people have long been a feature of English writing and Black British and British Asian writers have readily taken up this theme, largely to imagine a gregarious multicultural experience. But it was not just the colonisers who transported plants, and this chapter also considered the importance of African initiatives in creating Caribbean foodways and modes of cultivation which have relevance to modern gardens and allotments.

Black British and British Asian writers resemble their colonial-era literary forebears in the ways that they find solace in gardens. They also share their forebears' global sense of plants and gardens, but often with transrural visions of parallel geographic spaces, combined with a critical sense of British colonialism and its botanical legacies. Casting a net deep into British imperial history, a contemporary writer such as David Dabydeen has, for instance, thoroughly deconstructed the English cottage garden, while Grace Nichols has embraced that culture and made it her own. Gardeners have always been aware that plants reflect travel, but recent historical work and the transrural perceptiveness of Black British and British Asian writers have taken this awareness to new levels.

Endnotes

1. See Martin Hoyles, *Bread and Roses: Gardening Books from 1560-1960* vol. 2. (London: Pluto Press, 1995), pp. 167-177.

2. See Oxford Economics, *The Economic Impact of Ornamental Horticulture in the UK* (2018), www.rhs.org.uk/science/pdf/The-economic-impact-of-ornamental-horticultureand.pdf.

3. See Twigs Way, *The Cottage Garden* (Oxford: Shire Books, 2011), pp. 25-29. There were also fermes ornées, such as the one created by the poet William Shenstone (1714-1763) at Leasowes, rather more picturesque than practical.

4. Roy Campbell, *The Georgiad: A Satirical Fantasy in Verse* (London: Boriswood, 1931), pp. 46-47.

5. Seamus Heaney, 'Digging', *Death of A Naturalist* (London: Faber, 1966), pp. 13-14.

6. See Martin Hoyles, *Bread and Roses*, vol. 2, pp. 110-130.

7. Kathy Willis and Carolyn Fry, *Plants. From Roots to Riches* (London: John Murray, 2014), p. 7.

8. For the information on Sloane see James Delbourgo, *Collecting the World: The Life and Curiosity of Hans Sloane* (London: Allen Lane, 2017), pp. 136-137.

9. On the Chelsea Physic Garden see Vic Keegan, Lost London No. 71, www.onlondon.co.uk/vic-keegan-lost-london-71-chelsea-physic-garden.

10. James Delbourgo, *Collecting the World*, p. 157.

11. *Ibid.*

12. See Beth Fowkes Tobin, *Colonizing Nature: The Tropics in British Arts and Letters, 1760-1820* (Penn: University of Pennsylvania Press, 2005), and Jill H. Casid *Sowing Empire. Landscape and Colonization* (Minneapolis: University of Minnesota Press), pp. 45ff.

13. Delbourgo, op. cit., p. 99.

14. Casid, *op. cit.*, p. 47.

15. Long, cited in Elizabeth A. Bohls, 'The gentleman planter and the metropole: Long's *History of Jamaica* (1774)' in *The Country and the City Revisited. England and the Politics of Culture, 1550-1850*, edited by Gerald MacLean, Donna Landry and Joseph P. Ward (Cambridge: CUP, 1999), pp. 144-145.

16. Casid, *op. cit.*, p. 51.

17. See Tim Barringer, 'Picturesque Prospects and the Labour of the Enslaved', in *Art and Emancipation in Jamaica: Isaac Mendes Belisario and his Worlds* (New Haven: Yale Center for British Art, 2007), pp. 41-64. And see Krista A. Thompson, *An Eye for the Tropics: Tourism, Photography, and Framing the Caribbean Picturesque* (Durham: Duke University Press, 2011), pp. 27-91.

18. William Beckford, *A Descriptive Account of the Island of Jamaica –
    with Remarks Upon the Cultivation of the Sugar-Cane, Throughout the
    Year and Chiefly Considered from a Picturesque Point of View* (London:
    T & J. Egerton, 1790, facsimile ed.), vol. 2, pp. 183-184.

19. On Thistlewood more generally see Trevor Burnard, *Mastery, Tyranny
    and Desire: Thomas Thistlewood and his Slaves in the Anglo-Jamaican
    World* (Chapel Hill: University of North Carolina Press, 2004).
    The calculation of Thistlewood's rapes comes from Michael Taylor,
    The Interest: How the British Establishment Resisted the Abolition of Slavery
    (London: Bodley Head, 2020), p. 44.

20. See Douglas Hall, 'Botanical and Horticultural Enterprise in
    Eighteenth Century Jamaica', in *West Indian Accounts: Essays on the
    History of the British Caribbean and the Atlantic Economy in Honour of
    Richard Sheridan*, ed. Roderick A. McDonald (Barbados: UWI Press,
    1996), pp. 101-115.

21. Casid, *op. cit.*, p. 49.

22. Katie Donington, *The Bonds of Family. Slavery, Culture and Commerce
    in the British Atlantic World* (Manchester: MUP, 2020), p. 321.

23. Donington, *op. cit.*, p. 18 and p. 314.

24. Donington, *op. cit.* p. 321.

25. Roderick Flood, *An Economic History of the English Garden* (London:
    Allen Lane, 2019), pp. 126-158.

26. For Trengwainton gardens see www.nationaltrust.org.uk/treng
    wainton-garden.

27. See Michael Craton and James Walvin, *A Jamaican Plantation: The
    History of Worthy Park 1670-1970* (London: W.H. Allen, 1970), p. 183.

28. Sally-Anne Huxtable, Corinne Fowler, Christo Kefalus, and Emma
    Slocombe, eds., *Interim Report on the Connections between Colonialism
    and Properties now in the Care of the National Trust, Including Links
    with Historic Slavery*, (Heelis: National Trust, 2020), p. 105.

29. For Sir Rose Price see The Legacies of Slave Ownership: www.ucl.
    ac.uk/lbs/person/19625.

30. Casid, *op. cit.*, p. 52.

31. Casid *op cit.*, p. 52.

32. Casid *op cit.*, p. 55.

33. Casid op. cit., p. 65.

34. Advolly Richmond, 2020, 'Garden History Podcasts', https://
    advolly.co.uk/, accessed 19 October, 2020.

35. See Beth Fowkes Tobin, *Colonizing Nature*, pp. 33-35, quote on p.
    33, and see www.nationalarchives.gov.uk/pathways/blackhistory/
    journeys/voyage_html/voyage.htm, accessed 19 October, 2020.

36. See David E. Stannard, *The American Holocaust* (Oxford: OUP, 1992);
    and see Martin Hoyles, *Bread and Roses*, pp. 156-167 for the persistent

way that white America denied the existence of Native American Indian agriculture despite having been saved by it at various early points in settler history.

37. See B.W. Higman, *Jamaican Food: History, Biology, Culture* (Kingston, UWI Press, 2008), pp. 146-147.

38. Higman, *op. cit.*, p. 149.

39. Kathy Willis and Carolyn Fry, *Plants. From Roots to Riches*, p. x.

40. Natural History Museum, 2007, 'Slavery and the Natural World', https://www.nhm.ac.uk/content/dam/nhmwww/discover/slavery-natural-world/chapter-4-everyday-life.pdf, p. 8.

41. On the disciplining of the propertyless through the terrors of the law as a stage of capitalism see Peter Linebaugh, *The London Hanged: Crime and Civil Society in the Eighteenth Century* (London: Verso Books, 2006).

42. Kathy Willis and Carolyn Fry, *Plants. From Roots to Riches*, p. 26; and see Patricia Fara, *Sex, Botany and Empire: The Story of Carl Linnaeus and Joseph Banks* (London: Icon Books, 2003, 2017).

43. On the Opium wars and the importance of the trade to empire see Carl A. Trocki, *Opium, Empire and Global Political Economy: A Study of the Asian Opium Trade 1750-1950* (London: Routledge, 1999).

44. On the role of quinine see Lucille H. Brockway, *Science and Colonial Expansion: The Role of the British Botanic Gardens, Online*, Anthropocene online Library. On the export of Indian indentured labour from India see Hugh Tinker, *A New System of Slavery: The Export of Indian Labour Overseas 1830-1920* (London: OUP, 1974).

45. See Alan Eyre, *The Botanic Gardens of Jamaica* (London, Andre Deutch, 1966).

46. Jack Goody, *The Culture of Flowers* (Cambridge: CUP, 1993), pp. 11-24.

47. See Alistair Watt, *Robert Fortune: A Plant Hunter in the Orient* (London: Royal Botanic Gardens, 2017).

48. Joseph Hooker quoted in Willis and Fry (2014), *op. cit.*, pp. 116, 117.

49. Floud, *The Economic History of the English Garden*, pp. 142-144.

50. Theresa, M. Kelley, *Clandestine Marriage. Botany and Romantic Culture* (Baltimore: The Johns Hopkins University Press, 2012), p. 54.

51. Theresa, M. Kelley, *op cit.,* p. 182.

52. Kelley, *op cit.*, p. 166.

53. Kelley, *op cit.*, p. 194.

54. Kelley, *op cit.*, p. 195.

55. Kelley, *op cit.*, p. 199.

56. Casid, *op. cit.*, p. 49.

57. Casid, *op. cit.*, p. 51.

58. *Poems by the Rev. Mr. Cawthorn, Late master of Tunbridge School*, p. 116, quoted in John Dixon Hunt, *The Oxford Book of Garden Verse* (London: Oxford, 1993), p. xxvii.

59. Walpole, cited in Casid, *op cit.*, p. 51.

60. *The Poems of William Cowper*, vol. 2, Ed. John Baird and Charles Ryskamp (London: OUP, 1995), pp. 172-173.

61. Cowper, p. 173.

62. Douglas Dunn, *Barbarians* (London: Faber, 1979). Included in John Dixon Hunt, *The Oxford Book of Garden Verse*, pp. 315. Andrew Marvell's 'The Mower Against Gardens' is a satire spoken in the voice of the mower who is condemned to hard labour to produce the gardens of 'Luxurious Man' who ignores the beauties of Nature 'most plain and pure', for the artificiality of the science of horticulture.

63. M.M. Mahood, *The Poet as Botanist* (Cambridge, CUP, 2008), p. 22.

64. Mahood, *op. cit.*, p. 60

65. Mahood, *op. cit.*, p. 100.

66. See Donna Landry, *The Invention of the Countryside*, p. 207.

67. Mahood, *op. cit.*, p. 123.

68. Kelley, 'Clare's Common Plants', in *Clandestine Marriage. Botany and Romantic Culture,* p. 127.

69. Dominick Tyler, 2015, *Uncommon Ground. A Word-Lover's Guide to the British Landscape* (London: Arts Council England), p. 120.

70. 'Helpstone' by John Clare, 2008, *John Clare. Major Works* edited by Eric Robinson and David Powell (Oxford: OUP), p. 1.

71. 'Wild Flowers' in John Clare, 2008, *John Clare. Major Works* edited by Eric Robinson and David Powell (Oxford: OUP), p. 253.

72. Kelley, *op cit.*, p. 129.

73. Mahood, *op. cit.*, pp. 112, 122.

74. Mahood, *op. cit.*, p. 126.

75. Mahood, *op. cit.*, p. 127.

76. Advolly Richmond on Gardener's World, 'There's more to auriculas than meets the eye'. www. bbc.co.uk/programmes/m000j4f5.

77. See ONS Report, 'One in eight British households has no garden', www.ons.gov.uk/economy/environmentalaccounts/oneineight britishhouseholdshasno garden/2020-05-14.

78. For the information on average plot size see *House Beautiful*, 'Gardens are getting smaller', www.housebeautiful.com/uk/garden/a2124/21st-century-garden-shrinking-smaller.

79. See Steve Poole, *The Allotment Chronicles: A Social History of Allotment Gardening* (Kettering: Silver Link Publishing, 2006), pp. 13-14, from which this information, but not always the interpretation, has been taken.

80. For the Swing riots see E.J. Hobsbawn and G. Rude, *Captain Swing* (London: Lawrence & Wishart, 1969).

81. Poole, *op. cit.*, pp. 24-25, 26-27.
82. Poole, *op. cit.*, pp. 40-41.
83. Poole, *op. cit.*, pp. 37-39
84. Poole, *op. cit.*, p. 24.
85. See Thomas C. Holt, *The Problem of Freedom: Race, Labor, and Politics in Jamaica and Britain, 1832-1938* (Baltimore, Johns Hopkins UP, 1992), pp, 143-176.
86. For the material on the potato above, see Poole, *op. cit.*, pp. 48-50.
87. Poole, *op. cit.*, pp. 70-72
88. See Who Owns England, 'How the Extent of County Farms Has halved in 40 Years', https://whoownsengland.org/2018/06/08/how-the-extent-of-county-farms-has-halved-in-40-years/
89. For the Thorpe Report see Hansard, Allotments (Thorpe Report, Volume 787: debated on 17 July 1969. Available on line.
90. Poole, *op. cit.*, pp. 192-193.
91. 'A Ramble in St James's Park', *The Complete Poems of John Wilmot Earl of Rochester*, ed. David M. Vieth (New Haven: Yale University Press, 1962, 2002), p. 41.
92. Quoted in Hazel Conway, *Public Parks* (Risborough: Shire Publications, 1996), p. 4. See this title for a general history of public parks.
93. See a report by Comedia in association with Demos, *Park Life: Urban Parks and Social Renewal*, ed. Liz Greenhalgh and Ken Worpole (London & Stroud: Demos & Comedia, 1995), pp. 29-30, 51-52.
94. *Park Life: Urban Parks and Social Renewal,* p. 53.
95. See Hazel Conway, *op. cit.*, pp. 77-84.
96. Travis Elborough, *A Walk in the Park. The Life and Times of a People's Institution* (London: Jonathan Cape, 2016), p. 56.
97. Laurence Westgaph for the International Slavery Museum, 'Allerton Towers', 2020, viewed on 27 October, 2020.
98. For Katrina Navickas's website see www.historyofpublicspace.uk/tag/parks. Navickas makes the point that until the end of the century many parks were not free to enter, and thus shut out the poorest.
99. Quoted in Navickas, op. cit.
100. See Hazel Conway, *Public Parks*, p. 63.
101. Nan Hesse Dreher, *Public Parks in Urban Britain, 1870-1920: Creating a New Public Culture*, PhD, University of Pennsylvania 1993. Online: repository.upenn. edu/edisertations/2673.
102. Navickas, *op. cit.*
103. Report of the House of Commons Select Committee on Public Parks, February 2017. Online: https://publications.parliament.uk/pa/cm201617/cmselect/cmcomloc/45/4504.htm. The figures from the following paragraph are all drawn from this report.
104. Report of the House of Commons, PKS315.

105. Report of the House of Commons, Paragraph 73.
106. Nichols, 'In the Shade of a London Plane Tree', *Passport to Here and There* (Newcastle: Bloodaxe Books 2020), p. 33.
107. See English Heritage, Suburbs and the Historic Environment (2012), np. Online at https://thegardenstrust.org/wp-content/uploads/2016/ /11/EH-Suburbs-and-the-Historic-Environment-with-revision-note- 2012.pdf.
108. *Ibid*.
109. See Colin Ward, *Sociable Cities: The Legacy of Ebenezer Howard* (Chichester: John Wiley, 1998).
110. Ward, *op cit*. And see Standish Meacher, *Regaining Paradise: Englishness and the Early Garden Movement* (New Haven: Yale University Press, 1999), pp. 44-69.
111. Meacher, *op. cit.*, pp. 145-177.
112. See Eugene Byrne, From slums to suburbs: Britain's Council House Revolution, BBC History Extra. Online: https://historyextra.com/ period/20th-century/slums-suburbs-britain-council-house- revolution-social-housing/
113. George Orwell, *Coming Up For Air* ([1939] London: Penguin Modern Classics, 2010), p. 10.
114. Quoted in Twigs Way, *The Suburban Garden* (Stroud: Amberley Publishing, 2020), p. 32.
115. Alfred W. Crosby, *The Columbian Exchange* (Westport: Praeger, 1972, 2003).
116. Judith A. Carney and Richard Rosomoff, *In the Shadow of Slavery: Africa's Botanical Legacy in the Atlantic World* (Berkeley: University of California Press, 2011), pp. 67-68.
117. Carney and Rosomoff, p. 55
118. Carney and Rosomoff, pp. 76-78.
119. Carney and Rosomoff, pp 76-77.
120. *Electricity Comes to Cocoa Bottom* (Leeds: Peepal Tree Press, 1999), pp. 47-49.
121. Natural History Museum, 2007, 'Diet and Nutrition', www.nhm.ac.uk/content/dam/nhmwww/discover/slavery-natural- world/chapter-5-diet-and-nutrition.pdf, accessed 26th October 2020.
122. *Ibid*.
123. *Ibid*.
124. Israel Vibration, 'So Far Away', on the album *Praises* (1990).
125. B.W. Higman, quoted in Carney & Rosomoff, p. 129.
126. Carney & Rosomoff, pp. 132-133.
127. Roderick A. McDonald, *The Economy and Material Culture of Slaves: Goods and Chattels on the Sugar Plantations of Jamaica and Louisiana* (Baton Rouge: Louisiana State University Press, 1993), pp. 16- 49, 92-198.

128. See B.W. Higman, *Slave Populations of the British Caribbean 1807-1834* (Baltimore: Johns Hopkins UP, 1984), pp. 314-346.

129. Vincent Brown, *The Reaper's Garden: Death and Power in the World of Atlantic Slavery* (Cambridge, Mass.: Harvard UP, 2008), pp. 48-57.

130. See for instance Lydia M. Pulsipher, 'They Have Saturdays and Sundays to Feed Themselves: Slave Gardens in the Caribbean', *Expedition*, vol. 32. No. 2 (1990).

131. Richard Westmacott, African-American Gardens and Yards in the Rural South (Knoxville: University of Tennessee Press, 1992), pp. 87-100.

132. See Richard Wilk, 'Review of Candice Goucher's *Congotay! Congotay! A Global History of Caribbean Food*', New West Indian Guide, vol. 90 (1-2), 2016, pp. 149-150.

133. See Thomas Holt, *The Problem of Freedom: Race, Labor, and Politics in Jamaica and Britain, 1832-1938*, pp. 143-176.

134. Arlette S. Saint Ville, Gordon M. Hickey and Leroy E. Phillip, 'Addressing food and nutrition insecurity in the Caribbean through domestic smallholder farming system innovation', *Environmental Change* 15, 2014, pp. 1325-1339, p. 1326.

135. Research into the Reverend Thomas Freeman was conducted by Advolly Richmond in response to the first 'What's Happening in Black British History' conference in 2014.

136. The Garden Museum, 2019, 'Portrait of a Black Gardener', https://gardenmuseum.org.uk/collection/portrait-of-a-black-gardener/, accessed 29 October, 2020.

137. Jeffrey Green, 2016, 'Three Nineteenth-Century Black Gardeners in England', https://jeffreygreen.co.uk/132-three-19th-century-black-gardeners-in-england/, accessed 26 October, 2020 and School of African and Oriental Studies 'Black History Month', https://blogs.soas.ac.uk/archives/2019/10/04/black-history-month-2019-thomas-birch-freeman/, accessed 27th October 2020.

138. Jeffrey Green, 'Three 19th Century black Gardeners in England'.

139. Richard Mabey, *Food for Free* ([1973] London: Collins, 2012), p. 19.

140. Richard Mabey, *Flora Britannica* (London: Chatto & Windus, 1996), p. 7, p. 8.

141. Iain Sinclair's preface to Richard Mabey, *The Unofficial Countryside* ([1973] Toller Fratrum: Little Toller Books, 2010), p. 8.

142. Mabey, *The Unofficial Countryside*, p. 19.

143. Mabey, *The Unofficial Countryside*, p. 8.

144. Mabey, *The Unofficial Countryside*, p. 76 and p. 82.

145. Mabey, *The Unofficial Countryside*, p. 150.

146. Jackie Kay, 'Extinction', published in *The Guardian*, 15th May, 2019.
147. James Procter, *Dwelling Places. Postwar Black British Writing* (Manchester: Manchester University Press, 2003), p. 1.
148. Maya Chowdhry, 'Forest Garden', *Fossil* (Leeds: Peepal Tree Press, 2016), p. 20.
149. *Ibid*.
150. Mabey, *The Unofficial Countryside*, p. 157.
151. McClintock in Mabey, *The Unofficial Countryside*, p. 156. See too
152. Maggie Campbell-Culver, *The Origin of Plants* (London: Hodder Headline, 2001) which documents plant imports going back to 1000 AD.
153. George Monbiot, *Feral. Rewilding the Land, Sea and Human Life.* (London: Penguin, 2013,), p. 100.
154. Monbiot, *Feral,* p. 99.
155. Cobbett, *Rural Rides.,* p. 104. As Michael Taylor records in *The Interest,* Cobbett's hostility to returned planters was also turned on anti-slavery campaigners, whom he attacked because they distracted attention from the suffering of the white rural poor. Cobbett's language in referring to enslaved people was also crudely negrophobic.[152]
156. Kylie Mirmohamadi, 'Wog Plants Go Home: Race, Ethnicity and Horticulture in Australia', *Studies in Australian Garden History*, p. 98.
157. David Dabydeen, *Disappearance* (London: Secker & Warburg, 1993), p. 15. Subsequent references are given in parenthesis in the text.
158. Melvin Hunter, 'Racist Relics: An Ugly Blight on Our Botanical Nomenclature', *The Scientist*, November, 1991. Online.
159. Theresa Kelley, *Clandestine Marriage. Botany and Romantic Culture.*
160. Grace Nichols, 'Wild About Her Back Garden', *Piccasso, I Want My Face Back* (Tarset: Bloodaxe, 2009), p. 55.
161. *Passport to Here and There* (Tarset: Bloodaxe, 2020), p. 11.
162. *Ibid*.
163. V.S. Naipaul, *Miguel Street* (London: Andre Deutch, 1959).
164. John Keats, letter to Richard Woodhouse, 27 October, 1818, *John Keats Selected Letters*, ed. Robert Gittings (Oxford: Oxford World Classics, 2009), pp. 147-149.
165. Nichols, 'Ode to a Daffodil', *Passport to Here and There,* p. 41.
166. 'Robin Redbreast', *Passport to Here and There,* p. 36.
167. Louisa Adjoa Parker, 'Safe as houses', *Salt, Sweat and Tears* (Cinnamon Press: Blaenau Ffestiniog, 2007), p. 2.
168. Adjoa Parker, *Ibid*.
169. *Ibid*.
170. Degna Stone, 'Allotments', *Handling Stolen Goods* (Leeds: Peepal Tree Press, 2019), p. 19.
171. William Wordsworth, *The Excursion* ([1814] Ithaca: Cornell UP,

The Cornell Wordsworth, 2007), p. 70. ll. 725ff.

172. Roger Robinson, 'Brixton Flora', *A Portable Paradise* (Leeds: Peepal Tree Press, 2019), p. 19.

173. Shanta Acharya, 'Aspects of Westonbirt Arboretum' in Kay, Robinson and Procter, *Out of Bounds*, p. 229.

174. *Ibid.*

175. Seni Seneviratne, 'Remembered Raspberries', *Wild Cinnamon and Winter Skin* (Leeds: Peepal Tree Press, 2007), p. 23.

176. Seni Seneviratne, 'Returners', *Unknown Soldier* (Leeds: Peepal Tree Press, 2019), p. 48.

177. Seni Seneviratne, 'Dandelion Clocks', *Wild Cinnamon and Winter Skin*, p. 26.

178. Steve Ott, 2020, 'The Black Farmer Calls for Landowners To Make More Allotment Space Available.', *The Kitchen Garden Magazine*, 5 August, www.kitchengarden.co.uk/the-black-farmer-calls-for-landowners-to-make-more-allotment-space-available/, accessed 29 October, 2020.

179. *Another Crossing* (Leeds: Peepal Tree Press, 2014), p. 17.

180. Mary Isokariari, 2013, 'Jamaican Gardeners Sowing New Seeds', *The Voice*, https://archive.voice-online.co.uk/article/jamaican-gardeners-sowing-new-seeds, 10th November 2013, accessed 29th October, 2020.

181. Farmerama Radio, 'Land-reform, stewardship, community ownership and land justice.' A podcast at https://landinournames.community/how-we-work, accessed 29 October 2020.

182. Josina Calliste in 'The Green Soul Grace podcast 1', www//greensoulgrace.org/podcast, accessed 29 October 2020.

183. On the Diggers see John Gurney, *Brave Community: The Digger Movement in the English Revolution* (Manchester: Manchester UP, 2012). On Thomas Spence see *Thomas Spence: The Poor Man's Revolutionary*, ed. Alastair Bonnett and Keith Armstrong (London: Breviary Stuff Publications, 2014); on the Chartist Land Plan see Navickas, *Protest and Politics of Space and Place* (2016), pp. 247-250.

184. Land in Our Names' homepage, https://landinournames.community/how-we-work, accessed 29 October 2020.

185. Ibid.

186. 'Brixton Market', *Pepper Seed* (Leeds: Peepal Tree Press, 2013), p. 21.

187. 'Mulatto Girl', *Salt, Sweat and Tears*, p. 67.

188. *Ibid.*

189. Louisa Adjoa Parker, 'Where are you really from? The hidden lives of POC in the countryside.' www.cpre.org.uk/opinions/black-lives-matter-in-the-countryside/, accessed 29 October, 2020.

CREATIVE RESPONSES:

THE COLONIAL COUNTRYSIDE

FIELDS

Strawberries

1

Seth glared at the Parson's Way. Yet more cacti. He stared at the thick green pads and crimson blooms, then struck at them with his axe. Green juice oozed from the split skin and trickled between the spikes. He straightened up. Some hairline splinters had lodged in his palm. Should have brought gardening gloves. Should have brought lots of things. He stared at the prickly pears. They might hydrate him on the return journey. There was no turning back now. It was Helen's last chance.

Helen would be lying where he left her, shaded by a curtain of calico. No more antibiotics. No medicine. It was the end of vitamins, the end of nutrition. She needed strawberries and he'd set off to get them: the last strawberries in England.

When he kissed her goodbye she said,

"Where's your safari hat?"

Joking, always joking. Often at his expense, but this only increased his respect for her. Her forehead had been bone-dry. Seth had no idea why he hadn't been struck down like Helen and most of their neighbours. If hope could keep her alive, then leaving her alone was worth the risk. He'd counted out fifteen bottles of water by their bed and positioned them within easy reach. He'd re-counted them. Helen had peered at him through her thin fringe. She smiled when he looked back at her.

The Cotswold hills were colonised by prickly forests, the paths blocked. Seth's tongue was sandpaper-dry. He angled his body to strike at the thorns again. The axe pitched forwards. He lunged through the gap between two plants and yelped in pain as a spine pierced his thigh. His shorts were pinned to the flesh. Hopping, he recovered his balance and eased himself to the ground. Blood seeped from the wound. He moved to hug his knees like a boy, but the spine jabbed his other leg. He wouldn't be able to walk without removing it. He shuffled sideways, leaned against an acacia tree and shut his eyes. He'd need a piece of cloth to use as a bandage. Bandages, plasters – yet more things he hadn't considered bringing. This whole quest was laughable. Seth rubbed the stubble on his chin, then rummaged through the pockets of his backpack, eventually pulling out a tea towel, of all things. At least it was clean. He wrapped it around the spine, inhaled and screwed his eyes shut. Then he yanked hard. He opened his eyes and looked down. The spine had snapped in his hand. He couldn't stomach digging out the rest. He knotted the tea towel tightly around his leg.

Sparrows landed on a saltbush. They perched there like emissaries, some sort of advance guard. He glanced around him and frowned. This wasn't so much a clearing as a scene of devastation – mashed cacti and flattened nettles, snapped branches and mangled tree trunks. Above it all, a layer of dust simmering in the heat. This could only have been done recently. And by a machine of industrial proportions, possibly a combine harvester put to misuse. There was no fuel for vehicles anymore. Perhaps someone had tried the engine and discovered some diesel left in its tank. But why? He spotted a series of craters obliterating the old footpath. Some luck at last: whatever it was had beaten a path in the direction of Heathcote Manor, six miles west.

He rummaged in his rucksack and brought out the first of his reserve bottles, unscrewing the cap. Flies buzzed around the lip. He swiped at them and tipped water into his mouth. He screwed the cap back on and slouched against the acacia.

2

Seth jolted awake. The air fizzed with cicadas. Close by the sound of a nightjar lilted through the darkness. He tipped back his head and stared into the branches. He imagined the golden throat and black eyes of the speckled bird. He opened his palms and held them towards the sky. There was a rush of night air. Sleep was the body's healing miracle. Apart from the injury, he couldn't have planned things any better. Walking by night, by moonlight. The very fact he was having an adventure was keeping Helen alive, he was sure of it. And here was the nightjar, waking him at the perfect hour, showing him the purest, simplest way. He was immersed in fireflies. The hedgerows sparkled. Even the moon was guiding him.

Helen had heard the rumour of strawberries from Jan the journalist, who'd written from Warwickshire forty days earlier. Lord Vane had a secret hoard of water in underground vats. Jan's letter insisted that Vane was growing strawberries at Heathcote Manor. Strawberries meant vitamins, minerals, antioxidants. Folate, potassium, magnesium. And, apparently, these were no ordinary fruits but a rare Cotswold variety, plumping up nicely under the shade of a marquee at the edge of Hadley copse. Strawberries were Helen's last chance.

3

Seth's thigh throbbed as he crossed the furrows. Hours passed. The sun climbed higher. The heat was building.

He paused only when he saw Heathcote's Elizabethan chimney stacks bending in the heat. A field veered towards the stately grounds and the turrets of a marquee. Seth removed his ski-glasses and squinted, shading his eyes with his arm. There were figures bending and swaying under the canvas. They gave the impression of dancing peacocks. More colours fluttered into view: lime green, hot pink, spun gold. Women, stooping to pick what must be strawberries, their patterned veils ballooning like tents over the furrows. Who were they? Muslims, perhaps. Or Indian. He couldn't be sure. There they all were, picking strawberries as though it were a mild summer day. The younger women looked a bit flushed. They were making their way towards the courtyard. Seth stumbled after them.

The women were collecting their bikes from the yard. They must have come on the last serviceable road from the city. It was a long time since his village could be accessed by road. Seth wanted to ask them about conditions in the city, about their journey, why they still looked so healthy. But he was parched. Past it. He slumped onto a stone bench. There was a sudden clink of metal, a hot breath against his calf, a bark.

"Watch out!" a woman cried.

A bloodhound straining at the end of its chain, its teeth millimetres from his face. He fell backwards.

"Leopold! LEOPOLD! Leave him boy!"

Lord Vane came out in a green cravat. Seth squinted at the lord of the manor. He took in the sunken eyes, the Roman nose, the crisp shirt and smooth hands. Vane was frowning at the hound,

"Giving you trouble is he? Don't be silly, Leo. I expect this person's after a glass of water?"

"Erm, yes," said Seth. He picked himself up. "Do you really have an underground reservoir?"

"Built by my grandfather. I feel it shows some foresight on his part."

"And why the strawberries?"

"Quintessentially English. Some things are entirely worth preserving."

The women had wheeled their bikes away. A fleet of them flashed along the drive, veils streaming behind.

"Are those really the last strawberries?"

Lord Vane nodded, "Yes, I'm as sure as anyone can be in these blighted times. I'll fetch that water."

"Thanks."

Seth sat back on the stone bench, pondering the damaged clearing he had spotted on his way, the women, the hound.

Lord Vane re-emerged with a jug of iced water. He gave Seth a tight smile and set a glass down on the bench. Seth sloshed water into the glass. It misted up in seconds. He studied the whorls and arches of his finger-prints then drank, forgetting all his questions about the strawberries and the underground lake. He was conscious of Lord Vane's retreating steps but couldn't shake off his malaise. No invitation into the house then.

Alone in the courtyard he began to feel revived. He retrieved an empty bottle from his rucksack and filled it. After he'd filled three more bottles, Seth headed for the strawberry field. Vitamins for Helen. No time to lose.

Strawberries glistened like rubies in the furrows. He put one into his mouth and tasted full-fleshed sweetness. He filled his plastic container and eased it into his backpack. Then he ate four more, one by one, letting the juice dribble down his chin. He wiped his face and stooped to pick one last strawberry, which he cradled in his hand.

4

Seth skirted the scorched woodland then looked back at the manor. The injured leg had swollen and it chafed against his other thigh. He reached the clearing and gazed into those odd craters. He felt exhausted, decided to have a short nap. He set his watch alarm to ten minutes. Slept.

In his dream everything shuddered. There was a feverish shaking just yards to his left. He leapt to his feet. A tree crashed to the ground. He jerked his head in the direction of the copse. A mass of grey blocked the horizon, great bodies charged at him, beating the earth with drum-like feet. Giant ears flapped, ivory tusks glinted in the sun. He tried to run but felt his skull was about to split. His leg had stiffened too. Move. He had to move. Clay Hill was directly ahead: he could try clambering up and sliding down its steeper face. Elephants couldn't manage steep inclines. Could they? He couldn't think.

It was hard to remember what happened after that. Slithering down the hill, clutching his leg, glancing backwards. Branches fractured like bones. An elephant loomed, trunk aloft, vast folds of skin wobbling above the dust.

When he woke he wasn't sure how he'd escaped. Move, he told himself. If Helen was still alive she'd be sipping tepid water. Seth limped over the bald earth towards the village, reaching the lane and heading for the pine avenue. Shade. A whole aristocratic mile of it.

5

Everything had faded to sepia: the old churchyard, the shrivelled orchard, the village green. The dry stonewalls looked yellow, jurassic. When the cottage bounced into view Seth broke into a wounded lope, stopping only when he reached the gate. Opening his fist, he stared at the squashed strawberry in his palm. He glanced up at the bedroom. The window was still closed. He pushed himself forward and threw open the front door. It took seconds to climb the stairs, enter the room, lift the calico curtain. He knelt by Helen's side and called her name, rifling through his rucksack. His fingers closed around the strawberry tub. He grasped Helen's hand and she squeezed back. He flicked off the tub lid, held a strawberry to her lips.

"Thank you," she said.

Seth stroked her jaw as she ate, willing her to extract nutrients from the fruit. Her flesh was bruised like a plum. He placed his ski-glasses by the bed.

"Better eat them all."

He watched her eat them, then lie back against her pillows, exhausted by the effort.

"Time for a sleep," she said, "I could hardly rest while you were gone."

"I'll open the window," he said, but she was already asleep.

Seth crept across the carpet. He opened the window and stared at his favourite tree. Something stirred among the branches. A bee-eater, electric blue, its feathers gleaming iridescent. The bird hopped along the branch and trained its eye on him.

Seth's head throbbed and his thigh ached. His mind turned to the horrors they faced. The vegetation was closing in. Helen might be sleeping now, but there were no more strawberries, no more cures. He stared at the horse chestnut as it rattled in the wind.

GARDENS

Azaleas

Cotton bunting. Cut-glass bowls.
Strains of Grieg and silver knives.

Jairo thumps into the tearoom,
Rafael in tow.

Jairo bats at the bunting.
Rafael belly-laughs: people frown.

His father points at the cake list:
"Lemon drizzle. Two slices. Extra thick!"

Then he begins: "THIS IS A STORY ABOUT
SANTIAGO, SEBASTIAN AND SALVADOR!"

Eyes roll, lips tut.
"SO I'M TOO LOUD?"

He punches a cushion,
feathers fly.

Rafael is regaled
with tales of traders on high seas.

He picks at crumbs,
wide-eyed at battles with giant calamari.

"Here's the ship!"
A milk-jug dangles from his father's thumb.

There are gasps from surrounding tables.
Eyes avert, conversations resume.

Outside, father and son
conquer the lawn, charge at trees, raise a leaf-flag.

They are
bursts of azalea in an English wood.

GRAVEYARDS

Myrtilla

St. Lawrence Church Oxhill, 1705

Six men shoulder your pall,
servants with your complexion.
The coffin scrapes a buttress:
your knuckle raps the casket base.

Beauchamp's arm shoots up.
The procession halts.

Mr Beauchamp's called a gentleman,
you, his cargo,
shipped from Nevis Island
to Queen's Square.

You saw everything. Said nothing.
Gave away the tenderness you craved,
raised the masters Beauchamp,
nursed and cradled waifs of a life unlived.

Myrtilla, evergreen
with showers of gold.

Your tomb cold-shoulders the family plot
    Myrtilla
    Black Girl
    Negro Slave
Lichens grow. Earth breathes. Grasses weave.

HILLS

Cotswolds

Snowshill Village

The map confounds us.
We feed horses, follow walls, cross hobbled fields.

We peep over limestone:
buds smoke, bees drone.

Hamida climbs a wall.
Her veil's a flag I follow,
ignoring nettles, boundaries, Lana's pleas.

We enter a lavender field,
roam combed rows.

Hamida twists a stem
and hands Lana a sprig:
"*lavender arabica*" she says.

"Loot", I say.
We grin and get to work,
hugging armfuls, tugging roots.

"Reminds me of Provence!" I call.
"Matches my bathroom!" Hamida retorts.
We stop.

A tractor putters across the hill.

Voices: we are rabbits
fearing farmers, dogs, diesel, wire.

Words drift, cornstalks crunch, ramblers pass by.

"Got the lavender?" I ask.
"Loot", says Lana, brandishing her bunch.

Mirth grips us: the field weeps blue, indigo, violet.

Back on the footpath we steal a last look.
The lavender stands guard: stiff-stalked, club-headed.

MAYPOLES

Green Unpleasant Land
Or *John Bull slates Danny Boyle's London 2012 Opening Ceremony*

The Olympics opening ceremony
was your so-called brainchild.
Loved the Queen's bit;
amazed she was up for that.

Agree Jerusalem's our true anthem,
though Jesus never trod on English soil.
But why plonk black people on the turf
next to maypoles and milk churns?

Where was Nelson? Wellington? Churchill?
This is blatant historical engineering!
FYI: Blake wrote about satanic mills
centuries before the *Empire Windrush* docked.

I cringed at the black shepherdess
in bonnet-ribbon and flowery gown.
Applauded M.P. Burley's tweet:
multicultural crap!

The whole charade was glib, Boyle!
England's green and pleasant land
is our last refuge.
Sigh.

If you're still listening, here's my message
to all you pc hand-wringers out there:
Jerusalem will never get built
if you corrupt our heritage.

MOORLANDS

Heathcliff

A mother's grip. Fingertips.
The whip. The ship.
Docks. Cobbles. Rain.
An Inn.
Bracken. Gorse. Reeds.
Lamplight stares. Quarrels.
The dog's bed. A warm tongue.

Names:
Savage
Gypsy
Lascar
Moor.

Uplands.
His favourite spot.
No audience here.
Mire gleams. Heather hides.

Curlews pay tribute.
          Cry above this loved place.
Defy the wordless moorland.

PARKS

Kings Heath Park

Birmingham, England.

I pass them on my first lap:
three walkers in tracksuits and duffles.
India, Kashmir and Pakistan in suburban step.

On lap two,
they forage for mulberries,
probing branches with a walking stick.

On the third lap
the trio meet my eye
to welcome a companion to their ritual.

Running, I remember all the times
I've eavesdropped on their talk
of cancer and cricket,
a busman's strike,
visas denied,
footwear,
diabetes,
a faraway grave.

They smile at me on my last lap.
Sunset makes toggles gleam,
lights eye-wicks, smears cheeks with gold.

By the Spring
They've outstripped Gandhi along grass-fringed paths
where something new begins with crocus and celandine.

PASTORAL: A NEW CHRONOLOGY

1600
Shakespeare: *As You Like It*
Oaks are counsellors in Arden's court.
There are books in brooks, tongues in trees, sermons in stones.

1628
Robert Herrick: 'The Country Life'
The Maypole, the Morris, the shearing feast.
Unwitting pheasants strut through glades.

1770
Oliver Goldsmith: 'The Deserted Village'
Brook and bower and bloom:
Fleeing charms, lamented by town-bound folk.

1783
George Crabbe: 'The Village'
Nymphs and muses are tinsel trappings: abandon Virgil:
write about sterile soil, rank weeds, blighted rye.

1773
Phillis Wheatley: a black poet writes
'To a Gentleman on His Voyage to Great Britain'
No Elysian scenes here, only wishes for his good health.

1814
Jane Austen: *Mansfield Park*
Antiguan plantations,
dead silence.

1832
John Clare: 'Remembrances'
Corruption. Enclosure. Clearance.
Departing pulpits of poplar, oak, lime.

1847
Emily Brontë: *Wuthering Heights*
Nelly tells Heathcliff
he is not a "regular black."

1847
Charlotte Bronte: *Jane Eyre*
England, Jamaica, Bertha Mason
insanity hides in country houses everywhere.

1868
Wilkie Collins: *The Moonstone*
East India Company loot,
vengeful Indians menace a Yorkshire estate.

1874
Thomas Hardy: *Far From the Madding Crowd*
Sheep-washing. Shearing suppers. Market days.
Rubbled old ways.

1879
Gerard Manley Hopkins: 'Binsey Poplars'
A row of aspens are felled,
havoc is wrought on the rural scene.

1883
Elizabeth Barrett Browning: 'Aurora Leigh'
Herefordshire hills: dimpled, rippling verdure.
Best not mention the sugar that bought this estate.

1891
Thomas Hardy: *Tess of the D'Urbervilles*
Greenwood. Sparrows roost, rabbits hop.
Gunfields. Pheasants thump onto landowners' altars.

1939
Adrian Bell: *Men in the Fields*
Unhurried ways.
Harvestmen. Glass tankards. A roan cob.

1959
Laurie Lee: *Cider With Rosie*
Russet summer.
Cheeks burn with orchard wine.

1962
Sylvia Plath, 'Pheasant'
Kingly, divine.
Let it roam its native hills.

1973
Richard Mabey: *The Unofficial Countryside*
Landfills of canary grass
Grebes nest in old tyres.

1984
Derek Walcott: *Midsummer*
Schoolboy memories of *Piers Plowman*
A St. Lucian ploughs England's muddy verse.

1984
Kazuo Ishiguro: *The Remains of the Day*
Nazis drink from china cups.
Jewish maids are dismissed.

1987
V.S. Naipaul: *The Enigma of Arrival*
Stonehenge is not for the likes of men
who climb, like Wordsworth, from valley to crest.

1989
Ingrid Pollard: 'Pastoral Interludes'
I wander through the Lake District
armed with a bat.

1991
Paul Henry: The Village, a State of Untruth
Blunt words in a butcher's shop.
His apron is bloodstained: visit at your peril.

1993
David Dabydeen, *Disappearance*
Something lurks in cottage gardens:
devil's-bit scabious and Turk's cap.

1999
Roger Deakin: *Waterlog*
Wild swimming, water sprites.
Defy landowners and claim your frog's-eye view.

2000
Mahendra Solanki: 'In a Jar'
Into the Severn and out to sea
go human ashes, *paan* and flowers.

2005
Manzu Islam, 'Catching Pheasants'
This bird isn't native!
It's an Asian immigrant!

2006
John Agard, 'Moorish'
Morris is no English dance:
The Africans brought it.

2008
Kathleen Jamie, 'Pathologies'
Unseen landscapes within.
Pink liver on a slab like an estuary, a sandbank.

2009
Grace Nichols: 'Framing the Landscape'
Knights flashed their swords too long ago.
Now Black poets sow these fallow fields.

2009
Grace Nichols, 'Wild About Her Back Garden'
Buddleia, vine, cherry, bamboo:
English gardens are global conventions.

2010
Rommi Smith: 'Night River'
Follow Keats's bright star;
forge priestly waters without map or moon.

2012
Robert Macfarlane: *The Old Ways*
Holloways, halterpaths, trods:
footfall remembers ancient passage.

2014
Amma Asante: *Belle*
Children of the enslaved
roam the lawn, tend the chickens.

2015
Caryl Phillips: *The Lost Child*
The black Heathcliff beats bracken,
trails behind Mr Earnshaw, sugar merchant.

2019
Peter Kalu: 'Richard Watt I, Merchantt, of Speke Hall'
Once a nuisance hurricane depleted his slave-stock.
Now a philanthropist with country house and family crest.

PUBS

The Saracen's Head

The Black Boy Inn, Caernarfon
Roaring fires
Dining of distinction
Five centuries of charm.

The Turk's Head, Penzance
Oak beams
Cornish intrigue
Smugglers drank here.

Labour in Vain, Staffordshire
In the face of objections
Villagers vote to keep the sign
Of white people scrubbing a Black boy.

The Black Bitch, Linlithgow
Not a racist slur
Just a local legend about a hound
Which carried food to its jailed master.

Blacks Head Inn, Sussex
Owner sues journalist
For inflammatory headline:
Woman Hospitalized By Falling Pub Sign.

SEEDS

William Blathwayt, Secretary of Foreign Plantations

Dyrham Park, 1690

The seeds of empire arrive in envelopes:
maple, red cherry, hickory nuts,
America's bright heirlooms.

Blathwayt has them sown in beds.
They germinate out of sight,
wriggle through soil.

He sips chocolate from pots,
administers colonies from his hearth,
contemplates planting at home and abroad.

Time passes, profits grow.
He surveys his flowers.
Only the brightest are plucked.

The exotic blooms are much admired:
they stand to attention for state visitors.
But how they shiver in their delft vases.

WOODLANDS

An Escaped Slave

Yorkshire, 1709

They're hunting him.

He wades barefoot across the Wharfe.
Branches break their brittle bones,
scrape his swollen toes,
rake the riverbed,
roll the eyes of pebbles.

Night thickens.
He stares at the bruised clouds, willing them to cover the moon.

Sighs shift the debris of winter,
leaves flutter like pages in the Earl's library.

He's not the first to flee along this riverbank,
to lumber through these bars of beech.

He hears wailing hounds,
thudding hooves,
flying clods,
rasping stone.

Lamplight flares.

A lurch and leap,
a flash:
a gasp of gunpowder,
a blast of blood inside his collar

He halts by the rhododendron.
Round leaves dab his cheek
as he falls.

EPILOGUE

EPILOGUE

Historical and literary ideas about the countryside have shifted significantly in the last three decades. For a long time now, historians, social geographers and archaeologists have recognised that English rural landscapes are readable, showing up such things as Bronze Age forts and Roman roads. The countryside was not, until recently, considered to reveal much about the British empire. Nor was the empire seen as having much to do with enclosure, rural poverty or rural industry. All that has changed.

It is no coincidence that the landscape historian W.G. Hoskins quoted the poetry of William Wordsworth in his 1977 classic, *The Making of the English Landscape*. His justification for quoting the words of a writer is clear: 'poets make the best topographers'.[1] Writers make good researchers and observers too. This book has demonstrated that advances in academic research have been accompanied by a rural turn in writing by Black British and British Asian authors, whose work has questioned and expanded traditional views of rural England.

Rurality has become a touchy subject lately. So has British history. At the 2020 opening of the Being Human festival, David Olusoga observed that 'history exploded into everybody's lives' when Black Lives Matter demonstrators threw Edward Colston's statue into Bristol harbour, 'a man who died 299 years ago.' As Olusoga remarked, 'history is at the centre of enormous discussions that we're having… about our past, about where it's left us and where it's taken us, and about the ideas that it has hard-wired into our culture, like race.'[2]

A few weeks earlier, the National Trust had released its Interim Report on its houses' connections with colonialism and historic slavery. Government ministers and columnists protested loudly, but it was too late. The horse had already bolted: now everyone knew what historians and curators had known for some time. People had learned about empire's link to England's rolling hills and country estates, not just its cities and ports.

The British nation truly is at a crossroads. Britons can choose the path of division or else move forward in a spirit of collective discovery. Either way, older generations cannot assume that later generations will accept their outlook. Young Britons are unlike any previous generation. With family connections across the globe, children growing up in Britain today have the capacity and resource to interpret their local surroundings more expansively than ever before. Back in 2018, I worked with 100 ten-year-olds on 'Colonial Countryside: National Trust Houses Reinterpreted'. These children opened my eyes to new possibilities. One child remarked that an Afghan table at Kedleston Hall had the same stone, lapis lazuli, as her grandmother's jewellery in Pakistan. Another went to India with her parents after seeing a miniature of Tipu Sultan at Charlecote Park. She returned and explained that there are three contrasting versions of Tipu Sultan: the English version (preoccupied with East India Company battles), the Hindu nationalist version (preoccupied with forced conversion to Islam) and the view of a Muslim curator she met in India, who revered Tipu Sultan for developing an Indian silk industry. Another child on the project wondered how he would feel if his mother's skull were displayed – like one he saw – beside a thumb piano and a bit of mosque tile in a colonial cabinet of curiosities. 'You can avoid this history if you want to', another child said in a conference speech, 'but you can't stop me studying it.'

Whether we asked for it or not, we are living in an era of 'culture wars'. In the face of concerted political and journalistic pressure to desist from telling 'woke' history to the British public, and clinging dearly to the talisman of research rigour, it strikes me that it is not just the freedom to expand our historical knowledge which is at stake. Nor is it simply that historians and writers can help us to understand how we ended up where we are today. As the next generation shows us, there is no need for rancour. Modern Britain really can be a place where minds and cultures commune.

Endnotes

1. W.G. Hoskins, *The Making of the English Landscape* (London: Hodder and Stoughton, 1977), p. 25.
2. Being Human festival launch, 10th November 2020, www.bing.com/videos/search?q=Being+Human+festival+launch+2020 &&view=detail&mid=9B3606FB9CB7DE88FD159B3606FB9CB7DE88FD15&& FORM=VRDGAR, accessed 20 November 2020.

FURTHER READING

History: Empire and Rurality

John E. Archer, *By a Flash and a Scare: Arson, Animal Maiming, and Poaching in East Anglia 1815-1870* (London: Breviary Stuff, 2010).

Stephanie Barczewski, *Country Houses and the British Empire, 1700-1930*, (Manchester: Manchester University Press, 2016).

Caroline Bressey, 'Cultural Archaeology and Historical Geographies of the Black Presence in Rural England', *Journal of Rural Studies* 25, 2009, 386-395.

Judith A. Carney and Richard Rosomoff, *In the Shadow of Slavery: Africa's Botanical Legacy in the Atlantic World* (Berkeley: University of California Press, 2011).

Rachel Carson, *Silent Spring* (New York: Houghton Miffin, 1962).

Jill H. Casid, *Sowing Empire. Landscape and Colonization* (Minneapolis: University of Minnesota Press, 2005).

Neil Chakaraborti and Neil Garland, eds., *Rural Racism*, (London: Routledge, 2012).

Andrew Charlesworth, *An Atlas of Rural Protest in Britain 1548-1900* (Philadelphia: University of Pennsylvania Press, 1983).

Kathleen Chater, *Untold Histories: Black People in England and Wales During the Period of the British Slave Trade, C. 1660-1807* (Manchester: MUP, 2009).

William Dalrymple, *The Anarchy: The Relentless Rise of the East India Company* (London: Bloomsbury Publishing, 2019).

Mohammed Dhalech, 'Challenging Racism in the Rural Idyll. Final Report of the Rural Race Equality Project Cornwall, Devon and Somerset 1996 to 1998', (Exeter: National Association of Citizen's Advice 1999).

Emile de Bruijn, Andrew Bush and Helen Clifford, *Chinese Wallpaper in National Trust Houses*, (Swindon: The National Trust, 2014).

James Delbourgo, *Collecting the World: The Life and Curiosity of Hans Sloane* (London: Allen Lane, 2017).

Katie Donington, *The Bonds of Family. Slavery, Commerce and Culture in the British Atlantic World* (Manchester: Manchester University Press, 2019).

Nick Draper, *The Price of Emancipation. Slave-Ownership, Compensation and British Society at the End of Slavery* (Cambridge: Cambridge University Press, 2010).

Madge Dresser, *Slavery Obscured: The Social History of the Slave Trade in an English Provincial Port c. 1698-1833* (London: Continuum Books, 2001).

Madge Dresser and Andrew Hann, eds. *Slavery and the British Country House* (London: English Heritage, 2013).

Martin Empson, *'Kill All the Gentlemen': Class Struggle and Change in the English Countryside* (London: Bookmarks, 2018).

Chris Evans, *Slave Wales: Welsh and Atlantic Slavery 1660-1850* (Cardiff: University of Wales Press, 2010).

Patricia, Fara, *Sex, Botany and Empire: The Story of Carl Linnaeus and Joseph Banks* (London: Icon Books, 2003, 2017).

Margot Finn and Kate Smith, eds., *The East India Company at Home, 1757-1857* (London: UCL Press, 2017).

Roderick Flood, *An Economic History of the English Garden* (London: Allen Lane, 2019).

Alistair Fowler, *The Country House Poem* (Edinburgh: Edinburgh UP, 1994).

Peter Fryer, *Staying Power: The History of Black People in Britain* (London: Humanities Press, 1984).

Perry Gauci, *William Beckford: First Prime Minister of the London Empire* (New Haven: Yale UP, 2013).

Gretchen Gerzina, *Black England. Life Before Emancipation* (London: John Murray, 1995).

Simon Gikandi, *Slavery and the Culture of Taste* (Princeton: Princeton UP, 2014).

Richard Gill, *Happy Rural Seat: The English Country House and the Literary Imagination* (Newhaven: Yale UP, 1972).

John Gilmore, *The Poetics of Empire: A Study of James Grainger's The Sugar Cane (1764)* (London: The Athlone Press, 2000).

Priyamvada Gopal, *Insurgent Empire: Anticolonial Resistance and British Dissent*, (London: Verso, 2019).

Jack P. Greene, *Evaluating Empire and Confronting Colonialism in Eighteenth-Century Britain* (Cambridge: Cambridge UP, 2013).

Jeffrey Green, *Black Edwardians: Black People in Britain 1901-1914* (London: Routledge, 1998).

Catherine Hall, Nicholas Draper, Keith McClelland, Katie Donington and Rachel Lang, *Legacies of British Slave-Ownership: Colonial Slavery and the Formation of Victorian Britain* (Cambridge: Cambridge UP, 2016).

Nick Hayes, *The Book of Trespass* (London: Bloomsbury, 2020).

E.J. Hobsbawm and George Rudé, *Captain Swing* (London: Readers Union & Lawrence & Wishart, 1970).

W.G. Hoskins, *The Making of the English Landscape* ([1955] Toller Fratram: Little Toller, 2013).

Sarah Houghton-Walker, *Representations of the Gypsy in the Romantic Period* (Oxford: Oxford UP, 2014).

Alun Howkins, *The Death of Rural England: A Social History of the Countryside Since 1900* (London: Routledge, 2003).

Martin Hoyles, *Bread and Roses: Gardening Books from 1560-1960* vol.

2. (London: Pluto Press, 1995).

Joseph E. Inikori, *Africans and the Industrial Revolution in England: A Study in International Trade and Economic Development* (Cambridge: Cambridge UP, 2002).

C.L.R. James, *The Black Jacobins: Toussaint L'Ouverture and the San Domingo Revolution* (Secker and Warburg, 1938).

Miranda Kaufmann, *Black Tudors* (London: OneWorld, 2017).

Theresa Kelly, *Clandestine Marriage. Botany and Romantic Culture* (Baltimore: The John Hoskins University Press, 2012).

Kevin Le Gendre, *Don't Stop the Carnival. Black Music in Britain* (Leeds: Peepal Tree Press, 2018).

Peter Linebaugh, *Stop, Thief! The Commons, Enclosures, and Resistance* (Oakland: PM Press, 2014).

Jo Littler and Roshi Naidoo, eds. *The Politics of Heritage. The Legacies of "Race"* (London: Routledge, 2005).

Daniel Livesay, *Children of Uncertain Fortune: Mixed-Race Jamaicans in Britain and the Atlantic Family, 1733-1833,* (North Carolina: The University of North Carolina Press, 2018).

Richard Mabey, *The Unofficial Countryside* ([1973] Toller Fratrum: Little Toller Books, 2010).

Robert Macfarlane, *The Wild Places* (London: Granta, 2007).

Sumita Mukherjee, *Indian Suffragettes. Female Identities and Transnational Networks* (Oxford: OUP, 2018).

Stephen Mullen, *It Wisnae Us: The Truth About Glasgow and Slavery* (Edinburgh: EUP, 2009).

Katrina Naviskas, *Protest and the Politics of Space and Place, 1789-1848* (Manchester: Manchester UP, 2016).

J.M. Neeson, *Commoners: Common Right, Enclosure and Social Change in England, 1700-1820* (Cambridge: Cambridge UP, 1993).

David Olusoga, *Black and British: A Forgotten History* (London: Pan, 2017).

Onyenka, *Blackamoores. Africans in Tudor England, Their Presence, Status and Origins.* (London: Narrative Eye, 2013).

Steve Poole, *The Allotment Chronicles: A Social History of Allotment Gardening* (Kettering: Silver Link Publishing, 2006).

Oliver Rackham, *The History of the Countryside* (London: Dent, 1986).

Marion Shoard, *The Theft of the Countryside* (London: Maurice Temple Smith, 1980).

Guy Shrubsole, *Who Owns England: How We Lost Our Green and Pleasant Land & How to Take it Back* (London: William Collins, 2019).

Taylor, Michael, *The Interest: How the British Establishment Resisted the Abolition of Slavery* (London: Bodley Head, 2020).

Adrian Tinniswood, *The Polite Tourist: Country House Visiting Through the Centuries* (London: The National Trust, 1998).

E.P. Thompson, *Whigs and Hunters: the origins of the Black Act* (London: Allen Lane, 1975).

E.P. Thompson, *Customs in Common* ([1999] London: Merlin Press, 2010).

Dominic Tyler, *Uncommon Ground. A Word-Lover's Guide to the British Landscape* (London: Guardian and Faber, 2015).

Rozina Visram, *Ayahs, Lascars and Princes: The Story of Indians in Britain* (London: Pluto, 1986).

James Walvin, *Slavery in Small Things: Slavery and Modern Cultural Habits* (John Wiley and Sons: Chichester, 2017).

Alistair Watt, *Robert Fortune: A Plant Hunter in the Orient* (London: Royal Botanic Gardens, 2017).

Eric Williams, *Capitalism and Slavery*, (North Carolina: University of North Carolina Press, 1944).

Kathy Willis and Carolyn Fry, *Plants. From Roots to Riches* (London: John Murray, 2014),

Criticism and Literary History

Paul Alpers, *What is Pastoral?* (Chicago: Chicago UP, 1996).

William Atkins, *The Moor. Lives, Landscape, Literature* (London: Faber and Faber, 2014).

John Barrell, *The Idea of Landscape and the Sense of Place 1730-1840: An Approach to the Poetry of John Clare* (Cambridge: CUP, 1972).

Jonathan Bate, *John Clare: A Biography* (London: Picador, 2003).

Patrick Brantlinger, *Rule of Darkness: British Literature and Imperialism 1830-1914* (Cornell: Cornell UP, 1988).

James Buzard, *The Beaten Track: European Tourism, Literature and the Ways to "Culture" 1800-1918* (Oxford: OUP, 1993).

Glen Cavaliero, *The Rural Tradition in the English Novel, 1900-1939* (London: Macmillan, 1977).

Paul Chirico, *John Clare and the Imagination of the Reader* (London: Palgrave Macmillan, 2007).

William J. Christmas, *The Lab'ring Muses: Work, Writing and Social Order in English Plebeian Poetry*, 1730-1830 (Newark: University of Delaware Press, 2001).

Franca Dellarosa, *Talking Revolution: Edward Rushton's Rebellious Poetics 1782-1814* (Liverpool, Liverpool UP, 2014).

Margaret Doody, *Jane Austen's Names: Riddles, Persons, Places* (Chicago: University of Chicago Press, 2015).

Alistair M. Duckworth, *The Improvement of the Estate: A Study of Jane Austen's Novels* (Baltimore: Johns Hopkins, 1971).

Terry Gifford, *Pastoral* (London: Routledge New Critical Idioms, 2019).

Terry Gifford, *Green Voices*: Understanding Contemporary Nature

Poetry(Nottingham: CCCP, 2011).

Adam Hopkins, *The Moorlands of England* (Toronto: Key Porter Books, 1995).

Graham Huggan and Helen Tiffin, *Postcolonial Criticism: Literature, Animals, Environment* (London: Routledge, 2010).

Suvir Kaul, *Poems of Nation, Anthems of Empire: English Verse in the London Eighteenth Century* (New Delhi: Oxford University Press, 2000).

Donna Landry, *The Muses of Resistance: Laboring-CClass Women's Poetry in Britain 1739-1796* (Cambridge: CUP, 1990).

Donna Landry, *Invention of the Countryside: Hunting, Walking and Ecology in English Literature, 1671-1831* (Basingstoke: Palgrave, 2001).

Lucinne Loh, *The Postcolonial Country in Contemporary Literature* (London: Palgrave, 2013).

Gerald MacLean, Donna Landry and Joseph P. Ward, eds. *The Country and the City Revisited. England and the Politics of Culture, 1550-1850* (Cambridge: CUP, 1999).

M.M. Mahood, *The Poet as Botanist* (Cambridge, CUP, 2008).

Saree Makdisi, *Romantic Imperialism: Universal Empire and the Culture of Modernity* (Cambridge: CUP, 1998).

James Procter, *Dwelling Places. Postwar Black British Writing* (Manchester: MUP, 2003).

Edward Said, 'Jane Austen and Empire' in *Culture and Imperialism* (New York: Knopf, 1993), pp. 80-96.

Abigail Ward, *Caryl Phillips, David Dabydeen and Fred D'Aguiar. Representations of Slavery* (Manchester: MUP, 2011).

Gabrielle White, *Jane Austen in the Context of Abolition* (London: Palgrave Macmillan, 2006).

Raymond Williams, 1973, *The Country and the City*, (London: Chatto & Windus, 1973).

Literature, Film and Photography

Louisa Adjoa Parker, *Salt, Sweat and Tears* (Cinnamon Press: Blaenau Ffestiniog, 2007).

John Agard, *We Brits* (Tarset: Bloodaxe, 2006).

Amma Asante, dir., *Belle* (Twentieth Century Fox, 2014).

Simon Armitage, *Walking Home* (London: Faber, 2013).

Jane Austen, 2003 [1814], *Mansfield Park* (London: Penguin, 2003).

Jo Baker, *Longbourne* (London: Knopf, 2013).

John Barrell and John Bull, *The Penguin Book of English Pastoral Verse* (London: Penguin, 1975).

Charlotte Bronte, *Wuthering Heights,* ([1850] London: Penguin, 1995).

Maya Chowdhry, *Fossil* (Leeds: Peepal Tree Press, 2016).

John Clare, *Major Works* (Oxford: Oxford University Press, 2008)

William Cobbett, *Rural Rides. Volume I and II* ([1830] London: Dent n.d.).

David Dabydeen, *Hogarth's Blacks: Images of Blacks in 18ᵗʰ Century English Art* (Manchester: MUP, 1987).

David Dabydeen, *Disappearance* ([1993] Leeds: Peepal Tree, 2005).

David Dabydeen, *A Harlot's Progress* ([1999] London: Vintage, 2000).

Rita Dove, *Sonata Mulattica.* (New York: Norton, 2010).

Camille Dungy, *Black Nature: Four Centuries of African American Nature Poetry* (Athens, Georgia: University of Georgia Press, 2009).

Earth Shattering: Eco Poems, ed. Neil Astley (Newcastle: Bloodaxe, 2007).

Bernardine Evaristo, *The Emperor's Babe* (London: Penguin, 2001).

Paul Gilroy and Stuart Hall, *Black Britain: A Photographic History* (London: Saqi Books, 2011).

Tanika Gupta, *The Empress,* (London: Oberon, 2013).

Ted Hughes, 'The Rain Horse' in *Wodwo* (London: Faber and Faber, 1967).

Ted Hughes, *The Remains of Elmet* (London: Faber, 1979).

Catherine Johnson, *The Curious Tale of the Lady Caraboo* (London: Corgi, 2015).

Sandra Kemp, 'Introduction', *The Moonstone. Edited with an Introduction by Sandra Kemp* (London: Penguin, 1998).

Andrea Levy, *The Long Song* (London: Tinder Press, 2011).

Robert Macfarlane, *The Wild Places,* (London: Granta, 2017).

Adam Low, director, *A Regular Black. The Hidden* Wuthering Heights (Leeds: Lonestar productions, 2009).

VS. Naipaul, *The Enigma of Arrival* ([1987] London: Picador, 2011).

V.S. Naipaul, *Guerrillas* (London: Andre Deutch, 1975).

Susheila Nasta and Florian Stadler, *Asian Britain: A Photographic History* (London: The Westbourne Press, 2013).

Grace Nichols, *Passport to Here and There* (Bloodaxe: Tarset, 2020).

Out of Bounds, ed. Jackie Kay, James Procter and Gemma Robinson (Bloodaxe: Tarset, 2013).

Ingrid Pollard, *Postcards Home,* (London: Autograph, 2004).

Max Porter, *Lanny* (London: Faber and Faber, 2019).

Sene Seneviratne, *Wild Cinnamon and Winter Skin* (Leeds: Peepal Tree Press, 2007)

Sene Seniviratne, *Unknown Soldier* (Leeds: Peepal Tree Press, 2019).

Lemn Sissay, *Morning Breaks in the Elevator* (Edinburgh: Payback Press, 1999).

Dorothea Smartt, *ShipShape* (Leeds: Peepal Tree Press, 2008).

Testament, *Black Men Walking* (London: Oberon Books, 2018).

The Redbeck Anthology of British South Asian Poetry (Bristol, Redbeck Press, 2000).

INDEX

Green Unpleasant Land explores how the aftereffects of empire, slavery and colonialism remain visible in the British landscape and cultural heritage for those who care to look, but how amnesia, evasion and outright denial conspire to present an image of 'global' Britain at sharp variance with the truth. There are those who want to soften the past or propound a neo-imperialistic view of British greatness for whom such truth-telling is a challenge to the ideology of the British ruling classes and their apologists, past and present. Unlike the USA with its history of enslavement within its own borders, for Britain, there has long been the temptation to think that the exploitation of conquered and enslaved others happened somewhere else, a somewhere that could be put out of mind, or turned into comfortable and deceitful myths of a benign mission. But as *Green Unpleasant Land* documents, colonised Caribbean peoples, though across the distance of the Atlantic, were often being exploited by the same landowning and commercial elites who were driving British agricultural workers off the land through enclosures in order to increase rentable values and expand their vast country estates.

This selection of novels and collections of poetry published by Peepal Tree over the past four decades represents some of the attempts by contemporary Caribbean writers to tell the stories of what was happening across the Atlantic. In different ways, both directly and obliquely, they document, imagine and explore the inner meanings of enslavement and colonial overlordship as experienced by people in the Caribbean. Some of these books also track how the consequences of colonialism and enslavement remain deeply embedded in the most difficult aspects of contemporary Caribbean reality: in the narrow social pyramids of race, colour and class that are only just beginning to break down; in the malign economic consequences of mono-cultural plantation economies; in the continuing high levels of under- and unemployment and in the massive loss of skills through the consequent pressures to migrate; and in the ever sharper divisions of wealth that produce gated communities at one end, ghetto communities at the other, and rising crime inbetween. Yet, as many of these books reveal, and themselves make manifest, the Caribbean has long been the site of cultures of resistance, self-realisation and creative expression produced under the most oppressive circumstances, which have enriched the region and the world, and not least Britain.

James Carnegie
Wages Paid
ISBN: 9781845232153; pp. 128; pub. 1976, 2016; £8.99

Wages Paid is a short but powerful novel set on a sugar plantation in Jamaica during the years of slavery. It is remarkable for its form – brief, separate paragraphs that build up the tensions of the events of one day; the rhythmic, almost ritualistic quality of its language; and its acute sense of the meeting point between outward lives of total constriction and inner mind-worlds in which desires and rationality cannot be suppressed.

In a world where all persons, including the plantation manager, have become commodities, the body becomes the site of struggle and the mind/brain the only organ that cannot be wholly owned. Sex is at the heart of a paradox. Mr Johnson, the owner, commands the bodies of any of the women he wants; he also owns enslaved men as studs, and women as breeders. But it is precisely this connection through sex that provides one of the plot motives of the novel, when Mr Johnson suspects he may have caught a dose of the clap from Johnson, the dominant male in the community of the enslaved. There are other goals at work in this "huis clos" world. Mary, the cook has reason to want to humble Johnson for the way he has treated her, and then what role will Wiseman, the obeah man, whose assistance is sought by all, play in the day's unfolding events? Not least for what it has to say about gender in the context of slavery and the construction of masculinity, *Wages Paid* was and is a groundbreaking novel.

Kevyn Alan Arthur
The View from Belmont
ISBN: 9781900715027; pp. 222; pub. 1997; £8.99

The View from Belmont tells two stories: one through the letters of a young English widow who takes over her husband's cocoa estate in Trinidad in 1823; the other through the responses of a group of contemporary Trinidadians who are reading the letters at the time of the 1990 Muslimeen attempted coup. Clara's letters present the insights of a perceptive, independent-minded and generous-spirited young woman, who is nevertheless wholly committed to the institution of slavery. The letters give a sharp sense of Trinidadian society in the process of formation, but at their heart is an account of Clara's relationships with those with whom she shares her life on the estate, in particular Kano, a 'loyal' slave who she takes to her bed.

For the contemporary Trinidadians, the letters raise troubling questions about the nature of the national psyche, the absence of social consensus and the extent to which the history of that period still shapes the present. Is Clara a 'worthless white bitch –– no different from any of them men who was screwing their slave women' or a sensible woman taking charge of her life and looking for companionship? This is a comic, painful and moving novel. Its presentation of the cruelties, violence and affections of everyday relations under enslavement raise questions not only about the nature of Caribbean societies, but the nature of history and its interpretation.

Carl Jackson
Nor the Battle to the Strong
ISBN: 9780948833977; pp. 352; pub. 1997; £9.99

From Imfe who is taken into slavery from Africa, Zero and Quamina who live under slavery but never submit to being slaves, Bam and Jane who live to see Emancipation but discover that they have been given little but the freedom to starve, Tom and Louise who endure the injustices of the colonial years, to Rocky who takes part in the popular uprisings for freedom and democracy in the 1930s, *Nor the Battle to the Strong* is an unrivalled portrayal of the lives of five generations of a family in Barbados.

It is a powerful and imaginative work of grief and hope whose universality is pointed to in the title's reference to Ecclesiastes: 'The race is not to the swift, nor the battle to the strong, for time and chance happeneth to them all.' It takes the reader through horrors as elemental as those of the Greek tragedy, through the dark humour of those who endured generations of human injustice to arrive at a hard-won but liberating vision of the human capacity for freedom, love and forgiveness. Jackson sings a redemption song which transports the reader out of darkness into light.

Beryl Gilroy
Inkle and Yarico
ISBN: 9780948833984; pp. 160; pub. 1996; £8.99

As a young man of twenty, Thomas Inkle sets out for Barbados to inspect the family sugar estates. On the way he is shipwrecked on a small West Indian island inhabited by Black Caribs. He alone escapes as his shipmates are slaughtered, and is rescued by Yarico, a Carib woman who takes him as, 'an ideal, strange and obliging lover.' So begins an erotic encounter, explored with poetic, imaginative intensity, which has a profound effect on both.

Amongst the Caribs, Inkle is a mere child, whose survival depends entirely on Yarico's favour and protection. But when he is rescued and taken with Yarico to the slave island of Barbados, she is entirely at his mercy.

Inkle and Yarico is loosely based on a 'true' story which became a much repeated popular narrative in the 17th and 18th centuries. Beryl Gilroy reinterprets its mythic dimensions from both a woman's and a black perspective, but above all she engages the reader in the psychological truths of her characters' experiences.

Andrew O. Lindsay
Illustrious Exile
ISBN: 9781845230289; pp. 388; pub. 2006; £9.99

In 1786, the Scottish poet Robert Burns, penniless and needing to escape the consequences of his complicated love life, accepted the position of book-keeper on an estate in Jamaica. The success of his *Poems chiefly in the Scottish Dialect* made this escape unnecessary. Thus far is historical fact. In Andrew Lindsay's novel, Burns indeed goes to Jamaica and then to the Dutch colony of Demerara where, into the world of sugar and slavery, he brought his propensity for falling in love, his humanity and his urge to write poetry. In 1997 a small mahogany chest is found in a Wai Wai Amerindian village in Guyana. It contains Burns' journal from 1786 to 1796, when he died.

Andrew Lindsay's novel is a work of imaginative invention, poetic description and meticulous historical reconstruction. As a fellow Scot who has settled in Guyana, Lindsay brings an incomer's fresh eye to the Caribbean landscape and imaginative insights into how Burns as a man of his times might have responded to slavery. Not least, *Illustrious Exile* contains some brilliant versions of Burns' poems, as written in the Caribbean.

Kevyn Baldeosingh
The Ten Incarnations of Adam Avatar
ISBN: 9781845230005; pp. 452; pub. 2005; £10.99

Tell me if I am mad,' Adam Avatar, a copper-skinned man with startling green eyes, asks Dr. Surendra Sankar, a psychiatrist in Trinidad. Aged forty-nine, there is some urgency in his request, since he fears that, very shortly, when he reaches his fiftieth birthday, he will die at the hands of his nemesis, the Shadowman.

Adam believes he is nearly five hundred years old and has gone through nine previous incarnations, including living as a fifteenth century Amerindian, a Spanish conquistador, a Portuguese slaver and a Yoruba slave, a female pirate and a female stickfighter in nineteenth century Trinidad. Not unreasonably, Dr. Sankar reaches for his pad to prescribe drugs used to control delusional states. But when Avatar's narratives of the experiences of his past selves are revealed to have an authenticity that cannot be explained away, Dr Sankar's perplexity grows.

Set in Haiti, Jamaica, Barbados, Guyana and Trinidad, *The Ten Incarnations of Adam Avatar* is an epic account of the New World experience of colonialism, slavery and resistance, and a provocative enquiry into the nature of history and what it means to be a Caribbean person.

Edgar Mittelholzer
My Bones and My Flute
ISBN: 9781845232955; pp. 206; pub. 1955, 2015; £9.99

Only when he is on board the steamer halfway to their remote destination up river in Guyana does Milton Woodsley realise that there is more to Henry Nevinson's invitation to spend time with his family in their jungle cottage. Milton, an artist, thinks he has been invited to do some paintings for Nevinson, and possibly be thrust into the company of their daughter, Jessie. But when the Nevinsons mention a flute player that no one else can hear, Woodsley begins to glean that there is more to their stay.

Mittelholzer subtitled his 1955 novel "A Ghost Story in the Old-fashioned Manner", and there is more than a hint of tongue-in-cheek in this thoroughly entertaining work, though it rises to a pitch of genuine terror and has serious things to say about the need to exorcise the crimes of slavery that lie behind the psychic manifestations, that still echo into the present in the relationship between the light-brown, upper-class Nevinsons and their Black servant, Rayburn. Amongst the barks of baboons, rustles of hidden creatures in the remote Berbice forests, Mittelholzer creates a brilliantly atmospheric setting for his characters and their terrified discovery that this is not a place where they can be at home.

Jean Goulbourne
Excavation
ISBN: 9781900715119; pp. 98; pub. 1997; £7.99

When a group of Jamaican students and their lecturers begin an archaeological dig on the old estate of Plantation Plains, each has different expectations. For Professor Milton, returned home after years abroad, the dig is to be the crowning achievement of a distinguished career. For Kwame, a lecturer from Ghana, it is the opportunity to use his knowledge to help identify African survivals in the New World. For Rastafarian Akete, the dig is going to be part of his mission to bring a sense of their African heritage to his fellow sufferers in the ghetto, and for Carla the excavations on the site of the Big House and the slave quarters are potent reminders that her own ancestry is both black and white. For the two young Americans who join them, the dig is the first chance to put their archaeological skills into practice in an exotic new environment.

All who are brought together by the dig are changed by the experience, the result both of their encounters with the relics of the history of enslavement, and the personal encounters within the group. This is a dramatic and poetically written exploration of the interaction of past and present, and of the issues of age, race and gender which the excavation provokes.

Karen King-Aribisala
The Hangman's Game
ISBN: 9781845230463; pp. 220; pub. 2007; £8.99

A young Guyanese woman sets out to write an historical novel based on the 1823 Demerara Slave Rebellion and the fate of the English missionary who is condemned to hang for his alleged part in the uprising, but who dies in prison before his execution. She has wanted to document historical fact through fiction, but the characters she invents make an altogether messier intrusion into her life with their conflicting interests and ambivalent motivations. As an African-Guyanese in a country where a Black ruling elite oppresses the population, she begins to wonder what lies behind her 'ancestral enslavement', why fellow Africans had 'exchanged silver for the likes of me'. As a committed Christian she also wonders why God has allowed slavery to happen. Beset by her unruly characters and these questions, the novel is stymied. In an attempt to unblock it she takes up a family contact to spend some time in Nigeria, to experience her African origins at first hand...

There, she confronts an even more unruly seepage between the different worlds of the historical novel and Nigeria in the grip of army coups. As such the novel has as much to say about the Guyanese past as the nature of postcolonial power in both Africa and the Caribbean. And if *The Hangman's Game* is provocatively post-modern in its self-reflexivity, its ideas are dramatically communicated through a novel that is rich in tension, dark humour and complex, strikingly drawn characters.

Angela Barry
Goree: Point of Departure
ISBN: 9781845231255; pp. 210; pub. 2010; £9.99

A chance encounter at Kennedy Airport with her ex-husband, Saliou Wade, takes Magdalene and their now adult daughter, Khadi, on a visit to him and his new family in Senegal. Magdalene is understandably nervous about the return, remembering the pain of the mutual cultural incomprehension – she is a St Lucian – that ended the marriage almost twenty years before; but Khadi refuses to go without her. In Senegal, whilst the now cosmopolitan Dr Saliou appears to exist comfortably in multiple worlds, there are more complex relationships to manage with members of his large extended family. But the sensitivities are not merely social and cultural. A visit Khadi and her half-sister Maimouna make to the slave port of Gorée has consequences that lay bare unfinished business between West Indians and Africans, between Magdalene and Saliou, and Khadi and her parents.

Diana McCaulay
Huracan
ISBN: 9781845231965; pp. 294; pub. 2012; £10.99

Back in Jamaica after years away, Leigh McCaulay encounters the familiarity of home along with the strangeness of being white in a Black country, and struggles with guilt and confusion over her part in an oppressive history of white slave owners and enslaved Africans.

As Leigh begins to make an adult life on the island, she learns of her ancestors – Zachary Macaulay, a Scot sent as a young man to be a bookkeeper on a sugar plantation in 18th century Jamaica who, after witnessing and participating in the brutality of slavery, becomes an abolitionist; and John Macaulay, a missionary who comes to Jamaica in the 19th century to save souls and ends up questioning the foundations of his beliefs.

Part historical and part contemporary literary fiction, loosely based on the author's own family history, *Huracan* explores how we navigate the inequalities and privileges we are born to and the possibilities for connectedness and social transformation in everyday contemporary life. But it is also the story of an island's independence; of the people who came (those who prospered and those who were murdered); of crimes and acts of mercy; and the search for place, love and redemption.

David Dabydeen
Johnson's Dictionary
ISBN: 9781845232184; pp. 224; pub. 2013; £9.99

In a novel set in 18th century London and Demerara, that might be dreamed or remembered by Manu, a revenant from Dabydeen's epic poem, *Turner*, we meet slaves, lowly women on the make, lustful overseers, sodomites and pious Jews – characters who have somehow come alive from engravings by Hogarth and others. Hogarth himself turns up as a drunkard official artist in Demerara, from whom the enslaved Cato steals his skills and discovers a way of remaking his world.

The transforming power of words is what enlightens Francis when his kindly (or possibly pederastic) master gifts him a copy of Johnson's *Dictionary*, whilst the idiot savant, known as Mmadboy, reveals the uncanny mathematical skills that enable him to beat Adam Smith to the discovery of the laws of capital accumulation – and teach his fellow enslaved their true financial worth.

From the dens of sexual specialities where the ex-slave Francis conducts a highly popular flagellant mission to cure his clients of their man-love (and preach abolition), to the sugar estates of Demerara, Dabydeen's novel revels in the connections of Empire, Art, Literature and human desire in ways that are comic, salutary and redemptive.

V.S. Reid
New Day
ISBN: 9781845230906; pp. 360; pub. 1949, 2015; £13.99

On the eve of a measure of democracy for Jamaicans in 1944, John Campbell looks back. As a boy, he relives his brother Davie's involvement in the Morant Bay rebellion of 1865. As a young man he recalls Davie's ill-fated attempt to set up a Utopian commune after Governor Eyre's savage revenge on Paul Bogle's supporters. As an old man he reflects on his nephew Garth's attempts to harness the energy of the working-class uprising of 1938 towards Jamaican self-rule.

First published in 1949, *New Day* has been read as an historical novel about Morant Bay and the early nationalist movement. Now, nearly 70 years later, what stands out is its acute portrayal of one man's way of seeing, from the intensity of childhood, to the comfortable self-satisfaction of middle age and old age's vicarious looking-on. At the heart of what is a more complex and conflicted narrative is a richly lyrical treatment of the human body and the network of its relations to the natural world, and a tragic awareness of how those connections fade as John Campbell moves from the peasant world of his childhood to manhood in the counting house, managing and profiting from capitalist agricultural production.

V.S. Reid saw the making of the Jamaican nation in epic terms – a vision that drew him to create his own poetic version of Jamaican patwa, to celebrate his country's landscapes, fauna and flora, and to make some interesting intertextual connections to the Aeneid, Paradise Lost and the Bible.

David Dabydeen
The Counting House
ISBN: 9781845230159; pp. 180; 1996, 2005; £8.99

Set in the early nineteenth century *The Counting House* follows the lives of Rohini and Vidia, a young married couple barely surviving in a small, caste-ridden Indian village who are seduced by the recruiter's talk of easy work and plentiful land if they sign up as indentured labourers to go to British Guiana. There, however, they discover a harsh fate as 'bound coolies' in a country barely emerging from the savage brutalities of slavery. On an estate owned by the Gladstone family, where the use of violence to discipline labour persists, they must come to terms with their problematic encounters with the recently emancipated Afro-Guyanese population hostile to immigrant labour that is reducing its bargaining power, and with rebels such as Kampta who has abandoned Indian village culture. The reality they must confront is that of their uprooted condition.

Anthony Kellman
Tracing Ja Ja
ISBN: 9781845232993; pp.156; pub. 2016; £8.99

Based on actual events in the last quarter of the 19th century, when a West African king was sent into exile to first St Vincent and then Barbados, Anthony Kellman has created a warmly human work of historical fiction. He locates the narrative between the trace of a satirical folk song, ridiculing the old African king's affair with his Barbadian servant, and the official records of the illegal kidnapping and exile to the Caribbean of Jubo Jubogha, the King of Opobo, who stood in the way of British imperial interests in the palm-oil rich region of the Niger delta. The novel focuses on the last four months of Jaja's life and the ironies of his position in Barbados where whites dominated all aspects of life and race prejudice was nakedly expressed, but where many Black Barbadians were piqued to discover the presence of an African king amongst them.

At the heart of the novel is an entirely human drama in which, though his relationship with young Becka brings new life to his battered body and spirit, and the Barbadian landscape lifts his despair, the king never loses his sense of the injustice done to him or gives up on his urgent desire to return home.

Hazel D. Campbell
Jamaica on My Mind: Collected Short Stories
ISBN: 9781845234409; pp. 346; pub. 2019; £14.99

Here in these stories is a radical vision of Caribbean possibility combined with an apprehension of how reality so often falls short. Sharply observant of the continuing inequalities of Jamaican society, the writing is wholly unsentimental or judgemental over the way her characters so often make the wrong choices. And for a writer who recognises how much of the Jamaican soul is rooted in the nation's churches, what could be more natural than that the devil makes several appearances throughout the collection? But even Lucifer is no match for the sheer cussedness of Jamaican politics. In "Jacob Bubbles", Hazel Campbell weaves a double narrative crisscrossing from the days of slavery to the years of open gang warfare of the 1970s and '80s at the behest of rival political parties that pitted equally deprived communities against each other. The story asks, in all seriousness, the seemingly absurd question about which of her two Jacobs – the Jacob who is an enslaved stonemason, and the Jacob whose only skill is with a gun – is most free.

This work is drawn from earlier published collections, *The Rag Doll and Other Stories*, *Women's Tongue* and *Singerman*, and eight new stories. Across their range Jamaica emerges from colonialism to the present, years of struggle, violence but also of continuing hope in the people's capacity for both endurance and re-invention.

David Dabydeen
Turner
ISBN: 9781900715683; pp. 84; pub. 1994, 2002; £7.99

'Turner' is a long narrative poem written in response to JMW Turner's celebrated painting 'Slavers Throwing Overboard the Dead & Dying'. Dabydeen's poem focuses on what is hidden in Turner's painting, the submerged head of the drowning African. In inventing a biography and the drowned man's unspoken desires, including the resisted temptation to fabricate an idyllic past, the poem brings into confrontation the wish for renewal and the inescapable stains of history, including the meaning of Turner's painting.

'Turner' was described Caryl Phillips as 'a major poem, full of lyricism and compassion, which gracefully shoulders the burden of history and introduces us to voices from the past whose voices we have all inherited', and by Hanif Kureishi as 'Magnificent, vivid and original. The best long poem I've read in years.'

In addition to the title poems, *Turner* contains selections from David Dabydeen's two earlier books, *Slave Song* (1984) and *Coolie Odyssey*.

Kwame Dawes
Requiem
ISBN: 9781900715072; pp. 56; pub. 1996; £7.99

In these 'shrines of remembrance' for the millions of the victims of transatlantic slavery, Kwame Dawes constructs a sequence which laments, rages, mourns, but also celebrates survival. Focusing on individual moments in this holocaust which lasted nearly four hundred years, these poems both cauterize a lingering infection and offer the oil of healing. In these taut lyric pieces, Dawes achieves what might seem impossible: saying something fresh about a subject which, despite attempts at historical amnesia, will not go away. He does it by eschewing sentimentality, rant or playing to the audience, black or white. His poems go to the heart of the historical experience and its contemporary reverberations.

This sequence was inspired by the award-winning book, *The Middle Passage: White Ships/Black Cargo* by the American artist Tom Feelings.

Anthony Kellman
Limestone
ISBN: 9781845230036; pp. 202; pub. 2008; £9.99
Limestone is the epic poem of Barbados and a major development in an indigenous Caribbean poetics. Drawing on the folk music of Tuk, Anthony

Kellman invents his own forms of Tuk verse to write the story of his island from the destruction of the Amerindians to the present day. Part one uses both invented characters and actual historical persons such as Bussa and Nanny Grigg, the leaders of the 1816 slave revolt, to explore the epic of loss, survival and reinvention in the lives of enslaved Africans. Part two is set in the post-emancipation period up to the twenty-first year of independence. Through the voices of those who led the struggle against colonialism – Samuel Jackman Prescod, Charles O'Neal, Clement Payne, Grantley Adams and Errol Barrow – Kellman explores their inner anguish over the slow pace of advance and the inevitable compromises with external power. And as the queues of would-be emigrants at the American consulate lengthen, the island asks: when a white business class still dominates the economy, who has benefited from the people's struggles of the past?

Part three is set at the end of the twentieth century and tells the stories of Livingston, a young musician, and Levinia, an Indian-African Barbadian schoolteacher who has migrated to the USA. Their stories explore the complex relationship of contemporary Barbadians to their homeland: deep attachment and an equal frustration over the absence of opportunities.

Above all, *Limestone* is never other than a poem: a vast treasure house of images, sounds and rhythms that move, entertain and absorb the reader in its world.

Colin Channer
Providential
ISBN: 9781845232481; pp. 96; pub. 2015; £8.99

No one, since Claude McKay's folksy *Constab Ballads* of 1912, has attempted to tackle the unlikely literary figure of the Jamaican policeman. Now, over a century later, drawing on his own family knowledge of the world of the police, on the complex dynamic of his relationship with his father, and framed within the humane principles of Rasta and reggae, Channer has both explored the colonial origins of that police culture and brought us up to date in necessary ways. The collection roots the origins of the police force in the aftermath of the massacre of Jamaican peasants after the Morant Bay rebellion in 1865, and the recruitment of Black Jamaicans by the colonial government to police other Black Jamaicans. This historical vision lies behind poems that manage to turn the complex relationships between a man and his father, a man and his mother, and man and his country and a man and his children, into something akin to grace.

All these titles can be ordered online from
www.peepaltreepress.com

By phone +44 (0)113 245 1703

By mail from Peepal Tree Press, 17 King's Avenue, Leeds LS6 1QS,
UK